JOURNAL
of the
American Research Center in Egypt

VOLUME 56

2020

Published by

THE AMERICAN RESEARCH CENTER IN EGYPT

Contents

Ayman Mohamed Ahmed	The Milk Deity *IAt* (*Ꜣt*) in Ancient Egyptian Religion	5
Mohamed Hussein Ahmed and Richard W. Redding	Faunal Remains from Excavations in 2019 at the Menkaure Valley Temple (MVT-W)	17
Ashley F. Arico and Katherine E. Davis	An Ostracon Depicting a King at the Art Institute of Chicago (AIC 1920.255)	35
Kathryn E. Bandy	A Family of Lector-Priests at Edfu: Oriental Institute Stela E11455 and the *Ib* Family during the Early Eighteenth Dynasty	47
Georgia Barker	Animate Decoration in the Burial Chamber: A Comparison of Funerary Models and Wall Scenes	71
Bob Brier, Michael G. Morabito, and Stuart Greene	The Khufu I Boat: An Empirical Investigation into Its Use	83
Kim McCorquodale	The Hoopoe and the Child in Old Kingdom Art	101
Luca Miatello	On the Pairs of Shafts in the Pyramid of Khufu as Means for the Ascent to the *Akhet*	115
Wahid Omran	Virtuous or Wicked: New Occurrences and Perspectives on the Black Silhouette in Graeco-Roman Egypt	143
Dora Petrova	A Lost *Dipinto* from the Tomb of Ramesses III and New Insights into the Nature of the Architectural Feature *nfr.w*	169
Lisa Sabbahy	Did Akhenaten's Founding of Akhetaten Cause a Malaria Epidemic?	175
Luiza Osorio G. Silva	The Myth of the Mundane: The Symbolism of Mudbrick and Its Architectural Implications	181
Saleh Soleiman	The Dating of Heneni's False Door at Hildesheim	199
Anke Weber, Judith Bunbury, Klara Dietze, Willem Hovestreydt, Dora Petrova, Lutz Popko, Gareth Rees, Lea Rees, and Karin Schinken	Second Report on the Publication and Conservation of the Tomb of Ramesses III in the Valley of the Kings (KV 11)	213

* * *

Book Reviews

Giovanni R. Ruffini, *Life in an Egyptian Village in Late Antiquity* (Nicola Aravecchia) 245

Glennise West, *The* Tekenu *and Ancient Egyptian Funerary Ritual* (Christian Knoblauch) 247

Julia Budka (ed.), *AcrossBorders 2: Living in New Kingdom SAI* (Kate Liszka) 249

Reg Clark, *Securing Eternity: Ancient Egyptian Tomb Protection from Prehistory to the Pyramids* (Rita Lucarelli) 251

Roger S. Bagnall and Gaëlle Tallet (eds.), *The Great Oasis of Egypt: The Kharga and Dakhla Oases in Antiquity* (Ryan Evan Reynolds) 252

Marianne Eaton-Krauss, *Bernard V. Bothmer, Egyptologist in the Making, 1912 through July 1946* (Thomas Schneider) 254

Omar D. Foda, *Egypt's Beer: Stella, Identity, and the Modern State* (Paul Tchir) 257

The Milk Deity *IAt* (*Ꜣt*) in Ancient Egyptian Religion

Ayman Mohamed Ahmed
Damanhour University

Abstract

This paper addresses the question of the deity (Ꜣt/Ꜣty) in ancient Egyptian religion. To date, there has not been a comprehensive study of this deity. The author attempts to provide answers for questions concerning how the name was written, differentiating the male and female forms of the deity, outlining the deity's character, describing his/her physical appearance and attributes, and his/her link to divine birth and milk production. Several issues related to this deity, such as its dual nature, remain uncertain. For example, although textual resources indicate a female form of the deity, no female form is actually shown. This study, based on linguistic, theological, and archeological sources, presents more documentation of this little-known deity in hope that it will serve as the basis for further research.

ملخص

تضم هذه الورقة البحثية دراسة عن المعبود/ة إيات/إياتي في الديانة المصرية القديمة، حيث إنه لا توجد دراسة شاملة عن هذا الموضوع. وقد حاول الباحث الإجابة عن عدة تساؤلات تمثلت في تعرف طريقة كتابة اسم المعبود/ة، والتفرقة بين الهيئة الأنثوية والذكورية، ووصف الشكل والصفات الجسدية، وارتباط ذلك بعملية الولادة الإلهية وإمداد المولود بالألبان. فهناك كثير من التفاصيل الدقيقة ومنها على سبيل المثال ماهية الهيئة المزدوجة تحتاج لمزيد من الدراسة، فعلى الرغم من أن المصادر النصية تشير إلى هيئة أنثوية، إلا أنه لم تصور أي هيئة أنثوية في الفن المصري القديم. وقد تناول الباحث ذلك من خلال دراسة للمصادر اللغوية والدينية والأثرية؛ لتقديم مزيد من التوثيق حول هذا/ه المعبود/ة على أمل أن تكون بمثابة أساس لمزيد من البحث.

Deities Related to Milk

Several deities in ancient Egyptian religion are associated with milk, the best known being Isis who took care of Horus and breast-fed him,[1] and Hathor, who, in the shape of a cow, suckled the ruler. Hathor appears prominently in Queen Hatshepsut's divine birth scene at Deir el-Bahari where she shown in the process of feeding the ruler, and the Hathor cow followed by several other cows ready to be milked in order to feed the ka of the queen.[2] Another milk deity was Hesat (*ḥsꜢt*) , a cow deity whose name  *ḥsꜢt* means "milk."[3]

[1] J. K. King, "Biosemiotics in ancient Egyptian Texts: The Key Unlocking the Universal Secret of Sexuality and the Birth of the Limitless," in L. M. Araújo (ed.), *Eroticism and Sexuality in Ancient Egypt: Second International Congress for Young Egyptologists: Lisbon, 23 to 26 October 2006: Second International Congress for Young Egyptologists: Lisbon, 23 to 26 October 2006* (Lisbon, n.d.), 282.

[2] E. Naville, *The Temple of Deir el Bahari, Part II* (London, 1897), 17, 18, pl. LIII. For other scenes that represent the same idea see Naville, *The Temple of Deir el Bahari, Part IV* (London, 1901), 4–6, pls. CIV, CV that show Hatshepsut being suckled by the Hathor cow.

[3] R. Faulkner, *A Concise Dictionary of Middle Egyptian* (Oxford, 1991), 177; *Urk.* IV, 238.14.

Journal of the American Research Center in Egypt 56 (2020), 5–15
doi: http://dx.doi.org/10.5913/jarce.56.2020.a001

According to Christian Leitz, she represents a milk-cow.[4] *Ꜣt*, a little known deity that is the subject of this paper, provided newborns with milk.[5]

Milk in Religious Rituals

In addition to being the primary sustenance of a small child, milk was offered as a libation to the gods.[6] Milk was mentioned in the daily offering meal in the ritual of Amenhotep I: *irt.t gngn.(t) 2 Ỉmn m n.k,* "Milk, *gngn.(t)* vessels 2: (O)Amen, take to yourself…"[7]

Milk was also used to revive and rejuvenate the deceased king in the afterlife through divine breast feeding. In addition, milk was the source of nourishment for the baby Horus.[8]

The suckling of the king was a regular feature shown on the monuments of ancient Egypt, the scenes symbolizing him receiving divine character and legitimizing the king as Horus.[9] The scene appears twice at Deir el-Bahari, where Hatshepsut and her *ka* are shown being breast-fed by the cow-headed Hathor.[10] It is also represented two other times at the same temple: on the northern wall of the outer sanctuary of the shrine of Hathor, and on the southern wall of the inner sanctuary of the same shrine where Hathor is represented as a cow breast feeding Hatshepsut.[11] Similarly, in the first register on the western wall of the birth chamber at the Luxor temple, king Amenhotep III is shown being breast-fed by the Hathor cow.[12]

The Name and Gender of Ꜣt

Ancient Egyptian deities are differentiated by their names and by symbols that give information about their nature and the forms of their manifestation(s).[13] The word *Ꜣt* is known from the First Dynasty as attested on the Palermo Stone[14] (see further, below). It was written simply with a *wꜣs* scepter through the Third Dynasty.[15] Several variations from the Old Kingdom are attested such as , . These writings refer to the female milk deity.[16]

[4] C. Leitz, *Lexikon der ägyptischen Götter und Götterbezeichnunge: Band I: A-y*, OLA 110 (Leuven-Paris-Dudley, 2002), 483.

[5] S. Tawfieq, *The History of Architecture in Ancient Egypt: Luxor* (Cairo, 1990), 201.

[6] H. E. Davidson, "Milk and the Northern Goddess," in S. Billington and M. Green (eds.), *The Concept of the Goddess* (London - New York, 1996), 91.

[7] J. B. McClain and K. Cooney, "The Daily Offering Meal in the Ritual of Amenhotep I: An Instance of the Local Adaptation of Cult Liturgy," *JANER* 5 (2005), 54.

[8] W. Guglielmi, "Milchgott s. Iat," *LÄ* 4 (1982), 127–28; Milk was kept inside anthropomorphic vases in the shape of a woman's body emphasizing the breasts. These vases were in different shapes, even ones in the form of Isis breast feeding Horus, her milk flowing from little holes in the nipples; P. Veiga, "To Prevent, Treat and Cure Love in Ancient Egypt: Aspects of Sexual Medicine and Practice in Ancient Egypt," in L. M. Araújo (ed.), *Eroticism and Sexuality in Ancient Egypt: Second International Congress for Young Egyptologists: Lisbon, 23 to 26 October 2006: Second International Congress for Young Egyptologists: Lisbon, 23 to 26 October 2006* (Lisbon, n.d), 458. For more information about milk, its significance and its role in religious rituals as well as its association to Hathor the cow, see W. Guglielmi, "Milk," in D. Redford, (ed.), *Oxford Encyclopedia of Ancient Egypt*, vol. 2 (Oxford, 2001), 412–13.

[9] M. Ivanova, *Milk in Ancient Egyptian Religion* (Uppsala, 2009), 6.

[10] Naville, *The Temple of Deir el Bahari, Part II*, 17, 18, pl. LIII; J. H. Breasted, *Ancient Records of Egypt, vol. 2: The Eighteenth Dynasty* (Chicago, 1906), 85 (§210); S. Quirke, *Exploring Religion in Ancient Egypt* (Oxford, 2016), 33; J. Iwaszczuk, *Sacred Landscape of Thebes during the Reign of Hatshepsut Royal Construction Projects*, vol. 1: *Topography of the West Bank* (Warsaw, 2016), 54.

[11] Naville, *The Temple of Deir el Bahari, Part IV*, pls. CIV, CV.

[12] Al. Gayet, *Le Temple de Louxor*, MIFAO 15 (Paris, 1894), 104, pl. 66, fig. 185.

[13] D. Budde, "Epithets, Divine," in W. Wendrich (ed.), *Encyclopedia of Egyptology* (Los Angeles, 2011), 1.

[14] Wilkinson, *Early Dynastic Egypt* (Routledge, 2005), 287.

[15] J. Kahl, *Frühägyptisches Wörterbuch, Erste Lieferung A-f* (Wiesbaden, 2002), 9.

[16] *Wb*. 1, 26.16.

The important evidence that links the goddess *Ỉꜣt* to dairy and nursing is the writing for the milk goddess in Spell 578 of King Pepi's I Pyramid Texts[17] on the west and east walls of the vestibule, concerning becoming Osiris at dusk:[18]

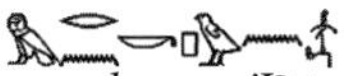
[19]

m rn.k pw n Ỉꜣ.t

"In this your name of Milk-goddess,"[20] which Allen translated as "in your identity of the Milk-Goddess."[21] This is relevant because the term *Ỉꜣtt*, which means "milk" or "cream," is written *Ỉꜣtt*[22] with the *wꜣs* scepter or[23] It is also written , with a vessel determinative, or in the form .[24]

Besides the *wꜣs* scepter and the sign that were used to write the name *Ỉꜣt*, there is another form, that appears in the related word *ḏsrt ỉꜣtt*[25] which Faulkner gives as *ḏsrt ỉꜣtt* and, and which he translates as a "milky ale."[26] This drink was mentioned in Pyramid Text Spell 146 of King Teti as *ḏsrt ỉꜣtt*[27] "sacred milk"[28] in the passage:

[29]

ḏd mdw sp 4 n ṯti pn fꜣt sp 4 ḏsrt ỉꜣtt ỉꜥb 2

"Recitation four times to this Teti to offer the offerings four times and two bowls of sacred milk."[30] Dimitri Meeks suggested another meaning for *ḏsrt ỉꜣtt*; a lotion made of milk.[31]

Based on the preceding information, different shapes of scepter that were used to refer to milk and for writing the name of the goddess include: , , and .

From the Old Kingdom, the name of the goddess was also written *Ỉꜣt*[32] with the determinative of the vulture (*mwt*) "mother," which, by extension, is related to milk. This writing appears in Spell 211 of the Pyramid Texts for a milk goddess responsible for nourishing and nursing the king:[33]

ẖnmtt pw nt Ỉꜣt

"foster-mother of the king is *Iat*." Faulkner referred to it in his translation as "a milk-goddess."[34]

---

[17] K. Sethe, *Ubersetzung und Kommentar zu den ältagyptischen Pyramidentexten*, vol. 2 (Hamburg, 1935–36), Spruch 578, 1537b. Hereafter Sethe, *Pyr* 2.

[18] J. P. Allen, *The Ancient Egyptian Pyramid Texts*. Writings from the Ancient World 23 (Atlanta, 2005), 184, recitation 520.

[19] Sethe, *Pyr* 2, Spruch 578, 1537b.

[20] R. O. Faulkner, *The Ancient Egyptian Pyramid Texts* (Oxford, 1969), 234, Utterance 578 §1537.

[21] Allen, *The Ancient Egyptian Pyramid Texts*, 184, Spell 520; Helck, *Bier im Alten Ägypten*, 19.

[22] Faulkner, *Concise Dictionary*, 7; A. H. Gardiner, *Egyptian Grammar* (Oxford, 1957), 509 (S 40); 503 (R19); D. Meeks, *Année lexicographique. Égypte ancienne* I, (Paris, 1980), 11 [77.0116)].

[23] Ivanova, *Milk*, 2.

[24] *Wb*. 1, 27, 1–4; Faulkner, *Concise Dictionary*, 7.

[25] *Wb*. 1, 27, 3.4.

[26] Faulkner, *Concise Dictionary*, 325.

[27] K. Sethe, *Ubersetzung und Kommentar zu den ältagyptischen Pyramidentexten*, vol. 1 (Hamburg, 1935), Spruch 146, 89b. Hereafter, Sethe, *Pyr.* 1.

[28] Faulkner, *Pyramid Texts*, 29, Utterance 146 §89.

[29] Sethe, *Pyr* 1, Spruch 146, 89b.

[30] Faulkner, *Pyramid Texts*, 29, Utterance 146 §89.

[31] D. Meeks, *Année lexicographique. Égypte ancienne* II (Paris, 1981), 13 (78.0126).

[32] *Wb*. 1, 26.16.

[33] Sethe, *Pyr* 1, Spruch 211, 131d; T. A. Wilkinson, *Royal Annals of Ancient Egypt: The Palermo Stone and its Associated Fragments* (London, 2000), 100; Helck, *Bier im Alten Ägypten*, 105.

[34] Faulkner, *Pyramid Texts*, 40, n.2, Utterance 211 §131.

Faulkner highlighted the link between the two written forms that appeared in the same manner and denoting the milk-goddess.[35] Leitz agrees that the writing refers to a goddess associated with milk.[36]

The name of the goddess also appears on pillars in the tomb of *Ḥtp-ḥr-n-Ptḥ* at Giza dating to the middle of the Old Kingdom[37] where it has the form[38] representing the *wꜣs* scepter crowned by the crescent and ostrich feather.

However, the Berlin dictionary gives the name *Ꜣ.ti(?)* without a determinative that it takes to refer to a male milk god attested from the Eighteenth Dynasty.[39] Earlier, Sethe and Helck mentioned the name of the milk god with the same writing.[40] Ivanova also gives the names *Ꜣty* and *Ꜣt* for male and female milk deities, respectively.[41] Hannig also cited the name in his list of deities as without a determinative.[42] This male form of the deity was depicted in the scene of the divine birth of Hatshepsut, as will be discussed below.[43]

Based on the preceding information, in the current study, the author will refer to the milk god (male form) as *Ꜣty* and to the milk goddess (feminine form) as *Ꜣt*.

Since the name of the goddess can be written with the *mwt* vulture, some argue that it should be read as *ꜣmwt* not *Ꜣt*.[44] The author, however, does not agree since *Ꜣt* was sometimes written without the vulture *mwt* as Hannig indicated by the form .[45] If the vulture was written, it was to be added at the end of the word as it is found in the Berlin dictionary: *Ꜣ.t* (?).[46] This means the word can be written with or without the vulture, which, in this case, is a determinative.

The Religious Significance of *Ꜣt* Based on the Textual Resources

The most important/earliest textual reference we have of the writing of *Ꜣt* is on the Palermo Stone where, in the fifth regnal year of an anonymous First Dynasty king, a divine image of *IAt* was fashioned or dedicated.[47]

Toby Wilkinson has discussed the meaning and reading of the second record of the Palermo Stone (fig. 1) that includes a reference to the fifth year of King Djer's rule stating: *šms-Ḥr mst Ꜣt mḥ 5 šsp1:* "Followers of Horus; creation of (an image of) *Ꜣt,* (Height of the Nile) 5 cubits and 1 palm measurement."[48] Heinrich Schäfer, however, transcribed it as *wḏ(yt) ḥrw ms(w)t sšꜣt* taking it as a reference to the birth of the goddess Seshat (*sšꜣt*) rather than *Ꜣt,* which he took to mean: Processional Tour of Horus, birth of Seshat (in the sense of creating an image of the deity).[49] Both Wilkinson and Schäfer agree that *mst* (birth) is used here to create an (image) to/for the deity.[50] Shih-Wei read the same text as *Yꜣm.t* and related it to the sixth year of King Djer's

---

35 Faulkner, *Concise Dictionary*, 7.

36 Leitz, *Lexikon der ägyptischen Götter und Götterbezeichnungen*, 96.

37 M. Baud and D. Farout, "Trois biographies d'Ancien Empire revisitées," *BIFAO* 101 (2001), 47 n. 25; See M. Baud, "The Birth of Biography in Ancient Egypt: Text Format and Content in the IVth Dynasty," in S. J. Seidlmayer (ed.), *Texte und Denkmäler des ägyptischen Alten Reiches*, Thesaurus Linguae Aegyptiae 3 (Berlin, 2005), 107.

38 *Urk.* IV, 231.6.

39 *Wb.* 1, 26.17; See *Urk.* IV, 23.15; Naville, *Deir el Bahri, Part II,* pl. 53.

40 *Urk.* IV, 231.15.

41 Ivanova, *Milk*, 3.

42 R. Hannig, *Großes Handwörterbuch: Ägyptisch-Deutsch* (Mainz, 2005), 1216 [43090].

43 Helck, *Bier im Alten Ägypten*, 105; Naville, *Deir el Bahri, Part II*, pl. 53.

44 W. Helck, "Iat (*iꜣt*)," in W. Helck (ed.), *LÄ* 3 (Wiesbaden, 1980), 114; T. Wilkinson, *Early Dynastic Egypt* (London-New York, 1999), 248. See J. Kahl, N. Kloth, and U. Zimmermann, *Die Inschriften der 3. Dynastie: Eine Bestandsaufnahme*, ÄA 56 (Wiesbaden, 1995), 204, 235.

45 Hannig, *Großes Handwörterbuch*, 1216 [43090].

46 *Wb.* 1, 26.16.

47 Wilkinson, *Early Dynastic Egypt*, 287. For an overview of work on early writing, see I. Regulski, "The Origins and Early Development of Writing in Egypt," Online Publication: 10.1093/oxfordhb/9780199935413.013.61 (2016), 1–28.

48 Wilkinson, *Royal Annals of Ancient Egypt*, 100.

49 H. Schäfer, *Ein Bruchstück altägyptischer Annalen: Palermo Stone* (Berlin, 1902), 3.

50 Wilkinson, *Royal Annals*, 100; Schäfer, *Ein Bruchstück altägyptischer Annalen*, 2.

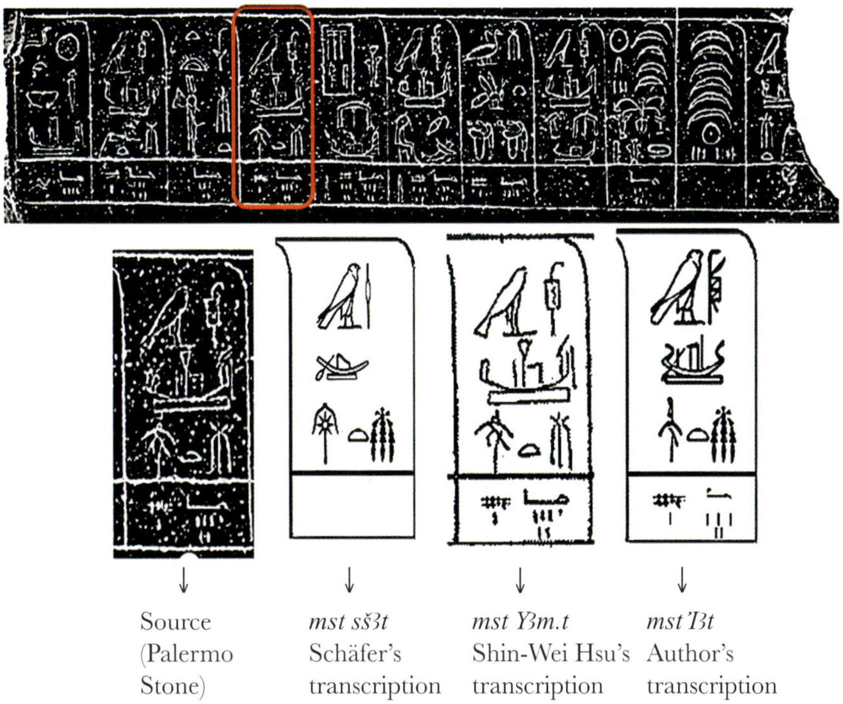

Fig. 1. A comparison of the transcriptions of the name of the goddess Ꞽꜣt in the second record of the Palermo Stone.

reign (fig. 2), not the fifth as indicated by Wilkinson, taking it as *šmsw Ḥr mst Yꜣm.t mḥ 5 šsp 1*, "the Followers of Horus and the birth of the goddess *Yꜣm.t* (Height of the Nile) 5 cubits and 1 palm."[51]

Based on the above arguments about the meanings and the reading of the word in the second record of the Palermo Stone, the author agrees with Wilkinson that the phrase refers to the goddess *Ꞽꜣt.* The writing of the name looks similar to that found in Pyramid Text 578 () and in the tomb of *Ḥtp-ḥr-n-Ptḥ* (), which was mentioned previously. In addition, the author deduces that the star sign () suggested by Schäfer for the Palermo Stone text, which he took as the symbol of the goddess Seshat *sšꜣt*, is not correct, the sign being () which is not the writing for Seshat.

The milk goddess is referred to in other Old Kingdom texts, such as Pyramid Text Spell 578 of King Pepi I, which was already referred to. It is part of the spells related to entering and leaving the tomb so that the deceased may become Osiris at dusk:[52]

[53]

ip.sn ṯw m rn.k pw n Ꞽnpw
n hꜣw nṯrw r.k m rn.k pw n Ꞽꜣt
ꜥḥꜥ.k r.k m ḫnt nt ntrw sꜣ smsw

[51] Shih-Wei Hsu, "The Palermo Stone; The Earliest Royal Inscription from Ancient Egypt" *Altorientalische Forschungen* 37.1 (2010), 82; through the linguistic investigation tackled in the paper for the name of the goddess.

[52] Allen, *Ancient Egyptian Pyramid Texts*, 173, recitation 520.

[53] Sethe, *Pyr* 1, Spruch 578, 1537a–b; 1538a.

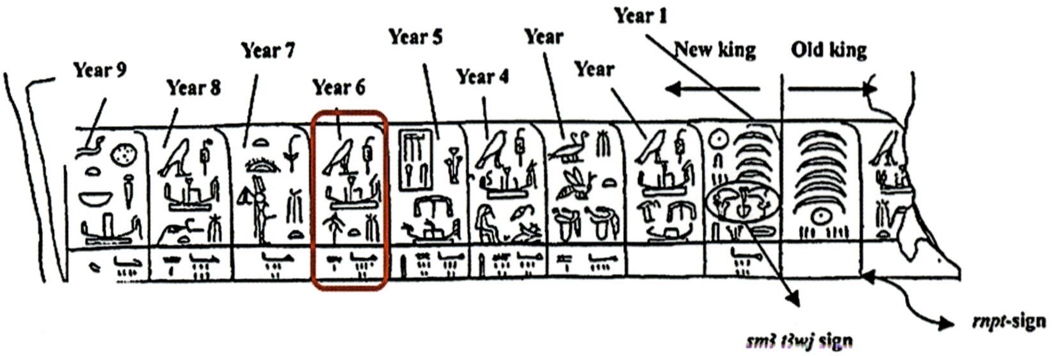

Fig. 2. The name IAt on the second record of the Palermo Stone in the sixth year of King Djer's reign. From Shin-Wei Hsu, "The Palermo Stone" (2010), 79, fig. 13.

> They will take account of you, in your identity of Anubis; and the gods will not go down against you, in your identity of the Milk-Goddess. So, you come to stand in the fore of the gods as the senior son.[54]

The name of the goddess is also mentioned in Spell 211, which was already referred to:

> It is indeed I who will give bread to those who exist, for my foster-mother is Iat, and it is She who nourishes, it is indeed she who bore me.[55]

The Male Form (*Ꞽꜣty*) of the Milk God

The documentation for the male form of the deity *Ꞽꜣty* dates from the Eighteenth Dynasty in a unique depiction of a man carrying a pot of milk on his head shown in the scenes of the divine birth in Hatshepsut's Temple.[56] The pot of milk on top of his head milk denotes his role as a god that who provides the baby with milk.[57]

The Function of *Ꞽꜣty* in the Divine Birth

The divine birth scene in Hatshepsut's Temple at Deir el-Bahari depicts the queen mother kneeling on a high bed or couch, underneath which is a row of *tyet* symbols. Before her, two cow-headed Hathors are suckling the baby-girl (Hatshepsut) and her *ka*. Below them are another two Hathor cows that will provide the infant with milk.

This scene depicts the nursing of Hatshepsut and her Twelve *Kas* who are held by twelve nurses. The last scene on the western wall depicts two gods, the one to the right presenting the divine baby and her *ka* to three seated gods who are dressed in Osirian attire. The other to the left is the milk god *Ꞽꜣty* who is identified by the milk jar on his head (fig. 3). Neither of the gods presenting the child and her *ka* are identified by texts.

Previously, Naville used the scene of the Divine Birth of Amunhotep III at Luxor Temple (fig. 4) [58] to identify the two unnamed gods at Deir el-Bahari. Because the gods at Luxor are clearly captioned as Hapy and Hekau,

---

[54] Allen, *Ancient Egyptian Pyramid Texts*, 184, recitation 520. See also Faulkner, *Pyramid Texts*, 234, Utterance 578 §1537.

[55] Faulkner, *Pyramid Texts*, 40, Utterance 211 §131.

[56] Naville, *Deir el Bahari Part II*, pl. LIII.

[57] Helck, *Bier im alten Ägypten*, 105.

[58] H. Brunner, *Die Geburt des Gottkönigs: Studien zur Überlieferung eines altägyptischen Mythos*, ÄA 10 (Wiesbaden, 1964), 138, scenes 13–14, pls. 13, 17; PM II, 349 [20.1, 2]; *Urk.* IV, 231.15.

Fig. 3. The Deity Iaty (left) in the Divine Birth, Hatshepsut's temple, Deir el-Bahari. Naville, Deir el Bahari, Part II, *pl. 53.*

he suggested that the gods at Deir el-Bahari were the same deities.[59] However, this is very unlikely. Although the figures identified as Hapi in the two temples differ in many ways (the abbreviated belt, the presence or absence of pendulous female breasts[60]), they share similarities making their identification plausible. But the identification of the god behind Hapi at Deir el-Bahari is portrayed in an entirely different way than the god in front of him (and the Luxor gods), and he is clearly identified as the milk god by the milk jug on his head.[61] Therefore, at Deir

[59] Naville, *Deir el Bahari, Part II*, 18.

[60] These pendulous breasts are usually without pronounced nipples. These breasts are distinguished from those of a normal or of a fat woman by their pendulous character, rendered by a line cutting sharply into the body below the breast. See J. Baines, *Fecundity Figures: Egyptian Personification and the Iconology of a Genre* (Warminster, 1985), 93.

[61] During a visit to the Temple of Hatshepsut on the West Bank on June 14, 2016, the author noted that the scene has degraded and the emblem of god *Ꜣty* is no longer visible.

Fig. 4. The Deity Heaku in the divine birth of Amenhotep III, Luxor temple. From Gayet, Le Temple de Louxor, *pl. 67, fig. 194.*

el-Bahari, the deities are the gods Hapy and *Ỉty* the milk-god,[62] rather than Naville's Hapi and Hekau. Ivanova agreed with this, also identifying the two gods as Hapy and *Ỉt.*[63]

Ỉty, as portrayed in the divine birth scene of Hatshepsut, is not associated with breast feeding because he is shown as a man, yet the milk jar on top of his head suggests that he provided the baby with milk. The texts of the divine birth scenes clearly differentiate his role from that of actually nursing the child, for Amun commands that the breast feeding goddesses—Nekhbet, Serket, Wadjet, Hathor, and the Hesat-cow—shall nurse the newborn queen:[64]

[65] 

wḏ.n [Imn n.s] n mnꜥ ḥmt.s ḥnꜥ kꜣw.s nbw
m ꜥnḫ wꜣs nb ḏdt nb snb nb ꜣwt-ib nb irt ḥḥw
m rnpwt ḥr st Ḥr n ꜥnḫw nbw ḏt

Amun has commanded you: to suckle her majesty together with all her *kas*. with all life, domination, all stability, all health and joy (in order) to make millions of years on the Horus-throne of all the living forever.[66]

62 H. Brunner, *Die Geburt des Gottkönigs*, 138, scenes 13–14, pls. 13, 17; PM II, 349 [20.1, 2]; *Urk.* IV, 231.15.
63 Ivanova, *Milk*, 5.
64 Ivanova, *Milk*, 6
65 *Urk.* IV, 230, 15–17.
66 Ivanova, *Milk*, 6.

Fig. 5. The limestone corner of the tomb niche of Akhet-hotep (Metropolitan Museum of Art 1958.123). Photo courtesy of The Metropolitan Museum of Art, Funds from Various Donors, and by exchange, 1958 (58.123).

The Emblem of *Ꜣty*

In the scene of the divine birth in Hatshepsut's temple, the deity *Ꜣty* is depicted with a milk jar with a leaf covering the milk above his head.[67] The leaf may have served to keep the milk clean. Such a method, using a piece of cloth or a leaf of a plant, is still used in Egyptian villages. The addition of the leaf in the divine birth scene indicates that the milk was for human use,[68] specifically to feed a baby. This also has parallels with practices in Egyptian villages, for if milk is to be used to feed animals, the villagers do not care about protecting it with a covering.

Priests of *Ꜣt*

A *sem*-priest of *Ꜣt* can be documented in the Third Dynasty by a text from Saqqara:[69] *tꜢ nb nsw m b(w) nb sm Ꜣ.t* [70] "…every secret of the king in every place (with) the *sem*-priest of Iat."[71]

Priests (*ḥm nṯr*) of the god are also attested. One is recorded on an inscribed block of a man named *Nis* that was found in the ruins of the tomb of Tesen (*ṯsn* sometimes written as). That text reads:[72]

---

[67] Gardiner, *Egyptian Grammar*, 530 (W20).

[68] Hannig, *Großes Handwörterbuch*, 106 [3555]; Faulkner, *Concise Dictionary*, 28.

[69] Kahl, *Frühägyptisches Wörterbuch*, 9.

[70] Kahl, *Frühägyptisches Wörterbuch*, 9; Kahl, Kloth, and Zimmermann, *Inschriften der 3. Dynastie*, 204. The researcher suggests using the preposition "with" in the translation "Every secret of the king in every place (with) the *sem*-priest of Iat" to clarify the meaning.

[71] Kahl, Kloth, and Zimmermann, *Inschriften der 3. Dynastie*, 205, 235, 245.

[72] S. Hassan, *Excavation at Gîza: With Special Chapters on Methods of Excavation, the False-Door, and Other Archaeological and Religious Subjects*, vol.

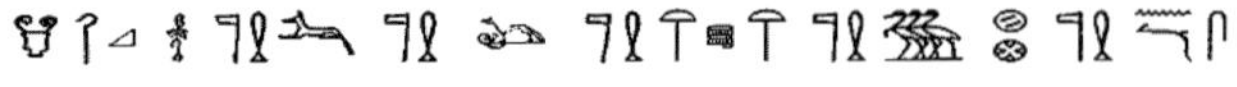

ḥk3 B3t ḥm nṯr Ꞽ3t ḥm nṯr Ꞽnpw ḥm nṯr Wp-w3t ḥm nṯr //// ḥm nṯr b3w nḫn ḥm nṯr Nis

"Ruler of the Bat-symbol,[73] Priest of Goddess *Ꞽ3t*, Priest of Anubis, Priest of Wepwawet, priest of …, Nes, Priest of the Souls of Nekhen."[74]

Another reference to a priest of *Ꞽ3t* is found on a corner block from the limestone chapel of Akhet-hotep from the reign of Snefru (fig. 5). It is decorated on two sides with the figure of the tomb owner along with his titles and name.[75]

The reliefs were so arranged that Akhet-hotep appeared emerging from the false-door niche (left) and entering it (right).[76] The complete list of Akhet-hotep's titles and epithets included many sinecures commonly carried by intimates of the pharaoh. The inscription on the right side of the block reads:[77] *sḥḏ s3 wr pr-ꜥ3 ḫrp ḫnt.jt n.t mjtr smk j3.t ḥm-nṯr-B3s.tjt ḥr.jt-ḫnt ḥm k3 3ḫ.t-ḥtp* "Inspector of the Great Phyle of the Palace, Director of the Miter-servants, Priest of Iat (*Ꞽ3t*), while the left inscription reads "Priest of Bastet who is upon the throne, *Ka*-priest, Akhet-hotep."[78]

Here, Iat, in the text on the right, is named as a complement to Bastet in the left text, and in the Pyramid Texts, they are both associated with providing milk. In Spell 508, Bastet is referred to as a mother who provides milk: *sd.n sw mwt.f B3stt*, "My mother Bastet has nursed me,"[79] while Iat is linked to birth, renewal, and breast feeding:[80] "The Milk-Goddess is his attendant. She is the one who will make possible for him to live."[81] Meanwhile Faulkner translates it as: "my foster-mother is Iat, and it is she who nourishes me..."[82] It seems therefore that Iat had the same function of nursing as did Bastet, thus she was mentioned with Bastet in the inscriptions of Akhet-hotep. According to Richard Wilkinson, the goddess Iat was naturally associated with infants.[83]

Conclusions

The present study uses texts and iconographical evidence to argue that the name of the deity is derived from *Ꞽ3tt* "milk."

The name of the milk goddess is written *Ꞽ3.t*  ,  with variations of the *w3s* scepter , and , or *Ꞽ3.t*  with the determinative of the mother goddess Mut. She is known from the First Dynasty, as attested on the Palermo Stone.

The name of the male milk god is written without a determinative as . He is known from the New Kingdom, during the Eighteenth Dynasty, as *Ꞽ3ty*.[84]

V (Cairo, 1944), 276.

73 W. A. Ward, *Index of Egyptian Administrative and Religious Titles of the Middle Kingdom with a Glossary of Words and Phrases Used* (Beirut, 1982), 130 [1110].

74 Hassan, *Gîza* V, 276; S. Hassan (276 n.1) refers to *IAt* as the milk goddess. The author agrees with Hassan's translation, because the writing of the name here corresponds to one of the ways in which the name of the goddess (female form) was written: .

75 Metropolitan Museum of Art 58.123, in P. F. Dorman, P. O. Harper, and H. Pittman, *Egypt and the Ancient Near East* (New York, 1987), 16. Akhet-hotep's small tomb is in northern Saqqara. The limestone block is 96 cm tall. See also C. Lilyquist and E. R. Russmann, "Egyptian Art," *BMMA* 41.3 (1984), 6.

76 R. A. Fazzini, J. F. Romano, and M. E. Cody, *Art for Eternity: Master Works from Ancient Egypt: Brooklyn Museum of Art* (London, 1999), 45, fig. 8.

77 N. Scott, "Two Reliefs of the Early Old Kingdom," *BMMA* 19 (1961), 194–95.

78 Translations from Niv Allon (2016), on the website of the Metropolitan Museum; https://www.metmuseum.org/art/collection/search/543912; N. Scott, "Two Reliefs of the Early Old Kingdom," 194–95, fig. 1; N. Cherpion, "The Human Image in Old Kingdom Non-royal Reliefs," in Metropolitan Museum of Art, *Egyptian Art in the Age of the Pyramids* (New York, 1999), 106, fig. 64.

79 Ivanova, *Milk*, 15; Faulkner, *Pyramid Texts*, 183, Utterance 508 §1111.

80 Helck, "*Iat (Ꞽ3t)*," *LÄ* 2, 114.

81 Allen, *Ancient Egyptian Pyramid Texts*, 30, recitation 144.

82 Faulkner, *Pyramid Texts*, 40, Utterance 211 §131.

83 R. Wilkinson, *The Complete Gods and Goddesses of Ancient Egypt* (New York, 2003), 145, 146.

84 *Wb.* 1, 26.17.

Based on the preceding information one may conclude that *Ꜣbt*, the milk goddess in its feminine form takes the determinative of the *Mwt*-vulture. She is associated with the process of fostering and breast feeding a baby as stated in the Pyramid Texts of King Teti, whereas, the male form of the deity, responsible only for providing the baby with milk, is *Ꜣbty*.

In the context of divine function, the deity also existed in two forms. The feminine form was linked to breast feeding the royal baby and king. The male form of the deity was associated with providing the royal baby and king with milk. The only iconographic attestation of the male form dates to the Dynasty Eighteen divine birth scenes of Hatshepsut at Deir el-Bahari (fig. 3).

The religious significance of the deity is indicated by the numerous times that he/she was mentioned in texts. References to the deity are found on the Palermo Stone, in the Pyramid Texts, and in some tombs. The texts also document the presence of priests who served the deity.

Faunal Remains from Excavations at the Menkaure Valley Temple (MVT-W), 2019

Mohamed Hussein Ahmed
Ministry of Tourism and Antiquities, Egypt

Richard W Redding
AERA, Giza Boston; Kelsey Museum of Archaeology, University of Michigan

Abstract

In 2019, Ancient Egypt Research Associates (AERA) re-excavated the western third of the Menkaure Valley Temple (MVT), which was first excavated by George A. Reisner in 1908–1910. Thick, dark layers that contained material culture, including large samples of faunal remains, were found during the excavations. These dark layers were deposited by Reisner, as fill, in the western third of the MVT-W. The material culture in these dark redeposited layers, including the bone fragments, came from rooms and silos in the central courtyard of the MVT and represent the consumption remains from inhabitants of the MVT courtyard. We test the hypothesis that inhabitants in the MVT courtyard are dependents of the temple receiving their provisions as part of their rights established by royal decree.

The majority of the bones came from cattle, with only three fish bones, and fifty-seven bird bones being identified; clearly cattle were the most significant food source. Most of the cattle were greater than 3.5 years of age. Forelimb fragments are over-represented and biased toward the right side. The sample of cattle probably represents the consumption of offerings. The diet of the inhabitants of the MVT courtyard differs from the diets of those inhabiting other parts of the Giza area.

ملخص

قامت جمعية ابحاث مصر القديمة في عام 2019 (AERA) باعادة اعمال الحفائر في الثلث الغربي من معبد الوادي للملك منكاورع (MVT) ، والذي تم عمل الحفائر بها سابقا لأول مرة بواسطة عالم الاثار جورج رايزنر في عام 1908–1910 حيث تم العثور على طبقات سميكة ذات الوان كاتمة تحتوي على اللقي والمواد الاثرية بما في ذلك مجموعة كبيرة من بقايا الحيوانات والتي تم اعادة ردمها قديما خلال اعمال الحفائر من قبل عالم الاثار جورج رايزنر في الثلث الغربي من المعبد حيث تم العثور علي لقي ومواد اثرية في هذه الطبقات المعاد ردمها من بينها بقايا العظام الحيوانية في غرف وصوامع الفناء الاوسط من المعبد وهي تمثل ما تبقي اثر استهلاك وغذاء سكان فناء المعبد كما اننا نقوم بتبني اختبار الفرضية القائلة بأن سكان فناء المعبد هم من الافراد (الاتباع) الذين يتلقون مؤنهم او غذائهم كجزء من حقوقهم المنصوص عليها بموجب مرسوم ملكي.

جاء اغلب بقايا العظام من الماشية مع ثلاث كسرات عظام من الاسماك فقط وتم التعرف علي 57 عظمة طائرويتضح لنا أن الماشية كانت المصدر الرئيسي للغذاء و كان عمر معظم الأبقار أكبر من 3.5 عام كما يتضح ان كسرات العظام من الارجل الامامية ممثلة بشكل مفرط واكثرها من الجانب الأيمن . ربما تمثل العينة التي تم دراستها من الابقار عبارة عن القرابين التي كان يقتاتون بها سكان هذا الجزء من المعبد كما انه يختلف النظام الغذائي لسكان فناء معبد الوادي لمنكاورع عن الأنظمة الغذائية لأولئك الذين يسكنون أجزاء أخرى من منطقة الجيزة.

Journal of the American Research Center in Egypt 56 (2020), 17–34
doi: http://dx.doi.org/10.5913/jarce.56.2020.a002

Introduction

In winter 2019, Ancient Egypt Research Associates (AERA) re-excavated the southern half of the western third of the Menkaure Valley Temple.[1] We designated this area as MVT-W (fig. 1). The MVT was first excavated by George A. Reisner in 1908-1910.[2] The AERA faunal team did not plan to analyze the animal remains recovered in the re-excavation as the material, we assumed, would not be in context, most likely being fill unknown sources. However, a great deal of material culture was found and, based on Reisner's photos and diary, the material recovered in the excavations was redeposited from the middle third, what appears to be the courtyard, of the MVT. In this courtyard Reisner found a series of structures and silos that he referred to as the Pyramid City of Menkaure.[3]

The fauna reflect activities of the people living within the temple compound who, based on three royal decrees recovered in the temple,[4] may have been provisioned by the central authority shortly after Menkaure's death. We decided to analyze the fauna from MVT in order to better understand the diet of the small group of people who occupied the temple for a period of time, after Menkaure's death, during the Fifth and Sixth Dynasty. We will test the idea that the inhabitants were provisioned by temple endowments as they were probably priests, or dependents of priests, of the cult of Menkaure. Their diet will be compared to the diet of different groups of people who lived at Heit el Ghurab, Giza, in the Old Kingdom.[5] This study will add to our knowledge of the regional economy of Old Kingdom Egypt and, in particular, the economic infrastructure of pyramids and temples. Documenting changes in the socioeconomic structure is important as such variations help us understand and explain the evolution of cultural complexity.

The Menkaure Valley Temple (MVT)

In 1908–1910, George Reisner excavated the MVT and left his field notes, drawings, and photographs with the Boston Museum of Fine Arts. These records are available online.[6] While Reisner was ahead of his time in systematic excavation and record keeping, archaeologists in this period, while, taking care of the complete artifacts, objects and architectural buildings, did not often save cultural material such as the broken pottery sherds, lithics and animal bones.

Fortunately, Reisner re-filled the western third of the MVT where he discovered the Menkaure dyad and triads—some of the most beautiful statuary of the Old Kingdom—with material removed from the middle third of the MVT, or courtyard. Reisner said, "With regret, I have determined to cover up all the back or western part of the temple. Perhaps in another century some archaeologist may wish to test the accuracy of our work or

[1] AERA's work in the Menkaure Valley Temple in 2019 was made possible by a generous grant from Dr. Walter Gilbert, and by grants from Charles Simonyi and Microsoft, Cameron and Linda Myhrvold, the Dr. Marjorie M. Fisher Fund, and contributions from Howard and Louise Phanstiel, Ed and Kathy Fries, Glen Dash, William Frank, Janice Jerde, Bruce Ludwig, and Matthew McCauley. We thank our anonymous donors who gave major support that made possible AERA's 2019 research and dissemination. We thank all our colleagues in the Ministry of Tourism and Antiquities, including Dr. Khaled El-Enany, Minister of Antiquities; Dr. Moustafa Waziri, General Director of the Supreme Council of Antiquities; Dr. Basem Gehad, Supervisor of Training and Training Centers, Dr. Nashwa Gaber, Director of the Department of Foreign Missions; Ashraf Mohedein, Director of Giza; Ahmed Eiz, Supervisor of Inspectors for AERA's Season 2019; Inspectors who represented the Ministry on the site: Shaima Abd El-Rahman and Mohamed Gamal; and Inspectors who represented the Ministry in AERA's Field Lab: Mohamed Salah and Dr. Sousan Ibrahim Fahmy. We also thank Dr. Ikram for her very useful comments on an earlier draft, and the anonymous reviewers for their comments. We thank Mark Lehner for his continued support of our research and his dedication to archaeology in Egypt.

[2] George Reisner, *Mycerinus: The Temples of the Third Pyramid at Giza* (Cambridge 1931).

[3] Reisner, *Mycerinus,* 47.

[4] Reisner, *Mycerinus,* 278–81.

[5] Richard Redding, "Status and Diet at the Workers' Town, Giza, Egypt," in D. Campana, P. Crabtree, S. DeFrance, J. Lev-Tov, and A. Choyke (eds.), *Anthropological approaches to zooarchaeology: Complexity, Colonialism, and Animal Transformations* (Oxford, 2010), 65–75.

[6] http://giza.fas.harvard.edu/, http://www.gizapyramids.org

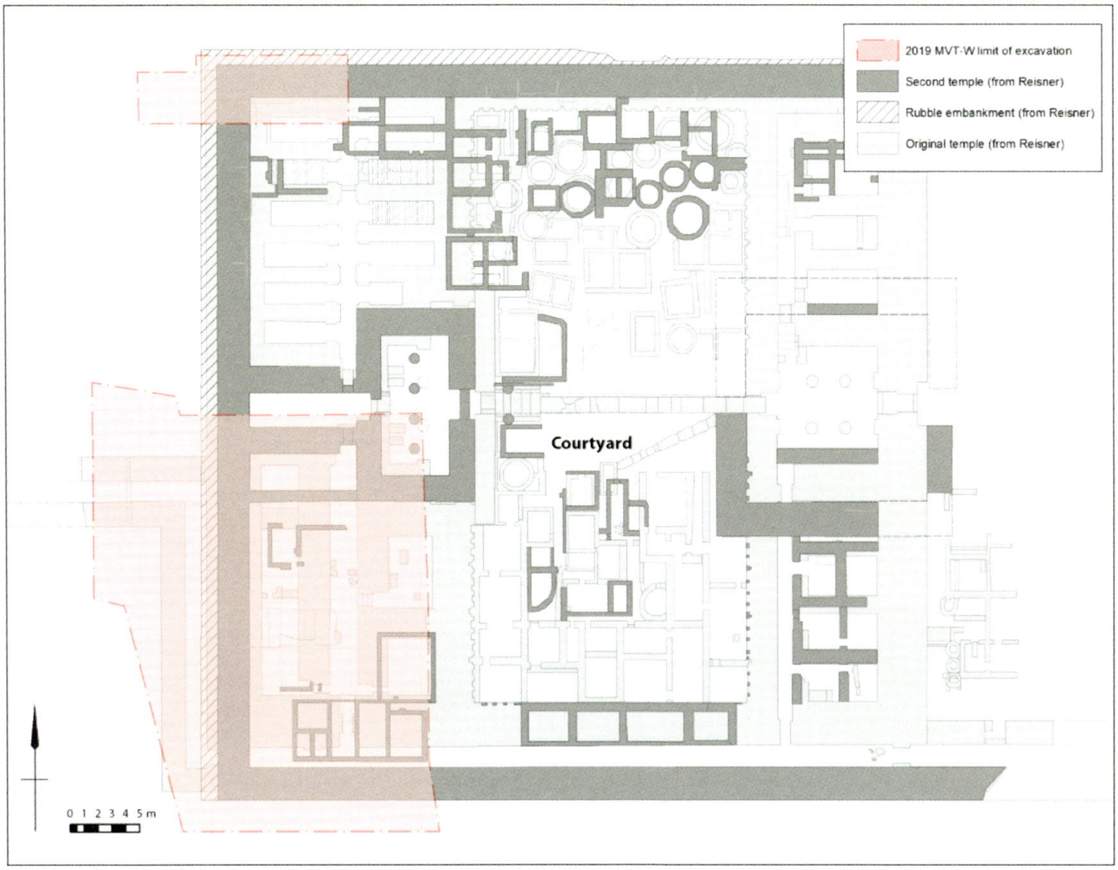

Fig. 1. Multi-phase Reisner plan of the MVT geo-rectified (corrected for position with respect to the Giza Plateau Mapping Project grid). Red rectangles indicate limit of excavation (LOE) in Season 2019. Map by Rebekah Miracle from AERA GIS.

to settle questions, which may come up later."[7] The material used to cover the western part of the temple came from the courtyard area:

> From February 8 onward the sand from the southern half of the court was thrown into the rooms in the southern part of the inner temple. I decided that the crude-brick walls could be saved from rapid decay only by covering again with sand.[8]

From photographs taken during Reisner's 1910 excavations (e.g., fig. 2), it appears that he filled the western third of the temple with cultural debris from the structures of the courtyard. Figure 3 is a section of some of the material redeposited in the western third of the MVT. Since the oldest layers were excavated last, they are on the top of the deposit. The stratigraphy is reversed.

AERA started the 2019 excavations in the west part of the temple and quickly realized what Reisner had done. His words proved prophetic. One hundred-and-eleven years after Reisner excavated MVT, the AREA specialists had the opportunity to study the redeposited cultural materials from the occupation in the courtyard.

---

[7] George Reisner Diary, February 8, 1910, p. 20.

[8] Reisner, *Mycerinus*, 38

Fig. 2. Reisner's excavation of the western and southern parts of the MVT court. His backfill and dumping (left) onto the western part of the temple consists of clean sand (white) and dense silt (dark). Photo. A339N-S. February 27, 1910, 111 years prior to our excavation of his dumps. View to the north.

Fig. 3. Clean sand and dark, dense, silty material in eastern section of the MVT-W excavations in 2019. Reisner's team dumped these materials in 1910 from their excavation of the settlement in the MVT court. Photo by Richard Redding, March 11, 2019.

As the faunal remains are associated with the structures in the courtyard, we can study the diet of people who lived in the MVT courtyard.

Who were these people? Reisner describes the structures in the courtyard as much like a "poor modern village."[9] He went on to conclude that the courtyard structures were a part of the pyramid city of Menakaure. Reisner found three inscribed stones in his excavations of the MVT that included royal decrees, two of which clearly establish the endowment of the MVT with offerings. The oldest is a decree by Shepseskaf that states he has endowed the temple of his father including a brief reference to bread.[10] It also established *pekher* offerings in the pyramid of Menkaure.[11] The *pekher* offerings referred to in the Shepseskaf text are reversion offerings and entitled the recipients to "daily deliveries of provisions from the reigning administration."[12] Ikram discusses the redistribution of offerings to the priests and their dependents.[13]

The later decree, by Pepy II, is similar to the decree of Pepy I that was found in the pyramid city of Snefru and continues the tradition of temple offerings reverting to priests.[14] Reisner goes on to conclude:

> By decree, the inhabitants, who were the priests of the pyramid temples and the trustees of the pyramid endowments, were granted certain privileges, exemption from taxes and from the exactions of administrative officials, probably as an additional inducement to maintain the offerings and services in the temple. These privileges made the pyramid cities very desirable for residence, and certainly everyone living in the neighborhood of such a city who could scrape up any pretext to an inherited right sought to gain a house in the city.... The Pepy decree may have been merely a renewal of some older decree; but it is certain that as long as the authority of that dynasty lasted, the pyramid city of Mycerinus was fully populated.[15]

Lehner and Hawass state that the structures in the courtyard were first built by Shepseskaf shortly after the completion of the MVT as an act of filial piety that would guarantee his succession.[16] The courtyard structures were rebuilt in the Fifth Dynasty during an expansion and renovation of the MVT.[17] A final phase of building in the courtyard is related to the Sixth Dynasty reconstruction, probably by Pepy II (c. 2246–2152 BC), after a flood heavily damaged the MVT.[18] Lehner extensively examined the question of who lived in the structures in the MVT courtyard and concluded that the structures, at least in the Fifth Dynasty occupation, were owned by highly ranked individuals and their estates, in order to claim a share of the temple offerings.[19] Lehner goes on to suggest that the actual occupants may have been dependents of these high ranking individuals.

Predictions

If the residents of the MVT courtyard structures were high status individuals receiving offerings of animals/meat, then what would these offerings consist? Based on tomb representations and actual offerings the most common gifts should be cattle.[20] We have visited large numbers of Old Kingdom tombs at Giza and Saqqara

---

[9] Reisner, *Mycerinus*, 49.

[10] Reisner, *Mycerinus*, 278.

[11] Nigel Strudwick, *Texts from the Pyramid Age* (Atlanta, 2005), 97.

[12] Hratch Papazian, *Domain of Pharaoh: The Structure and Components of The Economy of Old Kingdom Egypt* (PhD dissertation, University of Chicago, 2005), 260–62.

[13] Ikram, Salima. *Choice Cuts: Meat Production in Ancient Egypt* (Leuven, 1995), 220–23.

[14] Reisner, *Mycerinus*, 49.

[15] Reisner, *Mycerinus*, 49–50.

[16] Mark Lehner and Zahi Hawass, *Giza and the Pyramids* (Chicago, 2017), 276.

[17] Lehner and Hawass, *Giza and the Pyramids*, 277.

[18] Lehner and Hawass, *Giza and the Pyramids*, 279–80.

[19] Mark Lehner, "Shareholders: The Menkaure Valley Temple Occupation in Context," in Peter Der Manuelian and Thomas Schneider (eds.), *Towards a New History for the Egyptian Old Kingdom Perspectives on the Pyramid Age* (Leiden-Boston, 2015), 227–314, 306.

[20] Ikram, *Choice Cuts*, 41.

and the dominant animal represented in offerings indeed is cattle, *Bos taurus*.[21] Since this is a royal establishment, we would expect the consumption of sheep and goat to be minimal, given the relative desirability of beef compared to sheep-goat meat.[22] Additionally, an average adult, two-year old, steer/bull/heifer/cow, would produce 183.4 kg of edible product (EP) while a sheep would produce only 15 kg of EP.[23] This is enough beef for 815 portions of 225 g each, while a sheep would provide only 66 portions of 225 g. Larger establishments should slaughter cattle and smaller sheep-goats. We would expect pigs to be absent in the sample. Fish and birds, which are illustrated in offerings may be present in small numbers.

Cattle temple offerings primarily consist of heads and forelimbs.[24] In the Pottery Mound, cattle remains at the Workers' Town settlement at Giza, the predominance of hind limbs was identified as evidence of the "left-overs" from offerings.[25] If the *pekher* offerings coming to the MVT are pre-slaughtered packages, then we should see a sample dominated by heads and forelimbs. On the other hand, if live animals are brought to the MVT as *pekher* offerings, we should see a sample that reflects the bone distribution found in whole animals.

Methodology

The excavators recovered the bone from each feature by hand. Added to this handpicked sample were bone fragments found during screening of all deposits through a 0.2 cm screen. Finally, during a second wet screening, additional bone was added to the sample. Bone fragments were also found in the heavy fraction during flotation, but this material has not been included in this analysis.

We identified the animal remains by bag, dumping the contents into a small screen and sorting the bone fragments into three piles: fish, bird, and mammals. The fish fragments were sorted into two piles, one that contained potentially identifiable fragments and another that contained unidentifiable fragments. We identified the fish fragments in the first pile to body part and taxon, and then weighed each identified fragment. No unidentifiable fish remains were found in the sample.

As with the fish, we sorted the bird fragments into two piles: identifiable and unidentifiable. Those in first pile were identified and each fragment weighed. The other pile of unidentifiable fragments was sorted into limb, vertebra, rib, sternum/synsacrum, and skull fragments. We counted and weighted these piles.

We also initially sorted mammal fragments into two piles, again of identifiable and unidentifiable fragments. For the identifiable material, we recorded the taxon, body part, fusion/wear, evidence of burning, and other information. We then weighed each of the identifiable fragments. We sorted the unidentified fragments into limb, skull, vertebra, teeth, and rib by size (large, medium, and small). Then we counted and weighed the resulting piles.

Identification of the remains was aided by use of a modern skeletal comparative collection maintained in the AERA Lab.

In this report we use the "number of identified specimens" or "NISP" to refer to the abundance of bones. We define NISP as a simple count of the number of bones in each category.

---

[21] Ikram, *Choice Cuts*, 237–303; Salima Ikram, "Food and Funerals: Sustaining the Dead for Eternity," *Polish Archaeology in the Mediterranean* 20 (2011), 361–71. Salima Ikram, "Funerary Food Offerings," in Miroslav Barta (ed.), *Abusir XIII, Abusir South 2. Tomb Complex of the Vizier Qar, His Sons Qar Junior and Senedjemib, and Iykai* (Prague, 2009), 294–98.

[22] Redding, "Status and Diet at the Workers' Town, Giza, Egypt," 72.

[23] Richard Redding, "Cattle in Egypt" (unpublished manuscript, 2020), 30.

[24] Redding, "Status and Diet at the Workers' Town, Giza, Egypt," 73–74. Ikram, *Choice Cuts*, 129; Allan Allentuck, "An Acquired Taste: Emulation and Indigenization of Cattle Forelimbs in the Southern Levant," *Cambridge Archaeological Journal* 25 (2015), 45–62; Eslam Mohamed Salem, Mahmoud Hewedi, Aly Abdalla, Tamer Fahim, Fatma Khalil, "Food Heritage: Proximate Composition Analysis of Forelegs of Steers ("Oxen") and Their Pharaonic Cultural Context," *Journal of Ancient Egyptian Interconnections* 20 (2018), 58–70.

[25] Redding "Status and Diet at the Workers' Town, Giza, Egypt," 73.

The Faunal Remains from the 2019 Excavations at MVT

The animal bones from the excavations represent the redeposit of material resulting from the work of Reisner. It has been excavated twice and, hence, subjected to two events that would lead to fragmentation. Amazingly, the bone is in good condition. During the 2019 field season, we examined 6,611 fragments of animal bone from the excavations at MVT-W. We identified three of these fragments as fish, fifty seven fragments of bird, and 6,551 fragments as mammal.

Osteichthyes *(Fish)*

Only three fish bones, weighing 3.5g, were found and all were identifiable. The very low representation of fish in the sample, given the screening process described above, is not due to recovery or, we believe, preservation. The Nile perch (*Lates niloticus*), the *schal* (*Synodontis schal*) and the catfish (*Clarius gariepinus*) were each represented by one fragment. We cannot say much with only three fragments. Two (the Nile perch and the *schal*) were fished from deep waters, and one (the catfish) from shallow water. All were commonly consumed in pharaonic Egypt and are represented in Old Kingdom tomb scenes.[26] Probably the most interesting aspect of the sample is the low number of fish. It is possible that the absence of fish is due to the loss of material during the first excavation and redeposition. We consider this unlikely, as the complete sample was transferred only about twenty meters and dumped in mass. A quick examination of the wet-screen samples, not included in this report, does not show any increase in the amount of fish.

The ratio of identifiable mammal to fish is 260:1. Given that the mammals identified, cattle, sheep and goats, provide a minimum of 15 kg of edible product (EP) while a large Nile perch or catfish provides about 5 kg., the contribution of fish to the diet is non-existent.

Aves *(Birds)*

In the MVT-W sample we identified fifty-seven bird-bone fragments. We were able to identify eighteen of these bones, which weighed 14.2 g, to species. Forty-nine fragments that weighed 20.5 g were only identifiable to body part: thirty-six limb fragments and three sternum/synsacrum fragments. The ratio of identifiable mammal to identifiable bird is 29.0:1

Anas acuta

The pintail duck is represented by ten fragments from wing and leg elements. Pintails are common at archaeological sites throughout Egypt. The most commonly represented waterfowl in pharaonic Egypt was the pintail.[27] It is a desirable food item that was placed in tombs as offerings throughout Egyptian history.[28] They are easily domesticated and apparently were in the Old Kingdom.[29]

Anas Penelope

The European Wigeon is represented by two wing bones, an ulna and a carpometacarpus. It is found at archaeological sites throughout Egypt. It is not commonly represented in tomb scenes, although it appears as a hieroglyph.[30] It is highly desirable, and is common in the bird markets of Egypt at present.[31]

---

[26] Douglas Brewer and Renee Friedman, *Fish and Fishing in Ancient Egypt* (Warminster, 1989), 29, 38, 40, 49, 61, 62, 67, 68, 75, 76.

[27] Patrick Houlihan, *The Birds of Ancient Egypt* (Warminster, 1986), 71.

[28] Houlihan, *The Birds of Ancient Egypt*, 73; Ikram, *Choice Cuts*, 290.

[29] Houlihan, *The Birds of Ancient Egypt*, 72.

[30] Houlihan, *The Birds of Ancient Egypt*, 69.

[31] Houlihan, *The Birds of Ancient Egypt*, 70.

Anas crecca

Only one element, a humerus, was identified as from a green-winged teal. It is common in archaeological sites throughout Egypt. The flesh of this teal is considered the most desirable of any waterfowl.[32] The green-winged teal is well represented in tomb scenes and it has been found as offerings in tombs.[33] It is found in the bird markets of Egypt at present.[34]

Fulica atra

The coot is represented in the sample by a carpometacarpus. It is occasionally found in archaeological sites in Egypt. The flesh of the coot is not desirable, but it is edible, and it is common in the bird markets of Egypt at present. [35] It is rarely represented in the art of pharaonic Egypt.[36]

Columbia livia

The rock dove, or pigeon, is represented by four fragments. The sample includes three wing and one leg elements: a coracoid, an ulna, a carpometacarpus and a tarsometatarsus. Pigeons, surprisingly, are not common in archaeological samples from Egypt. Their occurrence in the MVT-W sample is a surprise. It is possible that pigeons did not become an important part of the Egyptian diet until the appearance of cotes in the Greco-Roman period. Pigeons are not common in pharaonic art, but they were eaten.[37]

Summary of the Birds

Birds were eaten by the residents of the MVT. It is curious that vertebrae, distal limb elements, and fragments of the sternum and synsacrum, largely are absent. The sample is too small to make a general statement, but it appears that slaughter of the birds may have occurred in some other area. The focus of consumption was on ducks that may have been domestic. Again, the contribution of birds to the diet of the residents in the courtyard is minimal.

The Mammals

We examined 6,551 mammal specimens, weighing a total of 42,009.0 g, and were able to assign 782 fragments, weighing 963.4 g, to at least the level of the genus. The unidentifiable mammals fragments numbered 5,769 and weighed 41,045.6 g. The counts (NISP) of identifiable fragments for each taxon are provided in Table 1. The identifiable sample is almost exclusively composed of cattle (*Bos taurus*).

Bos taurus

Cattle are the dominant animal in the archaeological sites, art, and hieroglyphs of pharaonic Egypt. Cattle meat, particularly from young cattle, is the most desirable among the domestic animals. At the Old Kingdom Workers' Village (Heit el-Ghurab) site at Giza, cattle meat was preferred, and preferential access was associated with higher status. The highest status individuals at the site consumed cattle, almost exclusively, and consumed very young animals, less than one-year of age.[38]

[32] Houlihan, *The Birds of Ancient Egypt*, 69.
[33] Houlihan, *The Birds of Ancient Egypt*, 69.
[34] Houlihan, *The Birds of Ancient Egypt*, 69.
[35] Houlihan, *The Birds of Ancient Egypt*, 91.
[36] Houlihan, *The Birds of Ancient Egypt*, 90.
[37] Houlihan, *The Birds of Ancient Egypt*, 101; Salima Ikram, "A Re-Analysis of Part of Prince Amenemhat Q's Eternal Menu," *JARCE* 48 (2013), 119–35.
[38] Redding "Status and Diet at the Workers' Town, Giza, Egypt," 73–74.

Table 1. Counts (NISP) of identified mammal from MVT-W presented by taxon

Taxon	Count (NISP)
Bos taurus	767
Ovis-Capra	8
Gazella sp.	3
Equus sp.	2
Oryx	1
Sus scrofa	1

Cattle (*Bos taurus*) are represented in MVT-W sample by 767 fragments that weighed 961.0 g. All of the cattle bones for which we have measurements fall in the range of domestic animals. Cattle are the dominate taxa as the ratio of cattle to sheep/goat fragments is 95.9:1. An adult young bull/steer/heifer produces 183.4 kg of EP and a sheep/goat produces 15 kg.[39] If we use the EP differential and recalculate the ratio to reflect EP contribution, we get a ratio of 1172.5:1. The contribution to the diet of sheep/goats or any other mammal is not significant.

Only two fragments, both parts of the pubis, could be sexed. One is male and the other female. We were able to record fusion data on 309 limb elements (Table 2). These data allowed us to construct a survivorship curve for cattle (fig. 4). The resulting curve trends down from birth to twenty-four to thirty months of age when the survivorship drops to 62.5%. The majority of the cattle (60.2%) had survived beyond 3.5–4 years when slaughtered.

We classified cattle bones into skull fragments and limb bones, we further classified the limb bones as proximal limb bones or distal limb bones. Proximal limb bones include the scapula, humerus, radius, ulna, pelvis, femur, patella, tibia, and lateral malleolus. These bones are usually associated with large cuts of meat and are considered meat-bearing bones. Distal limb bones included carpals, tarsals, metacarpals, metatarsals, phalanges and sesamoids. The bones have little meat but they are covered with tendons and cartilage, and the bones themselves are filled with marrow, and are considered non-meat bearing bones. Skull fragments, at sixty-four, represented 8.2% of the total number of cattle fragments. Cattle limb bones are represented by 703 fragments. The distal limb element fragments totaled 359 and proximal limb element fragments, 344. The meat-bearing limb fragments from cattle represent 48.9% of limb specimens and the non-meat bearing fragments represent 51%. If whole animals were brought to the area for slaughter, than 66% should be distal limb fragments and 34% proximal limb fragments. Distal limb elements are under-represented and proximal limb elements are slightly over-represented. It is possible that phalanges and podials were being utilized in other areas. Metatarsals are certainly under-represented.

Forelimb elements are represented by 357 fragments and hindlimb elements by 185 fragments. A bias toward forelimbs is apparent in the data. We tested whether this bias was significant using Chi^2. We assumed that the expected number of fore- and hind limb fragments would each be 271 as the number of hind limb to forelimb elements in a *B. taurus* is 1:1.1. The Chi^2 was 28.0 with one degree of freedom and the difference was highly significant (p=0.000). Forelimbs are over-represented and the difference is highly significant.

Table 3 presents the NISP for the forelimb elements by symmetry: right versus left. We would expect a 50:50 relationship: one right fragment for each left fragment. We tested the data in Table 3 using Chi^2. The test used the NISP for right fragments against the expected, that is if 50% of the total would have been from the right side. The Chi^2 was 14.632 with four degrees of freedom and the difference was highly significant (p=0.00552982). Table 4 presents the symmetry data from the hindlimb elements. We also tested these data using Chi^2. Again, we would expect a 50:50 relationship. We have tested the hind limb data using the Chi^2 with the right fragments versus the expected. The Chi^2 value is 2.791, with six degrees of freedom, and the test indicates the difference

[39] Redding, *Cattle in Egypt*, 30.

Table 2. Fusion data for cattle elements from MVT-W presented by fusion group

Group	Age of Fusion (months)		Element	Unfused	Fused	Group % Fused
1	7–10		Scapula	6	47	
		Group Total		6	47	88.7
2	12–18		Dist. Humerus	3	31	
			Prox. Radius	0	15	
		Group Total		3	46	93.9
3	18		First Phalanx	4	25	
	18		Second Phalanx	5	32	
		Group Total		9	57	86.4
4	24–30		Dist. Tibia	8	12	
			Dist. Metapodial	10	18	
		Group Total		18	30	62.5
4	42–48		Prox. Humerus	14	15	
			Dist. Radius	4	9	
			Prox. Ulna	2	4	
			Prox. Femur	8	9	
			Dist. Femur	4	11	
			Prox. Tibia	5	8	
		Group Total		37	56	60.2

from expected is not significant (*p*=0.83457591). The bias observed in the forelimb towards the right side is highly significant. There is no significant bias in the hindlimbs between the right and left sides.

Ovis-Capra

All of the sheep-goat remains must be from domestic animals because the wild ancestors of sheep and goat did not occur in Egypt.[40] Sheep-goats are represented in MVT-W sample by eight fragments that weighed 20.9 grams. The sample included fragments of a mandible, a right molar, an ischium, a distal metapodial, a proximal metacarpal, two first phalanges, and a second phalanx. Only the distal metapodial could be identified to genus and it was from a sheep. This is an extremely small sample

[40] Dale Osborn and Jana Osbornova, *The Mammals of Ancient Egypt* (Warminster, 1998), 186, 193.

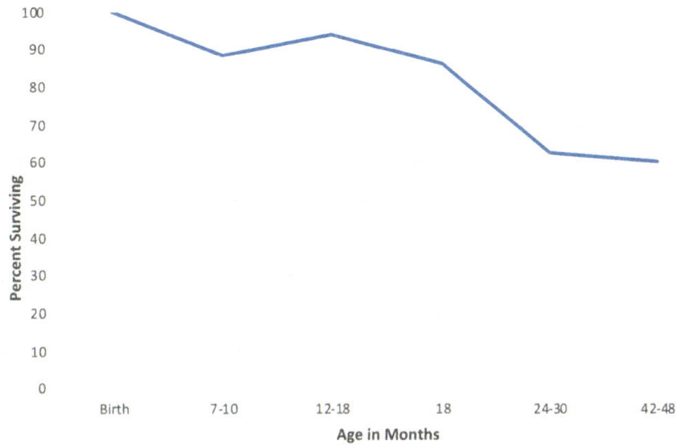

Fig. 4. Survivorship curve for the MVT-W cattle based on bone fusion data.

Table 3. Counts (NISP) by element by symmetry for fore limb fragments from MVT-W

Fore limb element	Right	left	Total	Expected
Scapula	54	19	73	36.5
Humerus	44	28	72	36.0
Radius	25	12	37	18.5
Ulna	15	17	32	16.0
Carpals	40	27	67	33.5
Metacarpals	22	20	42	21.0
Total	200	123	323	

Table 4. Counts (NISP) by element by symmetry for hind limb fragments from MVT-W

Hind limb element	Right	Left	Total	Expected
Femur	25	14	39	19.5
Patella	4	3	7	3.5
Tibia	19	19	38	19.0
Calcaneum	4	8	12	6.0
Astragalus	8	18	26	13.0
Tarsal	9	12	21	10.5
Metatarsals	4	7	11	5.5
Total	73	81	154	

Gazella *sp.*

Gazelles are wild and were probably found in the desert to the west of the Giza plateau during the Old Kingdom. We found only three fragments of a gazelle that could not be identified to species. These included a distal humerus and two 1st phalanxes. Six species of gazelle may have occurred in Egypt in the pharaonic period.[41] Since the most reliable way to differentiate these species is by horn core shape, we could not identify the fragments to species. It is likely that they represent the Dorcas gazelle, *G. dorcas*, or the slender-horned gazelle, *G. leptoceros*.

Equus *sp.*

An equid is represented in the MVT-W sample by two metacarpal elements. Both fragments, one from metacarpal III and one from metacarpal IV, were found in the same context and fit together. The equid represented by these fragments is most likely the donkey, *E. asinus*.

Sus scrofa

The pig occurred wild in pharaonic Egypt[42] but it is likely that the MVT-W pig is domestic. We identified only one fragment as from the pig: a distal second metacarpal.

Oryx dammah

The scimitar-horned oryx was found throughout the western desert into modern times and was well represented in pharaonic art. [43] It may have been tamed in the Old Kingdom. We found a single distal humerus that was identified as oryx. Since the straight-horned, beisa, oryx *(Oryx beisa)*, is limited to the southern extremes of Egypt, we have identified the fragments as from the scimitar-horned oryx.

Unidentifiable Mammal Fragments

The counts and weights of the unidentified mammal fragments are presented by category in Table 5.

Based on identifiable fragments, the ratio of cattle to sheep-goat is 95.9:1. Based on counts for large limb fragments, assuming all large limb fragments are cattle and all medium limb fragments are sheep-goat, the ratio of cattle to sheep-goat is 7.6:1. For rib fragments, the ratio is 19:1 and vertebra fragments it is 22.1:1. These figures are far short of the 95.9:1 based on identifiable fragments. Using the weight of identifiable fragments, the ratio for limb fragments is 60.3:1, for rib fragments it is 63.2:1, and for the vertebra fragments it is 76.3:1. Which number is the best estimate of relative abundance for cattle versus sheep-goat? Many factors affect these numbers. Larger limb bones may break into more identifiable fragments. Medium limb shaft fragments may be more common than identifiable sheep-goat might suggest. We think this problem is something that needs to be systematically explored.

Summary for the Mammals

Cattle dominate the MVT-W fauna to the point that the contribution of all other mammals is insignificant. Domestic sheep, goats, and possibly pig may have been consumed, but cattle contribute 136.3 kg of meat for each

---

[41] Osborn and Osbornova, *The Mammals of Ancient Egypt*, 175–80.

[42] Richard Redding, "The Pig and the Chicken: Modeling Human Subsistence Behavior in the Archaeological Record Using Historical and Animal Husbandry Data," *Journal of Archeological Research* 23 (2015), 330.

[43] Osborn and Osbornova, *The Mammals of Ancient Egypt*, 161–65.

Table 5. Counts (NISP) and weights (g) of unidentifiable mammal fragments presented by category

	Large limb	Medium limb	Large rib	Medium rib	Large vertebra	Medium vertebra	Large skull	Medium skull	Large teeth frags.	Medium teeth frags.
Counts	3164	419	478	25	376	17	184	28	246	1
weight	32095.8	532.2	2227.7	35.2	2945.5	38.6	1062.2	56.4	752.3	0.8

1 kg of sheep-goat meat. Some gazelle meat was possibly consumed but it appears to have been rare, possibly a trickle-down.

Sixty percent of the cattle were older than forty-eight months. This is unusually old for a harvest profile of males. The ideal time to harvest young males is before their second year when the growth curve begins to flatten and the second year of births increases labor requirements.[44] It is possible that a number of females that were being culled from the breeding herd might have been consumed.

The limb bone distribution for the cattle suggest that slaughter may not have occurred in the area of the courtyard because distal limb elements are under-represented, but it is possible that cattle may have been butchered in the area of the MVT courtyard with the distal limb fragments being removed from the area. These distal limb elements, which are covered with tendons and ligaments but contain desirable fatty marrow, were used to produce a knuckle bone stew/soup that may have been given to dependents and laborers not residing in the MVT courtyard. Ikram has discussed examples of these joints being offered in other Old Kingdom pyramid complexes at Abu Sir.[45] In present-day Egypt knuckle-bone stews/soup, *kawara*, is composed of the ends of limb bones of cattle, usually the feet, after the removal of any large muscles, leaving all the marrow, cartilage, and connective tissue. *Kawara* is a protein rich, high calorie dish (20 g of protein, 65.5 g of fat and 519 Kcal per 100 g[46]) that would have been ideal for individuals involved in heavy labor. Table 6 presents the Minimum Number of Animals (MNA) for each of the limb elements that we calculate as the NISP of the most common fragment of the element taking into account symmetry. Table 6 also includes the difference between the observed MNA for each element and the expected MNA, which is based on the element with the highest MNA. The absence of phalanges and the metatarsal bones is significant as the distal metatarsal/metacarpal and phalanges are the elements usually used to prepare *kawara*.

Cattle forelimb fragments are over-represented in the sample and the difference is highly significant. Cattle forelimbs are represented in tombs as the preferred offering.[47] The over-representation of forelimb fragments either represents the slaughter of whole animals in the courtyard plus an influx of some forelimb packages, or the preferential removal of hindlimb elements. Curiously, we found a bias in forelimb fragments to the right side of the animal. No symmetry bias was found in the hindlimb. These data would suggest that the over-representation of the forelimbs is due to the influx of forelimb packages, primarily from the right side.

---

44 Redding, *Cattle in Egypt*, 28.

45 Ikram, *Choice Cuts*. 136–37. Also see, De Mayer, M. and J. M. Serrano, "Cattle Feet in Funerary Rituals: A Diachronic View Combining Archeology and Iconography," in P. Piacentini and A. D. Castelli (eds.), *Old Kingdom Art and Archaeology 7, Proceedings of the International Conference Universita Degli Studi di Milano 3–7 July 2017* (2019), 402–7.

46 P. L. Pellett and Sossy Shadarevian, *Food Composition Tables for Use in the Middle East* (Beirut, 2013), 20.

47 Redding, "Status and Diet at the Workers' Town, Giza, Egypt," 73–74; Ikram, *Choice Cuts*, 129; Allan Allentuck, "An Acquired Taste: Emulation and Indigenization of Cattle Forelimbs in the Southern Levant" *Cambridge Archaeological Journal* 25 (2015), 45–62; Eslam Mohamed Salem, Mahmoud Hewedi, Aly Abdalla, Tamer Fahim, Fatma Khalil, "Food Heritage: Proximate Composition Analysis of Forelegs of Steers ("Oxen") and Their Pharaonic Cultural Context," *Journal of Ancient Egyptian Interconnections* 20 (2018), 58–70.

Table 6. Counts of limb elements compared to expected based on minimum number of animals (MNA) established from most frequently occurring element

Forelimb element	MNA expected	Observed	Difference	Hindlimb element	MNI expected	Observed	Difference
Humerus	20	20	0	Femur	18	15	-3
Radius	20	10	-10	Tibia	18	11	-7
Ulna	20	9	-11	Patella	18	4	-14
Radial carpal	20	6	-14	Lateral malleolus	18	3	-15
Intermediate carpal	20	8	-12	Calcaneum	18	8	-10
Ulnar carpal	20	5	-15	Astragalus	18	18	0
2nd+3rd carpal	20	12	-8	Central+4th tarsal	18	8	-10
Metacarpal	20	15	-5	Metatarsal	18	4	-14
First phalanx	76	31	-45				
Second phalanx	76	37	-39				
Third phalanx	76	0	-76				

Comparisons

We would like to compare the MVT-W fauna to two other faunas from the Workers' Town, also known as the Heit el Ghurab (HeG). The first fauna is the combined data for the two Galleries that AERA has excavated, Gallery III.3 and III.4 (fig. 5). The galleries at the HeG were believed to have housed workers involved in the construction of Menkaure's pyramid. Residents of the Galleries were provisioned.[48] The second fauna is from an area referred to as the Pottery Mound (PM) (see fig. 5). The PM is a garbage dump from one or more high status houses that included sealing fragments with high-ranking titles.[49] The PM fauna included two teeth from a leopard (*Panthera pardus*) which probably came from leopard-skin robes that included the head. Additional leopard teeth have been found in House 1, which the PM abuts. These robes are seen in tomb scenes worn by royals and priests.[50] We selected these two faunas for comparison because the Galleries had a low status, albeit, provisioned diet, while the PM had a high-status provisioned diet. [51]

A caveat regarding these comparisons: The Galleries and PM faunas are from the Workers' Town and are part of an integrated subsistence system. These faunas date to the reign of Menkaure, the last king of the Fourth Dynasty. The MVT-W fauna probably dates to the Fifth and Sixth Dynasties, and while it was part of an integrated subsistence system, it was not the same one.

Table 7 presents ratios between taxa for the Galleries, PM and MVT-W faunas. The ratio between cattle and sheep-goats for the Galleries, PM, and MVT-W shows cattle elements occurring at low levels in the Galleries and rising to a stunning 95.9:1 in the MVT-W. Given the relative contribution of edible product between cattle and sheep-goat, 184 kg for a steer/bull/heifer/cow to 15 kg for a sheep-goat, while cattle have an almost equal contribution to the diet in the Galleries, cattle are far more important than sheep-goat in the diet at the PM, and sheep-goat, compared to cattle, are an insignificant part of the diet at MVT-W. One caveat with the Galleries' sample of cattle: in terms of EP, cattle are probably much less important than we might assume based on the ratio, 0.1:1, because the cattle elements present are not the large meat bearing elements but the distal non-meat

[48] Redding, "Status and Diet at the Workers' Town, Giza, Egypt," 69.

[49] John Nolan, *Mud Sealings and Fourth Dynasty Administration at Giza* (PhD dissertation, University of Chicago, 2010), 357–82.

[50] Richard Redding, "Treasures from a High Class Dump," *AERAgram* 8.2, 6–7

[51] Redding, "Status and Diet at the Workers' Town, Giza, Egypt," 72–73.

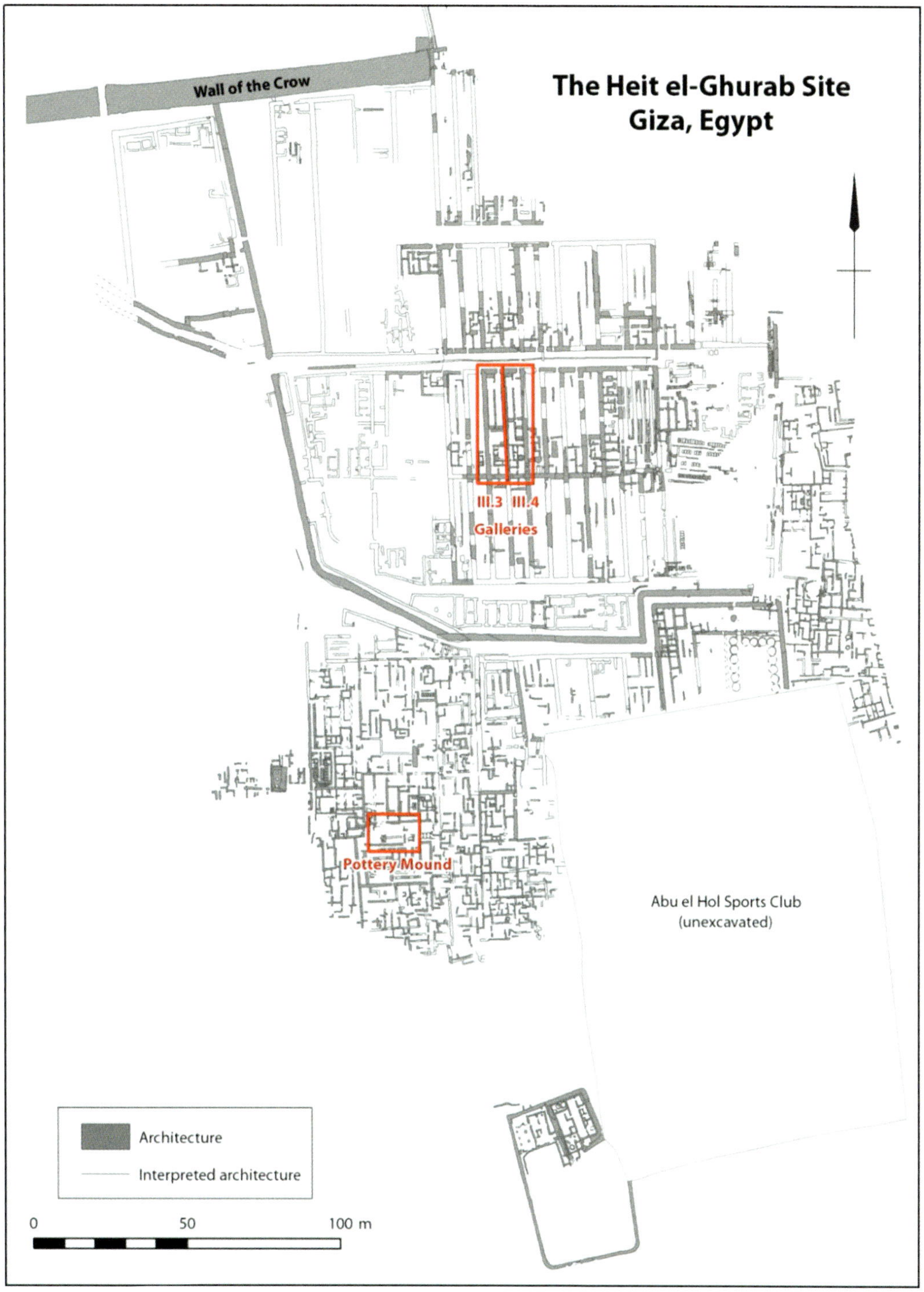

Fig. 5. The Workers' Town (HeG) with Galleries III.3, III.4, and the Pottery Mound located. Figure by Rebekah Miracle from AERA GIS.

Table 7. Comparison of ratios between taxa based on NISP for the faunas of the Galleries, PM and MVT-W

Ratio	Galleries	PM	MVT-W
Cattle to sheep-goat	0.1:1	7.4:1	95.9:1
Cattle to identified fish	0.8:1	3.1:1	255.6:1
Cattle to bird	4.4:1	1.2:1	13.5:1

bearing elements. This suggests that the residents of the Galleries were eating feet of cattle, a stew of distal limb elements, which, per unit of bone, makes smaller contribution to the diet, in calories, than the larger meat bearing bones, albeit a nutritious one.

The ratio of cattle fragments to identifiable fish fragments probably does not have much meaning in terms of contribution to the diet. Since an average fish yields only a small fraction of the EP of a steer/bull/heifer/cow, even if the ratio is 1:1, the contribution of fish is very small relative to that of cattle. The ratio can be used to changes in the diet between areas of a site or between sites. In the Galleries, the ratio of cattle to identified fish is 0.8:1 and rises to 3.1:1 in the PM. Residents in the galleries consumed much more fish than the individuals whose garbage was placed in the PM. For MVT-W, the ratio is 255.6:1 as only three identifiable fish fragments were recovered. The residents of the MVT courtyard were probably not eating fish. With the ratio of cattle to bird fragments we see a slightly different pattern. Birds are less important in the Galleries and the MVT-W faunas and most important in the PM fauna.

One of the most interesting ratios in the three faunas is cattle hindlimb to cattle forelimb. In the PM the ratio is 38.8:1 and the fusion data indicates that all the cattle were slaughtered before the age of twenty-four months and the majority before twelve months.[52] The PM sample represents the remnants of the carcasses of animals slaughtered for offerings.[53] The ratio of cattle hindlimb to cattle forelimb for the Galleries is also biased toward hindlimbs (5.1:1). Again, although the bias is not as great, we suggest that the residents of the Galleries were getting the tibias, tarsals, metatarsals, and phalanges left over from cattle slaughtered for offerings, probably to prepare as an ancient equivalent of *kawara*. The ratio for the MVT courtyard fauna, at 0.5:1, is biased toward forelimb fragments. The bias is not large, but is statistically significant. This suggests that the residents of the MVT courtyard were getting extra forelimbs from cattle slaughtered somewhere else or slaughtered locally with the rest of the body removed. The only other fauna that we excavated at Giza that has a ratio of cattle hindlimb to cattle forelimb that is biased toward forelimbs, at 0.1:1, is the sample from the Silo Building Complex (SBC).[54] The SBC is an installation occupied by individuals supporting the cult of Khafre and, hence, consumed offerings.[55]

The symmetry bias in cattle forelimbs to the right limb is curious. The SBC sample, although small (30 NISP) is also biased to the right side with nineteen forelimb fragments from the right side and eleven from the left. In some of the earliest studied "elite" burials from Hierakonpolis, the cattle, and indeed most of the species of animals found in the burials, are disproportionally represented by forelimbs, and further, they are biased to the right side.[56] Also, in an Eleventh Dynasty temple foundation deposit, the right forelimbs of cattle are disproportionally

52 Redding, "Status and Diet at the Workers' Town, Giza, Egypt," 73.

53 Redding, "Status and Diet at the Workers' Town, Giza, Egypt," 73.

54 Unpublished data.

55 Anonymous, "Conundrums and Surprises: The Silo Building Complex,"*AERAgram* 13 (2012), 9.

56 Wim Van Neer, Veerle Linseele, and Renée Friedman, "Animal Burials and Food Offerings at the Elite Cemetery HK6 of Hierakonpolis," in S. Hendrickx, R. Friedman, K. Cialowicz and M. Chlodnicki (eds.), *Egypt at Its Origins: Studies in Memory of Barbara Adams* (Leuven-Paris-Dudley, 2004), 106–8.

Fig. 6. Cattle heads and forelimbs as offerings in a scene from Luxor Temple east of the sanctuary. Photo by Richard Redding

represented.[57] The normative explanation for a right side bias is ritual.[58] We are reluctant to offer an explanation based on the data.

The last ratio we will examine is between cattle skull fragments and cattle limb fragments.

We have already discussed the use of cattle forelimbs as offerings, but the heads of cattle are almost equally portrayed as offerings (fig. 6). The Galleries have the greatest representation in the cattle samples of skull fragments with a ratio of cattle limb fragments to cattle skull fragments of 2.3:1. The MVT courtyard cattle sample has a ratio of cattle limb fragments to cattle skull fragments of 11.0:1 and the PM sample has a ratio of 69.6:1. If the PM sample is the leftovers from offerings, then the very low representation of skull fragments is congruent with that conclusion. The MVT courtyard residents should have had access to the EP associated with the skull, so we would expected it to have had the highest number of skull fragments relative to limb fragments. The question becomes why are the Galleries higher? It is possible that like the distal hindlimb elements that could be used to make *kawara*, the left-over low value EP of the skull, once the desirable brain, cheek, and tongue had been removed, were transferred to individuals of lower status than the occupants of the MVT courtyard.

The age structure of the PM cattle is extremely young with only four cattle older than twenty-four months, and 90% of the cattle were slaughtered before twelve months of age. The age structure of the Galleries also indicates a focus on young cattle with 70% less than twelve months of age and no evidence of any cattle surviving

[57] Laszlo Bartosiewicz, "Cattle Offering from the Temple of Montuhotep Sankhkara (Thebes, Egypt)," in M. Mashkour, A.M. Choyke, H. Buitenhuis, and F. Poplin (eds.), *Archaeozoology of the Near East IVB: Proceedings of the Fourth International Symposium on the Archaeozoology of Southwestern Asia and Adjacent Areas* (Groningen, 2000), 172.

[58] Michael MacKinnon, "Left Is Right: The Symbolism behind Side Choice among Ancient Animal Sacrifices," in D. Campana, P. Crabtree, S. DeFrance, J. Lev-Tov, and A. Choyke (eds.), *Anthropological Approaches to Zooarchaeology: Complexity, Colonialism, and Animal Transformations* (Oxford, 2010), 250–58; Simon Davis, "'Thou shalt take of the ram … the right thigh; for it is a ram of consecration …': Some Zoo-Archaeological Examples of Body-Part Preferences," *Uomini, piante e animali nella dimensione del sacro. Bari: Edipuglia* (2008), 63–70; Richard Madgwick and Jacqui Mulville, "Feasting on Fore-Limbs: Conspicuous Consumption and Identity in Later Prehistoric Britain," *Antiquity* 89 (2015), 629–44; László Bartosiewicz, "Cattle Offering from the Temple of Montuhotep Sankhkara (Thebes, Egypt), in M. Mashkour, A. M. Choyke, H. Buitenhuis, and F. Poplin (eds.), *Archaeozoology of the Near East IVB: Proceedings of the Fourth International Symposium on the Archaeozoology of Southwestern Asia and Adjacent Areas* (Groningen, 2000), 164–76.

beyond twenty-four months of age. The MVT-W fauna focusses on older cattle with 60% surviving beyond the age of forty-eight months. The older age of slaughter for the MVT-W fauna maybe the result of a use of more females who were culled from breeding populations.

Conclusion

The fauna from the MVT-W, which represents subsistence debris deposited by the occupants of the courtyard of the temple, exhibits characteristics associated with consumption of offerings by high-status individuals. First, the fauna is dominated by cattle; sheep and goats are effectively absent. This was our first expectation in our list of predictions. Second, the over-representation of forelimb fragments is consistent with offerings. What is not is the absence of heads. This, along with the absence of distal limb elements, is a new pattern we need to examine and explain. We suggest that this may be related to the individuals in the MVT courtyard consuming the most desirable meat portions and passing the heads—less brain, cheek, and tongue, and the distal limb elements, particularly from the hindlimb—on to lower ranking dependents who were residents of some other area. If this scenario is correct, we suggest that slaughter occurred in or near the courtyard and cattle parts were distributed from there. The lithic sample included large numbers of blades and fragments of knives, which would support this hypothesis.

Excavations by AERA continued in 2020 and an additional sample of bone was recovered. Further excavations are planned. We will test some of these hypotheses with data from future seasons.

The MVT-W faunal data present patterns in distribution of species, body parts and symmetry. These patterns are best understood as part of the overall subsistence system of the Old Kingdom, particularly provisioning by a central authority and the food infrastructure that supported pyramids construction and temple maintenance. They can only be explained with reference to faunal from excavations in other settlement areas of the Giza Plateau and other settlements areas of other Old Kingdom sites.

An Ostracon Depicting a King at the Art Institute of Chicago (AIC 1920.255)

Ashley F. Arico
Art Institute of Chicago

Katherine E. Davis
University of Michigan

Abstract

Publication of a figured ostracon held in the Art Institute of Chicago. Likely deriving from a western Theban context, the limestone flake bears a sketch of a king on the recto and textual inscriptions on the verso. An evaluation of the drawing, as well as an edition of the previously unpublished hieratic texts, is presented. The pristine surface of the figured recto in contrast to the multiple uses on the verso suggests that the object had a complex use history. Uses as a ritual object and for scribal practice are considered.

ملخص

نشرٌ لأوستراكا مصورة تحمل رسمًا لشخص محفوظة بمعهد شيكاغو للفنون. تحمل تلك كسرة الحجر الجيري ، التي يُحتمل أن تكون قادمة من موقع بغرب طيبة، رسمًا لملك على الوجه وكتابات على الظهر. تُقدم هذه المقالة تقييماً للرسم وتحقيقاً للنصوص الهيراطيقية التي لم تنشر من قبل. يشير وجه الأوستراكا الذي يحمل رسماً في حالة جيدة من الحفظ، والظهر الذي تم إعادة استخدامه مراتاً عديدة، ، إلى أن هذا الأثر لديه تاريخ استخدام معقد ويناقش هذا المقال هذه الأوستراكا كأثرًا شعائريًا، مع استخدامها لأغراض التدريب على الكتابة.

Introduction

Figured ostraca are limestone flakes or potsherds repurposed as surfaces for illustration rather than or in addition to writing.[1] These miniature artworks, which range from rough sketches to the fully realized designs of master artists, depict a variety of subjects including the flora and fauna of Egypt, glimpses of daily life, divine images, and depictions of the king. An example of the latter type can be found at the Art Institute of Chicago (AIC) (figs.

We thank Maria Kokkori, PhD, Associate Scientist for Scholarly Initiatives, Art Institute of Chicago; Kelly Keegan, Associate Paintings Conservator, Art Institute of Chicago; and Rachel Sabino, Objects Conservator, Art Institute of Chicago for their assistance with studying and imaging the ostracon. We also thank Richard Jasnow and Karen (Maggie) Bryson for their thoughtful suggestions, and Emily Teeter, whose earlier research on this object was invaluable.

[1] Numerous studies have been dedicated to the topic of figured ostraca, both within specific museum collections and more generally. See, for example, Emma Brunner-Traut, *Die altägyptischen Scherbenbilder (Bildostraka) der deutschen Museen und Sammlungen* (Wiesbaden, 1956); Bengt E. J. Peterson, *Zeichnungen einer Totenstadt: Bildostraka aus Theben-West, ihre Fundplätze, Themata und Zweckbereiche mitsamt einem Katalog der Gayer-Anderson-Sammlung in Stockholm* (Stockholm, 1973); William H. Peck and John G. Ross, *Egyptian Drawings* (New York, 1978); Emma Brunner-Traut, *Egyptian Artists' Sketches: Figured Ostraka from the Gayer-Anderson Collection in the Fitzwilliam Museum, Cambridge* (Leiden, 1979); Anne Minault-Gout, *Carnets de pierre: L'art des ostraca dans l'Égypte ancienne* (Paris, 2002).

Journal of the American Research Center in Egypt 56 (2020), 35–46
doi: http://dx.doi.org/10.5913/jarce.56.2020.a003

Fig. 1. Recto of Ostracon with a Sketch of a King, New Kingdom, Dynasty 19–20. Photo courtesy of The Art Institute of Chicago.

Fig. 2. Verso of Ostracon with a Sketch of a King. Photo courtesy of The Art Institute of Chicago.

1 and 2).[2] In its present state, the limestone flake measures 24.1 x 15.2 cm with a maximum thickness of 3.2 cm. On the smooth, slightly convex surface of the recto, a skilled artist has drawn an unnamed king. The jagged verso has had a more complex history of use, with portions of three separate hieratic inscriptions and a large hieratic crocodile sign preserved. This face of the ostracon has not previously been published.

James Henry Breasted purchased the ostracon from the well-known antiquities dealer Ralph Huntington Blanchard on behalf of the Art Institute of Chicago in 1919. In a letter to the museum's president, Charles L. Hutchinson, written from Cairo, Breasted described his acquisition as an "Artist's preliminary study of standing figure of a king drawn in ink on limestone, an exquisite sketch."[3] Assigned the accession number 1920.255, it remains the most ancient drawing in the museum's collections.[4]

A Royal Image

At first glance the ostracon's decorated face presents a very traditional depiction of a New Kingdom monarch. The king stands facing right. Although he is not named, his status as a ruler is indicated by the khepresh (or Blue

[2] Thomas George Allen, *A Handbook of the Egyptian Collection* (Chicago, 1923), 44; Emily Teeter, "Ostracon with a Sketch of a King" (unpublished manuscript, November 11, 2018), Microsoft Word file, Department of Arts of Africa, The Art Institute of Chicago.

[3] James H. Breasted to Charles L. Hutchinson, December 4, 1919, Directors' Correspondence, Box 032, Oriental Institute Museum Archive, University of Chicago.

[4] The object was on long-term loan to the Oriental Institute Museum of the University of Chicago from August 1949 to January 1993. While there, it bore the registration number E18214.

Fig. 3. Depiction of a standard-bearing statue of Seti I. After Amice M. Calverley, The Temple of King Sethos I at Abydos, vol. 1, The Chapels of Osiris, Isis and Horus *(London-Chicago, 1933), pl. 30.*

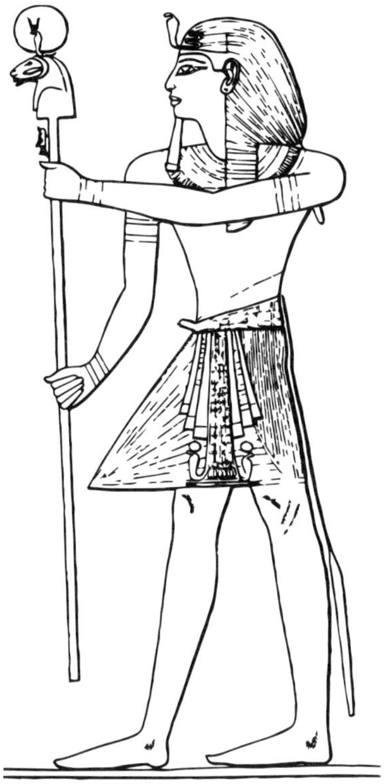

Fig. 4. Depiction of Ramesses III presenting the standard of Amun-Re. After The Epigraphic Survey, Medinet Habu, vol. 5, The Temple Proper, pt. 1, *OIP 83 (Chicago, 1957), pl. 330.*

Crown) that adorns his head, complete with a coiled uraeus above his brow and a streamer falling from the nape of his neck. The king wears a mid-calf-length kilt with a looped sash and longer sheer garment. His chest is bare save for the plain broad collar around his neck, which is paired with an armlet and bracelet on each arm. More unusual is the staff that he supports with his left arm, signaling his role as a standard bearer of Amun-Re. As an emblem of that god, the standard is topped with a ram's head crowned with a large solar disk.

Standard bearers appear with some regularity in the art of the New Kingdom within both the royal and private realms.[5] Depictions show a striding individual—often the king, but sometimes also an official, or even the queen—with a divine standard in the form of a shoulder-height staff surmounted by the head of a god or other sacred image.[6] The motif is perhaps most familiar in the form of standard-bearing statues, which were produced from the middle of the Eighteenth Dynasty through the end of the New Kingdom. In these three-dimensional works, the standard usually rests against its bearer's shoulder, secured in the crook of his or her elbow in a manner akin to that depicted on the ostracon.[7] When represented in two dimensions, however, the pose of these statues is much more rigid: the standard is held out before the individual who grasps the staff with both hands,

[5] B. van de Walle, "Le pieu sacré d'Amon," *Archiv Orientální* 20 (1952), 111–35; Marianne Eaton-Krauss, "Concerning Standard-Bearing Statues," *SAK* 4 (1976), 69–73; Helmut Satzinger, "Der Heilige Stab als Kraftquelle des Königs: Versuch einer Funktionsbestimmung der ägyptischen Stabträger-Statuen," *Jahrbuch der Kunsthistorischen Sammlungen in Wien* 77 (1981), 9–43; Catherine Chadefaud, *Les Statues Porte-enseignes de l'Égypte ancienne (1580–1085 avant J.C.): Signification et insertion dans le culte du Ka royal* (Paris, 1982).

[6] In some instances two standards appear.

[7] Occasionally the standard is held in front of its bearer, as in a fragmentary statue depicting Ramesses VI (Leiden F. 1941/12/1. See Simone Burger Robin, *Late Ramesside Royal Statuary* (Wallasey, UK, 2019), 70–74.

resting its bottom securely on top of the statue base (fig. 3).[8] Human (that is to say non-statue) standard bearers are frequently shown in a similar pose when raising their standards in presentation to the gods (fig. 4).

These complementary contexts for two-dimensional depictions of the king as a standard bearer raise the question of how the subject of the drawing currently under discussion should be understood—is it a representation of the ruler, or of a statue portraying him? Unfortunately, a break at the bottom of the stone has removed the king's feet, and with them any clues to interpretation that might have been provided by the presence of a statue base or groundline. The content of his right hand provides an important hint, however. Here, the king holds a short, horizontal object—almost certainly the document case that is a well-attested feature of royal statues, including contemporary examples showing the king as a standard bearer.[9] The presence of an object in this hand, which is usually used to stabilize the staff, together with the placement of the standard vis-à-vis the king indicate that he is stationary, if not a static work of stone outright.[10] Indeed, the image aligns more closely with the actual appearance of a standard-bearing statue, in which the subject rests the standard against his body as a matter of necessity, protecting the relatively thin staff from breakage, rather than the usual presentation of the statue type in paint or relief, which reflects the intended interpretation of the composition, namely that the person depicted is presenting the standard.[11] Although it is possible that the artist was drawing from another source of inspiration when creating the image,[12] based on the present evidence its interpretation as a sketch of a statue seems most probable.[13]

Great care was taken in preparing the image, which was laid out first in red, and then finished in black.[14] The lines were drawn with the sure hand of a skilled draftsman, although the work was not without revisions—noticeable particularly in the shape of the ram's uraeus, which has been enlarged, and the position of the king's neckline. The artist chose a limestone flake with a smooth, pristine surface for his composition, which is centered on and scaled to the size of the stone. The appropriateness of the image for this particular piece of limestone may have been influenced by the shape of the stone itself, the rounded top of which could be seen as evoking the shape of a round-topped stela.

The use of ostraca as stelae is a well-attested phenomenon in western Thebes, particularly in the worship of local deities, such as Meretseger and Amun, or those with close ties to the scribes who interacted with ostraca in the course of their daily lives, such as Ptah and Thoth.[15] While this image of a monarch differs slightly from the

[8] Such depictions can be found both in private tomb reliefs and on temple walls e.g., the depictions of a standard-bearing statue of Thutmose IV in the tomb of Amenhotep-Sise (TT 75) and in the king's festival courtyard at Karnak (Dimitri Laboury, "On the Master Painter of the Tomb of Amenhotep Sise, Second High Priest of Amun under the Reign of Thutmose IV (TT 75)," in Richard Jasnow and Kathlyn M. Cooney (eds.), *Joyful in Thebes: Egyptological Studies in Honor of Betsy M. Bryan* (Atlanta, 2015), 331–34, with further references).

[9] Henry G. Fischer, "An Elusive Shape within the Fisted Hands of Egyptian Statues," *MMJ* 13 (1978), 20–21; Jacques Vandier, *Manuel d'Archéologie Égyptienne, vol. 3, Les grandes époques: La statuaire* (Paris, 1958), 421.

[10] For a similar pose where the opposite hand is used to stabilize the standard, see a scene from the tomb of Amenemhab (TT44), where the priest of the standard is shown supporting it while the tomb owner censes and libates before it (Satzinger, "Der Heilige Stab," 18–19, fig. 10; Hassan el-Saady, *The Tomb of Amenemhab No. 44 at Qurnah* (Warminster, 1996), 16–17, pls. 9–12).

[11] Further support for the identification of the drawing's subject as a statue rather than a flesh-and-blood monarch may be found in the chapel of Paser at Medinet Habu, which seems to present a standard-bearing statue of Ramesses III in a similar pose, although in that instance the scene, which depicts several statues of the king, has been heavily restored. See: Siegfried Schott, *Wall Scenes from the Mortuary Chapel of the Mayor Paser at Medinet Habu*, SAOC 30 (Chicago, 1957), 4, pl. 1.

[12] For example, Teeter has put forth the suggestion that the scene may reflect a festival procession witnessed by the artist firsthand (Teeter, "Ostracon with a Sketch of a King").

[13] Drawings of statues are elsewhere attested on ostraca, e.g., an image of a kneeling figure on a base presenting an image of the king (Jeanne Vandier d'Abbadie, *Catalogue des ostraca figurés de Deir el Médineh (Nos 2256 à 2722)*, DFIFAO 2 [Cairo, 1937], 84, pl. 58 [no. 2406]). A similar depiction of a kneeling king presenting an altar of Amun lacks a base, but likely also represents a statue (Annie Gasse, *Catalogue des ostraca figurés de Deir el-Médineh (Nos 3100–3372)*, DFIFAO 23 [Cairo, 1986], 14, pl. 15 [no. 3169]; Annie Gasse, "Comme des bêtes! La comédie humaine selon les ostraca figurés de Deir el-Medina," in Hanane Gaber, Laure Bazin Rizzo and Frédéric Servajean (eds.), *À l'oeuvre on connaît l'artisan … de Pharaon! Un siècle de recherches françaises à Deir el-Medina (1917–2017)* [Milan, 2017], 114).

[14] Preparatory drawings in red are a not uncommon feature of figured ostraca (Brunner-Traut, *Egyptian Artists' Sketches*, 3). On the AIC example, the entire image was planned in red first.

[15] Ostraca were a common substitute for carved stelae (Brunner-Traut, *Egyptian Artists' Sketches*, 7–8). While many followed the format of more traditional stelae, others were simpler, sometimes consisting solely of an image, e.g., an ostracon depicting Thoth (Bengt E. J. Peterson, *Zeichnungen aus einer Totenstadt*, 75, pl. 16 [no. 23]).

content of those more obvious ostraca-stelae, it is worth noting that divine standards, as manifestations of the deities they represent, were a familiar focus of worship within the community in their own rights, adding further weight to this image of a king.[16] That the surface was not reused or added to at a later date points towards a more substantial significance behind the artwork. Furthermore, the fact that the opposite face was used several times suggests that the ostracon was in circulation for some period of time.

Textual Analysis

The verso of the ostracon has a far rougher surface than the recto and is a palimpsest with faded ink from at least three texts. Traces of a washed older text (Older Palimpsest) remain and two short texts (Text A and B) are arranged perpendicularly. Additionally, a hieratic crocodile sign is written in the bottom right corner, oriented in the same direction as Text B. There are numerous difficulties in reading due to fading of the ink, interference from the older text, and the uneven surface. Both infrared imaging and D-Stretch were used to clarify ink traces, although only infrared added anything significant to our understanding.

Older Palimpsest

Traces of a fairly thoroughly washed palimpsest can be seen in the top half of the verso, extending through the space occupied by Text A. An infrared image (fig. 5) reveals at least five lines above Text A. Unfortunately, even with the infrared image, these traces are largely unreadable. In the few instances where the ink has not been as thoroughly washed, some traces can be read as numbers (for example, the numerals for 12 appear twice in left middle). Traces belonging to the palimpsest, as they are largely illegible, have been left untranscribed to distinguish them from Text A and B (figs. 6, 7). The text may have been an administrative or account text of some kind. What is clear is that the hand is noticeably smaller than either of the two later texts and is likely from a different scribe.

Text A

Transliteration

1 ꜣbd 1 ꜣḫt sw 3 hrw pn sḫꜥy
2 [nswt] (jmn-ḥtp)| ꜥ.w.s r pꜣ sw(?) …
3 j[…] mn(?) … […

Translation

1 First month of Akhet, day 3. This day: the appearance in procession of
2 [King] Amenhotep, lph, at the time…
3 …

[16] They too were sometimes the subjects of ostraca decoration. On one example a ram-headed standard is flanked by kneeling figures (Jeanne Vandier d'Abbadie, *Catalogue des ostraca figurés de Deir el-Médineh (Nos 2734 à 3053)*, DFIFAO 2 [Cairo, 1959], 194, pl.105 [no. 2885]). Another presents the ibis-headed standard of Thoth (Vandier d'Abbadie, *Catalogue des ostraca figurés [Nos 2734 à 3053], 220, pl.158 [no. 3002]*). For the cult surrounding divine standards, see Satzinger, "Der Heilige Stab," 18–20.

Fig. 5. Infrared image (1.0–1.1µm) of top of verso of Ostracon with a sketch of a king. Image courtesy of the Art Institute of Chicago.

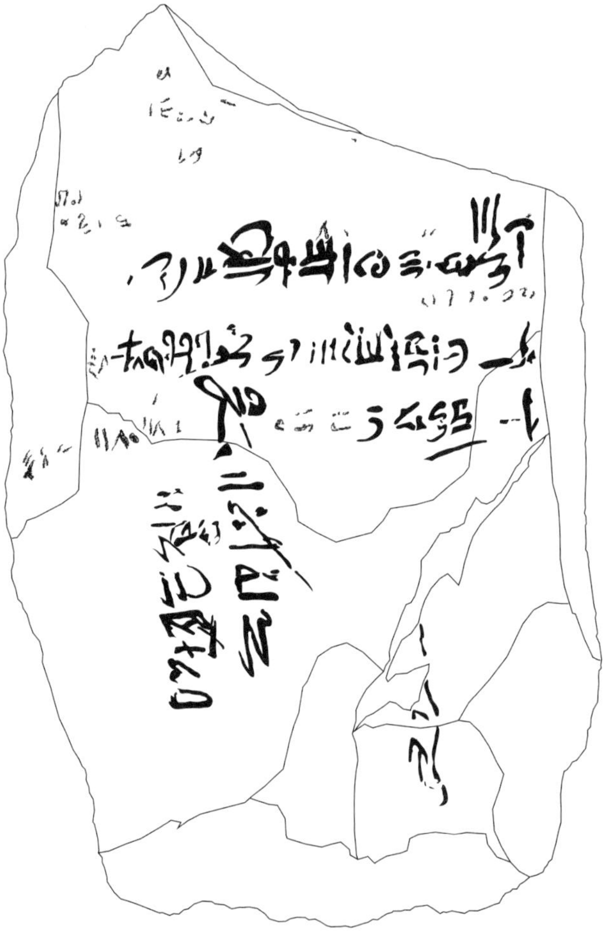

Fig. 6. Digital line drawing of verso. Drawing by Katherine E. Davis.

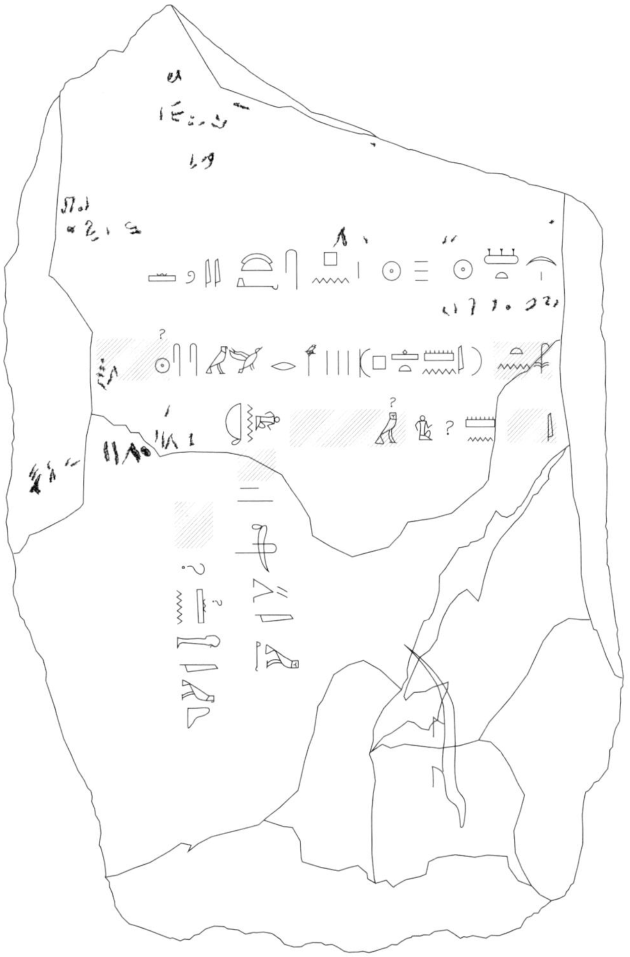

Fig. 7. Hieroglyphic transcription of Text A and B. Drawing by Katherine E. Davis.

Philological Commentary

l. 1 *sḫꜥ* "to cause appear, to be in procession" or as a noun "appearance in a procession."[17] As a verb, it can be used intransitively of a god appearing in procession. It also refers to the king appearing at the coronation or in a festival.[18]

l. 2 Traces at the beginning are quite damaged. However, there does appear to be an initial tall stroke, which could fit a writing of *nswt*. Other references to the divine Amenhotep I use the phrase *nswt jmn-ḥtp*.[19] The traces could also match *jn* "by," though the next line may also contain a group that could be read as such.

The end of this line is difficult, potentially with some interference from the older text. After the *r*, we suggest *pꜣ sw* "at the time…" A similar writing occurs in one of the oracular amuletic decrees: *jw=tn jn n=s jmn r pꜣy=f sw* "we shall bring Amun to her at his time," which Edwards suggests is referring to

[17] *Wb.* 4, 236.12–237.20; Leonard Lesko and Barbara Lesko, *A Dictionary of Late Egyptian*, 2nd ed. (Providence, 2002), II, 68.

[18] Donald B. Redford, *History and Chronology of the Eighteenth Dynasty of Egypt: Seven Studies* (Toronto, 1967), 3–27.

[19] René van Walsem, "Month-Names and Feasts at Deir el-Medina," in Robert J. Demarée and Jac. J. Janssen (eds.), *Gleanings from Deir el-Medîna* (Leiden, 1982), nos. 56–57, 68–71, 82–83.

the statue of the god during an oracle, potentially a similar situation as we have here.[20] A long tail, as from an *f*, is visible after the *pꜣ*, but it is difficult to say if this due to the ink being smudged, traces from the older text, or a writing of *pꜣ=f* for *pꜣy=f*. After *pꜣ sw*, it is tempting to read *nfr* but this is far from certain. Unfortunately, these potential readings do not have parallels with other texts that refer to the cult of the divine Amenhotep I.[21]

l.3 This line is also quite difficult. The beginning contains a clear vertical stroke, likely a reed leaf. This may be *jn* "by," which would suggest that the subsequent word(s) was a title or personal name.[22] However, there are two problems. First, there is the tail of what might be an *f*, although this could be attributed to the Older Palimpsest, and *jn=f* "by him" is grammatically unsatisfying, as the only potential antecedent is Amenhotep himself. And second, the signs that directly follow appear to be a writing of *mn*, but they do not quite match the *mn* in Amenhotep's name, and the subsequent signs are difficult to resolve.[23] It remains unclear where exactly this line ends, as the end of the first line of the perpendicular Text B encroaches. There are no traces that suggest there was a fourth line to the text.

Text B

Transliteration

1 mj sšm=j n=k

2 qꜣj n ? [...

Translation

1 Come, let me show you
2 the character of ? [...

Philological Commentary

l. 1 There are traces of two vertical strokes after the *sšm* sign. An *m*-owl would be expected after it, but the traces appear too vertical. Perhaps they are simply strokes. There is space for a determinative, likely the walking legs, although almost no traces remain.

l. 2 This is a writing of *qj* "form, manner" with the typical New Kingdom spelling *qꜣj*.[24] The *ꜣ*, however, appears more like a quail chick, and the standing mummy determinative has a somewhat odd shape. The bookroll determinative is expected in addition to the mummy, but the sign here does not conform to the typical shape with a dot above it. If this is not a bookroll determinative, this group may instead be a set of horizontal signs (perhaps  or 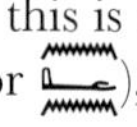), but its interpretation eludes us. The final phrase is unfortunately too damaged to read.

[20] Iorwerth E.S. Edwards, *Hieratic Papyri in the British Museum. Fourth Series: Oracular Amuletic Decrees of the Late New Kingdom* (London, 1960), 11, pl. 3 (Pap. L. 1, vs 47=P. BM 10083, vs. 47). Per Edwards' interpretation, the 1st person plural pronoun is exceptionally written *tn* in several of the amuletic decrees.

[21] We might expect an epithet after Amenhotep's name, but *pꜣ nb pꜣ dmj* "the lord of the town," *n pꜣ wbꜣ* "of the court," *n pꜣ kꜣmw* "of the garden," etc. do not fit the traces. See Jaroslav Černý, "Le culte d'Amenophis I chez les ouvriers de la Nécropole thébaine," *BIFAO* 27 (1927), 162–64; LGG I, 333–35; and Gabi Hollender, *Amenophis I. und Ahmes Nefertari: Untersuchungen zur Entwicklung ihres posthumen Kultes anhand der Privatgräber der thebanischen Nekropole* (Berlin, 2009), 10–13.

[22] E.g., the settlement text of Henuttawy at Karnak in Robert Ritner, *The Libyan Anarchy: Inscriptions from Egypt's Third Intermediate Period* (Atlanta, 2009), 138–43 (line 1).

[23] It is tempting to see this as a personal name given the seated man. Perhaps *mnnꜣ*? See Benedict G. Davies, *Who's Who at Deir el-Medina: a Prosopographic Study of the Royal Workmen's Community*, Egyptologische Uitgaven 13 (Leiden, 1999), 163–67; Ranke, *PN* I, 152.

[24] See Wb. V, 15 and Lesko and Lesko, *A Dictionary of Late Egyptian, II, 145–46.*

General Commentary on Texts

The chronological relationships between the texts are fairly clear. The Older Palimpsest was written first and then washed off. Its illegibility prevents us from determining whether or not the break at the top right, corresponding to the bottom of the recto, occurred before or after its repurposing as a writing surface. Text A and Text B were written next. Text A, the dated text, was likely written before Text B as the former text occupies the full width of the ostracon, while the first line of the latter ends before it intersects with the second line of the dated text. The crocodile was likely written around the same time as Text B, but its precise place in this sequence is impossible to determine.

The reference to the cult of Amenhotep I indicates that the ostracon originated in Deir el-Medina or its western Theben surroundings and dates to the New Kingdom, all of which accords with the image on the recto. Unfortunately, no more can be said about its original location based on the internal textual evidence. Paleography places the text in the Ramesside Period, but cannot narrow the time frame any further. Similarly, the absence of a regnal year and the lack of any prosopographic information precludes a more specific dating on the basis of content.

Perhaps the most intriguing element of these texts is that Text A references a procession of Amenhotep I. Festivals and processions associated with the divine Amenhotep I occur frequently in Deir el-Medina documents.[25] However, there are two aspects of this account in the AIC ostracon worth further discussion.

First, the date of I Akhet 3 does not match up with the attested festivals of Amenhotep I. The closest parallel in terms of date comes from two brief texts, O. Cairo 25275,2 and O. Cairo 25276,1, which refer to a festival of Amenhotep, *ḫʿ-n-jmn-ḥtp*, in the first month of Akhet, but on day 29 and 30, respectively.[26] Additionally, the third month of Peret is associated with a feast of Amenhotep, known as *p(ꜣ)-n(y)-jmn-ḥtp*, which is also used simply as the month name in certain Deir el-Medina documents.[27] And finally, a festival *ḫʿ nswt jmn-ḥtp* is attested in the third month of Shemu.[28] The date of I Akhet 3 is sometimes associated with the New Year's festival which can span the first month of Akhet, days 1–3.[29]

Second, the use of the term *sḫʿ* does in fact suggest that this is merely speaking of a procession, not necessarily a festival. The term does not occur in names of feasts or festivals during this period, in contrast to terms like *ḫʿ*, *ḥb*, *p(ꜣ)-n(y)*, and *ḫnw,* which are frequent elements of feast/festival names in Deir el-Medina texts. Instead, *sḫʿ* refers to the specific act of appearance (i.e., the ritual event of the cult image carried by the priests),[30] rather than as part of the name of the event. The closest parallel to the AIC ostracon's phrasing comes from an oracular

---

[25] Černý, "Le culte d'Amenophis I," 159–203 and van Walsem, "Month-Names," 215–43; Heidi Jauhiainen, "'Do Not Celebrate Your Feast Without Your Neighours': A Study of References to Feasts and Festivals in Non-Literary Documents from Ramesside Period Deir el-Medina" (PhD dissertation, University of Helsinki, 2009). A couple more recently published attestations: ODM 10051, verso 3–4 (absence journal), see Pierre Grandet, *Catalogue des ostraca hiératiques non littéraires de Deîr el-Médînéh: Tome X Noss 10001–10123*, DFIFAO 46 (Cairo, 2006), 55–56, 241; and ODM 10269, recto 4 (list of offerings for various festivals), see Pierre Grandet, *Catalogue des ostraca hiératiques non littéraires de Deîr el-Médînéh: Tome XI Nos 10124–10275*, DFIFAO 48 (Cairo, 2010), 148–52, 374–75.

[26] Van Walsem, "Month-Names," 223 (nos. 56–57); Černý, "Le culte d'Amenophis I," 182.

[27] O. BM 29560 vs. 8; O. Louvre E 3263,9; O. Cairo 25688,1; ODM 434 vs. 2; and ODM 1265 col. 1, 22. See van Walsem, "Month-Names," 219 (nos. 16–20), 222 (nos. 44–48, for undated attestations of this feast); Jauhiainen, "Do Not Celebrate Your Feast without Your Neighbours," 131–40.

[28] Van Walsem, "Month-Names," 226 (nos. 82–83).

[29] Wolfgang Helck, "Feiertage und Arbeitstage in der Ramessidenzeit," *JESHO* 7 (1964), 156. Helck's reconstruction of the Deir el-Medina festival calendar relies on whether or not a particular day was a work day or free. Based on his corpus of journal entries, absence lists, and similar sources, I Akhet 1 was always free, while only some texts recorded day 2 or day 3 as free. For the three day duration of the New Year's festival, see, e.g., I *ꜣḫt 1 sw 2 sw 3 ʿḥʿ.n tꜣ jst m wsf n wpt-rnpt*; ODM 209, vs. 20. In contrast, O. Ashmolean 11 gives I *ꜣḫt* 3 as a work day. For a more updated treatment of the Deir el-Medina festival calendar, see Jauhiainen, "Do Not Celebrate Your Feast without Your Neighbours." ODM 739 references five men who were at a feast (*ḥb*) on I Akhet 3, which is likely a reference to the New Year's festival, but is not specific.

[30] Derchain makes a similar observation for the later use of *sḫʿ* in the Canopus decree: "*sḫʿy* signifie en effet couramment en égyptien 'porter solennellement en procession'; c'est un sorte de term technique." Philippe Derchain, "Un sens curieux de ἔκπεμφις chez Clément d'Alexandrie," *CdE* 26 (1951), 278.

stela dating to the reign of Ramesses VI. Here *sẖꜥ* describes the appearance of Amun-Re in the Opet festival in a caption for the upper register scene where priests carry the divine bark.[31]

> *sẖꜥ ḥm nṯr pn šps jmn-rꜥ nswt-nṯrw nb pt m ḥb nfr n jpt*
>
> "Appearance in procession of the majesty of this noble god Amun-Re, king of the gods, lord of the sky, in the beautiful feast of Opet"

And the term recurs on the same stela in the dated text in the third register (line 2), again describing the appearance of Amun-Re in the Opet.

> *hrw pn m tr n dwꜣt sẖꜥꜥ ḥm nṯr šps jmn-rꜥ nswt-nṯrw m ḥb.f nfr n jpt ꜥḥꜥ.n smj n=f wꜥb n mꜣꜥt mry-mꜣꜥt m-ḏd...*
>
> "On this day at the time of morning, the majesty of the noble god Amun-Re, king of the gods, appeared in procession in his beautiful feast of Opet. The wab priest of Maat Mery-maat reported to him, saying..."

This example makes it clear that *sẖꜥ* is the processional action in the scene, while the name of the event is, of course, the Opet Festival and the act of addressing the god for the oracle is covered by the verb *smj* "to report."[32] However, this use of *sẖꜥ* is not typical of Deir el-Medina documentary texts, which instead either use *ẖꜥ* "appearance" either as the name of the feast or as a reference to the/a processional event[33] or specify the oracular action of addressing the god.[34]

Thus, while the overall context for Text A might be a festival event, the terminology simply specifies a procession, likely arranged for oracular purposes.[35] The dates of oracular consultations with Amenhotep I fall on both feast days/weekends and also non-feast days, indicating that the cult image of Amenhotep could be brought out on an ad hoc basis.[36] While there are no oracular texts dated to I Akhet 3, there is evidence that some legal proceedings could occur on that date, as O. Michaelides 47 records a *qnbt* session occurring then,[37] which suggests that oracular proceeding is possible.

Text B is an excerpt from a miscellany text, although its specific phrasing does not quite match any extant example. Our text is a variant of the phrase *mj sḏd=j n=k* "Come, let me tell you," which occurs in numerous examples.[38] This introduction followed by *qj* "manner, character"[39] is attested in two texts. The closest parallel comes from the Satirical Letter (P. Anastasi I, 8,8): *mj sḏd=j n=k qj n sẖꜣw ry* "Come, let me tell you the character of the scribe Ray,"[40] for which a variant *mj sšm*… "come, let [me] show…" exists.[41] Another close parallel can

---

[31] JE 91927 in Pascal Vernus, "Une texte oraculaire de Ramsès VI," *BIFAO* 75 (1975), 104, 107.

[32] Similarly, *hrw pn sẖꜥ nṯr pn šps nb nṯrw jmn-rꜥ* in P. Brooklyn 47.218.3, Richard Parker, *A Saite Oracle Papyrus from Thebes in the Brooklyn Museum* (Providence, 1962), 7.

[33] E.g., *ꜥḥꜥ.n tꜣ jst n pꜣ ẖꜥ n jmn-ḥtp* "the gang was absent in the Appearance of Amenhotep," ODM 10051, Grandet, *Catalogue des ostraca, Nos. 10001–10123*, 55. For name of feast vs. name of event, see Jauhiainen, "Do Not Celebrate Your Feast," 176.

[34] In ostraca, petitioners typically *smj* "report" to Amenhotep I: e.g., O. BM 5625, rt. 1 in Aylward M. Blackman, "Oracles in Ancient Egypt II," *JEA* 12 (1926), 181–82; O.Cairo 25242 in Černý, "Le culte d'Amenophis I," 179; or O. UC 39622 (O. Petrie 21) in Jaroslav Černý and Alan Gardiner, *Hieratic Ostraca* (Oxford, 1957), pl. 16,4, but also sometimes *ꜥš* "call" which also occurs in O. UC 39622 or *ꜥḥꜥ* "stand," e.g., O. BM 5624, vs. 5 in Blackman, "Oracles," 177.

[35] For oracles generally, see Jaroslav Černý, "Egyptian Oracles," in Parker, *A Saite Oracle Papyrus*, 35–48.

[36] Sven P. Vleeming, "The Days on which the *Ḳnbt* used to Gather," in Robert J. Demarée and Jac. J. Janssen (eds.), *Gleanings from Deir el-Medîna* (Leiden, 1982), 183–92; Jauhiainen, "Do Not Celebrate Your Feast," 159.

[37] Hans Goedicke and Edward Wente, *Ostraka Michaelides* (Wiesbaden, 1962), 17, pl. 50; K*RI* III, 514–15.

[38] P. Chester Beatty V (BM 10685), rt. 6,13; P. Anastasi III (BM 10246), rt. 5.6; 5.9; and 6.3; P. Anastasi IV (BM 10249), rt. 9.4 and 9.7–8; P. Anastasi I (BM 10247) 9.9; 27.2; and 28.8.

[39] Related phrases include *ḏd=j n=k qj* (BM EA 10247, 9,7 and 28,7) and *wḥꜥ=j n=k qꜣj* (BM EA 10247, 18.6 and BM EA 9994, rt. 5.8).

[40] Also paralleled in P. Turin CGT 54011, x+1.4. For both, see Hans-Werner Fischer-Elfert, *Die Satirische Streitschrift des Papyrus Anastasi I.*, KÄT (Wiesbaden, 1986), 87.

[41] ODM 1069. See Fischer-Elfert, *Die Satirische Streitschrift*, 87 and Georges Posener, *Catalogue des ostraca hiératiques littéraires de Deir el Médineh. Tome I, Nos 1001 à 1108*, DFIFAO I (Cairo, 1938), 18, pl. 39.

be found in O. BM 50716, not just to this particular phrasing but to the overall content of the ostracon. Just as on the AIC ostracon, the British museum example contains both an administrative text and a miscellany text, written perpendicular to each other. It also contains the line drawing of a bull. The miscellany text on the British Museum piece is as follows: *mj sḏd=j n=k pꜣ qj n sẖꜣw ꜥḥꜥ r-rw*[*ty*]… "Come, let me tell you the character of a scribe who stands outside…".[42]

Literary excerpts on ostraca are usually understood to be the product of scribal education. Although the AIC ostracon does not exhibit the most traditional hallmarks of a New Kingdom scribal exercise (i.e., several lines of a "classic" Middle Egyptian literary text, sometimes with verse points, mistakes, and a colophon),[43] excerpts from the Miscellany texts do occur on ostraca and occasionally include a date which acts as a clear marker of a scribal exercise.[44] Further indications that Text B might be a scribal exercise include the slight oddities in orthography[45] and the writing of the hieratic crocodile, which is suggestive of sign practice.[46]

Use History

The discrepancy between the recto and verso, not just in subject matter but in the nature of their use and reuse, requires some explanation. Why did the recto, whose face provided a vastly superior work surface, only have a single use, while the verso, with its jagged texture, experienced repeated reuse? The answer almost certainly lies in its original purpose. Given that there is no evidence of an earlier text or image on the recto, the drawing of the king must have constituted its first use, as no scribe or artist would have chosen the poor quality of the verso if given the option. Moreover, it appears that in this particular instance, the power associated with the image of a king carrying an emblem of Amun-Re prevented any erasure or interference even as the other face saw repeated use.[47]

In light of this, we propose the following reconstruction of use history: 1) A skilled artist drew the image of the king, likely with the intent that the image would have a ritual purpose. 2) An administrative text (Older Palimpsest) was added to the verso. The recto was left untouched. 3) Despite providing a poorer writing surface than that on the recto, the adminstrative text (Older Palimpsest) was removed in preparation for the addition of new texts.[48] That the opposite side remained untouched further points to the value and significance of the image it bears. 4) A dated administrative text (Text A) related to the procession of Amenhotep I was added. 5) The ostracon was rotated 90 degrees and the miscellany text (Text B) was added. Two events cannot be placed within this cycle with any certainty. First, the break at the bottom of the recto/top of the verso likely occurred before step 4, but it is not clear whether this was before or after a scribe wrote the Older Palimpsest. And second, at some point after the initial administrative text was removed, the crocodile was added.

Given such a history, the ostracon was likely used by multiple individuals. While the artist who sketched the image may have been the same individual who wrote the Older Palimpsest, Text A and B are clearly written in a much larger hand, as mentioned above. Thus at least two, potentially three individuals, made use of it. Yet

---

42 Robert J. Demarée, *Ramesside Ostraca* (London, 2002), 32, pls. 108–109. See also, Hans-Werner Fischer-Elfert, *Lesefunde im literarischen Steinbruch von Deir el-Medineh* (Wiesbaden, 1997), 40–43.

43 For the traditional overview of this topic, see Hellmut Brunner, *Altägyptische Erziehung* (Wiesbaden, 1957), 17–27. But for a more critical take that questions the divide between Middle Egyptian literary excerpts on ostraca as the work of beginner scribes and the Late Egyptian miscellanies as the work of advanced apprentices, see Andrea McDowell, "Teachers and students at Deir el-Medina," in Robert J. Demarée and Arthur Egberts (eds.), *Deir el-Medina in the Third Millennium AD: A Tribute to Jac. J. Janssen* (Leiden, 2000), 217–33.

44 For example, Černý and Gardiner, *Hieratic Ostraca*, pls. 10.3, 41.1.

45 Although this may simply be due to the poor state of preservation.

46 Other examples of hieratic crocodiles likely written as sign practice: ODM 1779 and 1781, see Annie Gasse, *Catalogue des ostraca littéraires de Deir al-Medina, Nos. 1775–1873 et 1156*, DFIFAO 44 (Cairo, 2005), 15, 17; see also Jeanne Vandier d'Abbadie, *Catalogue des ostraca figurés de Deir el Médineh (Nos 2001 à 2255)*, DFIFAO 2 (Cairo, 1936) 49, pl. 33 (no. 2237).

47 In contrast, for an example of a drawing of a king that was erased in order for the surface to be reused for a text, see BM 50711 in Demarée, *Ramesside Ostraca*, 31, pl. 104. It is important to note that the original drawing of this king was in red ink and may never have been finished, which is not the same situation as on the AIC ostracon.

48 On a purely practical note, the verso must have been washed with a damp cloth or in some other manner that would have left recto unmarred.

these individuals may have been in quite different stages of their careers. The artist from the recto was skilled, while the scribe of Text A and B might have still been a student/apprentice. That an object might have moved between such different hands is a reminder that while modern scholarship often treats education as separate from the daily lives of workers, there was likely no such divide within a community like Deir el-Medina.

By and large, the recto and verso of an ostracon need not have any connection to each other. In particular, there are numerous examples where a figured drawing bears no relationship to a text on its opposite face.[49] Nonetheless, there are ostraca where such a relationship does exist.[50] Given the above proposed interpretations of the image on the AIC ostracon as representing a statue of a king and Text A as an account of the appearance of King Amenhotep I, likely in the form of a statue in procession, it is worthwhile to consider a potential link between these two episodes of use for the ostracon.[51] Indeed, Text A might have been written on this ostracon precisely because of the image on its recto. While Text A clearly does not serve as a caption for the image, not least because the Older Palimpsest would have been written before it, a looser link might have existed. Perhaps the scribe witnessed the procession and used this specific ostracon because its royal image felt apropos.

Conclusion

While each aspect of the ostracon, when considered individually, fits into a well-represented genre—be it figured images of kings, administrative texts, or excerpts from literary texts—the object as a whole presents an intriguing example of reuse that illuminates the complexity of a use cycle that likely saw the ostracon passed through several different hands and used for varied purposes. It is also a case study in why an object must be studied as a material whole, not divided into its constituent visual and textual parts.

[49] E.g., BM 8507 in which the recto contains a scene of a monkey and the verso several lines of a legal text or BM 50711 whose recto preserves a palimpsest of a letter written over a washed drawing and whose verso contains a drawing of a man with a knife. For both, see Demarée, *Ramesside Ostraca*, 22, pls. 50–51 and 31, pls. 104–105, respectively.

[50] E.g., OIM E13951, which depicts a satirical scene with a boy, mouse, and cat on one side and the hieratic inscription "the cat and mouse bring in the boy" on the other (Emily Teeter, "Satirical Scene," in Jean M. Evans, Jack Green, and Emily Teeter (eds.), *Highlights of the Collections of the Oriental Institute Museum* (Chicago, 2017), 99).

[51] It should be noted, however, that the processional image of Amenhotep I likely took a different form, as no standard-bearing statues of that king are known. As mentioned above, the statue type does not appear within New Kingdom statuary until the middle of the Eighteenth Dynasty.

A Family of Lector-Priests at Edfu: Oriental Institute Stela E11455 and the *Ỉb* Family during the Early Eighteenth Dynasty

Kathryn E. Bandy
Tell Edfu Project

Abstract

This article presents the study of two stelae from Edfu dating to the early Eighteenth Dynasty that represent members of the same extended family of lector-priests from Edfu (Oriental Institute E11455 and Princeton Y1993-151). The texts of both stelae were published in the early Twentieth Century; however, neither stela has been comprehensively published. The two stelae present the opportunity to revisit the family's genealogy and chronological position. The study also considers dating criteria for late Second Intermediate Period and early Eighteenth Dynasty stelae and assesses the contemporary positioning and role of lector-priests. Finally, it briefly addresses the influence of documentary scribal culture on monumental inscriptions vis-à-vis the late Second Intermediate Period–early New Kingdom Tell Edfu Ostraca.

ملخص

تتناول هذه المقالة دراسة للوحتين قادمتين من إدفو ومؤرختين ببدايات عصر الأسرة الثامنة عشر. تُظهر اللوحتان أعضاءً من نفس العائلة الممتدة لكبار الكهنة المرتلين من إدفو (معهد الدراسات الشرقية E11455 وبرينستون Y١٩٩٣-١٥١). نُشرت نصوص اللوحتين في أوائل القرن العشرين؛ ومع ذلك، لم يُقدم نشرٌ علميٌ شاملٌ لأي من اللوحتين حتى الآن. تتيح اللوحتان الفرصة لإعادة النظر في سلسة نسب العائلة ووضعها من الناحية التأريخية. كما تتناول هذه الدراسة المعايير التأريخية للوحات في أواخر عصر الانتقال الثاني وبدايات عصر الأسرة الثامنة عشرة، وتُقيّم مكانة ودور كبار الكهنة المرتلين آنذاك. ختامًا، تتناول المقالة بإيجاز أثر ثقافة الكتابات التوثيقية في النقوش التذكارية في سياق أوستراكا تل إدفو المؤرخة بأواخر عصر الانتقال الثاني وبدايات عصر الدولة الحديثة.

Introduction

Edfu, the capital of the second nome of Upper Egypt, preserves one of the most extensive monumental records for local and regional officials from the late Middle Kingdom through the early New Kingdom.[1] Through these monuments, genealogical histories and the succession of officials in key administrative positions have been reconstructed, providing important insight into Edfu's administration and social history as Egypt transitioned into and out of the Second Intermediate Period.[2]

---

[1] This study was funded by an Oriental Institute Collections Research Grant, made possible through the generous donation of Mr. Jim Sopranos. I would like to thank the Oriental Institute for support of the project. I would also like to thank Emily Teeter, who first brought the stela to my attention, and the Oriental Institute Museum's Registrar, Helen McDonald, who facilitated my access to the stela.

[2] Most notable is P. Vernus "Edfou du début de la XIIe Dynastie au début de la XVIIIe Dynastie: Études philologiques, sociologiques et historiques d'un corpus documentaire de l'Égypte Pharaonique" (PhD dissertation, Université Paris: Sorbonne, 1987). More recent studies include S. Kubisch, *Lebensbilder der 2. Zwischenzeit: Biographische Inschriften der 13.–17. Dynastie*, SDAIK 34 (Berlin, 2008), and M. Marée, "Edfu under the Twelfth to Seventeenth Dynasties: The Monuments in the National Museum of Warsaw," *BMSAES* 12 (2009), 31–92.

Journal of the American Research Center in Egypt 56 (2020), 47–69
doi: http://dx.doi.org/10.5913/jarce.56.2020.a004

At the very end of the Second Intermediate Period and into the early Eighteenth Dynasty, Edfu's priesthood is particularly well represented. Of note is an extended family of officials, many bearing the names *Ἰwf* and *Ἰb*, whose members served as lector-priests and held the position of chief lector-priest over several generations. The family is represented on at least eight monuments, including stelae, offering tables, and statues.

Monuments of the Chief-Lector Priest Ἰb

Oriental Institute stela E11455 (fig. 1) does not have a specific find-spot and was described by G. Daressy as one of a series of Middle Kingdom monuments from "le kom d'Edfou."[3] This is typical for the late Second Intermediate Period and early New Kingdom material from the site. Unlike many of the late Middle Kingdom and early Second Intermediate Period pieces that can be situated in the Isi Complex, the places in which the later funerary monuments at Edfu were erected remains uncertain. Recent finds from the 2018 season of the Tell Edfu Project (The Oriental Institute, The University of Chicago) indicate that at least some of the monuments may have come from ancestor shrines in early New Kingdom villas.[4]

Oriental Institute E11455 was initially accessioned by the Cairo Egyptian Museum as TR 9/16/18/25.[5] James Henry Breasted subsequently purchased it for the Oriental Institute Museum from the Cairo Egyptian Museum in February of 1920. G. Daressy's 1919 publication reproduced only its text, along with a brief description of its decoration, without images.[6]

Oriental Institute E11455 is a round-top, limestone stela, measuring 39 cm x 25.5 cm. The stela is complete, without any breaks or damage. It is divided into four parts—a decorated lunette with wadjet eyes flanking a shen ring sits above two registers with offering scenes, with two lines of text at the bottom. Each offering scene depicts a seated couple before an offering table and a standing son pouring libations. All six individuals are identified by name and a short, narrative text accompanies the first scene. The figures are executed in low relief and the text is sunk. A frame surrounds the two offering scenes, with thin lines separating the text below. The inclusion of two offering scenes on a single stela is unusual at Edfu.

The sides, bottom, and back of the stela have been roughly dressed. The upper edges of the sides have been smoothed, but short, oblique chisel marks are visible. The stela's bottom is uneven. It would not have stood on its own and would have been set into a larger monument or construct. The back is also roughly hewn; however, the stela does lay flat. There is a small, circular hole drilled into the center of the stela's top toward the back. Three round holes, presumably for display in modern times, have been drilled into the back of the stela.

Lunette

The wadjet eyes flanking the central shen ring are comparable in size, with the left sitting slightly higher than the right. Neither eye has a delineated pupil. The canthus of the right eye almost abuts the right side of the shen ring, with only a small amount of space separating the two. By contrast, the canthus of the left eye is at a further

[3] G. Daressy, "Monuments D'edfou Datant Du Moyen Empire," *ASAE* 18 (1919), 50–52 [IX]. The stela was subsequently included by P. Vernus in his study of the Edfu corpus; however, he did not have physical access to the stela or images of it (Vernus, "Edfou," 368–70 [112]). "Le kom d'Edfou" refers to the remains of the ancient town. Now referred to as "Tell Edfu" it is currently being excavated by the Tell Edfu Project under the direction of Drs. N. Moeller and G. Marouard (Tell Edfu was affiliated with The Oriental Institute, The University of Chicago until June 2020, and is now under the umbrella of Yale University).

[4] A villa excavated in 2018 preserved an ancestor shrine, including a statue, stela, and ancestor bust ("New Discoveries of a Domestic Shrine for Ancestor Worship of the Early New Kingdom (ca. 1500 BCE) at Tell Edfu." See Louise Lerner, "Ancient urban Villa with Shrine for Ancestor Worship Discovered in Egypt," UChicago News, January 4, 2019 (https://news.uchicago.edu/story/ancient-urban-villa-shrine-ancestor-worship-discovered-egypt). The material is being studied by N. Moeller and G. Marouard.

[5] The Cairo registration number is visible in black ink on the stela's left edge and upper back. The number 17 is also written in faded red on the stela's front, above the left wadjet eye. It does not correspond to any known field registration number, museum registration number or Daressy's publication.

[6] G. Daressy, "Monuments D'edfou Datant Du Moyen Empire," *ASAE* 18 (1919), 50–52 [IX]. The stela was subsequently included by Vernus in his study of the Edfu corpus; however, he did not have physical access to the stela or images of it (Vernus, "Edfou," 368–70 [112]).

Fig. 1. Oriental Institute Stela E11455. Photo (D. 19113) courtesy of the Oriental Institute of the University of Chicago.

distance. Spacing between the elements of the individual eyes is not consistent—the distance between the arch of the brows and the eyes differs between the two and the lines vary in thickness.

As is common in the New Kingdom, the shen ring sits above the bottom line of the wadjet eyes.[7] A lightly etched line extending from the shen ring towards the left wadjet eye may have been intended to indicate its placement.

Register 1: Ꞽb, Tꜣ-šri(.t), and Ꞽd

The seated couple is identified as the *ẖry-ḥb(.t) tpy Ꞽb* and the *nb.t-pr Tꜣ-šri(.t)*.[8] The couple's names are placed above their heads. Neither is straight, angling slightly up to the right. *Ꞽb* holds a triangular lotus flower to his nose with his left hand and a fold of cloth in his right. He wears a knee-length short kilt, with a long over-kilt, reaching down to mid-calf, terminating in an extended point above his left ankle. He is bare-chested, with a plain rounded collar.

Tꜣ-šri.(t), seated behind *Ꞽb*, wraps her left arm around his shoulder and places her right hand on his upper arm. The individual fingers of her left hand are incised, but those of her right are not. She wears a single-strap dress that extends down to mid-calf. A single curved line below her neck indicates the top of a collar.

[7] R. Caminos and H. Fischer, *Ancient Egyptian Epigraphy and Palaeography* (New York, 1976), 46–47; A. Ilin-Tomich, *From Workshop to Sanctuary: The Production of Late Middle Kingdom Memorial Stelae*, MKS 6 (London, 2017), 5.

[8] See below for the name of *Ꞽb*'s wife.

The couple is seated on a high-back chair, which extends up to *Tꜣ-šri(.t)*'s shoulder and curves slightly outward at the top.[9] The outward curve of the chair's back is distinguished only by a lightly etched line that extends up and over the scene's frame—the line of the frame respects the chair back, suggesting that the scene was planned, laid out, and then not adjusted despite it being clear that the chair, as designed, would not fit in the available space delineated by the frame.[10]

The table before the couple is heaped with offerings. The bottom layer consists of a round loaf of bread preceding two stacked, oblong loaves, and then a crescent before the final round loaf. This crescent may be a correction, its addition intended to keep the final loaf circular, avoiding excessive negative space, and matching the first loaf in shape and size.

Ỉb's son, the *ẖry-ḥb(.t) Ỉd*, stands behind the table. He wears the same attire as his father and pours libations.[11] He is explicitly identified as performing the offering ritual for his father in four columns of text above the offering table, filling the entirety of the space below the right wadjet eye and top of the offerings. The text is in sunk, relatively deep, and slightly uneven hieroglyphs. The inclusion of text narrating the actions of the dedicator is otherwise unattested at Edfu. The narration is directed to *Ỉb* by *Ỉd*—the offering is carried out "by your son" (*sꜣ=k*) for "your ka" (*kꜣ=k*).

> (1) *ir.t ḥtp-di-ny-sw.t* (2) *ḫꜣ m ḫ.t nb(.t) nfr.t* (3) *n kꜣ=k in sꜣ(4)=k ẖry-ḥb(.t) Ỉd*
> Performing the *ḥtp-di-ny-sw.t*, a thousand[a] of all good things for your ka,[b] by your son, the lector-priest[c] *Ỉd*[d]

a) The sign was copied by Daressy as .[12] The form is abnormal. Its top is rounded and was added secondarily. The vertical stroke is square at the bottom, rather than the rhizome, and there is a rectangular cross-stroke in the middle.

b) The *kꜣ* arms have distinct circular loops for hands. This contrasts with the more oblong hands in the offering formula below, which are more the norm in the Edfu corpus. The use of loops instead of distinct hands is encountered elsewhere in Egypt during this time but is not restricted to a specific location or workshop.[13]

c) The has only a single loop at the top, above a vertical line that terminates in the two ends of the twisted cord. This form matches that in the titles identifying the other figures in the offering scenes, but differs from the form in the offering text below. There, the top loop is followed by three, short, oblique strokes in place of a vertical line.

H̱r and *ḥb* lack internal details. Again, this follows the titles accompanying the figures in the scenes, but, in the case of *ẖr*, not the offering text below.

d) Rather than originating at the shoulder, the front arm of emerges from the head and extends straight out, with only a slight curve indicating the bend of the elbow. This is the case for all examples of the determinative in the stela, as well as (A17) in the name of *Ỉb*'s wife. Only , also in her name, has the forward arm

---

[9] Similar high-backed chairs at Edfu tend to date to the Second Intermediate Period and into early New Kingdom (including Cairo CG 20499, Cairo CG 20537, Cairo JE 38917, Cairo JE 46200, Cairo JE 46785, Cairo JE 46988, Hildesheim 1261, Hildesheim 1896, Warsaw 141262, and the Clère stela). Cairo JE 38917 and Cairo JE 46988 name king Dedumose of the Sixteenth Dynasty. The chair back cannot be used as a sole dating criterion, as low-backed chairs continue into the early/mid-Eighteenth Dynasty at Edfu (e.g., Birmingham 70'96 and Cairo JE 46199).

[10] This contrasts with the chair in the lower scene, which terminates abruptly with less of a curve, directly abutting the edge of the frame, hinting at the order in which the various elements of the stela were laid out and carved. This suggests that the first register was laid out, and possibly lightly etched, with the draughtsman then recognizing the problems and correcting them prior to work on the second register. The positioning of the chair back in the first register contrasts with the register line below the figures, which deviates from 180, most notably below the libation water and *Ỉd*'s front foot.

[11] Pouring libations becomes more common in the Eighteenth Dynasty (Ilin-Tomich, *From Workshop to Sanctuary*, 6). Examples from Edfu all date to the Eighteenth Dynasty (Birmingham 70'96, Cairo JE 46201, Hildesheim 1896, and a stela seen in the Tadross antiquities shop, whose current location is unknown (Vernus, "Edfou," 332–35 [100]).

[12] G. Daressy, "Monuments D'edfou Datant Du Moyen Empire," *ASAE* 18 (1919), 50.

[13] M. Marée, "A Sculpture Workshop at Abydos from the Late Sixteenth or Early Seventeenth Dynasty," in M. Marée (ed.), *The Second Intermediate Period (Thirteenth-Seventeenth Dynasties): Current Research, Future Prospects*, OLA 192 (Leuven, 2010), 255.

beginning below the head, which is necessary to distinguish it. This trait, evoking a more "cursive" form, is not exclusive to the late Second Intermediate Period and is common in monuments from the end of the Seventeenth into the Eighteenth Dynasty (up to ca. Amenhotep III).[14]

The bottom line of the seated figure is unusually long, extending well beyond its front arm.

Register 2: Ỉd, T3-wr.t, and Ỉwf

The second register is separated by a thick horizontal, raised line. The couple, the *ẖry-ḥb(.t) Ỉd* and the *nb.t-pr T3-wr.t*, sit before an offering table, with libations poured by their son, the *ẖry-ḥb(.t) Ỉwf*. The couple's names are in two short vertical columns before *Ỉd* and the near edge of the offering table. As above, they sit at a slight angle and are roughly aligned with the top of the figures' heads. Unlike above, there is no space behind *T3-wr.t* for her name. The slight angle of her name avoids overlap with *Ỉd*'s lap – had her name extended straight down, the signs would have abutted *Ỉd's* knees.

Ỉd holds a lotus flower in his left hand and a folded cloth above his lap in his right. He wears the same set of kilts as his father above; however, unlike above, the fold of the short under-kilt is visible as a diagonal line on his right thigh without visible top knot.

T3-wr.t embraces her husband. The orientation of the couple is reversed from that of *Ỉb* and his wife above. Here, *T3-wr.t*'s full legs are visible, obscuring *Ỉd*'s hips behind her lap.

Unlike the couple above, the couple's feet sit on a low, rectangular footrest that extends from behind her heels, past his feet, and under the offering table. The chair upon which *Ỉd* and *T3-wr.t* sit has longer chair legs than that of the first register, while the legs of both couples are roughly comparable in length. The footrest compensates for the additional height of the second chair.

There are no beer jars present below the table in this second scene due to the spatial restrictions imposed by the footrest.

Ỉd's son, the *ẖry-ḥb(.t) Ỉwf*, stands behind the offering table and is identified in two vertical columns before him. No text narrates the performance of the offering ritual. *Ỉwf* wears the same set of kilts and pours libations.

The Offering Text

Below the second register are two lines of text with the offering formula, separated by thin, uneven, incised lines. The top line, separating the second register and text is uneven, curving up at the end, to avoid leaving space between the socles of the chair and the register line.

The text is in evenly spaced blocks, without any haphazardly placed signs. The hieroglyphs vary slightly in depth, but, generally, are not as deeply carved as those in the offering scenes above.

There are no indications that the offering text was carved first with the names of the deceased and his son added later. The final signs in both lines are closer together; however, this reflects a desire to align the text with the frame and avoid breaking up units of the offering formula. It appears that the entire text was known prior to being carved, resulting in the deliberate spacing of the hieroglyphs and individual blocks of text and phrases.

> (1) *ḥtp-di-ny-sw.t Ḥr Bḥd.t Wsir ḥry-ib Bḥd.t di=sn pr.t-ḫrw iḥ.w 3pd.w* (2) *ḫ.t nb.t nfr(.t) wꜤb(.t) n k3 n ẖry-ḥb(.t) tpy Ỉb s3=f ẖry-ḥb(.t) Ỉd*
>
> (1) A gift that the king gives[a] and Horus of Behdet[b], and Osiris[c] who is in Behdet, that they give[d] invocation offerings[e] of bread and beer, and cattle and fowl, and (2) every good, pure thing for the *k3* of the chief lector-priest,[f] *Ỉb*[g] (and) his son, the lector-priest *Ỉd*.

[14] P. Vernus, "Trois Statues De Particuliers Attribuables a La Fin De La Domination Hyksos," in J. Vercoutter (ed.), *Livre Du Centenaire, 1880–1980*, MIFAO 104 (Cairo, 1980), 185–86.

a) The offering formula uses the contemporary *ny-sw.t-di-ḥtp,* lacking the *t* phonetic complement. The newer form of the offering formula was largely in place by the end of the Sixteenth Dynasty. The omission of the *t* with *ny-sw.t* was not universal at Edfu and is attested at the site in the late Seventeenth Dynasty.[15]

The central element of the *ḥtp* is a tall, thinner loop than in the text in the first register, which is more bulbous, utilizing a smaller amount of space. The *t* phonetic complement is also quite small, but matches the size and form of the *t*'s in the remaining offering formula. It is notable that the *ḥtp* sign is not one of the anomalous forms attested at Edfu during the Second Intermediate Period.

b) The combination  is overly long and attenuated in both cases, with a rather flat *d*. This is also the case with the other long, horizontal block of text, *di=sn*, later in the line. These attenuated forms allow for a more even spacing of the remainder of the offering formula and avoid any awkward breaking up of the text.

The *d* in *Ỉd*'s name at the end of line 2 is shorter than in *Bḥd.t*. While there is space for the elongated form, the *d* in *Ỉd*'s name is the final sign group at the edge of the stela and no longer needs to be elongated to accommodate the text. The shorter form allows it to respect the edge of the text in the line above, which also respects the vertical frame of the scenes. The final *d* also differs in that the palm and bottom fingers of the hand are a thin, downward-curving single line, with a comparatively short wrist, similar to the contemporary hieratic.

c) Osiris is written with the throne rather than the portable seat.

d) The *di*-cone is carved separately from the hand, sitting above the palm and atop thumb, which is carved separately.

e) *T* and *ḥnq.t* are placed below *pr.t-ḫrw*, contrary to the late Middle Kingdom-Second Intermediate Period shift that separates them, with their own plural strokes. This "reversion" is consistent with a general trend of archaizing the offering formula in the Eighteenth Dynasty.[16] This may also be a result of spacing—including separate plural strokes would have required either wrapping cattle and fowl, which respect the back leg of the chair above, onto the following line or extending the text beyond the scene's frame.

The cattle and fowl signs are stacked vertically, sharing a single set of plural strokes. Again, potentially due to spatial restrictions, rather than archaizing.

f) The top loop of 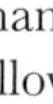 is hollow, with three short, oblique lines in lieu of the two central loops in the first register.

g) *Ỉb*'s name lacks a determinative, as in Register 1 and with *Ỉd*'s name in Register 2. All other names, including those of depicted figures, have determinatives. The inclusion of determinatives for represented individuals becomes more common in the Second Intermediate Period.[17]

Cairo Offering Table CG 23015

Cairo CG 23015 (fig. 2) names two series of individuals, *Ỉb*'s immediate family and an additional group not present on Oriental Institute E11455.[18] The *ḥry-ḥb(.t) Ỉb* and his wife, , are named on the left.[19] On the right are, *Ḏḥwty*, *Ỉwf*, *Ḏḥwty,* and *Ỉd*, of ambiguous relation.

The name of *Ỉb*'s wife is not identically rendered on Oriental Institute E11455 and Cairo CG 23015  and , respectively). A third woman, bearing the same name as that of Cairo CG 23015, , is present on stela Birmingham 70'96, belonging to the *wꜥb*-priest *Nb-it,* also of Edfu.[20]

[15] Marée, "Edfu under the Twelfth to Seventeenth Dynasties," 58–59.

[16] P. Vernus, "Sur Les Graphies De La Formule 'L'offrande Que Donne Le Roi'," in Stephen Quirke (ed.), *Middle Kingdom Studies* (New Malden, MA, 1991), 150–51.

[17] Ilin-Tomich, *From Workshop to Sanctuary*, 23–24; Vernus, "Edfou," 566–91, esp. 578.

[18] A. Kamal, *Tables D'offrandes, CG 40* (Cairo, 1906–1909), vol. 1, 14 and vol. II, pl. 8; Vernus, "Edfou," 316–16bis.

[19] According to A. Kamal, the image of the offering table in the Catalogue Générale is reversed (Kamal, *Tables d'offrandes*, vol. 1, 14).

[20] J. Ruffle, "Four Egyptian Pieces in Birmingham City Museum," *JEA* 53 (1967), 41–44.

Fig. 2. Cairo offering table CG 23015. From A. Kamal, Tables d'offrandes, *vol. 2), pl. VIII.*

Several different readings of her name have been put forward–*Tꜣ.i-šri(.t)*,[21] *Tꜣ-i-(ẖ)rd*,[22] *Tꜣ-ird*,[23] and *Tꜣ-imrd*.[24] None are entirely satisfactory, and all three examples are in restricted space. The inclusion of *rd* on Cairo CG 23015 was clearly important to the artist, as the female determinative at the end of the column is cramped. The blank space following the seated male determinative for *Ỉd*, on the other side indicates that the artist was not concerned with negative space. The space behind the wife's head on Oriental Institute E11455 is also restricted, although would have fit in the horizontal line, providing space for *rd* before the determinative.

---

[21] H. De Meulenaere takes *rd* on CG 23015 as a corruption of for , pointing to the use of *ẖrd* in the Middle Kingdom (H. De Meulenaere, "Contributions a la prosopographie du Moyen Empire [1. - Le Vizir Imeny. 2. - Quelques anthroponymes d'Edfou du Moyen Empire. 3. - Une stele d'Elkab]," *BIFAO* 81.1 (1981), 81). However, *šri* becomes more common in the New Kingdom (H. Ranke, *Die ägyptischen Personennamen II* (Gluckstadt, 1952), 10). De Meulenaere ("Contributions a la prosopographie," 81) notes the name on Birmingham 70'96, but does not equate the two women.

[22] D. Franke, *Personendaten aus dem Mittleren Reich (20.–16. Jahrhundert V. Chr.)*, ÄA 41 (Wiesbaden, 1984), 67 [49].

[23] Ranke, *Die Agyptischen Personennamen I*, 354 [8].

[24] Vernus points to the early New Kingdom masculine variant, *Pꜣ-imrd*, positing an association through the verb *rd* "to grow" with a prefix *m* (Vernus, "Edfou," 369). The inclusion of the *m* is encountered in two out of three attestations on the stela of a man bearing the name, dated to the early Eighteenth Dynasty (Leiden V 49; 14 P. Boeser, *Die Denkmäler des Neuen Reiches dritte Abteilung Stelen*, LEI 6 (Haag, 1913), pl. XI [14]). is encountered again in the name a Memphite priest from the time of Amenhotep I in the Third Intermediate Period genealogy of *ʿnḫ=f-n-Sḫm.t* (stela Berlin 23673). Vernus also does not rule out the possibility of its being foreign. Foreign names are rare in both the contemporary monumental and hieratic records at Edfu. Neither the feminine nor masculine variants are present in the Tell Edfu ostraca corpus. For the potential of *Pꜣ-imrd* being foreign, see T. Schneider, *Asiatische Personennamen in ägyptischen Quellen des Neuen Reiches*, OBO 114 (Freiburg, 1992), 103–4.

The name on Birmingham 70'96 is squeezed between the legs of the woman and the preceding man. The personal names in the second line of figures on Birmingham 70'96 utilize lapidary hieratic forms, presenting the possibility that an error was made in transcription.[25] A corruption on two separate monuments, not from the same artistic atelier is difficult, but, nevertheless, a corruption of *TꜢ-šri.t* seems the best option.

The other individuals on Cairo CG 23015 have no explicit relationships to either *Ỉb*'s family or one another. Unlike with the first group, the text is not all oriented in the same direction. The title *ḥm-nṯr* concludes the column of text, with the following horizontal line containing the juxtaposed names . The final short column, *wꜥb Ỉd*, returns to the standard orientation and is separated from the names above by a thin horizontal line, creating a visual barrier between them.

The absence of a determinative following the name *Ỉwf* creates ambiguity as to the number of individuals present. P. Vernus identifies three: *ḥm-nṯr Ḏḥwty, Ỉwf*, and *Ḏḥwty*.[26] In taking the first *Ḏḥwty* and *Ỉwf* as two individuals, he suggests that the orientation creates a group of three persons related directly to one another, and not necessarily *Ỉb* and his wife. The separation and change in orientation of the *wꜥb*-priest *Ỉd* then associates him with *Ỉb* and his wife, perhaps to be equated with his son on Oriental Institute E11455.[27] The orientation provides the filiation, as there is not enough space for *sꜢ=f*.

D. Franke contrarily identifies a couple: *Ỉwf*, a *ḥm-nṯr* priest of Thoth, and a woman *Ḏḥwty*, tentatively identifying *Ỉwf* as the son of *Ỉd* and grandson of *Ỉb*, of Oriental Institute E11455, with both father and son bearing other priestly titles before later becoming lector-priests,[28] contrary to all three generations of Oriental Institute E11455 bearing the title lector-priest. This requires the omission of *Ỉd*'s wife, *TꜢ-wr.t*, but the inclusion of *Ỉwf*'s presumed wife, *Ḏḥwty*, who is otherwise unattested. Although the cult of Thoth increased in popularity during the Second Intermediate Period, the title *ḥm-nṯr Ḏḥwty* and surviving evidence for a contemporary cult of Thoth at Edfu are lacking. More likely, this is simply a priest named *Ḏḥwty*, resulting in three individuals.[29]

Neither interpretation resolves the question as to the identification of these individuals and their ties to *Ỉb* or one another. Given the presence of another woman, *Ḏḥwty*, the absence of *Ỉd*'s wife is surprising. The omission of determinatives following personal names is not unique to Cairo CG 23015 and their absence, along with any clear familial affiliations, could simply be a result of available space. Their presence together does not necessitate a genetic relationship; however, the naming patterns of the family are suggestive, and the individuals were unquestionably close to one another, even if not direct relations.

An equation of the same individuals and generations between the monuments also presents the prospect of identifying two elements from the same funerary monument—its stela and associated offering table. Paleographically, the two exhibit clear differences. There are some similarities between the stela and the offering table, particularly with the offering text in the first register of Oriental Institute E11455. The *ḥtp* sign is rather bulbous, the *ḥ* of the offering text in the first register of Oriental Institute E11455 consists of a single top loop, with vertical line and tails, missing the two central loops, and the *kꜢ* arms lack distinct thumbs. However, there are differences. On Cairo CG 23015, the arm of the seated man determinative emerges from the head, but is more sharply bent at the elbow rather than curving, the horizontal writing of the phonetic elements of *ẖry-ḥb(.t)* vs. , *bḥ*, , has a stronger upward curve, the eye for Osiris lacks a canthus, and the divine determinative following Osiris is less schematic. This does not preclude their originating from the same spot, but does not allow for an assignment to the same contemporary artists.

25 The contemporary hieratic record from Edfu only utilizes in the name *Ḥr-šri*. Instead, is used in all other names.

26 Vernus, "Edfou," 316.

27 Vernus, "Edfou," 316bis (d) and (f). In this case, *Ỉd* would have been promoted from *wꜥb* to *ẖy-ḥb.t*.

28 Franke, Personendaten, 62 [38] and 131 [64].

29 Masculine and feminine theophoric names invoking Thoth are attested in the Tell Edfu Ostraca.

Statue Cairo TR 9/6/18/28

Cairo TR 9/6/18/28 belongs to an untitled man named *ỉd*, and was dedicated by his son, the *ẖry-ḥb(.t) ỉwf*.[30] No photograph is available and only a description of the statue and its text have been published. The statue was found at the kom and published at the same time as Oriental Institute E11455 and Cairo TR 9/6/18/26 by G. Daressy, who makes no comment as to if they were found together or in the same area of the site, although this cannot be ruled out.[31] The shared names of *ỉwf* and *ỉd* correspond to the father and son combination in Oriental Institute E11455.

Stela Birmingham 70'96 and ỉb's In-Laws(?)

Birmingham 70'96, belonging to the *wꜥb*-priest *Nb-it*, has no archaeological provenance, but is attributable to Edfu by its offering formula and personal names.[32] The name of Nb-it's sister's directly matches that of the wife of *ỉb* on Cairo CG 23015. Should these two women and that of Oriental Institute E11455 be one and the same, then we can identify *ỉb*'s brother-in-law as a *wꜥb*-priest named *Nb-it*, evidencing the broader intermarriage patterns of priestly families. Further, such an equation may provide identifications for the *ḥm-nṯr Ḏḥwty, ỉwf,* and *Ḏḥwty* of Cairo CG 23015. It is not inconceivable that these two men and one woman may be in-laws of *ỉb*.

Birmingham 70'96 may, potentially, be further associated with Cairo CG 20623, belonging to the *imy-rꜣ šnw.ty n Ḥr Bḥd.ty Ḏḥwty*, who has two untitled sons named *Ḥr-ḥtp* and *Nb-it*, potentially the brothers from Birmingham 70'96, further extending *Tꜣ-šri.t*'s family lineage.[33]

ỉb's Extended Family and Their Monuments

Eight stelae, offering tables, and statues from Edfu, including those of *ỉb* and his wife, contain individuals holding the title of *ẖry-ḥb(.t)* or *ẖry-ḥb(.t) tpy* and the names *ỉwf, ỉb,* or *ỉd* (Table 1).[34] P. Vernus has reconstructed two

---

[30] Daressy, "Monuments D'edfou Datant Du Moyen Empire," *ASAE* 18, 51 [X]; Vernus, "Edfou," 371 [113]. Vernus equates the statue with Cairo JE 49565 and cites B. Hornemann's publication Types of Ancient Egyptian Statuary I–III (Copenhagen, 1957), no. 529). Subsequent publication of photographs of Cairo JE 49565 indicate that the two are not the same piece (M. Eaton-Krauß, "A Very Unusual Statue Said to Come from Edfu" in M. Eaton-Krauß, C. Fluck, and G. van Loon (eds.), *Egypt 1350–AD 1800: Art Historical and Archaeological Studies for Gawdat Gabra* (Wiesbaden, 2011), 63–74).

[31] The second group of monuments from Edfu published by G. Daressy is described as recently arriving at the Cairo Museum (Daressy, "Monuments D'edfou Datant Du Moyen Empire," *ASAE* 18, 49). The date of their publication and registration numbers is not necessarily indicative that they were found in the same spot at Edfu.

[32] Ruffle, "Four Egyptian Pieces," 41–44; Vernus, "Edfou," 328–31 [No. 99].

Both examples of *Nb-it* on the stela reverse the *f* and *t*. This inversion is not encountered in other stelae or the ostraca from Edfu (see Figure 6b, col. 1, 6).

[33] P. Vernus suggests a possible familial association between the two based on the shared names of brothers, *Nb-it* and *Ḥr-ḥtp*, as well as stylistic and paleographic similarities between the two stelae (Vernus, "Edfou," 330–31). Should this be the case, and should Birmingham 70'96 include *ỉb*'s wife, then *ỉb*'s in-laws can be extended back a further three generations, identifying his father-in-law as the Overseer of the Granary (or double granary; *imy-rꜣ šnw.ty n Ḥ r Bḥd.ty*). However, this would require the omission of *Tꜣ-šri.t* from her father's stela (Cairo CG 20623), which identifies at least two other daughters.

[34] Birmingham 70'96, and Walters 22.313 have not been included in Table 1 due to the absence of explicit ties. Walters 22.313, a statue, belongs to an untitled man named *ỉwf*, dedicated by his brother, the *ḥm-nṯr* priest *ỉwf*. The father bears no title and his name, which is effaced, was read by P. Vernus as *Ḥr* (Vernus, "Edfou," 347–48). The *ḥm-nṯr ỉwf,* follows *ir.n Ḥr* without any clear relation (*n kꜣ n ỉwf* in *sn=f sꜥnḫ rn=f ḥm-nṯr ỉwf ir.n Ḥr(?) ḥm-nṯr ỉwf*). This may be the same *ỉwf* to whom the statue was dedicated. If so, then two generations are present: the father, *Ḥr*, and two brothers, sharing the name *ỉwf*, at least one of whom was a *ḥm-nṯr* priest. No definitely identifiable members of the *ỉb* family bear the title *ḥm-nṯr*. *Ḏḥwty* of offering table Cairo CG 23015 is a *ḥm-ntr*; however, his relationship to the family is unclear. The naming pattern and the involvement of the individuals in the temple is highly suggestive that they represent members of the extended family (whether known or unknown relations not preserved in the textual record). The statue was published by G. Steindorff (*Catalogue of the Egyptian Sculpture in the Walters Art Gallery* [Baltimore, 1946], pl. 9 [no. 58]) and is currently on display in the Walters Art Museum. The statue's back, containing the dedicatee, Iwf, faces a wall and is inaccessible. I would like to thank Dr. Lisa Anderson-Zhu for providing information about the statue and photographs of the three visible sides.

family trees, likely interrelated, totaling at least six generations.[35] Cairo JE 46200 and Oriental Institute E11455 present the longest family histories, three generations each.

Table 1. *Ἰb* Family Monuments.

Monument	Owner	Provenance at Edfu	Publication
Cairo CG 23015	*ẖry-ḥb(.t) Ἰb*	Unknown	Kamal, *Tables d'offrandes*, 14 and pl. 8; Vernus, "Edfou," 316–316bis [93]
Cairo JE 43362	*ẖry-ḥb(.t) Ἰwf*	Sebbakh	Daressy, "Monuments d'Edfou datant du Moyen Empire," *ASAE* 17, 242–43 [V]; Vernus, "Edfou," 310–13 [91] and pl. 59
Cairo JE 46200	*ẖry-ḥb(.t) tpy Ἰb*	Tell	Daressy "Monuments d'Edfou datant du Moyen Empire," *ASAE* 17, 237–39 [I]; Kubisch, *Lebensbilder*, 234–39 and fig. 20; Vernus, "Edfou," 287–91 and pl. 54
Cairo JE 46203	*ẖry-ḥb(.t) Ἰb*	Unknown	Daressy, "Monuments d'Edfou datant du Moyen Empire," *ASAE* 17, 239 [II]; Vernus, "Edfou," 292–94 [87] and pl. 55
Cairo TR 9/6/18/28	*Ἰd*	Tell	Daressy "Monuments d'Edfou datant du Moyen Empire," *ASAE* 18, 51 [X]; Vernus, "Edfou," 371 [113]
Cairo TR 9/6/18/26	*ẖry-ḥb(.t) Ἰwf/Ἰb*	Tell	Daressy, "Monuments d'Edfou datant du Moyen Empire," *ASAE* 17, 49–50 [VIII]; Kubisch, *Lebensbilder*, 244–47 [Edfu 22]; Vernus, "Edfou," 314–15 [92]
Oriental Institute E11455 (Cairo TR 9/6/18/25)	*ẖry-ḥb(.t) tpy Ἰb*	Tell	Daressy, "Monuments d'Edfou datant du Moyen Empire," *ASAE* 18, 50–51 [IX]; Vernus "Edfou," 368-370 [112]
Princeton Y1993-151	*ẖry-ḥb(.t) Ἰwf*	Unknown	Engelbach, "Steles and Tables," 118–19; Vernus, "Edfou," 303–5 [89] and pl. 57

Stela Princeton Y1993-151

Princeton Y1993-151 (fig. 3) is a round-topped stela measuring 52.2 cm x 36.0 cm x 4.0 cm. The upper left corner and far bottom right corner of the stela are broken away, missing a segment of the offering formula and the end of the third son's name. The upper corner was missing at the time it was first seen by R. Engelbach.[36]

Princeton Y1993-151 was first published R. Engelbach in 1922 without photographs[37] and subsequently included by P. Vernus, with a photograph, in his study.[38] Both R. Engelbach and P. Vernus encountered the stela in an antiquity shop in Cairo, without any archaeological provenance.[39] The inclusion of Horus of Behdet in the offering formula and the personal names attribute it to Edfu.

The round-topped stela has six horizontal lines of text above a scene of a seated man before his standing wife and son, all of whom are identified by name. Two additional sons are identified only by name on the far right of the stela. The lunette is empty and there are no visible traces of any pigmentation.

35 Vernus, "Edfou," 906–9 and 913.

36 R. Engelbach, "Steles and Tables of Offerings of the Late Middle Kingdom from Tell Edfu," *ASAE* 22 (1922), 119.

37 Engelbach, "Steles and Tables," 118–19.

38 Vernus, "Edfou," 303–5 and pl. 57.

39 Vernus saw the stela in Cairo in 1972. The stela was donated to the Princeton Art Museum, by Dr. Alvin E. Friedman Kien ("Acquisitions of the Art Museum 1993," *Record of the Art Museum, Princeton University* 53, no. 1 (1994), 80–81). I would like to thank Dr. Michael Padget, Curator of Ancient Art at the Princeton Art Museum, for providing information about the stela.

Fig. 3. Stela Princeton Y1993-151. Photo courtesy of Princeton University Art Museum / Art Resource, NY.

The bottom of the stela is not evenly cut. While it appears that the bottom is eroded or broken, the socles of both chair legs, as well as the feet of *Iwf* and his wife, are present.

The Text

Six lines of text dominate the upper half of the stela. Only the first two have uneven horizontal separation lines below them. A final horizontal line, at a slight angle, separates the end of the text from the scene below. These lines are uneven with faintly etched lines above all three, all of which are straighter than the final product. There are no lightly etched lines between lines 3 to 6 of the text to indicate an intention to include them.

The overall quality of the carving for the scene versus the hieroglyphs is marked. In contrast with the human figures, most of the hieroglyphs lack detail. In many cases, signs do not sit flat and are carved at an angle. The text is uneven in terms of spacing and alignment and exhibits a propensity for breaking sign groups and combining words. In some places, there is significant space between blocks of text and standard blocks are broken up, such as with …*tꜣ di=sn*… in line 3 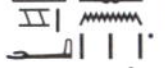. In other places, the hieroglyphs are simply not straight, angling up to the right, or properly aligned (e.g., *nṯr.w imy.w* in line 2 and *nṯr.w im=sn* in line 5). Vertically stacked horizontal signs are similarly not aligned (e.g., the water determinative of *Ḥʿpy* in line 6). The text is meticulous in its inclusion of feminines and plurals.

(1) *ḥtp-di-ny-sw.t Ḥr Bḥd.t Wsir* [*ḥr-ib*]
(2) *Bḥd.t nṯr.w imy.w p.t nṯr.w imy.w*
(3) *tꜣ di=sn pr.t-ḫrw t ḥnq.t iḥ.w ꜣpd.w ḥtp.w-nṯr nb*

(4) *ḥr=s sšr snṯr mrḥ.t ḫ.t nb.t nfr.t*
(5) *wꜥb.t ꜥnḫ.t nṯr.w im=sn dd.t pt qmꜣ.t tꜣ*
(6) *ỉnn.t Ḥꜥpy m ḥtp.w(t)=f nfr.t n kꜣ n wꜥb*
(7) *ẖry-ḥb(.t) Ỉwf*
(1) A gift that the king gives[a] and Horus[b] of Behdet,[c] and Osiris[d] [who is in][e]
(2) Behdet and the gods who are in[f] heaven and the gods who are in
(3) the land, that they give[g] invocation offerings of bread and beer[h] and cattle and fowl and all offerings
(4) including cloth, incense, oil and, every good
(5) and pure thing[i] on which the gods[j] live, which the sky gives,[k] which the land produces,
(6) and which Hapy brings,[l] as his good offerings for the *kꜣ* of[m] the *wꜥb*-priest (sic.?) (and?)
(7) lector-priest[n] *Ỉwf*[o]

a) Written *ny-sw.t-di-ḥtp* with phonetic complement. The *ḥtp* sign has two horizontal ticks. This is encountered as early as the Thirteenth Dynasty and continued in use, often in association with the older variation of the offering formula (*ny-sw.t-ḥtp-di*), into the late Second Intermediate Period and early Eighteenth Dynasty.[40] This is particularly prevalent in southern Upper Egypt.[41]

b) In contrast to the form of the Horus falcon used in the name of *Ḥri* below and all other birds, the falcon's feet are represented as small, abutting X's resting atop the horizontal line etched below. The falcon thus has three "legs," corresponding to the three peaks of the Xs. The same form is encountered once in the Clère stela (line 6). The Clère stela and Princeton Y1993-151 bear some similarities; however, the two are largely paleographically distinct.[42]

c) is inverted in both examples (lines 1 and 2). The mirror-reversal of signs is encountered during the Second Intermediate Period.[43] This inversion is not seen in any other monuments belonging to the extended *Ỉb* family at Edfu, but is attested at the site in the late Middle Kingdom-early Second Intermediate Period (the stelae of *Bbi-rsy* (British Museum EA1371),[44] *Rn=f-rsy* (current location unknown),[45] and *Rni-snb* (private collection Paris).[46]

Bḥd.t is more frequently written in either a single block, as in Oriental Institute E11455, or two blocks of two signs. In Princeton Y1993-151, both examples of the city determinative are oversized and placed independently, behind the phonetic signs. This cannot be an issue of transcription from hieratic—the scribe would have ligatured the t and determinative. Unlike other blocks of text, there is also significant space between the determinatives and following words. This placement is particularly unusual given the artist's attempts to avoid separated small signs in the text below (note j). Further unlike other sign combinations below, the *t*s are not centered below *Bḥd* (e.g., *nb.t* and *inn.t*). Rather, they sit to the right side, leaving ample space for the determinative or, alternatively, oblique strokes to render *Bḥd.ty*. A solution may be found in that the artist initially carved a *t* below *bḥ* on the left, perhaps to be followed by the *niw.t* sign, with the sign block following the inversion of. The correction of *t* to *d*, incorporating the *t* into the base of the thumb of *d*, then altered the spacing. He then used the same layout in the subsequent line. There, however, the *niw.t* sign is not as oversized and would have fit below the *d*.

d) Written with the seat (Q9) rather than the throne (Q1). The inversion of the seat is a Second Intermediate Period trend.[47]

---

40 Vernus, "Edfou," 629–32.
41 Ilin-Tomich, *From Workshop to Sanctuary*, 16 and Table 5.
42 The Clère dates to ca. Kamose: Marée, "Edfu under the Twelfth to Seventeenth Dynasties," 58–66 and fig. 16.
43 Kubisch, *Lebensbilder*, 123.
44 E. Budge, *Hieroglyphic Texts from Egyptian Stelae &c., in the British Museum Part V*, HTBM 5 (London, 1914), 7 and pl. 16.
45 M. Alliot, Rapport Sur Les Fouilles De Tell Edfou, 1933, FIFAO 10:2 (Cairo, 1935), pl. 17 [4].
46 Engelbach, "Steles and Tables of Offerings," 122–23; Vernus, "Edfou," 150–52 [47] and pl. 22b.
47 D. Franke, *Egyptian Stelae in the British Museum from the 13th to 17th Dynasties*. Volume I, Fascicule 1: *Descriptions*, M. Marée (ed.), (London, 2013); Ilin-Tomich, *From Workshop to Sanctuary*, 8–9.

e) The far bottom right of the divine determinative following Osiris is preserved. Following this, the obvious restoration is *ḥr-ib*, completing *ḥr-ib Bḥd.t*, which concludes on the following line. While, it seems that there would be excessive space for the compound preposition alone, the overall spacing and size of the hieroglyphs indicates the two signs were placed next to one another and not vertically stacked, filling the entire space. Compare the size of *ḥr* in line 4.

f) The legs of the quail chick are more like those of a standing human figure or compared to those of the quail chicks in the personal names *Ꞽwf* and lack the horizontal line below the feet.

g) Instead of constituting a single block, *di=sn* is separated and combined with the preceding *tꜣ* . Contrary to dd.t in line 5, the verb is written with rather than .

h) The items of the offering formula are all separated with their own plural strokes.

Rather than a beer jar, a milk jar with a plume of steam is used. This substitution is common from the late 13th Dynasty and is not restricted to Edfu.[48] At Edfu, it continues through the early Second Intermediate Period, and into the Seventeenth Dynasty (e.g., Cairo JE 46785 and Cairo TR 16/2/22/22).

The bread loaf is oblong, with three shallow oblique strokes. The same form is used in the determinative of *ḥtp.w=f* (line 6).

The cattle and fowl signs are tall, taking up the full height of block of text, necessitating the placement of plural strokes behind the signs. This is a Second Intermediate Period trend.[49]

i) *Ḫt nb.t* is separated into two blocks. *Ḫt* has a papyrus roll determinative.[50] All its subsequent modifiers include a *t*.

j) The use of the plural *nṯr.w*, and not singular, is unusual at Edfu. It is otherwise attested on the late Seventeenth Dynasty Clère stela of the *ḥm-nṯr n Ḥr Bḥd.ty Nb-it*, which utilizes plural strokes.

k) The spacing of *ḏd.t p.t qmꜣ.t tꜣ* breaks standard sign groups. The *t*s of the verbs are added to the top of the sign groups of the following nouns. Again, this is not an issue of transcription from the hieratic, but rather the artist's desire to avoid isolated signs. The *t* of the preceding *ꜥnḫ.t* is separated due to its being surrounded by vertical signs.

The formula is attested on six other stelae from Edfu dated to the late Middle Kingdom through the end of the Seventeenth Dynasty (British Museum EA 1371, Cairo CG 20537, Cairo JE 46784, Cairo JE 48230, Cairo TR 9/6/18/26, and the Clère stela).

l) The form of *in* deviates in that the body of the pot sits atop and not below the horizontal line representing the jar rim. The 16th Dynasty (reign of *Ḏd-ḥtp-Rꜥ Ddw-msw*) stela of *Ḫnsw-m-Wꜣs.t* from Edfu uses the same form (Cairo JE 38917). Cairo JE 38917 is also one of the few Edfu stelae in which the figures are executed in raised relief; however, there are significant paleographic deviations between the two in other sign forms (including diagnostic signs such as the seated man determinative and *ḥtp*).

m) *Wꜥb* follows *n kꜣ n*. The form matches that in the preceding line. As observed by P. Vernus, the *wꜥb* sign is carved over .[51] The same hieroglyphs are then carved below *wꜥb*, providing *Ꞽwf*'s title of lector-priest. There are no traces of a *b,* and it would not have fit at the end of the line. Spacing and sign placement alone cannot be the explanation, as the artist clearly had no problem breaking the signs up in the following title. Either, there was an error in carving or *Ꞽwf* is identified as both a *wꜥb* and *ḫry-ḥb(.t),* potentially first as a *wꜥb*-priest before his promotion to lector-priest (which may explain its initial omission). The presence of both on a single monument is abnormal, but not without precedent. Officials holding both positions on the same monument are encountered in the Thebaid.[52]

n) The title is determined with .[53]

o) All examples of have the front arm emerging from the head, which is more rectangular in shape. The elbow of the front arm is sharply bent and not curved.

---

48 Marée, "A Sculptural Workshop," 254.

49 Ilin-Tomich, From Workshop to Sanctuary, 21; Marée, "A Sculptural Workshop," 255.

50 Ilin-Tomich, *From Workshop to Sanctuary*, 22–23; Vernus, "Edfou," 549–54.

51 Vernus, "Edfou," 304 (f).

52 Vernus, "Edfou," 908 and n. 17.

53 Vernus, "Edfou," 910–12.

The wide (D54), with a swooping forward leg finds parallel in the contemporary hieratic, which often has a wide stance.

The Scene of Ỉwf and His Family

Ỉwf is shown seated before his wife, *Ỉwf*, and son, *Ḥri*. He wears a round, striated collar and is bare-chested with a defined bellybutton. His kilt lacks details other than a clear waistband.[54] He sits on a low-back chair, holding a lotus flower to his nose with his left hand. The lotus blossom is tripartite, with striations in the central portion, a form otherwise not attested at Edfu. The stem is short, extending only slightly beyond his left hand. Proportionally, his two arms are short in relation to his torso, as well as the arms of his wife and son. This is contrary to the more typical trait of longer, attenuated limbs encountered during the Second Intermediate Period.[55]

Ỉwf's wife, also named *Ỉwf*, stands before him, named in a short horizontal line of text above her head. She wears a single-strapped dress, round, striated collar and has a bracelet on her left wrist. Both of her arms and her fingers are longer and more attenuated than those of her husband.

Ỉwf's son *Ḥri*, stands behind his mother, and is named, without title, above his head. The space behind his name is not damaged; however, there is a slight depression in the stone, creating an uneven surface. There would have been space for a title had the artist utilized this surface; however, he chose not to do so as the back of the determinative, incorrectly carved as a seated woman, coincides directly with the point at which the surface dips. *Ḥri*'s right arm is extended forward towards his mother's left hand, barely touching her wrist. His figure is damaged below the waist, with the lower part and foot of his front leg, the bottom right of his kilt, and his entire back leg missing.

Behind *Ḥri* is a column of text, identifying two more sons: *Ỉd*[56] and Q*ꜣw*.[57] Neither bears a title. There is not enough space for any titles the men may have held or the names of additional children.

Cairo Stela TR 9/6/18/26

Stela Cairo TR 9/6/18/26 is fragmentarily preserved—its top, including any depictions of the deceased and family and much of the offering formula, is purportedly gone. To date, no photograph or facsimile of the stela is available.[58] The text used for all studies is that reproduced by G. Daressy, who offered few comments on its execution and style.[59] The stela belongs to the *<ḫry-ḥb(.t)> tpy n Ḥr Bḥd.ty Ỉwf*, who is further identified (*ḏdw*) with a name partially lost in a break at the end of x+2, with x+3 preserving .

According to Daressy's copy, lines x+3, and those following, are complete, which leaves space for only a single block of text at the end of x+2. Elsewhere, the phonetic elements are present for the name *Ỉb*. The result is a man *Ỉwf*, who goes by *Ỉb* (*Ỉwf/Ỉb*), son of the *<ḫry>-ḥb(.t) Ỉwf* and *the nb.t-pr Ỉwf*. No other family members are identified.

---

[54] What appears to be a pleat at knee-level is a surface scratch.

[55] Kubisch, *Lebensbilder*, 122.

[56] *Ỉd* is written with a censor and not the standard cow ear, through confusion with the verb *idi*, "to cense" or *id.t* "fragrance" (*WB* I, 152, 9).

[57] The top of the second bird's head is more rounded and like the quail chick in *Ỉwf*'s name than the preceding aleph. The names Q*ꜣw*, Q*ꜣ*, Q*ꜣ.wy*, and Q*ꜣi* are well attested at Edfu during late Second Intermediate Period and Eighteenth Dynasty in the Tell Edfu Ostraca. Q*ꜣꜣ* and Q*ꜣw* are also attested in on stelae Birmingham 70'96 and Hildesheim 1896.

[58] Vernus, "Edfou," 314–15 [No. 92]; Daressy, "Monuments D'edfou Datant Du Moyen Empire," *ASAE* 18, 50–51 [IX]; Kubisch, *Lebensbilder*, 244–47 [Edfu 22].

S. Kubisch notes that, at the time of her study, the stela was inaccessible in the basement of the Cairo Egyptian Museum and that the proper registration number is TR 9/6/18/26 and not TR 9/6/18/20 (Kubisch, *Lebensbilder*, 244, n. 906). As of 2018, the stela remains unavailable.

[59] Daressy, "Monuments D'edfou Datant Du Moyen Empire," *ASAE* 18, 50–51 [IX].

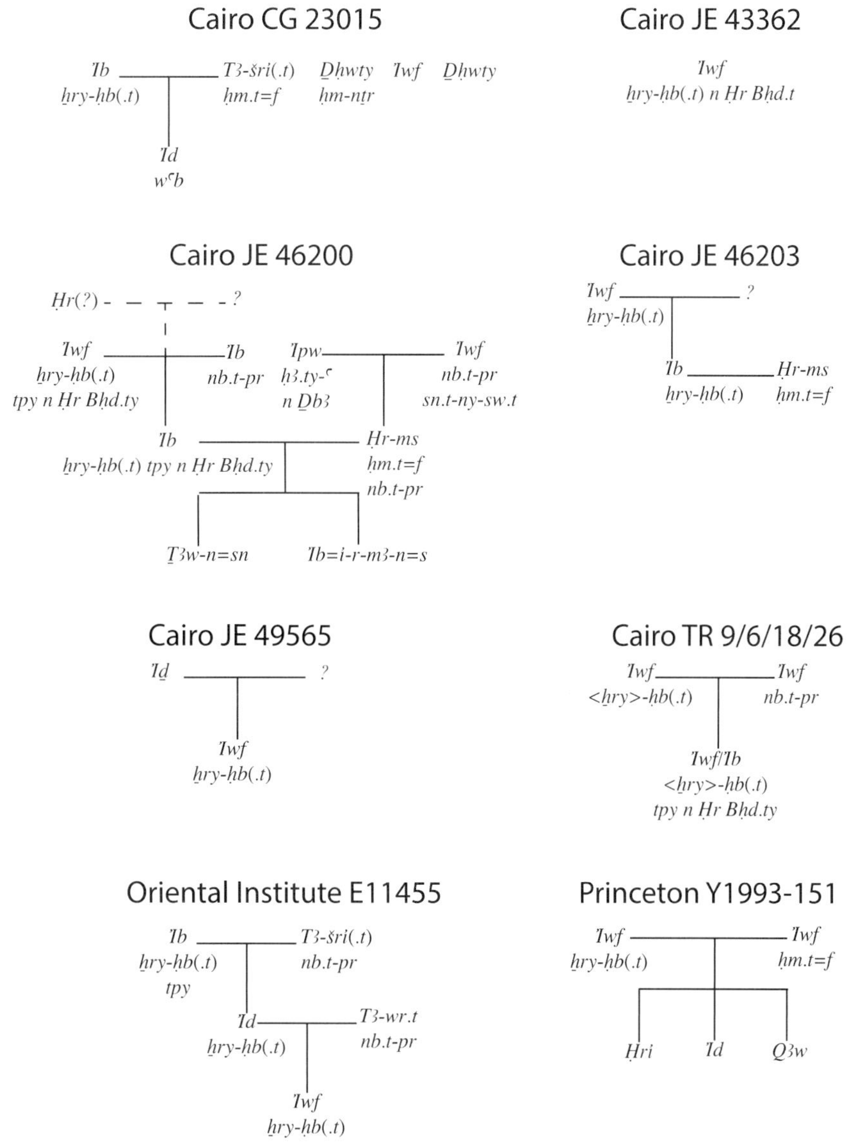

Fig. 4. Lineages of individual monuments belonging to the ꜤIb family.

G. Daressy describes the hieroglyphs as "dessinés gauchement, mal proportionnés," but gives only the example of the *n*, which is executed by a simple line.[60] The execution of the hieroglyphs of Princeton Y1993-151 can be similarly characterized, the *n* is a straight line, but there are diagonal downward strokes on each end of the sign. There are also variations between the two—despite the inclusion of the passage *dd.t p.t* … in both, Princeton Y1993-151 is more meticulous with regard to verbal forms. Further, unlike Princeton Y1993,151, the text of Cairo TR 9/6/18/26 is located at the bottom of the stela rather than the top.[61]

[60] Daressy, "Monuments D'edfou Datant Du Moyen Empire," *ASAE* 18, 49.

[61] The location of the scene is not an absolute criterion, the placement of the scene at the bottom of the stela continues into the Eighteenth Dynasty (Vernus, "Edfou," 487–88).

Stela Cairo JE 46200

Cairo JE 46200 belongs to the *ḫry-ḥb(.t) tpy n Ḥr Bḥd.ty Ỉb* and identifies at least three generations of the family. Both *Ỉb* and his father, *Ỉwf* of Cairo JE 46200 are identified as chief lector-priests and *Ỉb*'s wife, *Ḥr-ms*, is identified as the daughter of a local mayor, *Ỉpw*, and the niece of an unnamed king.[62] The only children present on *Ỉb*'s stela are two daughters, *Ṯ3w-n-sn* and *Ỉb=i-r-m3ʿn-s*, neither of whom is attested elsewhere. *Ỉb*, his wife, *Ḥr-ms*, and father, *Ỉwf,* are also on Cairo Offering Table JE 46203, which names no additional family.[63]

A potential fourth generation is present in the filiation of *Ỉb*'s father, written in subscript between lines four and five. Following the name *Ỉw[f],* including its determinative, is a single bird, which does not conform to either the *s3* bird or Horus falcon earlier in the line. P. Vernus reads *wr*, identifying the eldest member of the family as a man named *Ỉwf-wr*.[64] Alternatively, the bird has been proposed to be a Horus falcon, identifying *Ỉwf*'s father, *Ḥr* (*Ỉw(f s3) Ḥr*).[65] Should this be, *Ḥr* lacks a title, filiation, and determinative, which is odd given the presence of all three for *Ỉwf* and adequate space for their inclusion. Given the absence of other men bearing the name on the stela, qualifying *Ỉwf* as the elder (*wr*) is seemingly unnecessary. Perhaps, *Ỉwf* had a son named *Ỉwf* (brother of *Ỉb*, absent on the stela) or other contemporary family member bearing the name, requiring his qualification as *wr*.

Reconstructing the Family and Edfu's Administrative Chronology

The family tree, its internal chronology, and chronological placement are entirely dependent on the content and style of its monuments. All include traits recognized as diagnostic of the late Second Intermediate Period through early Eighteenth Dynasty and exhibit a range in specific elements and quality of production.[66] All studies to date situate the family at the very end of the Seventeenth Dynasty and into the Eighteenth Dynasty, which is certainly correct.

While there is some overlap between the monuments naming the same figures, a "clean" lineage including all monuments cannot be reconstructed (fig. 4).[67] Two distinct groups can be identified—an early sequence of three generations (Cairo JE 46200 and Cairo JE 46203) and a later sequence of three generations (Cairo CG 23015, Cairo TR 9/6/18/28, and Oriental Institute E11455), with no clear ties between them (fig. 5). Cairo JE 43362, Cairo TR 9/6/18/26, and Princeton Y1993-151 are isolates. Both Cairo TR 9/6/18/26 and Princeton Y1993-151 include couples sharing the name *Ỉwf*; however, they share no common children.

Stelae Cairo TR 9/6/18/26 and Cairo JE 46200 have traditionally served as linchpins for the early family lineage. Critically, neither stela owner identifies any male children or siblings. P. Vernus identified Cairo JE 46200 as the earliest family monument, tentatively identifying *Ỉwf,* married to *Ỉwf,* of Cairo TR 9/6/18/26 as a son of *Ỉb* of Cairo JE 46200, who was omitted from the stela. In his reconstruction, *Ỉwf/Ỉb* of Cairo 9/6/18/26 tentatively becomes the *Ỉb* of Oriental Institute E11455, named after his grandfather.[68] Contrarily, S. Kubisch equates *Ỉwf/Ỉb* of Cairo TR 9/6/18/26 with *Ỉwf* of Cairo JE 46200, pointing to the almost verbatim copying of two textual passages between the stelae, adding an earlier generation to the family.[69] The owner of Cairo TR 9/6/18/26 thus moves from being the child of to the parent of the owner of Cairo JE 46200.

62 *Ḥr-ms*'s mother, *Ỉwf,* is identified as a royal sister (sn.t-ny-sw.t), providing her husband with the title *s3-ny-sw.t ʿq*.

63 George Daressy, "Monuments D'edfou Datant Du Moyen Empire," *ASAE* 17 (1917), 239–40 [III]; Vernus, "Edfou," 292–94 and pl. 55 [No. 87].

64 Vernus, "Edfou," 289 (g).

65 Daressy, "Monuments D'edfou Datant Du Moyen Empire," *ASAE* 17, 240; Franke, *Personendaten*, 62 [39]; L. Morenz, *Beiträge zur Schriftlichkeitskultur im Mittleren Reich und in der 2. Zwischenzeit*, ÄAT 29 (Wiesbaden, 1996), 172 (E); Kubisch, *Lebensbilder*, 236.

66 For Second Intermediate Period traits, see, recently, Marée, "A Sculpture Workshop at Abydos"; Ilin-Tomich, *From Workshop to Sanctuary*.

67 Figure 4 lists only those family ties explicitly identified in the monuments. Individuals without explicit ties are listed separately.

68 Vernus, "Edfou," 907–8.

69 Kubisch *Lebensbilder*, 238. The shared passages are *ʿq r ḥ3.t pr ḥr pḥ.wy* (Cairo JE 46200, l. 6; Cairo 9/6/18/26, x+3–4) and *wʿb ʿ.wy ḥr ir.t ḫ.t* (Cairo JE 46200, 8; Cairo TR 9/6/18/26, l. x+5). These two passages do not immediately follow one another, and the intervening text is not identical between the two stelae.

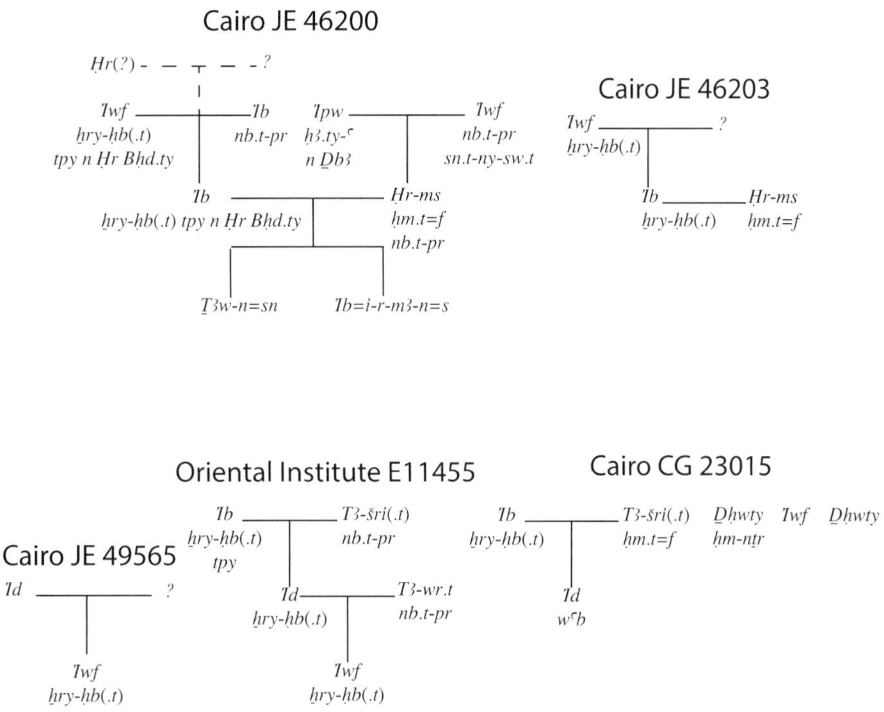

Fig. 5. Lineages of the earliest and latest generations of the family of ꜥꞽb.

That *ꞽwf/ꞽb*'s parents share the same name may suggest that he is a child of *ꞽwf* and *ꞽwf* of Princeton Y1993-151, as identified by Vernus.[70] However, no son named *ꞽwf* or *ꞽb* is present on the stela and there is not enough space for a fourth son's name. Presumably *Ḥri*, the only depicted son on the stela, was the eldest and would have succeeded his father in office.[71] For Cairo TR 9/6/18/26 to be a son absent from Princeton Y1993-151, requires the passing of the office between the untitled *Ḥri* and the absent *ꞽwf/ꞽb*, despite the presence of *ꞽd* and *Q3w*.

Highly speculative is the equation of *ꞽwf* and *ꞽwf*'s son, *Ḥri*, (Princeton Y1993-151) with the potential *Ḥr*, grandfather of *ꞽb*, on Cairo JE 46200. Should this be the case, then an additional generation could be added to the earlier family history— *ꞽwf* and *ꞽwf* of Princeton Y1993 thus being the great-grandparents of *ꞽb* of Cairo JE 46200, constituting the oldest generation. *Ḥr/Ḥri* would thus have named his son after his father, *ꞽwf*, who then married an unattested woman named *ꞽwf*, with whom he had a son *ꞽb*. Should there be only one couple named *ꞽwf* and *ꞽwf*, parents to *ꞽwf/ꞽb* and *Ḥri*, *ꞽd*, and *Q3w*, then *ꞽwf/ꞽb*'s office of chief lector-priest would have passed on to his nephew *ꞽwf*, son of *Ḥr/Ḥri*. Based on S. Kubisch's reasoning, Cairo TR 9/6/18/26 and Cairo JE 46200 are roughly contemporary requiring Princeton Y1993-151 to also be a contemporary work. While prosopographically tempting, we are still confronted with the reality that such a family tree requires multiple family members to be absent across a history of family monuments, which would be extraordinary.

Such a backward extension of the family history would put it in chronological proximity to a series of lector-priests who married into the late Middle Kingdom-early Second Intermediate Period *Ḥri* family of mayors via the marriage of a daughter of the mayor *ꞽbi-iꜥw, S3.t-Ḥr*, to a lector priest, *Ḥri* (Cairo JE 46199).[72] The couple

---

[70] Vernus, "Edfou," 315.

[71] An additional lector-priest named *Ḥri* is known from an obelisk at Edfu; however, it dates to earlier in the Second Intermediate Period and belongs to another priestly family (EDBY 121; D. Farout, "Trois Nouveaux Monuments De La Famille Des Gouverneurs D'edfou a La Deuxieme Periode Intermediaire," *RdE* 58 (2007), 41–69).

[72] The stela dates to the Second Intermediate Period. Vernus, "Edfou," 198; Marée, "Edfu under the Twelfth to Seventeenth Dynasties," 52.

had a son named *Ỉwf-snb*. While tempting to identify the son, *Ỉwf-snb*, as an elder family member of the late Second Intermediate Period-Early New Kingdom priestly family, he is untitled, and a different son, *Sbk-ḥtp*, bears the title of lector-priest. No examples of men bearing the name *Ỉwf-snb* also identify with the shortened *Ỉwf*. An extended familial relationship would result in a sequence of officials stretching from the end of the Thirteenth Dynasty through the Second Intermediate Period and into the early Eighteenth Dynasty.

Should the families be related, then the sequence of mayors during the late Second Intermediate Period and their marriage into the royal family prevents its projection too far into the past. The paternal cousin of the lector-priest *Ḥri*'s wife, *Sbk-m-sꜣ=f*, married Nubkheperre Intef VII, in the middle of the Seventeenth Dynasty (Cairo TR 16/2/22/23).[73]

As tempting as such ties are, they are speculative at best and rely entirely on a series of popular personal names and shared titles, which hardly constitute a safe means of identification. A further backwards projection of the family is unlikely. Challenges aside, the *Ỉb* family cannot be missing too many "middle" generations given the relative duration of the end of the Second Intermediate Period and estimations as to generational longevity.[74]

The king to whom *Ḥr-ms* of Cairo JE 46200 was related is unknown and no further family information is available about her father, the mayor *Ỉpw*. What is certain, however, is that he must be a successor of the *Ḥri* family of mayors, whose tenure can be dated through at least the reign of Nubkheperre Intef VII of the mid-Seventeenth Dynasty, establishing a terminus post quem for the mayor *Ỉpw*.[75]

It has been suggested that the nephew of the mayor *Ḥr-ḥr-ḫw.t=f*, an untitled *Ỉwf* (Cairo CG 20329), may be equated with the later mayor and overseer of the half-domain (*ḥꜣ.ty-ꜥ imy-rꜣ gs-pr*) *Ỉwf* (Cairo JE 63949), whose only known family member is a brother, *Mnṯw-nḫt*.[76]

However, such ties are complicated chronologically by the presence of an additional mayor, *M-ḥb* (Cairo JE 49566), whose career and military exploits date to the reign of Kamose, imposing an even later terminus post quem.[77] Other than his mother, *Bim*, *M-ḥb* has no known relations and it is most likely that he is to be located somewhere in between *Ỉwf* and *Ỉpw*. A familial relation between these mayors is possible, but their existence presents a necessary break in a potential extended lineage linking the *Ḥri* family of mayors, a contemporary line of lector priests, and the later priestly *Ỉb* family.

Further complicating the mayoral sequence at Edfu is the recent discovery of a stela naming a mayor and overseer of priests *Ḥr-nḫt* and his wife, the *iry.t-pꜥ.t Nfr.t-wbn=s*, outside the recently excavated Eighteenth Dynasty villa at Tell Edfu, inserting another mayor into Edfu's official chronology.[78] The personal names have been hacked and the representations of *Ḥr-nḫt* and his wife defaced, perhaps suggesting that there was local upheaval in the office of mayor or shift in power among the local elite families.[79]

---

[73] The precise duration of the early 17th Dynasty remains uncertain, but was not a long period of time, see D. Polz, *Der Beginn des Neuen Reiches: Zur Vorgeschichte einer Zeitenwende*, SDAIK 31 (Berlin, 2007).

[74] Generational durations have been suggested to be between twenty and thirty years (C. Bennett, "A Genealogical Chronology of the Seventeenth Dynasty," *JARCE* 39 (2002), 240; M. Bierbrier, *The Late New Kingdom in Egypt (c. 1300–664 B.C.): A Genealogical and Chronological Investigation* (Warminster, 1975), xvi; J. Quaegebeur, "The Genealogy of the Memphite High Priest Family in the Hellenistic Period," in D. Crawford, J. Quaegebeur, and W. Clarysse (eds.), *Studies on Ptolemaic Memphis* (Leuven, 1980); K. Jansen-Winkeln, "The Relevance of Genealogical Information for Egyptian Chronology," *ÄuL* 16 (2006), 257–75; T. Schneider, "Das Ende der Kurzen Chronologie: Eine Kritische Bilanz der Debatte zur Absoluten Datierung des Mittleren Reiches und der Zweiten Zwischenzeit," *ÄuL* 18 (2008), 299–301). See J. Elias, "Coffin Inscription in Egypt after the New Kingdom: A Study of Text Production and Use in Elite Mortuary Preparation" (PhD dissertation, Chicago: The University of Chicago, 1993), 27–51, for an extended discussion on the complications in using generational counts.

[75] For the family and its monuments, see K. Bandy, "Town and District: Local and Regional Administration During the Second Intermediate Period" (PhD dissertation, Chicago: The University of Chicago, 2016), 49–57; Farout, "Trois Nouveaux Monuments"; Vernus, "Edfou," 843–47.

[76] Vernus, "Edfou," 842–43. Vernus equates the men through the stylistic dating of *Ỉwf*'s stela (Cairo JE 63949). The stela dates to the Seventeenth Dynasty (Kubisch, *Lebensbilder*, 218; D. Franke, *Das Heiligtum des Heqaib auf Elephantine: Geschichte eines Provinzheiligtums im Mittleren Reich*, SAGA 9 (Heidelberg, 1994), 84, n. 277).

[77] No known descendant of any other attested mayor bears the name *M-ḥb* or *Ḥr-m-ḥb*.

[78] See n 4.

[79] *Ḥr-nḫt* and *Nfr.t-wbn=s* cannot be placed chronologically in the known mayoral families or equated with individuals attested in the monumental record outside Edfu, but the writing of the *ḥtp-di-ny-sw.t* formula on the stela is indicative of a Second Intermediate Period-early New Kingdom date.

Edfu's mayoral sequence indicates that the earliest attested members of the *Ỉb* family must have lived, at the very earliest, contemporary with or, far more likely, after the reign of Nubkheperre Intef VII by at least one generation. This comports with the stylistic dating of the early family monuments. Stylistically, Cairo JE 46200 can been dated to the very end of the Seventeenth or early Eighteenth Dynasty.[80] As with Princeton Y1993-151, the *niw.t* signs are oversized, and the text is not always evenly spaced, sized, or distributed; however, the text of Cairo JE 46200 is not as haphazardly organized.[81] The associations between Cairo JE 46200 and Cairo TR 9/6/18/26 necessitate that it too be included in the early family monuments. While these three stelae cannot be assigned to the same workshop and, based on the description and copied text of the latter, exhibit distinct differences, the few identifiable similarities are suggestive of a closer chronological proximity than with Oriental Institute E11455.

This identification does not resolve the relationship(s) between these monuments and Oriental Institute E11455. The middle generation(s) remain murky—there are no explicit ties between the individuals and the name *Ỉwf* was hardly rare.[82] Oriental Institute E11455 is thus left "floating" in relation to earlier generations, but can be safely dated to the early Eighteenth Dynasty. Based on style and parentage Oriental Institute E11455, Cairo CG 23015, and Cairo TR 9/6/18/28 constitute the end of the known family history.

The Social Position of Lector-Priests in the Late Second Intermediate Period–Early Eighteenth Dynasty

Unlike *wʿb*- and *ḥm-nṯr* priests, who participated in seemingly "secular" activities in areas such as production facilities, lector-priests are generally understood to have served almost exclusively as ritual actors and keepers of ritual texts and materials.[83] Within the realm of the temple, they were involved in the maintenance of and activities in its library or scriptorium.[84] Their ritual activities were not restricted to "official" temple affairs—lector priests were also involved in healing and other magical activities.[85]

The men of *Ỉb*'s family were not only lector-priests, but they held the office of chief lector-priest over several generations. The daily duties and responsibilities of the position are uncertain, but it can be stated that they served at the top of the hierarchy of ritualists within the local temple. It has been previously questioned if the position existed at every temple, with an individual holding the bare title *ẖry-ḥb(.t)* potentially serving in capacity of chief lector at some sites, sans official designation.[86] The preserved monumental record for provincial centers is limited and the absence or sporadic preservation of monuments attesting to the title at other sites need not indicate the absence of the position in any given locality or temple.[87]

---

80 Kubisch, *Lebensbilder*, 235; Marée, "Edfu under the Twelfth to Seventeenth Dynasties," 53, n. 88; Vernus, "Edfou," 291.

81 Kubisch, *Lebensbilder*, 123. Kubisch points particularly to the spacing of *pr.t-ḫrw*.

82 The recent discovery of a statue naming a district scribe (*sš spꜣ.t*) *Ỉwf*, son of the *sꜣb Ỉwf* and *Nꜣi*, in an early New Kingdom Villa at Tell Edfu further substantiates the local popularity of the names.

83 The Abu Sir papyri identify their primary role as ritualists (H. Vymazalová, "The Administration of the Royal Funerary Complexes," in J. Moreno García (ed.), *Ancient Egyptian Administration*, HdO1 104 (Leiden, 2013), 191–92). The Twelfth Dynasty stela of the lector-priest *Ttw* (Cairo CG 20088) relates that he "wrote in the temple" (*iw sš.n=i m ḥw.t-nṯr tn n.t Ḫn.ty-imn.tyw*).

84 See, for example, the extensive discussion by Morenz on Edfu's cultural importance during the late Middle Kingdom and Second Intermediate Period (Morenz, *Beiträge*, 176–81). The presence of literary texts, including copies of the Hymn to the Nile and Instruction from a Man to his Son, in the Tell Edfu Ostraca corpus are indicative of the continuation of scribal culture and education at Edfu in the late Second Intermediate Period and early New Kingdom and not a cultural breakdown during a time of political tumult.

85 R. Ritner, *The Mechanics of Ancient Egyptian Magical Practice*, SAOC 54 (Chicago, 1993), 220–21; S. Sauneron, *The Priests of Ancient Egypt* (New York, 1960), 61–64.

86 S. Quirke, *Titles and Bureaux of Egypt, 1850–1700 BC* (London, 2004), 125. S. Quirke points specifically to the Lahun papyri, where the bare title *ẖry-ḥb(.t)* and "regular" lector priest (*ẖry-ḥb(.t) ʿꜣ*) are the most frequently attested. At least one clear example of the title *ẖry-ḥb(.t) tpy* is present at Lahun. Papyrus Cairo JE 71581 (=Berlin 10017) relates the acquisition of meat offerings. Listed among the recipients are the mayor, phyle director, and chief lector priest (U. Luft, *Urkunden zur Chronologie der Späten 12. Dynastie: Briefe aus Illahun*, CCEM 7 (Vienna, 2006), 113–17 and pl. 35).

87 Contra R. Forshaw, *The Role of the Lector in Ancient Egyptian Society* (Oxford, 2014), 12 regarding the "conspicuously few" examples of lectors in the New Kingdom comparative to earlier periods.

Evidence for any administrative activities carried out by lector-priests, even within the temple, is limited. There is a relative paucity of seals and sealings belonging to lector-priests. A lector priest of Wah-Sut (*ẖry-ḥb(.t) n Wꜣḥ-Sw.t*) was found in the sealings deposit associated with the temple of Senwosret III in Abydos.[88] At least three seal impressions identifying a regular lector-priest (*ẖry-ḥb(.t) ꜥšꜣ*) were found at Lahun.[89] The Lahun sealings can be identified as jar sealings by their shape, perhaps reflecting their responsibility for maintaining ritual supplies.[90] An additional sealing belonging to the seal bearer and lector priest (*ḫtm.ty-*[…] *ẖry-ḥb(.t)*) was also found at Lahun.[91] Reconstruction of the excavations by C. Gallorini has identified some of the sealings deposits as from in or around the temple area.[92]

The status of the position of chief lector-priest is, from the early Middle Kingdom, exemplified in its being held by local nomarchs in Middle Egypt.[93] This changed at some point in the late Middle Kingdom, when the title of chief lector-priest is more often individually held. Documentary evidence indicates lector-priests held positions of status. Papyrus UC 32166, a household list (*wp.wt*) of the *ẖry-ḥb(.t) ꜥšꜣ Snfrw* from Lahun, attests to the resources and relative status of even regular lector-priests.[94] Listed among the house are a series of dependents (*ḏ.t=f*), many of whom are women. Should this *Snfrw* be the same man as the *ẖry-ḥb(.t)* attested on the sealing from Lahun discussed above, then we can speak to a single man using both titles, perhaps only the abbreviated *ẖry-ḥb(.t)* on his seal due to spacing.[95]

S. Quirke has suggested that *Snfrw*'s house was one of the eleven large residences at Lahun.[96] If so, then *Snfrw*'s economic resources can be quantified archaeologically. As calculated by B. Kemp, the large households at Lahun, together, could have sustained the population of the town.[97] The Late Middle Kingdom Papyrus Ramesseum E also includes at least two lector-priests among the individuals associated with regional grain holdings.[98]

Papyrus Cairo JE 71580 (=Berlin 10005) from Lahun, an account of *ꜥqw* and its use for the payment/expenditure (*sšm*) to temple staff, indicates that *Snfrw*'s circumstances were not exceptional.[99] The highest paid individuals are the mayor and overseer of the temple, followed by the chief lector priest and libationer, who

88 J. Wegner, *The Mortuary Temple of Senwosret Iii at Abydos*, PYE 8 (New Haven, 2007), 347, fig. 157 [no. 53]. The image of the sealing suggests that it was either attached to a basket or peg, perhaps from a container holding ritual goods or equipment. Its shape is not that of a papyrus document or jar sealing.

89 Now in the Ashmolean (1889.1156; G. Martin, *Egyptian Administrative and Private-Name Seals: Principally of the Middle Kingdom and Second Intermediate Period* (Oxford: Griffith Institute, 1971), 54 [650] and pl. 38 [14]; W. Petrie, *Kahun, Gurob, and Hawara* (London, 1890), pl. 10 [18].

90 G. Martin identifies them as jar sealings (Martin, Seals, 54 [650]). One example on display at the Ashmolean is clearly a jar sealing, with the seal stamped into the top of the jar stopper. It would not have been, even potentially, broken upon its removal, unlike with a sealing affixed to other objects. Nevertheless, it still would have been indicative of the last authorized individual to access the vessel's contents.

91 Martin, Seals, 125 [1622] and pl. 47 [18]; W. Petrie, *Illahun, Kahun, and Gurob* (London, 1891), pl. IX [11]. The back-type and current location are not known. Petrie states that the majority of sealings from the deposit were from boxes, vessels, and bags (Petrie, *Illahun, Kahun, and Gurob*, 14).

92 C. Gallorini, "A Reconstruction of Petrie's Excavation at the Middle Kingdom Settlement of Kahun," in S. Quirke (ed.), *Lahun Studies* (New Malden, 1998), 43–49 and 54.

93 As attested at Beni Hasan, Deir el-Bersheh, and Meir. For the role and status of the chief lector priest in the early Middle Kingdom, see H. Kees, "Die Priesterliche Stellung Des Monthemhet," *ZÄS* 87 (1962).

94 M. Collier and S. Quirke, *The UCL Lahun Papyri: Religious, Literary, Legal, Mathematical and Medical* (Oxford, 2004), 116–17; F. Griffith, *The Petrie Papyri: Hieratic Papyri from Kahun and Gurob Principally of the Middle Kingdom* (London, 1898), 25–29 and pls. 10–11.

95 The potential equation of the two men was first observed by F. Griffith (Griffith, *The Petrie Papyri*, 26).

96 Quirke, *Titles and Bureaux*, 125.

97 B. Kemp, *Ancient Egypt: Anatomy of a Civilization*, 2nd ed. (London, 2006), 215–17. As calculated by B. Kemp, the Southern House at Lahun had a capacity of 316.40 cubic meters, providing 1091 "minimum ration units," calculated as taking 0.29 cubic meters per person (Kemp, *Anatomy of a Civilization*, 216, Table 1; B. Kemp, "Large Middle Kingdom Granary Buildings," *ZÄS* 113 (1986), 131–33). This would have more than adequately supported the more than 20 individuals in *Snfrw*'s family and staff.

98 Many of the entries are damaged and the majority of those preserved consist of fragmentary male names with few associated titles, particularly priests. The lector priests are present on Sheet 3, vol. 1, 3–4. A summation of the account is provided by S. Quirke, *The Administration of Egypt in the Late Middle Kingdom: The Hieratic Documents* (New Malden, Surrey: SIA, 1990), 190; A. Gardiner, "A Unique Funerary Liturgy," *JEA* 41 (1955), 9). Photographs of the papyrus are available in the Ramesseum Papyri Catalogue (an online research catalogue of the British Museum) (R. Parkinson, "Online Research Catalogues. The Ramesseum Papyri," (The British Museum)).

99 L. Borchardt, "Besoldungsverhaltnisse Von Priestern Im Mittleren Reich," *ZÄS* 40 (1902), 113–17.

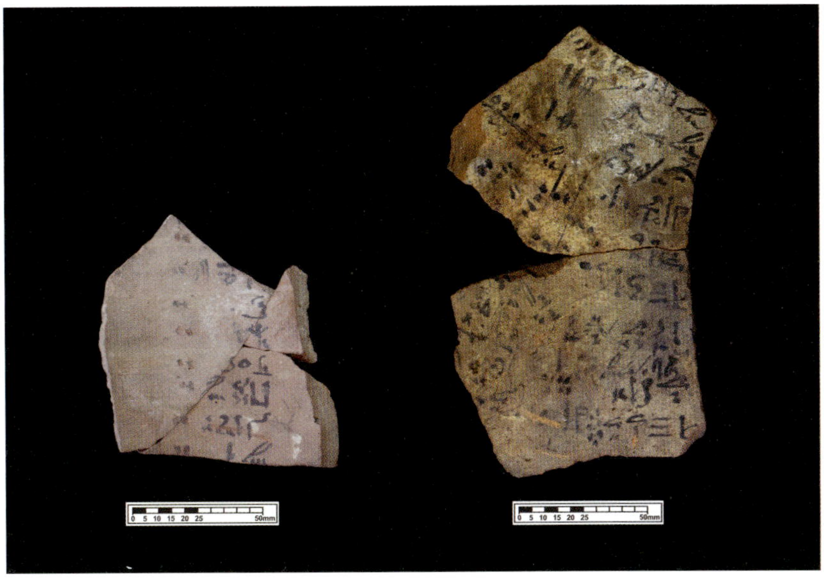

Fig. 6. Tell Edfu Ostraca 39 (verso) and 48 (recto). Photo: K. Bandy, Tell Edfu Project.

receive the same amount, the regular lector-priest and royal *wˁb*-priest, who receive the same amount, and then the phyle director.[100]

The economic prosperity and social standing of the position continued into to the Second Intermediate Period and early New Kingdom. The manifest number of stelae from Edfu attest to their continuing ability to afford quality funerary monuments. Further, the early Eighteenth Dynasty (Ahmose-Amenhotep I) tomb of the second lector priest (*ẖry-ḥb*(*.t*) *snw*) of Horus of Edfu, *S3-t3-im3w*, at Hagr Edfu (HE 1) speaks to his available resources. An inscription in his tomb relates his attachment to a statue within the temple and its associated income, including foodstuffs, and at least 40 auroras of land.[101]

Similar social standing is further indicated by marriage patterns. *Ib*'s family, as well as that of the earlier lector-priest of Edfu *Ḫri*, intermarried with the local mayoral family. These marriages extended even to direct members of the royal house. *S3-t3-im3w*'s in-laws held positions affiliated with the queen mother and the title *s3-ny-sw.t*.

Excursus: The Tell Edfu Ostraca and Edfu's Monumental Record

Excavations at Tell Edfu have found more than 250 hieratic ostraca from archaeological contexts ranging from occupation levels to old excavation debris.[102] The majority of the ostraca can be dated to the late Second Intermediate Period into the mid-Eighteenth Dynasty (Thutmose III/Hatshepsut) based on archaeological, paleographic, and prosopographic grounds. The texts primarily consist of name lists and payment records, with occasional larger institutional records relating to storage and production. They served as internal institutional documents and, in most cases, lack rubrics that would provide clear, institutional affiliations for the named workers.

---

100 The chief lector-priest is the only religious official in the list who is "permanent," the others are all qualified as being in their month of service (*imy 3bd=f*).

101 W. Davies, "The Tomb of Sataimau at Hagr Edfu: An Overview," *BMSAES* 20 (2013), 54 and fig. 18.

102 The ostraca were the subject of my dissertation (Bandy, "Town and District"). Their full publication is in preparation.

Potential Correlations between the Extended ꞽb Family and the Contemporary Documentary Record

The Tell Edfu Ostraca provide an extensive dataset for local names and naming patterns during the period in which *ꞽb* and his family lived. The local popularity of many of the names from the priestly families encountered in the monumental record is substantiated in the Tell Edfu Ostraca. *ꞽwf, ꞽb, ꞽd, Nb-it* (as well as the female variant, *Nb.t-it*), Q*ꜣw* (and its variants), and *Ḏḥwty* are all common at Edfu during this time.[103] *ꞽwf* is attested for both men and women in the ostraca corpus, although most often is male.

Several coherent groups of workers can be identified through the repeated occurrence of the same names together (including names with titles and/or filiations), documented by the same scribe. One of these groups, identified as "Worker Group B," is large and diverse, including untitled men and women, scribes, an unnamed *ḥry*, as well as *wꜥb* and *ḥm-nṯr* priests (fig. 6 right). Priests are frequently, but not always, identified by their name and title.[104] Given the absolute absence of the title *ẖry-ḥb*(*.t*) in the entire corpus, it is unlikely that any "hidden" lector-priests are present.[105]

A potential association between the ostraca and the monumental record may exist between the individuals tentatively identified as *ꞽb*'s in-laws (Birmingham 70'96) and the other individuals found on Cairo Offering Table CG 23015. Individuals sharing the names of both a *ḥm-nṯr* priest *Ḏḥwty* (Cairo CG 23015) and a *wꜥb*-priest *Nb-it* (Birmingham 70'96) are present in Worker Group B (fig. 6 right, col. 1.4 and col. 1.6). While it is possible that these are the same men, extreme caution must be used, and several mitigating factors must be kept in mind: (1) Depending on the relationships between the individuals on the monuments, *Nb-it* and *Ḏḥwty* may have been separated by at least one generation and, depending on the exact relationship between *Ḏḥwty* and *ꞽb*, potentially two generations, whereas the two priests in the ostraca are contemporaries. (2) Both names are extraordinarily common at Edfu. Other individuals bearing the names and lacking titles are found in the contemporary ostraca that do not document Worker Group B, the later Eighteenth Dynasty ostraca, and the monumental record. (3) Filiations providing the name of an individual's father or mother are common in the ostraca, but are rarely included with the priests and never with any priests bearing the names *Nb-it* or *Ḏḥwty*.

Nevertheless, the naming patterns, titles, and chronological placement of the Tell Edfu Ostraca are suggestive. It is very possible that the priests in the ostraca are members of the same extended family (or families), albeit of an indeterminate generation, who may (or may not) be documented in the contemporary monumental record. Barring further discovery of ostraca with explicit filiations for the priests, definitive equations of individual priests in the monumental and documentary records of Edfu will remain elusive despite their chronological proximity and suggestive naming patterns.

"Documentary" Scribal Culture at Edfu

The increasing influence of so-called "documentary scribal culture" on private monuments during the late Middle Kingdom and into the Second Intermediate Period is well-known.[106] Shifts in orthography, sign shape, and distribution are well attested in Upper Egypt, including Edfu. In addition to having one of the largest provincial monumental records during this period, Edfu now also has the most extant provincial hieratic record for the late Second Intermediate Period and early New Kingdom. The exact contemporaneity of the hieratic and monumental records cannot be established, but the two can be dated to the same general period. Thus,

103 Despite the relative paucity of theophoric names invoking the god Horus in the monumental record, this was not a local trend at the time. Names such as *Ḥr, Ḥri, Ḥr-ꜥꜣ, Ḥr-ḥtp, Ḥr-šri, Šd-Ḥr*, etc. are present in the ostraca.

104 While it is possible that some of these represent two individuals bearing the same name, this is not true for all cases. A man bearing the name *ꞽb-tti* is only identified as a *ḥm-nṯr*-priest twice.

105 The title is not present in any of the ostraca excavated to date. Although not a significant portion of the corpus, the institutional records present largely relate to commodities, storage, and production—areas of activity in which one would not expect to find lector-priests. This follows the general pattern of sealings distribution from Wah-Sut. Institutionally, *ḥm-nṯr* and *wꜥb*-priests are encountered in storage and production facilities (Bandy, "Town and District," 104–5 and 200–202).

106 See recently, Marée "A Sculpture Workshop at Abydos," 249, n. 52, who notes the quick spread of documentary traits in Upper Egypt, particularly the Thebaid.

Edfu, provides one of the few examples of relatively substantial, parallel hieratic documentary and monumental scribal cultures for comparison.

Despite this, a direct comparison between the two to evaluate any hieratic influence remains difficult. The ostraca do not include many of the elements (particularly words and phrases from offering formulae) exhibiting documentary culture in the monumental record for comparison due to the nature of their content. Further, the relatively limited corpus of late Middle Kingdom hieratic at Edfu allows for only a limited study of the development of local script and documentary scribal culture over time and any influence it may have played on the changing local monumental written culture. P. Vernus[107] and S. Kubisch[108] have both noted hieratic trends among some of the Edfu monuments, particularly among the corpus of the very late Middle Kingdom and early Second Intermediate Period, predating the monuments in this paper and most of the Tell Edfu Ostraca.

The Tell Edfu hieratic finds parallels in the Seventeenth and Eighteenth Dynasty hieratic of Thebes, including the contemporary ostraca from Deir el-Ballas[109] and later Eighteenth Dynasty ostraca from Deir el-Bahari[110] and papyrus Louvre E 3226.[111] In general, the script is larger and more rounded than the administrative scripts of the late Middle Kingdom.[112] Edfu's hieratic of the late Middle Kingdom through mid-Eighteenth Dynasty is not as heavily ligatured (Figure 6). Signs are stacked vertically and often abbreviated in form, but, generally, are more cursive.

Nevertheless, a few observations can be made. Many of the signs displaying hieratic tendencies noted by P. Vernus and S. Kubisch are abbreviated or highly cursive in the Tell Edfu Ostraca. Figure 6 includes Tell Edfu Ostraca 39 and 48, two ostraca from the same stratigraphic level, dated to the early Eighteenth Dynasty, which are representative of the corpus at large. In all cases, ( ) is abbreviated (fig. 6 right, col. 1.1) and ( ) typically includes the top loop followed by one to three oblique strokes (fig. 6 left, x+6).

The clearest concordance between the monumental and hieratic corpora is the positioning of the arm in some signs of male figures. Examples of ( ) on the very late Seventeenth and Eighteenth Dynasty monuments from Edfu frequently have the forward arm emerging from the head of the figure and not the shoulders, most visible in the determinatives accompanying male personal names. This is not observable in the ostraca, as determinatives for male and female personal names are abbreviated.[113] The emergence of the arm is observable, however, in other seated and standing figures of men in hieratic. (A24) and (A28) are the most frequently encountered full male figures. For , the head is usually, but not always, indistinguishable (a single vertical stroke represents the head and body). The arms of ( ) in the personal name Wrd (Figure 6b, col. 1, 2) emerge from the very top of the sign.[114] By contrast, ( ) almost always has a distinct head (fig. 6 left, x+4). This is only the case in the administrative ostraca—the literary ostraca from Tell Edfu utilize different forms.[115]

---

107 Vernus, "Edfou," 619–23.

108 Kubisch, *Lebensbilder*, 128–31.

109 Königliche Museen zu Berlin, *Hieratische Papyrus aus den Königlichen Museen zu Berlin III: Schriftstücke der VI. Dynastie aus Elephantine, Zaubersprüche für Mutter und Kind, Ostraka* (Leipzig, 1911), pl. 42

110 W. Hayes, "A Selection of Tuthmoside Ostraca from Der El-Bahri," *JEA* 46 (1960).

111 M. Megally, Le Papyrus Hiératique Comptable E. 3226 Du Louvre, *BdÉ* 53 (Cairo, 1971).

112 Not to be confused with the local literary hand. The two literary ostraca from Tell Edfu (TEO 131 and 135) are paleographically distinct from the administrative documents, being even larger and more rounded.

113 As is .

114 All three attestations of the name were written by the same scribe.

115 The few signs of men, all of which hold sticks, have their forward arm emerging from midway down the vertical stroke, in the approximate area of the shoulders.

Animate Decoration in the Burial Chamber: A Comparison of Funerary Models and Wall Scenes

Georgia Barker
Macquarie University

Abstract

The exclusion of animate beings from the scenes displayed on the walls of Old Kingdom burial chambers has long been understood as a means to protect the deceased from any potential harm the figures might pose. Funerary models likewise depict people and animals from everyday life, yet they were included in burial chambers for a more expansive time period. This paper raises this apparent contradiction and conducts a comparative analysis of the two artistic media in order to highlight the unique properties and role of the funerary model. It is here proposed that during a time of instability, the model offered a more practical safeguard for the tomb owner's eternal sustenance and so it became the preferred mode of representation for the burial chamber.

ملخص

لطالما فُهم استبعاد الكائنات الحية من المناظر المصورة على جدران غرف الدفن بعصر الدولة القديمة باعتباره وسيلة لحماية المتوفى من أي ضرر محتمل قد تشكله هذه الكائنات. وبالمثل نجد النماذج الجنائزية تُصور الأشخاص والحيوانات من الحياة اليومية، ومع ذلك، فقد وضعت هذه النماذج في غرف الدفن لفترة زمنية أطول. تتناول هذه المقالة هذا التناقض البيّن، وتُجري دراسة مقارنة بين هاتين الوسيلتين الفنيتين من أجل تسليط الضوء على الخصائص الفريدة للنماذج الجنائزية ودورها. يقترح مؤلف هذه المقالة أنه في أثناء فترات عدم الاستقرار وفرت النماذج الجنائزية حماية بقدر أكبر من الناحية العملية للقوت الأبدي لصاحب المقبرة، وهكذا صارت الأسلوب المفضل للتصوير لأجل استخدامها في غرفة الدفن.

The burial chamber formed a vital part of the tomb, serving as the house of the deceased for eternity.[1] It was intended to be secure and access to it was blocked after interment. During the Old and Middle Kingdoms, this isolated section of the tomb was rarely decorated with scenes as it was presumably feared that the living beings depicted would come to life and potentially cause harm to the deceased.[2] Instead, the representations were focused in the above-ground chapel which was accessible to the living for the continuation of the funerary cult. While there are some Old Kingdom burial chambers that feature animate beings in their wall scenes, a deliberate effort to avoid these creatures is clearly apparent. Yet, despite this concern of living figures, funerary models, which likewise depict animate creatures, were housed in burial chambers during the late Old and Middle Kingdoms. In an apparent contradiction, these three-dimensional representations of humans and animals could be included alongside the body in the substructure for a longer period than animate wall scenes. While scholarship

[1] I am grateful to Prof. Naguib Kanawati for his helpful comments on the drafts of this manuscript, as well as to those who provided feedback after my presentation of an earlier version of this paper at the 2019 Annual Meeting of the American Research Center in Egypt.

[2] A. Bolshakov, *Man and His Double in Egyptian Ideology of the Old Kingdom* (Wiesbaden, 1997), 118; N. Kanawati, *The Tomb and Beyond: Burial Customs of Ancient Egyptian Officials* (Warminster, 2001), 113; K. Dawood, "Animate Decoration and Burial Chambers of Private Tombs during the Old Kingdom: New Evidence from the Tomb of Kairer at Saqqara," in L. Pantalacci and C. Berger-El-Naggar (eds.), *Des Néferkarê aux Montouhotep: Travaux archéologiques en cours sur la fin de la VIe dynastie et la Première Période Intermédiaire* (Lyon, 2005), 111.

Journal of the American Research Center in Egypt 56 (2020), 71–81
doi: http://dx.doi.org/10.5913/jarce.56.2020.a005

regularly emphasizes the similarities between the two artistic media, there are some key differences that are yet to be properly acknowledged. It is here proposed that the unique properties of the model caused it to become the preferred mode of representation for the burial chamber. The model's appearance in the substructure coincides with a period of instability in the country and so it seems that for some tomb owners, a heightened need for security outweighed the dangers posed by the three-dimensional human and animal figures.

The first examples of burial chambers decorated with animate wall scenes may be dated to the late Fifth Dynasty, perhaps to the reign of Djedkare or Unis.[3] Prior to this, walls were completely void of decoration, although some coffin and sarcophagi bore inscriptions or geometric designs.[4] During this earliest phase of decoration, the scenes in the substructure closely resembled those of the tomb-chapel, with people and animals from everyday life prominently displayed.[5] The most extensive example may be found in the tomb of Kaiemankh at Giza where animate beings feature prominently on all four walls of the burial chamber, including figures of the tomb owner, offering-bearers, officiants performing ceremony, butchers slaughtering oxen, musicians and dancers, preparers of food, agricultural and animal workers, and crews operating boats.[6] However, a significant change in decoration soon took place, perhaps at the end of the reign of Unis, when human and animal figures were deliberately removed from the designs.[7] During this middle phase of decoration, which extended until the end of the reign of Pepy I, scenes in substructures concentrated on offering-lists and piles of food and drink, as can be found, for example, in the burial chamber of Mereruka at Saqqara.[8] Moreover, hieroglyphic signs representing humans and animals were either avoided or truncated. In the offering-formulae of Mereruka's burial chamber, the jackal determinative for the name of Anubis was initially inscribed but was soon replaced by the phonetic writing of the god's name.[9] This practice of altering hieroglyphic signs of living creatures was further advanced during the reign of Pepy II, the final phase of decoration, when dangerous reptiles were also mutilated.[10] The tomb of Pepyankh-hery-ib at Meir contains two decorated burial chambers: one for the tomb owner and one for his wife, Hewetiaah. In her offering-list, harmful snakes and vipers were initially transcribed, but their heads were later systematically cut off by scratching the paint near the head to eliminate any threat that they might pose to the deceased (fig. 1).[11] The safety of the tomb owner was of paramount importance and this deliberate move away

---

[3] The precise origin of this practice is dependent upon the dating of tombs that feature animate beings in their designs. Many tombs with this decoration do not allow for absolute dating, and so a chronology of this practice must be flexible in considering variations in date. Dawood, "Animate Decoration and Burial Chambers," 109–10; N. Kanawati, "Decoration of Burial Chambers, Sarcophagi and Coffins in the Old Kingdom," in K. Daoud, S. Bedier and S. Abd El-Fatah (eds.), *Studies in Honor of Ali Radwan*, vol. 2 (Cairo, 2005), 55; N. Kanawati, *Decorated Burial Chambers of the Old Kingdom* (Cairo, 2010), 45.

[4] Bolshakov, however, sees the "ceiling stelae" of some Second Dynasty tombs as the formative stage of development in the decoration of the burial chamber. Bolshakov, *Man and His Double*, 112–13; Kanawati, *Decorated Burial Chambers*, 21.

[5] The phases of decoration adopted here are taken from Kanawati, *Decorated Burial Chambers*.

[6] H. Junker, *Giza, band 4, Die Mastaba des K3jmꜥnḫ (Kai-em-anch)* (Vienna-Leipzig, 1940), pls. 2–17. Various dates have been proposed for this tomb, spanning the Fifth and Sixth Dynasties, but it seems likely that it belongs to the earliest phase of animate decoration in the burial chamber. For a discussion on the proposed dates for this tomb, see M. Lashien, "The Ultimate Destination: Decoration of Kaiemankh's Burial Chamber Reconsidered," *ET* 26.1 (2013), 403–15; A. Woods, "Contribution to a Controversy: A Date for the Tomb of *K3(=i)-m-3nḫ* at Giza," *JEA* 95 (2009), 161–74.

[7] One unusual exception may be found in the burial chamber of Remni at Saqqara, dated to the early Sixth Dynasty. Although human figures have been distinctly avoided in the scenes, a live calf is curiously depicted aboard four of the boats on the east wall. This tomb owner must not have considered this animal harmful. N. Kanawati, *The Teti Cemetery at Saqqara*, vol. 9, *The Tomb of Remni* (Oxford, 2009), pl. 52a; Kanawati, *Decorated Burial Chambers*, 53, 60–61.

[8] This tomb may be dated to the reign of Teti at the beginning of the Sixth Dynasty. All four walls of the substructure are decorated with scenes: on the east wall are slaughtered animals, granaries and items of food and drink; on the west wall are jars and chests; and on the north and south walls are identical scenes of food items and offering-formulae. P. Duell, *The Mastaba of Mereruka, vol. 2 (Chambers A 11–13, Doorjambs and Inscriptions of Chambers A 1–21, Tomb Chamber, and Exterior* (Chicago, 1938), pls. 200–208; Kanawati, *Decorated Burial Chambers*, 54; N. Kanawati, A. Woods, S. Shafik, et al., *Mereruka and His Family*, vol. 3.2, *The Tomb of Mereruka* (Oxford, 2011), pls. 94–111.

[9] Interestingly, the jackal determinative remained for the word *s3b* 'judge' in Mereruka's titles. Kanawati, *Decorated Burial Chambers*, 66–68; Kanawati, Woods, Shafik, et al., *Mereruka and His Family* 3.2, pl. 94.

[10] In fact, most examples of decorated burial chambers date to the reign of this king. Dawood, "Animate Decoration and Burial Chambers," 110; Kanawati, *Decorated Burial Chambers*, 55.

[11] Kanawati, *Decorated Burial Chambers*, 71.

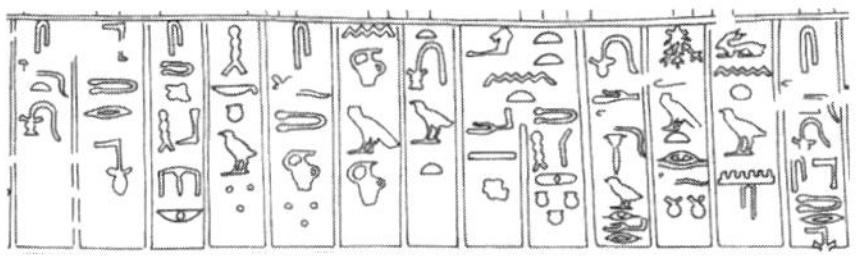

Fig. 1. East wall of the burial chamber of Hewetiaah (D2) at Meir, late Sixth Dynasty. N. Kanawati, The Cemetery of Meir, vol. 1, The Tomb of Pepyankh the Middle *(Oxford, 2012), pl. 96 [detail]. Reproduction by permission of the Australian Centre for Egyptology.*

from representing animate figures seems to highlight the severity of the threat posed by living creatures depicted in the burial chamber.

Funerary models, on the other hand, display many similarities with animate wall scenes, yet experience a more prolonged period of use in the substructure. This artistic medium comprises small three-dimensional sculptures which likewise depict objects, people and animals from everyday life. They first appear in the form of serving statuettes in tombs of the Fourth and Fifth Dynasties where they consist of single figures carved of stone, usually performing tasks associated with food production.[12] These statuettes were housed in the serdab which was positioned within the superstructure of the tomb.[13] During the late Sixth Dynasty, however, a transformation of the funerary model occurred. The sculptures were now fashioned of wood, comprised groups of figures arranged on a single base, and portrayed a wider range of tasks. Significantly, the models were also moved to the burial chamber where they were housed alongside the body of the deceased.[14] Ideally, they would be placed to the east of the coffin, directly next to the eye-panel, but they could also be positioned on the floor of the chamber or on top of the coffin.[15] Models feature prominently in burials of the Middle Kingdom, but rapidly disappear after the time of around Senusret III.[16] This is certainly a much longer and more consistent use of decoration in the burial chamber than animate wall scenes.

In order to understand this contrasting length of appearance in the substructure, a comparison of the two media needs to be conducted. The model must have had its own unique features that contributed to its prolonged inclusion in the burial chamber. Although the two- and three-dimensional representations exhibit many similarities in design, a fact which is regularly emphasized in scholarship,[17] there are some important differences that are yet to be properly acknowledged. Firstly, the type and range of themes represented forms a key difference. The scenes commonly displayed on tomb-chapel walls have been divided by Kanawati into seven broad categories: the tomb owner and his family; rural life; fishing, fowling and the desert hunt; professions and industries; sport and recreation; funerary rites; and the afterlife.[18] Similarly, the models have been classified by Tooley according to five main themes: agriculture and animal husbandry; food preparation; industrial processes; offering-bearers;

---

[12] Roth has proposed the designation of "serving statues" rather than "servant statues" in order to prevent the identity and purpose of the individuals depicted from being assumed. The term "statuette" is preferred here to reflect the typically smaller size of the figures. The most common motif illustrated by these sculptures is that of a female miller grinding grain on a quern stone. A. Tooley, "Middle Kingdom Burial Customs: A Study of Wooden Models and Related Material," vol. 1 (PhD dissertation, University of Liverpool, 1989), 4; A. Roth, "The Meaning of Menial Labor: 'Servant Statues' in Old Kingdom Serdabs," *JARCE* 39 (2002), 103.

[13] Tooley, "Middle Kingdom Burial Customs 1," 3; Roth, "Meaning of Menial Labor," 103.

[14] J. Breasted, *Egyptian Servant Statues* (Washington, 1948), 2–3; Roth, "Meaning of Menial Labor," 117–18; G. Eschenbrenner-Diemer, "From the Workshop to the Grave: The Case of Wooden Funerary Models," in G. Miniaci, M. Betrò and S. Quirke (eds.), *Company of Images: Modelling the Imaginary World of Middle Kingdom Egypt (2000–1500 BC). Proceedings of the International Conference of the EPOCHS Project Held 18th–20th September 2014 at UCL, London* (Leuven, 2017), 172.

[15] The precise location of the models was dependent upon the amount of available space in the chamber. Tooley, "Middle Kingdom Burial Customs 1," 83; A. Tooley, *Egyptian Models and Scenes* (Princes Risborough, 1995), 14; J. Podvin, "Position du mobilier funéraire dans les tombes égyptiennes privées du Moyen Empire," *MDAIK* 56 (2000), 287.

[16] Tooley, "Middle Kingdom Burial Customs 1," 67.

[17] The concept that models were simply substitutes or duplicates of the wall scenes pervades throughout scholarship. Schäfer, for example, writes that the content of wall scenes was transformed into three-dimensional form in models. Similarly, Tiradritti states that models were a "three-dimensional transposition" of the scenes. Taylor, alternatively, notes that the scenes were "augmented" by models. Even further, Malek labels the models as "three-dimensional equivalents" of tomb scenes. Such statements presuppose the similarities between the two media and do not address the notable differences between them. H. Schäfer, *Principles of Egyptian Art*, rev. ed. (Oxford, 1986), 38; J. Malek, *Egyptian Art* (London, 1999), 146; J. Taylor, *Death and the Afterlife in Ancient Egypt* (London, 2001), 99–100; F. Tiradritti, *Egyptian Wall Painting* (New York-London, 2008), 173–74.

[18] Kanawati, *Tomb and Beyond*, 85–108.

Fig. 2. Granary model from the tomb of Meketre (TT 280) at Thebes, early Twelfth Dynasty. The Metropolitan Museum of Art, New York: 20.3.11.

and boats.[19] While there are clearly many parallels between these two classifications, some key points of difference are noticeable. Firstly, the models are more condensed in the range of themes they represent. The scenes encapsulate a wide spectrum of everyday life activities and portray many tasks in which the tomb owner himself participated. Models, conversely, concentrate on activities that will provision the deceased in the afterlife, most notably the production of food and transportation. Additionally, the tomb owner rarely appears in models, with the activities in which he partakes largely excluded from the three-dimensional repertoire.[20] Secondly, the models are more condensed in the range of motifs incorporated within each theme. In that of agriculture, for example, wall scenes display several stages of the cycle, including ploughing and sowing, harvesting, transportation on donkeys, threshing, winnowing and sieving, and storage in granaries. Models, in contrast, only exhibit the motifs of ploughing, transportation and storage, with the final process significantly more popular (fig. 2).[21] While this is partially a result of the technical limitations of the three-dimensional medium,[22] it also reflects the desire to

[19] A. Tooley, "Models," in D. Redford (ed.), *Oxford Encyclopedia of Ancient Egypt*, vol. 2 (Oxford, 2001), 425.

[20] In scenes, the tomb owner takes an active role in fishing and fowling in the marshes, the desert hunt, and at the offering-table. These motifs are excluded from the three-dimensional repertoire. However, the tomb owner does occasionally appear in models, and when he does, he is most often found on model boats. See, for example, a sailing boat from Meir where the living owner is seated on deck beneath a canopy while enveloped in a white cloak. Reisner, CG 4798–4976 et 5034–5200, pl. 7. Or, his presence on the boat may be suggested by his coffin, as in one of the funerary boats of Ukh-hotep from Meir. The Metropolitan Museum of Art, New York: 12.183.3. Additionally, the tomb owner appears in two unusual three-dimensional examples of the rendering of accounts theme. Musée des Beaux-Arts de Lyon: 1969–404; H. Winlock, *Models of Daily Life in Ancient Egypt from the Tomb of Meket-Re' at Thebes* (Cambridge, 1955), pl. 13; G. Barker, "Classification of a Funerary Model: The Rendering of Accounts Theme," *JARCE* 55 (2019), 5–13.

[21] G. Barker, "Funerary Models and Wall Scenes. The Case of the Granary," *GM* 254 (2018), 8.

[22] Some of the intermediary stages of the agricultural cycle would have been very difficult to fashion in three-dimensions. For example, the thin stems of the crop which formed an integral aspect of harvesting scenes would have required exceptionally fine carving.

emphasize the final product which would nourish the deceased in the afterlife. These differences in design clearly show that the models were not exact replicas of the scenes, but maintained their own unique repertoire.

The media's contrasting locations within the tomb help to explain these individual design choices. Positioned in the above-ground chapel, scenes not only contributed to the tomb owner's well-being in the afterlife, but also functioned as a proclamation of his earthly life.[23] Visitors would see the large figures of the owner, be impressed by his achievements and superior status, and perhaps be greater encouraged to present offerings. The more expansive range of themes and prominent portrayal of the tomb owner himself were suited to public display. Models, on the other hand, being housed in the burial chamber, were not visible to any visitors to the tomb and so solely functioned for the benefit of the tomb owner's afterlife rather than attracting visitors. The focus on provisions witnessed in the three-dimensional repertoire is understandable as these were of prime importance for the deceased's afterlife. Each medium was specifically designed according to its unique role within the tomb, and for the model, this was to provision the deceased for eternity.

A second difference between the media is noticeable in the utilization of accompanying inscriptions. Text formed an important part of wall scenes with captions integrated into the images to identify specific individuals, record the dialogue of the workers and describe the activities taking place.[24] Funerary models, conversely, very rarely include any type of text. It was not possible for the sculptor to integrate inscriptions into the model in the same way that the artist of the wall scene could achieve so easily. The serving statuettes housed in serdabs of the Fourth and Fifth Dynasties occasionally include labels inscribed on their bases. These texts identify the figures as specific individuals, usually family members or dependents of the tomb owner, yet they still carry out the tasks of servants.[25] This has led Roth to suggest that they not only provided for the deceased by producing food, but also shared in the offerings that were presented to him.[26] Once the models moved to the burial chamber, text featured even more rarely. Of the limited number of Middle Kingdom examples known that do include inscriptions, most are representations of granaries where it is the type of grain being stored that is notated.[27] Occasionally, offering-bearers or boats include a short caption which may identify the tomb owner or more rarely the workers themselves,[28] but the vast majority of models remain uninscribed.

While this may suggest that Middle Kingdom models solely depict generic workers, it should also be noted that not all human and animal figures in wall scenes are labeled with captions. It is also common for such figures to remain anonymous. This could lead to the conclusion that all unnamed characters are generic figures, but it is also possible that we are unable to detect the subtle distinguishing details.[29] The activities displayed in scenes are usually understood as typical actions that could have occurred at any time and in any place.[30] However,

[23] Kanawati, *Tomb and Beyond*, 116.

[24] N. Kanawati and A. Woods, *Artists in the Old Kingdom: Techniques and Achievements* (Cairo, 2009), 30–31.

[25] The largest surviving group of inscribed serving statuettes belongs to the tomb of Niaku-inpu at Giza, today housed in the Museum of the Oriental Institute of the University of Chicago. Amongst the group are named sons, daughters, and a dependent who are engaged in tasks related to the preparation of food. Roth, "Meaning of Menial Labor," 116.

[26] It was through their service that the individuals depicted increased their chances of sharing in a successful afterlife. Roth, "Meaning of Menial Labor," 116.

[27] In the model granary from the tomb of Gemniemhat at Saqqara, for example, an inscription is found on the papyrus document resting on the lap of the scribe. Ny Carlsberg Glyptotek: AEIN 1630. Alternatively, a hieratic docket may be painted onto the wall of the granary, recording the types of grain being stored, as is found above each silo in a model from Aswan. British Museum, London: EA 21804. C. Jurman, "To Show and to Designate: Attitudes towards Representing Craftsmanship and Material Culture in Middle Kingdom Elite Tombs," in G. Miniaci, J. Moreno Garcia, S. Quirke, et al. (eds.), *The Arts of Making in Ancient Egypt: Voices, Images, and Objects of Material Producers 2000–1550 BC* (Leiden, 2018), 104–5.

[28] In a model female offering-bearer from the tomb of Hepi-kem at Meir, the name and titles of the tomb owner are recorded on the load carried on her head. Museum of Antiquities, Eton College: ECM.1591–2010. Alternatively, on one of the funerary boats of Ukh-hotep from Meir, the four figures surrounding the bier are individually labeled with their own names and titles. The Metropolitan Museum of Art, New York: 12.183.3.

[29] M. Lashien, "Narrative in Old Kingdom Wall Scenes: The Progress through Time and Space," *BACE* 22 (2011), 102.

[30] G. Gaballa, *Narrative in Egyptian Art* (Mainz am Rhein, 1976), 5, 27–28; K. Weeks, "Art, Word, and the Egyptian World View," in K. Weeks (ed.), *Egyptology and the Social Sciences* (Cairo, 1979), 61; H. Groenewegen-Frankfort, *Arrest and Movement: An Essay on Space and Time in the Representational Art of the Ancient Near East* (New York, 1987), 33; W. Davis, *The Canonical Tradition in Ancient Egyptian Art* (Cambridge, 1989), 192–94.

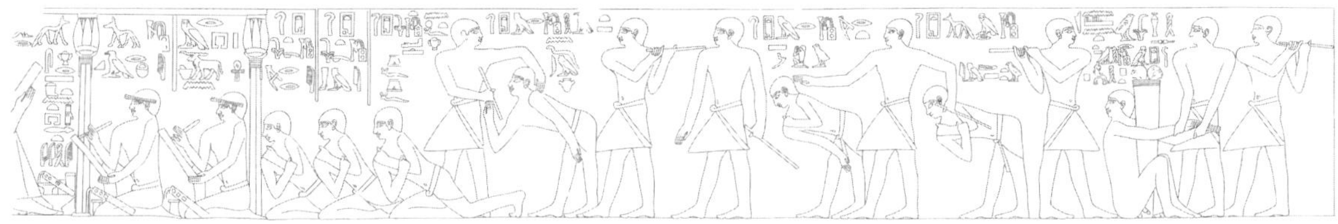

Fig. 3. West wall of room A4 in the tomb of Mereruka at Saqqara, early Sixth Dynasty. N. Kanawati, A. Woods, S. Shafik, et al., Mereruka and His Family, vol. 3.1, The Tomb of Mereruka *(Oxford, 2010), pl. 78a. Reproduction by permission of the Australian Centre for Egyptology.*

Fig. 4. Fourth register, north wall of the tomb of Amenemhat (no. 2 upper cemetery) at Beni Hassan, Twelfth Dynasty. N. Kanawati and L. Evans, Beni Hassan, vol. 3, The Tomb of Amenemhat *(Oxford, 2016), pl. 96 [detail]. Reproduction by permission of the Australian Centre for Egyptology.*

elements of specificity are clearly identifiable in many scenes, indicating the depiction of particular individuals engaged in specific events. In the rendering of accounts scene displayed on the west wall of room A4 in the tomb of Mereruka at Saqqara, seven accused men are brought forward for questioning, one of whom is beaten on a whipping post (fig. 3). The scribes and culprits are individually labeled with names and titles, but the guards ushering forward the offenders are unnamed. With the identification of specific individuals and the first known illustration of the whipping post, this scene is not a copy of an earlier one, but a depiction of a specific, likely well-known, event.[31] Although the guards are unlabeled, there is no reason to assume that they too were not depictions of specific people. Rather, they seem to be secondary characters in the narrative.[32] Alternatively, the motif of the presentation of animals before the tomb owner is especially common and is regularly standardized. The depiction of certain animals and people, however, can individualize the event. In the Twelfth Dynasty tomb of Amenemhat at Beni Hassan, for example, a herdsman in the fourth register of the north wall displays signs of physical deformities, walking with unnaturally bent legs, while leading forward an ox with a distorted horn (fig. 4). Neither the herdsman nor the ox is named, but their distinct appearance distinguishes them from the rest of the procession. These deformities were presumably rather uncommon, so it is likely that they are identifying features of specific individuals, both man and animal.[33] Although discernible characteristics are not always obvious to our eye, this does not mean that all nameless figures were considered generic by the ancient Egyptians. Rather, it may be that only those individuals considered most important were labeled. The same situation may be true for models. The absence of inscriptions in the three-dimensional medium may rather be on account of the threat posed by dangerous reptiles, such as snakes and vipers, which commonly appear in the hieroglyphic script. Indeed, some tomb owners mutilated these signs on their burial chamber walls in order to be protected from harm.[34] In conjunction with the technical difficulty of integrating inscriptions into a three-dimensional art-

[31] N. Kanawati, "Specificity in Old Kingdom Tomb Scenes," *ASAE* 83 (2009), 264.

[32] Kanawati, "Specificity," 264.

[33] Kanawati, "Specificity," 264.

[34] See, for example, the burial chamber of Hewetiaah from Meir, as discussed above.

work, the model figures were free from any threat posed by dangerous signs and may have been representations of known individuals who were trusted by the tomb owner.

A third distinction between the two media is in their accessibility to the population. The construction and decoration of a tomb was dependent upon the status and wealth of each individual tomb owner.[35] While designs varied according to tomb-types and building materials, the ideal monument comprised both a superstructure and substructure.[36] Only the highest elite, however, could afford extensive decoration. Many tombs in fact did not have a chapel, and amongst those that did, only a small number were decorated with scenes.[37] Conversely, all tombs had a burial chamber where the body of the deceased was housed. Funerary models were not as costly to produce as wall scenes which required the smoothing, plastering, painting and/or carving of tomb walls, and so could be stored in substructures of individuals of a wide range of status. One of the highest officials with preserved models is the Eleventh Dynasty chancellor Meketre of Thebes who housed twenty-four models in his tomb.[38] Although his chapel has suffered significant damage, fragmentary remains indicate that it was originally decorated with painted scenes.[39] At the other end of the scale, models are extensively known from burials of lower officials who could not afford an elaborate funerary structure. The lower cemetery at Beni Hassan was found to contain almost nine hundred burials, the vast majority of which do not have superstructures. During his excavation of the cemetery in 1902–4, Garstang found a multitude of models belonging to these tomb owners who would have served the provincial governors interred in the grand tombs of the upper cemetery.[40] Moreover, the quantity and quality of models could be adaptable to the wealth of each individual owner. In poorer burials, a single model could suffice and in these instances, the sculpture is usually crudely fashioned of pottery.[41] Alternatively, wealthy tomb owners could afford several models and could commission statuettes of superior craftsmanship. The largest known assemblage belongs to the governor Djehuty-nakht of El-Bersha, comprising at least one hundred models.[42] Significant variation in quality is noticeable amongst this corpus, but some are particularly finely carved, most notably the so-called Bersha Procession (fig. 5). The three-dimensional medium was certainly accessible to much more of the population than wall scenes and in many cases comprised the only form of decoration within the tomb.

Fourthly, the media differ in their ease of construction. The execution of scenes on the walls of burial chambers was required to occur within the substructure itself. In most cases, working conditions would have been particularly poor, with artists operating in limited lighting. This may be contrasted with the chapel where natural light flooded in, allowing scenes to be finely executed. This created a distinction in quality, with the subterranean scenes often not as finely or precisely executed as those in the chapel. In fact, all known burial chambers with

---

[35] A. Dodson and S. Ikram, *The Tomb in Ancient Egypt: Royal and Private Sepulchres from the Early Dynastic Period to the Romans* (London, 2008), 48.

[36] Kanawati, *Tomb and Beyond*, 76.

[37] At El-Hawawish, for example, Kanawati has noted that of the more than 880 rock-cut tombs, only about sixty have decorated chapels. Kanawati, *Decorated Burial Chambers*, 10.

[38] Unfortunately, as the vast majority of nomarchal tombs have been plundered, the extent to which this top echelon furnished their graves with models is unknown. However, the fact that some have preserved models demonstrates that the three-dimensional medium was a valued type of decoration for high officials and not just for the lower classes. R. Freed and D. Doxey, “The Djehutynakhts’ Models,” in R. Freed, L. Berman, D. Doxey, et al. (eds.), *The Secrets of Tomb 10A. Egypt 2000 BC* (Boston, 2009), 151.

[39] Winlock, *Models of Daily Life*, 9–13. Another example is found in the tomb of the overseer of Upper Egypt Niankh-pepy-kem of Meir who may be dated to the late Sixth Dynasty. At least twenty-six models were found in the tomb, one of the largest pre-Middle Kingdom model assemblages known. He also utilized painted decoration with scenes spanning the walls of his chapel. A. Blackman and M. Apted, *The Rock Tombs of Meir*, vol. 5, *The Tomb-Chapels of A, No. 1 (that of Ni-'ankh-Pepi the Black), A, No. 2 (that of Pepi'onkh with the 'Good Name' of Heny the Black), A, No. 4 (that of Hepi the Black), D, No. 1 (that of Pepi), and E, Nos. 1–4 (those of Meniu, Nenki, Pepi'onkh and Tjetu)* (London, 1953); Tooley, “Middle Kingdom Burial Customs 1,” 11–12; N. Kanawati, L. Evans, M. Lashien, et al., *The Cemetery of Meir*, vol. 3, *The Tomb of Niankhpepy the Black* (Oxford, 2015).

[40] J. Garstang, *The Burial Customs of Ancient Egypt as Illustrated by the Tombs of the Middle Kingdom* (London, 1907).

[41] These models often take the form of offering-trays, soul houses or fertility figurines. Tooley, “Middle Kingdom Burial Customs 1,” 373–77.

[42] There were in fact two occupants of this burial: the governor and his wife, also named Djehuty-nakht. The tomb was found plundered, with the grave goods scattered throughout the chamber. It is thought that the model corpus was originally divided into two groups, but determining which models belonged to which owner is an impossible task. Even if divided, each group is still an exceptionally large corpus. Today, the models are housed in the Museum of Fine Arts, Boston. Freed and Doxey, “Djehutynakhts’ Models,” 151–52.

Fig. 5. Model of a procession of offering-bearers ('The Bersha Procession') from the tomb of Djehuty-nakht (Reisner 10A) at El-Bersha, late Eleventh or early Twelfth Dynasty. Photograph © 2020 Museum of Fine Arts, Boston: 21.326.

scenes are simply executed in painting, with a total absence of relief.[43] In the tomb of Mereruka, for example, the scenes of the chapel are intricately carved in relief and colored with paint, while those of the burial chamber are only executed in black ink except for the east wall which was finished in color.[44] On the other hand, models were created in workshops and only transported to the tomb upon completion. This allowed their construction to be conducted in more favorable conditions, with the potential of creating a higher quality and quantity of artworks. This ease of construction may have impacted each tomb owner's choice of decoration for his tomb.

These four key differences of theme, text, accessibility and ease of construction may explain the preference for the three-dimensional medium in the burial chamber. Firstly, the themes represented by the model were almost entirely concerned with provisions. These were of prime importance for the afterlife and so there was a desire to protect them within a sealed section of the tomb. Secondly, model figures may have represented known and trusted individuals and, with the absence of inscriptions, no threat was posed from dangerous hieroglyphic signs. Thirdly, the medium was accessible to more of the population and could be incorporated more easily into a wider range of burials. This was particularly significant for those who could not afford elaborate funerary structures. Fourthly, models were fashioned in workshops away from the tomb where conditions were more favorable for artistic creation. These distinguishing properties highlight the unique advantages of the model and demonstrate why it became the preferred mode of representation for the substructure.

However, tomb owners could still choose to depict living creatures on the walls of their burial chambers. In the tombs of the First Intermediate Period and early Middle Kingdom, a total of seventeen burial chambers decorated with animate wall scenes have been identified by Dawood.[45] A further two tombs may be added to

[43] Bolshakov, *Man and His Double*, 117.

[44] Duell, *Mastaba of Mereruka* vol. 2, pls. 200–208; Kanawati, Woods, Shafik, et al., *Mereruka and His Family* 3.2, pls. 36–57; Kanawati, *Decorated Burial Chambers*, 63–64.

[45] Dawood, "Animate Decoration and Burial Chambers," 111.

this list with the recent discovery of the decorated burial chambers of Baqet I and Baqet II at Beni Hassan by the Australian Centre for Egyptology.[46] Similar to the earliest phase of decoration in the Fifth Dynasty, these tombs make no attempt to mutilate or remove the living creatures from their designs, but rather feature them as the main part of the decoration. In the burial chamber of the Eleventh Dynasty female tomb owner Kemsit at Thebes, for example, the walls are decorated with scenes featuring animate beings, including the tomb owner and attendants, offering-bearers, butchers slaughtering an ox, a procession of cattle, and a man milking a cow.[47] Consequently, the practice of depicting living creatures on the walls of burial chambers was not completely abandoned, but continued to be sporadically adopted by some high officials even into the Middle Kingdom. The elimination of animate beings was not consistent across all tombs and so may have been a personal choice of the tomb owner rather than strictly dictated by religious belief. Funerary models, however, were a more popular choice, not only maintaining their presence in substructures throughout the First Intermediate Period, but becoming even more common and widespread during the Middle Kingdom.[48] As models became increasingly prevalent, animate wall scenes only occasionally appeared, with the three-dimensional medium forming the favored type of decoration for the burial chamber.

Tomb owners not only had to consider the risk posed by depicting animate creatures in the substructure, but also that posed by turmoil in the country. During the late Old Kingdom, Egypt experienced a period of significant instability. Increasing evidence has demonstrated that turmoil began as early as the Fifth Dynasty, perhaps with the reign of Nyuserre.[49] As high-ranking officials attained more power, there was a growing tendency for enrichment. Elite tombs became larger and more lavishly constructed and decorated, with some even adopting royal architectural elements.[50] Not only was it during this period that the practice of decorating the burial chamber with models and wall scenes began, but decoration was also introduced to royal substructures. The pyramid of Unis at the end of the Fifth Dynasty was the first to adopt this practice, with the walls inscribed with the Pyramid Texts. Although this decoration is textual while that of private tombs is largely figurative, there is some correlation in their origins.[51] It seems that one of the first more securely dated examples of private burial chambers decorated with scenes belongs to Senedjemib-inti of Giza who served as the vizier under Djedkare. However, it is likely that his tomb was created by his son during the reign of Unis, thus aligning with the first use of the Pyramid Texts.[52] Although the reasons for the origin of this practice are not completely known, they should perhaps be considered alongside the need for greater security.[53] There were a number of factors that contributed to both political and economic instability, including the weakening of divine kingship, the growing

[46] The two tombs, dated variously between the Ninth and Eleventh Dynasties, feature animate beings on the walls of their burial chambers. Baqet I's substructure is unfortunately poorly preserved due to significant water damage, but traces of a figure of the tomb owner holding a staff can still be seen. In contrast, the burial chamber of Baqet II is very well-preserved, with painted decoration appearing on all four walls. The living creatures displayed include offering-bearers, officiants performing ceremony, animals led forward in procession and three representations of the tomb owner himself.

[47] E. Naville and H. Hall, *The Eleventh Dynasty Temple at Deir el-Bahri*, vol. 3 (London, 1913), pls. 2–3; PM I.1^2, 385–86.

[48] Tooley, "Middle Kingdom Burial Customs 1," 62.

[49] Bárta has argued that the increasing strength of high officials is already witnessed during the reign of Nyuserre. These men accumulated more wealth and official duties, and many significant offices had already become hereditary. As a result, each king from Djedkare onward introduced administrative reforms that aimed to preserve centralized kingship and curb the power of these officials. M. Bárta, Journey to the West: The World of the Old Kingdom Tombs in Ancient Egypt (Prague, 2011), 173; M. Bárta, "Egyptian Kingship during the Old Kingdom," in J. Hill, P. Jones and A. Morales (eds.), *Experiencing Power, Generating Authority: Cosmos, Politics, and the Ideology of Kingship in Ancient Egypt and Mesopotamia* (Philadelphia, 2013), 271–72.

[50] The tomb of the vizier Ptahshepses at Abusir, dated to the reign of Nyuserre, incorporates several royal architectural elements, including a monumental columned portico, a statue room with three niches, an east-west oriented cult-chapel, a boat room, and an angular vaulted ceiling over the burial chamber. He was the first private individual to utilize these features, but other viziers and high-ranking officials of the Fifth and Sixth Dynasties continued this tradition. Bárta, *Journey to the West*, 175–78; Bárta, "Egyptian Kingship," 268–69.

[51] D. Vischak, "Common Ground between Pyramid Texts and Old Kingdom Tomb Design: The Case of Ankhmahor," *JARCE* 40 (2003), 135; Dawood, "Animate Decoration and Burial Chambers," 109.

[52] Although dating tombs with decorated substructures often causes difficulties, Dawood has noted that there is no concrete evidence to suggest that private burial chambers were decorated prior to the introduction of the Pyramid Texts. E. Brovarski, *The Senedjemib Complex*, vol. 1, *The Mastabas of Senedjemib Inti (G 2370), Khnumenti (G 2374), and Senedjemib Mehi (G 2378)* (Boston, 2000), 79–81; Dawood, "Animate Decoration and Burial Chambers," 109–10, 116; Kanawati, *Decorated Burial Chambers*, 45.

[53] Dawood, "Animate Decoration and Burial Chambers," 109; Kanawati, *Decorated Burial Chambers*, 43–44.

power of officials, a decline in the resources of the central government and climatic changes.[54] As a result, the guarantee of the provision of offerings became less secure and so tomb owners looked for other means to ensure a continual supply. With the belief that funerary artistic representations would magically come to life and serve the deceased, artworks became an important safeguard.[55] Although this came in different forms, the decoration of the burial chamber served as a significant precautionary measure for the tomb owner's supply of goods for the afterlife.

The need for security continued in the First Intermediate Period when, alongside a collapse of central authority, there was a rise in the influence of the provinces. Egypt was divided into several units with provincial rulers acting more or less independently of the central government and who had the ability to raise their own armies.[56] It was a time of disorder with severe famine, economic crisis and civil war.[57] The autobiography of Ankhtifi of Mo'alla evokes the atmosphere of the period, describing how "Upper Egypt was dying of hunger and people were eating their children" and that in response to the violence Ankhtifi "caused a man to embrace (even) those who had killed his father or brother."[58] With such instability, not only was the fear that provisions would not continue for the deceased paramount, but tomb robbery became an expected phenomenon.[59] The burial chamber, positioned below ground and sealed after interment, maintained an important role in providing protection for the tomb owner's supply of goods for the afterlife, and indeed, models are known from substructures throughout this period.

However, the protection of the burial chamber was not ensured. Housing objects of value, it was regularly targeted by thieves and so several measures were taken to make the substructure more secure, including extending the depth of the shaft, using a portcullis to block the entrance and placing the mouth of the shaft outside the chapel.[60] Alternatively, some tomb owners created sealed rooms within their tomb for the storage of models. This offered an additional safeguard in case the substructure was interfered with,[61] and also provided some separation between the body of the deceased and the animate figures. For example, the overseer of Upper Egypt Niankh-pepy-kem at Meir stored his assemblage of models in a one meter deep niche cut into the floor of the burial chamber that was sealed with a stone slab before the shaft was filled with rubble.[62] Alternatively, the models of Meketre were crowded in a small, roughly cut, square room carved into the side of the corridor of his tomb at Thebes.[63] Both of these sealed chambers in fact avoided theft with the model assemblages found undisturbed and in a relatively fine state of preservation. The creation of these sealed rooms shows that security was a driving factor in the design and decoration of the tomb. Models could be easily stored in these compact locations and were less likely to be interfered with by thieves. The three-dimensional artworks therefore functioned as an important additional safeguard for the tomb owner's supply of goods for the afterlife.

During a period of instability, tomb owners looked for increasing ways to protect their eternal supply of provisions. The guarantee of an on-going mortuary cult could not be ensured as turmoil increased within society. Accordingly, tomb owners utilized artistic representations as a precautionary measure for their eternal nourishment. Two risks were therefore simultaneously considered by each tomb owner: that posed by instability in the

---

[54] N. Kanawati and J. Swinton, *Egypt in the Sixth Dynasty: Challenges and Responses* (Wallasey, 2018), 221–23.

[55] Dodson and Ikram, *Tomb in Ancient Egypt*, 15.

[56] W. Grajetzki, *Burial Customs in Ancient Egypt: Life in Death for Rich and Poor* (London, 2003), 36; J. Moreno Garcia, "The Territorial Administration of the Kingdom in the 3rd Millennium," in J. Moreno Garcia, (ed.), *Ancient Egyptian Administration* (Leiden-Boston, 2013), 148.

[57] The First Intermediate Period has recently been reexamined by scholars in order to reassess the designation of the period as a 'dark age.' See the discussions of S. Seidlmayer, "The First Intermediate Period (c. 2160–2055 BC)," in I. Shaw (ed.), *The Oxford History of Ancient Egypt* (Oxford, 2000), 108–36; N. Moeller, "The First Intermediate Period: A Time of Famine and Climate Change?," *AeUL* 15 (2005), 153–67; H. Willems, "The First Intermediate Period and the Middle Kingdom," in A. Lloyd (ed.), *A Companion to Ancient Egypt* (West Sussex, 2010), 81–100; M. Bárta, "Long Term or Short Term? Climate Change and the Demise of the Old Kingdom," in S. Kerner, R. Dann and P. Bangsgaard (eds.), *Climate and Ancient Societies* (Copenhagen, 2015), 177–95.

[58] Seidlmayer, "First Intermediate Period," 118–23; Kanawati and Swinton, *Egypt in the Sixth Dynasty*, 209–11.

[59] D. Brewer and E. Teeter, *Egypt and the Egyptians*, 2nd ed. (Cambridge, 2007), 42–44.

[60] Kanawati, *Decorated Burial Chambers*, 13–19.

[61] Tooley, "Middle Kingdom Burial Customs 1," 77.

[62] Tooley, "Middle Kingdom Burial Customs 1," 11.

[63] Winlock, *Models of Daily Life*, 12–13.

country and that caused by depicting living creatures in the burial chamber. It seems that for many tomb owners, the fear that offerings would be terminated outweighed the danger of representing animate beings. The lack of consistency in the choice of decoration suggests that each individual determined which risk was more significant. For those that selected to include artistic representations in the burial chamber, the funerary model seems to have offered a more practical safeguard. The distinctive properties of the three-dimensional medium demonstrate that it served a unique role in the tomb, designed to ensure the deceased was safely provisioned for eternity.

The Khufu I Boat: An Empirical Investigation into Its Use

Bob Brier
Long Island University/LIU Post

Michael G. Morabito
United States Naval Academy

Stuart Greene
Houston, Texas

Abstract

Although the Khufu I Boat is one of the oldest, largest, and best-preserved vessels from antiquity, there has been no empirical experimentation to determine its nautical properties or its function. This paper presents results of the first tank testing of a model of the Khufu I Boat in 1995, and then suggests the vessel's probable use.

ملخص

مُلخَّص: على الرغم من أن المركب الأول للملك خوفو هو أحد أقدم وأكبر مراكب العصر القديم وأفضلها حفظًا، لكنه لم يخضع من قبل لأي اختبار تجريبي لتحديد خصائصه الملاحية أو وظيفته. يناقش هذا المقال النتائج الأولى للإختبار الذي أجري عام ٥٩٩١ لنموذج المركب الأول للملك خوفو بصهريج مياه، ويُقدم تصوراً للإستخدام المحتمل للمركب.

Introduction

When the Khufu I[1] Boat (also known as the Cheops Boat) was first discovered in 1954 by the Egyptian architect/Egyptologist Kamal el-Mallakh, it created a sensation. Here was the best-preserved boat of the ancient world, but its purpose was far from clear. Part of the reason for the uncertainty was that it was in 1,224 pieces, in thirteen layers at the bottom of a pit. However, even before the pieces were removed, Jaroslav Černý published an article speculating on the boat's purpose.[2] He based his discussion partly on photographs of the upper layer in the boat pit (fig. 1) and partly on Egyptian mythology. His conclusions were heavily influenced by the number of boat pits surrounding the Khufu pyramid. He quickly dismissed the theory that the boat was solar because Egyptian mythology dictated that there were only two solar boats—one for the day and one for the night—and there are five pits clustered around the Great Pyramid. Černý never discussed the possibility that two of the boats were solar and the other three were for other purposes. Černý then discusses other possibilities, based on mythological texts, but never considers the possibility that the boat could have had an actual, practical use. Since Černý's article, there has been little discussion of the practical use of the boat in the Egyptological literature. This paper

[1] From the time of the boat's discovery, it has been called the "Cheops Boat" by Egyptologists and the public. Because the Japanese have now excavated a second boat pit and we have two boats, they are now called "Khufu I" and "Khufu II," respectively.

[2] Jaroslav Černý, "A Note On The Recently Discovered Boat of Cheops," *JEA* 41 (1955), 75–79.

Journal of the American Research Center in Egypt 56 (2020), 83–99
doi: http://dx.doi.org/10.5913/jarce.56.2020.a006

Fig. 1. Pieces of Khufu I in pit.
Photo: Supreme Council of Antiquities.

provides a discussion of some engineering analyses of the boat, which we hope will assist in understanding its capabilities.

It would be two full years before the pieces of the boat were consolidated and removed from the pit (fig. 2). Then it would be nearly ten more years before the boat was reconstructed in the first attempt at seeing what it originally looked like. However, before any reconstruction was attempted, the only major Egyptological report on the boat was published, "The Cheops Boats."[3] This report had four authors, each writing a chapter. Zaki Nour wrote a chapter on the discovery of the boat at Giza, but somehow never mentions the discoverer, Kamal el-Malek. Mohammad Salah Osman's chapter is on "Engineering Works" and describes how the blocks from the pit were lifted. Zaki Iskander, the well-known chemist and expert on materials in ancient Egypt, wrote a chapter on the conservation of the wood, the chemicals used, and the state of the wood when discovered. The last chapter, written by the conservator, Ahmad Youssef Mustafa, describes how he reinforced and lifted the pieces out of the pit, moved them to the restoration shed, and arranged them in the order they were found. This is where the book ends. The boat had not been reconstructed yet, and nothing about its possible use or religious significance is discussed. This is pretty much how it has remained until recent times. The book was officially titled *The Cheops Boats: Part I*, but no sequel ever appeared.

The first and most important of the post-reconstruction publications was Paul Lipke's monograph on the Khufu I Boat.[4] In it, he records the various pieces of the boat and goes into detailed discussions of the various techniques used to hold the pieces together. Lipke, a naval historian, focuses on the boat's construction, but offers little discussion of the ship's purpose in ancient Egypt. Although his interest is not Egyptological, this is a seminal, fact-based work, crucial to anyone interested in Khufu I. The first reconstruction of the boat was completed in 1968, more than ten years after its discovery. Before this reconstruction, Hag Ahmed Youssef Mustafa, the conservator responsible for the boat, spent years apprenticing in shipyards and carving models of the boat's pieces so he could practice the reconstruction before he attempted it on the full-scale boat. Still, five attempts to reconstruct the boat were necessary[5] before Hag Ahmed was satisfied that he had it right, primarily because ancient Egyptian techniques were unique, lacking any parallels to known traditional or modern boat construction (fig. 3); so it was not till the 1970s that data-based work on the boat could be conducted.[6] The difficult and painstaking reassembly of the boat has been recounted in Nancy Jenkins' book, *The Boat Beneath the Pyramid*,[7] which, while intended for a popular audience, contains many details not found elsewhere.

At the time of Lipke's publication, the boat's discovery was now thirty years old and few scholars were interested in discussing the boat's purpose. Subsequent publications by naval historians continued Lipke's focus and concentrated on the ship's construction—how the planks were held together by a combination of mortises and

[3] Zaki Nour, Mohamed Zaki, et al., *The Cheops Boats* (Cairo, 1960).

[4] Paul Lipke, The Royal Ship of Cheops: A Retrospective Account of the Discovery, Restoration and Reconstruction. Based on Interviews with Hag Ahmed Youssef Moustafa (Oxford, 1984).

[5] See Lipke, *The Royal Ship of Cheops*, 63–93, for descriptions of the five reconstructions.

[6] We should point out that even today we can't be absolutely certain how the boat originally looked. For example, there is still discussion of how to place the five pairs of oars found in the pit. The way they are placed today, in oarlocks crafted of rope, is an invention of Hag Ahmed. See Samuel Mark, "A different Configuration for the Quarter-Rudders on the Khufu I Vessel (c. 2566 BC), and Egyptian Methods of Mounting Quarter-Rudders and Oars in the 4th and 5th Dynasties," *International Journal of Nautical Archaeology* 41 (2011), 84–93, for additional discussion.

[7] Nancy Jenkins, *The Boat Beneath the Pyramid* (New York, 1980).

Fig. 2. Pieces of Khufu I being removed from the pit.
Photo: Supreme Council of Antiquities.

Fig. 3. Reconstruction of Khufu I. Photo: Supreme Council of Antiquities.

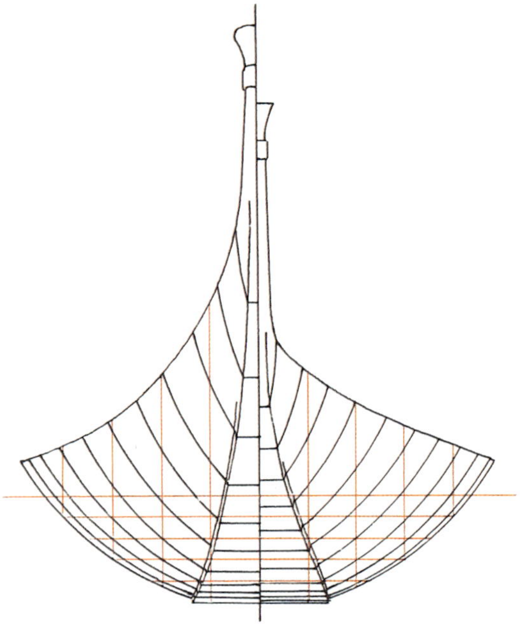

Fig. 4. Body plan use to produce model of Khufu I. Photo from Landström, Ships of the Pharaohs, *30).*

tenons and lashings.[8] Today, six decades after the boat's discovery, its purpose is still debated. It is our hope that the publication of our work will shed more light on the purpose that the Egyptians intended the boat to serve.

It is important to note what was not among the 1,224 pieces found the boat pit, as this may help determine some possibilities for the boat's use. Most important, there was neither a mast nor sails. Nor is there a place on the deck suitable for accommodating a mast. From this, it is reasonable to conclude that Khufu I did not sail. We will discuss this issue later in the paper.

So how was the boat used? In 1994 the opportunity arose to take a significant step towards answering this question. Bob Brier was Director of the National Endowment for the Humanities "Egyptology Today" program, and one of the students, Howard Nepo, wrote his paper on Hatshepsut's ships. As part of the project, he carved a half model of one of the boats shown on her mortuary temple at Deir el-Bahri. It was an impressive model and Brier showed it to some of his colleagues at the Webb Institute for Naval Architecture, a school on Long Island specializing in Naval Architecture and Marine Engineering. One of the professors asked if Nepo could carve a full model so the ship's nautical properties could be tested in Webb's model tank. (It turns out that both Howard Nepo and his father were world-class model carvers.) Nepo pointed out that not much could be learned by carving a model of Hatshepsut's boat because the wall reliefs did not give accurate ship lines. Thus, it was decided to substitute Khufu I. Here we had the actual boat to look at and could also use the drawings in Landström's *Ships of the Pharaohs*[9] as a starting point (fig. 4 and Table 1).

Table 1. Principal characteristics of the model as tested

	Model	Ship
Scale	1/20	-
Length, Overall, LOA (m)	2.169	43.38
Length, at waterline, LWL (m)	1.407	28.14
Max Beam, B (m)	0.295	5.89
Depth, minimum to deck (m)	0.084	1.68
Draft, tested, T (m)	0.064	1.27
Test Displacement, freshwater (kg)	8.534	68,274
Surface Area, S (m2)	0.289	115.6

8 See Cheryl Ward Haldane, "Ancient Egyptian Hull Construction" (PhD dissertation, Texas A&M University, 1993); Samuel Mark "The Construction of the Khufu I Vessel (c. 2566 BC): A Re-Evaluation," *International Journal of Nautical Archaeology* 38 (2009), 133–52, and Samuel Mark, "New Data on Egyptian Construction Methods in the Khufu I Vessel (c. 2566 BC) from the Paul Lipke Collection," *International Journal of Nautical Archaeology* 40 (2011), 18–38.

9 Björn Landström, *Ships of the Pharaohs: 4000 Years of Egyptian Shipbuilding* (New York, 1970).

The Khufu I Boat Model

The father and son Nepos created a 1:20 model that was designed to be tested in the Webb model tank. The completed boat model (figs. 5 and 6) was over two meters long (Table 1) and was not intended as an exact replica, but was intended to reproduce the lines and everything necessary for testing in a towing tank. The model was built of pine and allowed for the twelve oars (five on each side, and two at the stern) to be removed. Thus, the boat could be tested with and without oars in the water. With this model in hand, we hoped the purpose of Khufu I would be clarified.

The Robinson Model Basin at Webb Institute is 28.3 m long, 3.05 m wide, and approximately 1.5 m deep. Scale ship models are towed by an overhead monorail and a cable drive at a constant speed. Instrumentation records the forces and motions of the model, such as the amount of towing force required to move the hull through the water. The tests were made using the Webb Institute Yacht Dynamometer. Figures 7 and 8 show photographs of the test apparatus connected to a modern yacht model. Drag force, side force, heeling moment, and yawing moment were measured.

The model was tested in the spring of 1995 as part of the Senior Thesis of one of the students, Stuart Greene. Although the findings were important, the only publication of the results was a brief news summary in *Science*.[10] The reason was that Greene was one of the few Webb students who, upon graduation, did not continue in the maritime industry. Brier did not have the technical knowledge to see the research through publication, so the data languished for twenty-five years. In 2018, Michael Morabito, also a Webb graduate, e-mailed Brier to ask if there were a project on which they could work together. The Stuart Greene data immediately came to mind and now we are able to finally present the data to the Egyptological community.

There have been some notable advances in the scholarly record in the period since the physical model tests were conducted, especially in the understanding of hull construction techniques, but no new surveys on the final outside hull shape from which the test model was built. The results presented here are from a comprehensive reanalysis of the experimental data, combined with new hydrostatic calculations based on an updated three-dimensional computer model of Khufu I.

Fig. 5. Khufu I Test Model.

Fig. 6. Khufu I test model being ballasted in towing tank (note position of the removable oars).

[10] C. Holden, "The Boat in the Tomb," *Science* 267/5203 (March 10, 1995), 1426

Fig. 7. Webb Institute yacht dynamometer towing a typical model of a modern hull. Photo courtesy of Engineering Laboratory Technician Jamie Swan.

Fig. 8. Webb Institute yacht dynamometer, showing a typical test of a modern hull at fixed angle of heel. Photo courtesy of Engineering Laboratory Technician Jamie Swan.

Hull Shape

At the time that the physical model was constructed, there were two published hull geometries to choose from, one by Landström and one by Lipke. Since that time, there has not been a laser scan of the hull, or other careful surveys as it sits in its museum. Neither Landström or Lipke had access to the final measurements of the hull in-situ.

Landström stated that his lines drawing is made on the basis of his own measurements, with some corrections because the planking had not yet been pressed into its final shape.[11] Lipke based his on measurements of the 1/20th scale model built by Hag Ahmed Youssef Mustafa, stating that the model, "is not altogether accurate either in form or in construction."[12] Table 2 shows the differences in published dimensions from selected references. The main differences are in the displacement, or weight (to be discussed later) and in the beam, or maximum width of the boat.

Figure 9 shows a comparison between Landström's cross section (used to build the physical model), and one based on Lipke's measurements of the model. The hull below the waterline (the important part for towing tests) is nearly identical. Regardless of these differences in shape, the physical model tests should be reflective of the real performance.

The differences in maximum beam affect the calculation of when water might come over the side of the boat. This is addressed later by computing the boat's stability for Landström's geometry, as well as a modified version using the beam and depth reported by Lipke.

Table 2. Khufu I boat principal characteristics from four references

	Landström (1970)	Abubakr (1971)	Jenkins (1980)	Lipke (1984)
Length, Overall (m)	43.40	42.32	43.4	43.63
Beam, maximum (m)	5.90	5.66	5.9	5.66
Depth, minimum to deck (m)	1.68	1.78	1.78	1.78
Estimated Max. Draft (m)	-	1.48	1.48	1.18
Estimated Min. Freeboard (m)	-	0.3	0.3	0.6
Hull Weight (t)	40.0	50.0	45.0	39.1
Deadweight (t)	-	100	-	54.7
Max. Displacement (t)	-	150	-	93.8

Weights and Stability

Greene's tests were at a weight corresponding to 68,200 kg in the full-size boat. This included approximately 40,000 kg of hull weight, based on estimates by Landström and Lipke, and an additional cargo and passenger weight of approximately 28,200 kg. The test weight was lower than previously estimated values of maximum displacement shown in Table 2. Abubakr had estimated a total weight of 150,000 kg. Lipke revised this value to 93,800 kg, considering the final geometry of the hull, as well as the requirement for reserve buoyancy (having the sides of the hull a bit higher than the water surface, to prevent flooding). The value of 68,200 kg was chosen because Lipke's value was for a maximum overload case, rather than a typical operational condition.

As part of the present reanalysis of the test data, a three-dimensional computer model of Khufu I was also tested numerically, to see how it would float at various weights. Figure 10 shows a rendering of such a condition. The computer simulation indicated that at approximately 9–11 degrees, the 68,200 kg ship would flood. This angle is known as the "downflooding" angle. The physical model flooded at a 10-degree angle, so both the physical model test and the computer simulation are in close agreement. This flooding is exacerbated because the

[11] Landström, *Ships of the Pharaohs*, 31.

[12] Lipke, *The Royal Ship of Cheops*, 97.

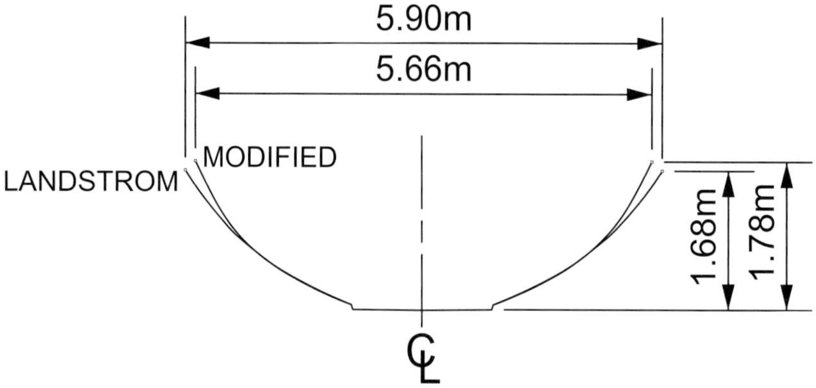

Fig. 9. Midship section based on Landström (1970), with modifications in beam and depth from Lipke, The Royal Ship of Cheops: A Retrospective Account of the Discovery, Restoration and Reconstruction.

deck is open, unprotected from the water (fig. 11), confirming that Khufu I was never intended for open waters such as the Red Sea or Mediterranean. While this has not been previously suggested, it is important to eliminate as a possibility. The sides of the hull would need to be higher (mainly at mid-length, where the lowest point is located), or the deck would need to be solid and watertight, if a boat similar to this were to operate on open waters.

Figure 12 shows the effect of the total weight on the downflooding angle. The thickness of the line represents a range of possible solutions accounting for small variations in hull dimensions that have been provided in the literature by Lipke and Landström, discussed earlier. The figure shows that as the weight increases, the ship is more likely to downflood at smaller angles. Even at the lightest expected displacement considered at the time of the model tests (the hull weight from Landström and Lipke of 40,000 kg, with no additional cargo), the downflood angle is less than 20 degrees, which makes the design unsuited for open waters. This graph of weight versus downflooding angle has convinced the authors that the 68,200 kg test was probably too large, and that the boat was never intended to haul much weight. While previous literature has not suggested that the boat would haul heavy cargo, implicit in the previous large estimates for maximum loaded weight is the assumption that the boat would be carrying something.

The complete details of the stability analysis have been presented more fully in an engineering paper before the Society of Naval Architects and Marine Engineers.[13] A few of the major findings include:

(1) A detailed weights analysis has been provided, indicating that the hull weight may be lower than the value of 40,000 kg predicted by Landström and Lipke. The hull weight (known as lightship weight) including a 10% uncertainty margin, was 32,500 kg, but more study is recommended.

(2) Khufu I can pass modern U.S. Coast Guard stability regulations for intact stability and downflood angle in protected waters,[14] provided the total weight is less than around 45,000 kg. The boat fails criteria for open waters. This is further confirmation that the boat was never intended for use in open waters, and that it was intended to be lightly loaded.

(3) Even though the boat pit did not include a mast, the possibility of sailing the boat was considered from a powering and stability standpoint, including estimates of the required sail area and boat speed. Because of the small angle at which flooding occurs, it is strongly argued that the Khufu I Boat would not be appropriate for

[13] M. G. Morabito, B. Brier, B., S. Greene, "Preliminary Stability and Resistance Analysis of the Cheops Boat," *Journal of Ship Production and Design* 36/1 (February 2020), 14–40.

[14] The specific criteria checked include the United States Code of Federal Regulations (CFR) 46 CFR 170.170 wind criteria, 46 CFR 170.173.e righting arm criteria in protected waters, and 46 CFR 170.050 passenger crowding, assuming 25 passengers. These are the initial checks that a Naval Architect would do when working on a new design to check the stability of the hull, but there are many other requirements to be coast guard certified.

Fig. 10. Computer rendering of Khufu I in downflood condition at 40,000 kg displacement.

Fig. 11. Khufu I, showing open deck along the side of the hull. Photograph by Jon Bodsworth.

sailing, even though it is possible from the standpoint of speed and power. This is because the sails cause the vessel to heel over toward the side. Having low sides and an open deck would risk downflooding when the boat was sailing.

Both the physical model tests and the computerized hydrostatics analysis indicated that the hull design was quite suitable for river use. The stability analyses indicated that while the boat should not have been used to carry heavy cargo, like stone blocks, the boat is likely a real design for use in protected waters while not heavily loaded. The question now became what could that use be?

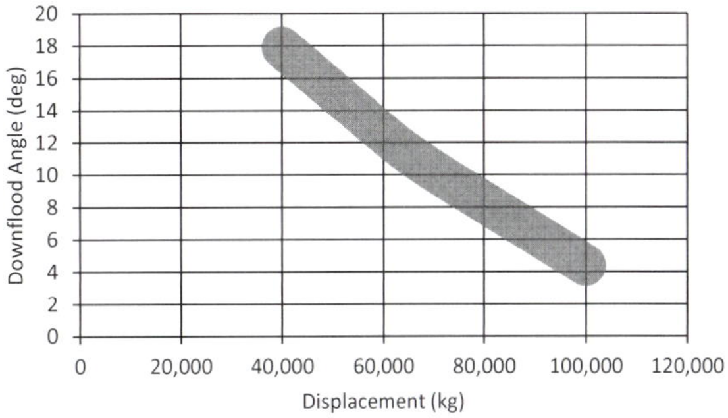

Fig. 12. Effect of total weight (hull + cargo) on downflooding angle.

Towing, Rowing, and Sailing Performance

The possible uses were explored in towing tank tests on the physical model. Typical ship resistance tests involve towing in the upright position to simulate propulsion with an engine (or with oars in this case). The tests on Khufu I also included runs at various degrees of heel, to simulate how the boat would respond if it were fitted with sails.

Figure 13 presents a graph of resistance versus speed for Khufu I at the 68,200 kg tested weight, as derived from towing measurements on the scale model, and expanded to full-size using the International Towing Tank Conference 1957 method. The details of the tests are provided more fully in Morabito, Brier and Greene's article.[15] The curve marked "Total" is

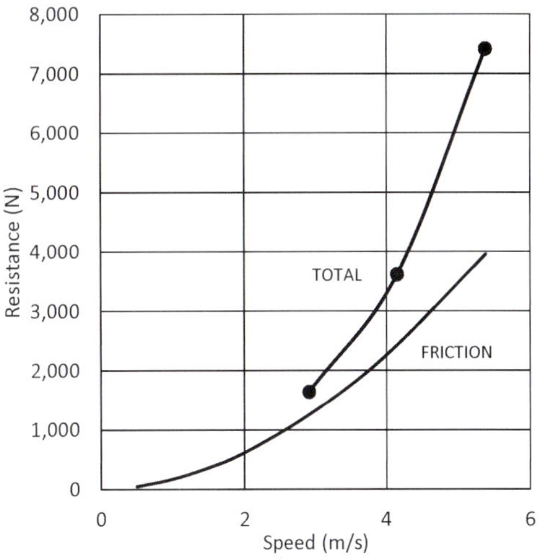

Fig. 13. Resistance versus speed for Khufu I boat at 68,200 kg total weight, based on scale model test results.

[15] Morabito, Brier, and Greene, "Preliminary Stability and Resistance Analysis of the Cheops Boat."

the force needed to tow the boat. The difference between the "Total" resistance curve and the curve marked "Friction" comes from the boat making increasingly large waves at higher speeds.

As mentioned, the Khufu I Boat had at total of twelve oars. However, there were no seats for the rowers, nor was there any accommodation for seats on the deck. Still, we wanted to see if it were possible to row the boat with the number of oars found in the pit. Our tank tests showed how much force was required to tow the Khufu I Boat. Next, we estimated the performance of rowers, the effects of winds, the river currents, and then combined them.

Zamparo estimated that the useful propulsion power of a person rowing is about 0.1 kilowatts (kW). [16] Coats considered the effect of duration (extending from a few minutes to more than 12 hours). He shows that regular rowers in fixed-seat boats can produce 0.1 kW for about 1 hour. [17] More trained crews in well-tuned boats can produce this power output for much longer durations. Stone provides a description of the variable river currents before the Aswan Dam was constructed:

> Early in June of each year the flow is the least. The current near Cairo has then a rapidity of only a little more than one mile per hour (1.6 km/h). Before the end of June, the annual rise commences; and by the end of September the rapidity of the current reaches nearly, if not quite, three and a half miles per hour (5.6 km/h). Late in October, or early in November, it commences a somewhat rapid decline until January, when the decline becomes more gradual and regular; this gradual decline continuing until about the end of May, when the minimum flow is again reached.[18]

Figure 14 shows the speed of the boat with different numbers of rowers. The solid black line is the speed of the 68,200 kg hull with no headwind. The lower dashed line includes a 20 km/h headwind. The range of expected Nile river currents is labeled. We saw earlier that the tested displacement is higher than we would propose now based on our new weights and stability estimates, so the boat should go a bit faster than this prediction.

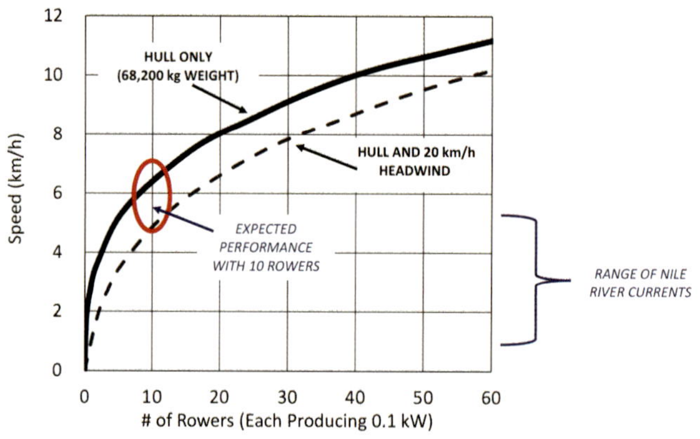

Fig. 14. Plot of number of rowers versus speed.

Could the boat be rowed with ten rowers and two steering oars? Technically yes, in the ideal calm conditions usually seen on the Nile. The boat could make progress against a headwind, but windy conditions may make controlling the boat difficult. The boat would be frustratingly slow traveling upriver during the Nile's flood stages. In the unlikely event of fighting a current and wind from the same direction (not usually the case on the Nile) the boat would actually move backwards. Increasing the number of rowers would be recommended.

Could the boat have been sailed? Possibly. We saw earlier that the low sides of the hull promote flooding at relatively small angles of heel. The force on the sails may cause the boat to heel over too far and flood in a sudden gust. The sailing performance is similar to other traditional sailing boats discussed by Palmer.[19] Sailing calculations based on the physical model testing of the Khufu I hull form[20] show that the hull could likely sail

[16] P. Zamparo, et al., "Energy balance of locomotion with pedal-driven watercraft," *Journal of Sports Medicine* 26/1 (January 1, 2008), 75–81.

[17] J. Coates, "Power and Speed of Oared Ships," in C. Westerdahl (ed.), *Crossroads in Ancient Shipbuilding. Proceedings of the Sixth International Symposium on Boat and Ship Archeology Roskilde 1991.* Oxbow Monograph 40 (Oxford, 1994), 249–55.

[18] C. P. Stone, "The navigation of the Nile," *Science* 4/93 (November 14, 1884), 456–57.

[19] C. Palmer, "Windward Sailing Capabilities of Ancient Vessels," *International Journal of Nautical Archeology* 38.2 (2009), 314–30.

[20] Morabito, et al. "Preliminary Stability and Resistance."

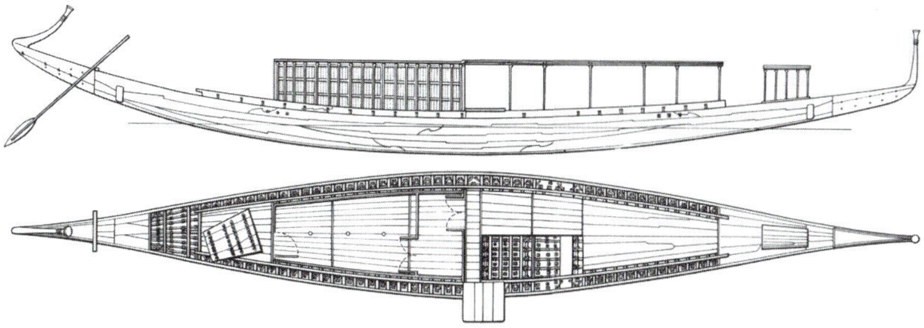

Fig. 15. Profile and plan view of Khufu I (from Landström 1979, 30–31). Note: Bow is to the right.

Fig. 16. Deck of Khufu I. Photograph by Ovedc, distributed under a CC BY-SA 4.0 license.

between about 91 and 103 degrees into the wind (mostly side-to side and downwind). Fixing the oars in position as leeboards (see fig. 6) improved angle to 79–92 degrees relative to the wind, meaning that it might be able to sail slightly upwind in ideal conditions. The hull shape of Khufu I, like other ancient sailing vessels, could be sailed mostly downwind, and would need to be rowed to go upwind.[21]

How Were the Oars Used?

How does the arrangement of Khufu I reflect on its use? Figure 15 shows a profile and plan view of it. Note the enclosed deckhouse with two chambers shown in the plan (and in figs. 16, 17), as well as the canopy. The two steering oars are shown in the diagram, but not the ten other oars found in the pit. Hag Ahmed attached the

[21] For the sailing and rowing performance observed in trials of a hypothetical reconstruction of an ancient Egyptian ship for use on the Red Sea, see P. Couser, C. Ward, and T. Vosmer. "Hypothetical Reconstruction of an Ancient Egyptian Sea-Going Vessel from the Reign of Hatshepsut, 1500BCE," Historic Ships Conference 2009. Royal Institution of Naval Architects. 19–20 November 2009 (London, 2009), 1–11.

Fig. 17. Workmen erect the bulkhead between the two chambers of the deckhouse of the Khufu I. Photo: Supreme Council of Antiquities.

oars near the canopy for display purposes (see fig. 11). The oars weighted somewhere around 57 kg each, and had lengths of 6.58–8.35 m[22] which could make them difficult to use.

As a point of comparison, modern sweep oars for competitive rowing are sold in lengths ranging from around 3.6 m to 3.8 m. The oars on the replica of the Greek Trireme Olympias were 4.2 m long, though Shaw argues for a slight increase in length.[23] Rodgers gives sketches and rowing arrangements analysis of a reconstruction of an ancient Greek Pentekonter with 4.6 m oars for single rowers, and 6.7 m oars for rowing in pairs.[24]

The Khufu I arrangements may be compared with typical Egyptian boats, such as those shown in the mastaba of Ti in Saqqara (fig. 18). The boats in the top of figure 18 have oars that are smaller than the steering oars and have loops connecting them to the long plank that runs along the deck on each side of the boat. Other reliefs show oars set in notches along this plank.[25]

The right-hand image in the second row of figure 18 shows paddlers kneeling on the deck, facing forward. These paddles have a broader blade than the oars. Perhaps Khufu I could be paddled with people kneeling on the deck in a similar way? The bottom two images in figure 18 show boats sailing. The rowing oars are raised up and laid across the boat and the rowers are seated together in the shade of the canopy.

[22] Lipke, *The Royal Ship of Cheops,* 103.

[23] T. Shaw, "Towards a Revised Design of a Greek Trireme of the Fourth Century BC: advantages of a long stroke," in B. Rankov (ed.), *Trireme Olympias, The Final Report* (Oxford, 2012), 76–81.

[24] W. L. Rodgers, *Greek and Roman Naval Warfare* (Annapolis, 1937), 37–40.

[25] See Figure 1 of S. Mark, "Graphical Reconstruction and Comparison of Royal Boat Iconography from the Causeway of Egyptian King Sahure (c. 2487–2475 BC)," *International Journal of Nautical Archeology* 42 (2013), 270–85.

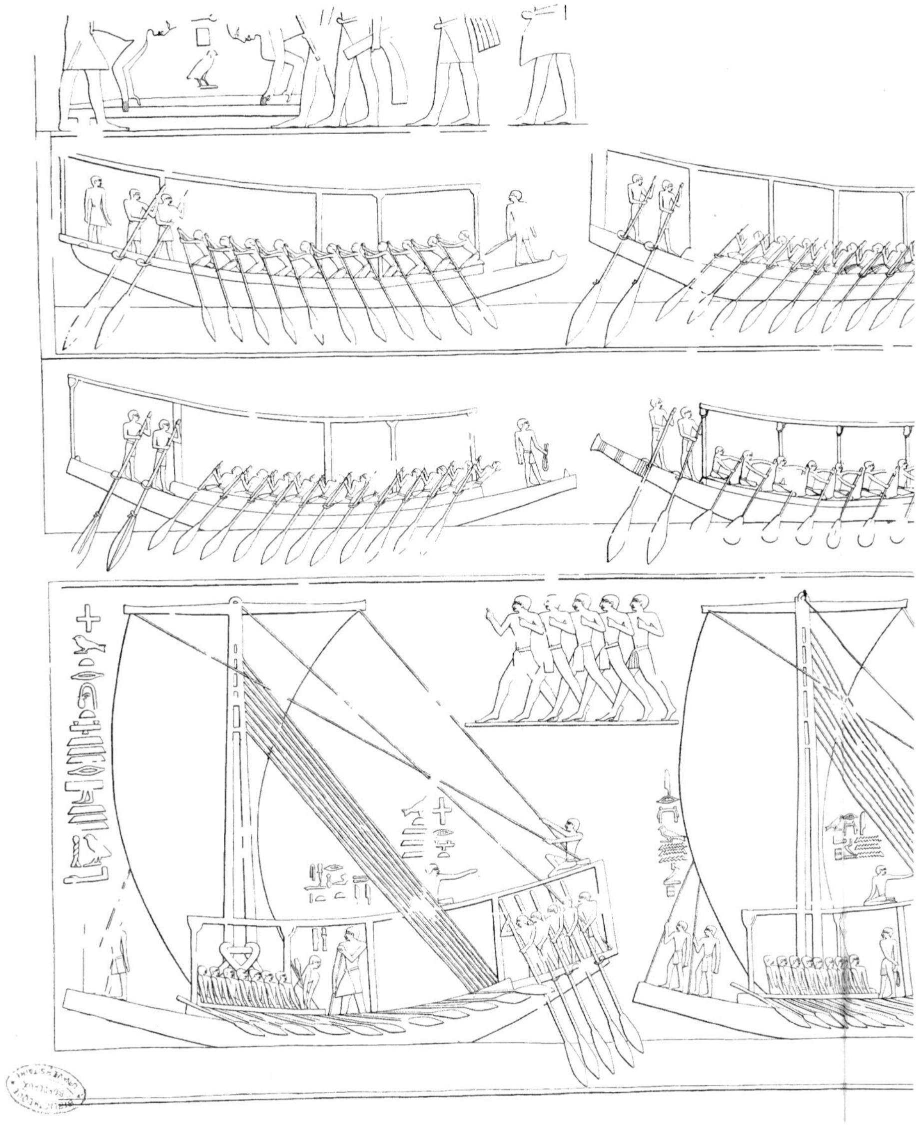

Fig. 18. Boats from the tomb of Ti (mid-Fifth Dynasty). From L. Epron, Le tombeau de Ti: Les approaches de la chapelle *(Cairo, 1939), pl. 49.*

Where does this leave us? Samuel Mark argues strongly and convincingly that what we had been calling oars were really quarter-rudders that were used for steering the vessel rather than propelling it.[26] He also points out that the "oars" are too long and heavy to have been used as such. While we have shown that the vessel could have been propelled by oars, we have not demonstrated that it was. Although Mark does not discuss the purpose of Khufu I, his conclusions are relevant to such a discussion. With no oars to propel it and no mast or sails, this strongly suggests that if Khufu I was used, it was towed.

Figure 19 recalls the pilgrimage of Sennefer and his wife to Abydos during the reign of Amenhotep II. Their private boat is being towed by another boat full of rowers. Newberry documented tomb paintings showing the

[26] Mark, "A different Configuration for the Quarter-Rudders on the Khufu I Vessel," 84–93.

Fig. 19. Pilgrimage of Sennefer and his wife to Abydos (TT96) showing their boat being towed by an oar-propelled boat. Photo by Luigi Tripani.

Fig. 20. Funeral procession of Kyky (Simut) showing funerary boat towed by oar-propelled boat (TT409). Photo by Thierry Benderitter.

annual stock-taking of the herds noting, "…it was the custom for a great man, in order to avoid the unpleasant neighborhood of the sailors, to put the crew into a separate boat, which towed his own finely-furnished dahabîyeh, the latter being without mast or oars."[27] Figure 20 shows a similar towing arrangement from the funerary voyage of Kyky (Simut) to Abydos. The spectacle of towing ceremonial boats was so widespread that funerary processions and religious observances made over land frequently included a miniature bark, towed across the ground on a sledge.[28]

Discussion

The results of our tests, both tank and computer simulated, have convinced us of two things. First, Khufu I was never used on the open sea. This was demonstrated by its flooding at less than 20-degree heel, and is further confirmed by the absence of a mast or sail. Second, we are convinced that Khufu I was built to be used, but not on open waters. Here we should say something about the speculation that it was a ceremonial boat, never intended for actual use.

---

[27] P. E. Newberry, *El Bersheh Part I (The Tomb of Tehuti-Hetep)*, Archeological Survey of Egypt 3 (London, 1895), 27, pls. 12, 18. See also P. E. Newberry, *Beni Hasan Part II*. Archeological Survey of Egypt 2 (London, 1893), pl. 12.

[28] P. P. Creasman, and N. Doyle, "Overland Boat Transportation During the Pharaonic Period: Archeology and Iconography," *Journal of Ancient Egyptian Interconnections* 2/3 (2010), 14–30.

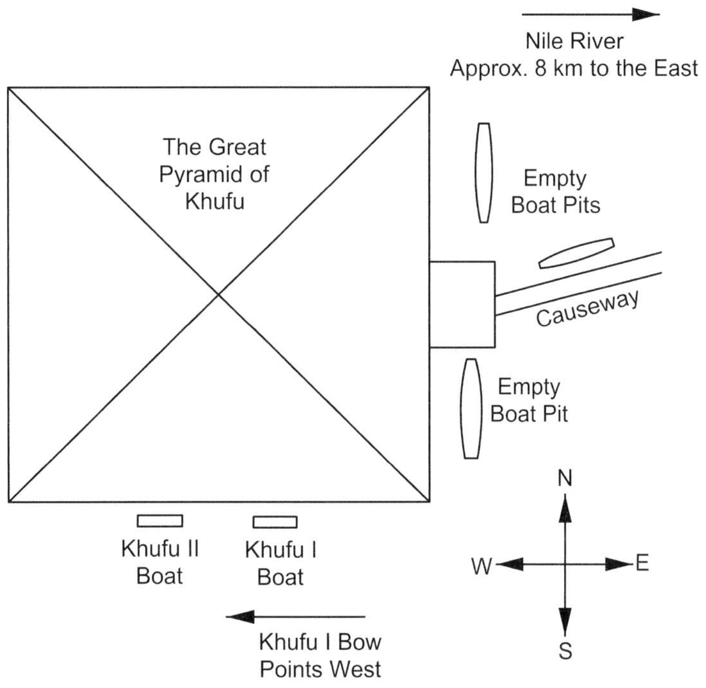

Fig. 21. Boat Pits Surrounding the Great Pyramid.

As mentioned above, Černý believed Khufu I was a ceremonial boat. Because there are five boat pits surrounding the Khufu pyramid (fig. 21), Černý suggested that four of the boats were symbolic, one for each of the four points of the compass so the pharaoh could journey wherever he chose in the next world. Černý believed that Khufu I was one of these boats. Černý speculated that the fifth boat was the actual boat that ferried the mummy of Khufu across to Nile for burial. When Černý made his suggestion, Khufu I and II were still in their pits, so the details of their construction were not known. After the reconstruction, and from our tests, it seems clear this was no ceremonial boat. It is larger and better constructed than such boats. As Ward points out, the fourteen boats at Abydos didn't have mortise and tenon joins necessary to hold them together, because they were merely ceremonial boats.[29] Further, there are no frames inside the hulls to make them rigid and suitable for water. Khufu I, on the other hand, has structural strength and nothing has been spared on it—it was built to be used.

So, if Khufu I couldn't have been used in open waters, but was clearly designed for use on the water, it must have been a Nile craft. This brings to mind two possible uses. First is the Abydos pilgrimage. Its lack of mast and sail might seem to rule out this possibility. With no sails, how could it go south against the current? The answer to this is that numerous tomb reliefs and paintings depict Abydos pilgrimages where the pilgrimage boat being towed by another boat with sails. Thus, when going south, the towing boat has its sails up, and the pilgrimage boat would need neither sail nor oars. On the return trip, the oars could be placed in the water to help navigate, but would not have to be used to propel the boat. So, the lack of mast and sails do not rule out the possibility that the Khufu I Boat was used for the Abydos pilgrimage.

The second possibility for Khufu I is that it was a funerary barge intended to ferry Khufu from the realm of the living on the east bank of the Nile to the west bank, the realm of the dead. We have ample tomb depictions of funerary boats being towed by a boat with sails up or with rowers (see figs. 20 and 22). These depictions are

[29] Cheryl Ward, "Boat-Building and its Social Context in Early Egypt: Interpretations from the First Dynasty Boat-Grave Cemetery at Abydos," *Antiquity* 80 (2006), 118–29.

Fig. 22. Funerary boat being towed by an oar-propelled boat shown in the tomb of Neferhotep (TT49). From Norman de Garis Davies, The Tomb of Nefer-hotep at Thebes, *vol. 1, PMMA 9 (New York, 1933), pl. 22.*

for funerals of commoners, but from the Great Harris Papyrus, we know they took place for pharaohs also ("He was rowed in his king's barge on the river and rested in his eternal house west of Thebes").[30]

Thus, we have two possible Nilotic uses in which Khufu I could have been towed: The Abydos pilgrimage and the funeral of the pharaoh. There is, however, one aspect of Khufu I that argues against the Abydos Pilgrimage. As Altenmüller points out in his important survey of Old Kingdom boat pits,[31] the two Khufu boats on the south side of the Great Pyramid were buried one behind the other, as if in tandem in a convoy of two. Further, they were oriented east-west (the bow of Khufu I to the west). This is paralleled by the two boat pits on the south side of the Khafra pyramid, also in tandem and oriented east-west. This is not an accident; the ancient Egyptians were very careful about orientation. The Abydos pilgrimage was a north-south journey, but the pharaoh's journey from the land of the living to the next world, was from east to west. We believe that the orientation of the Khufu boats suggests their funerary use, to take the body of Khufu from the east to the west. We might also point out that the two east-west boats, one behind the other, argues against Černý's idea that Khufu I was one of the four symbolic boats for the four points of the compass.

The sewn construction method used for Khufu I supports the ability to disassemble, transport, and reassemble the boat. It is reasonable to ask, "Why construct Khufu I so that it could be taken apart, if it was only going to be placed on the Nile and would never have to be transported in pieces?" The recent finds at Wadi al-Jarf, on the coast of the Red Sea, dating to the reign of Khufu, include long storage galleries suitable for storing disassembled components of boats, as well as worked timbers, pieces of tenons, and parts of oars.[32] Creasman and Doyle explain that perhaps there were insufficient resources on the coast of the Red Sea to support a boat-building industry. Parts of boats could be transported over land to remote sites and then reassembled.[33] Why use this method for a Nile River craft? We should point out that the sewn construction method of Khufu I is seen in many other boats that were not intended to be transported over land. The causeway of Sahure's pyramid depicts his fleet of ships that sailed the Mediterranean and the reliefs show external lashings, indicating that they too were "sewn" boats.[34]

Again, Why? Mediterranean ships didn't have to be carried. There are really three answers. First, the sewn construction method made the ships easier to repair; replacements could be modular. Second, wood was a very

[30] Harris Papyrus, British Museum EA 9999, Plate 76. Translation after J. H. Breasted, *Ancient Records of Egypt: Volume IV The Twentieth to the Twenty-Sixth Dynasties* (Chicago, 1906), 200.

[31] Hartwig Altenmüller, "Funerary Boats and Boat Pits of the Old Kingdom," *Archív Orientální* 70/3 (2002), 270.

[32] P. Tallet and G. Marouard, "An early pharaonic harbor on the Read Sea Coast," *Egyptian Archaeology* 40 (2012), 42.

[33] P. P. Creasman, and N. Doyle, "Overland Boat Transportation" 14.

[34] S. Mark, "Graphical Reconstruction" 278–79.

valuable commodity in Egypt and such construction made recycling easier, with little damage to the planks.[35] Third, metal fasteners were very expensive at the time, and so lashing planks may have been a more effective use of limited resources. Since the discovery of Khufu I, maritime archeology is revealing increasing numbers of sewn boats from around the Mediterranean, including sixty-four wrecks described by Pomey and Boetto.[36] Sewn boats have been discovered outside the Mediterranean in Britain, Oman, India, Sri Lanka, Vietnam, southern China, the Maldives, and other locations. Lashing planks together was deeply imbedded in shipbuilding, so it is not surprising that Khufu I was tied together.

Conclusion

This paper has summarized recent research into the function of the Khufu I Boat, including the stability and flotation characteristics, handling under sail, rowing capabilities, construction method and design arrangements. The results clearly indicate that this type of hull form, with its low sides and open deck, was not suited to carrying heavy cargo, carrying sails, or operating in rough conditions, which could cause the side of the hull to become immersed and to flood. The results have shown that the boat would be capable of safely being rowed or towed on the Nile River with light cargo on board.

Because of its construction, lack of mast and sails or propulsion oars, and its east–west orientation when buried, we feel confident that the Khufu I Boat was intended to be used for the pharaoh's funeral. Preliminary investigations by the Japanese team who are excavating Khufu II have led them to estimate that there are about seventy-eight oars in the pit.[37] These include many short oars (approximately 3.5 m long, and suited for propulsion) and a smaller number of longer oars (approximately 7 m long) that could be used for steering oars or quarter rudders. The large number of propulsion oars would provide adequate power for propelling Khufu II while also towing Khufu I. It is not clear whether Khufu II includes a mast or not. Future excavations will reveal this.

[35] For an interesting discussion of this, see S. Mark, "Notes on the Mediterranean and Red Sea Ships and Ship Construction from Sahure to Hatshepsut," *Journal of Ancient Egyptian Interconnections* 6/2 (2014), 43–44.

[36] P. Pomey, P. and G. Boetto, "Ancient Mediterranean Sewn-Boat Traditions," *International Journal of Nautical Archeology* 48/1 (2019), 5–51.

[37] Takahashi Toshimitsu 高橋寿光, "Materials Revived from the Pit" ピットからよみがえる部材 Presentation given at The 5th Sun Boat Symposium 第5回太陽の船シンポジウム "よみがえれ！太陽の船の部材たち, June 20, 2016, Waseda University, Tokyo, Japan. (http://www.solarboat.or.jp/report.html (accessed 27 March 2020).

The Hoopoe and the Child in Old Kingdom Art

Kim McCorquodale
Macquarie University, Sydney

Abstract

Hoopoes are highly distinctive birds in Egyptian art. They have been attributed with a special link to children, and it has been claimed that in the Old Kingdom, a naked child who holds a hoopoe is the eldest son and the heir of the deceased. However, a broader examination of all children of the tomb owner and a larger corpus do not support these assertions. Hoopoes are held by both male and female adults as well as both male and female children. They are held by eldest and younger sons in almost equal numbers and in the majority of cases, where a younger son holds a hoopoe, the eldest son is present in the same scene but does not hold a hoopoe. It appears that hoopoes are just attractive birds that are held by both adults and children in much the same way as geese, ducks, pigeons, golden orioles, and other small birds.

ملخص

يعد طائر الهدهد من الطيور المميزة للغاية في الفن المصري القديم. وقد نسبت إليه علاقة خاصة بالأطفال، وقيل إنه في عصر الدولة القديمة إذا صُوّر طفلٌ عارٍ يمسك بطائر الهدهد فهو الابن الأكبر للمتوفى ووريثه. ومع ذلك، فهناك دراسات واسعة النطاق تناولت كل أبناء صاحب المقبرة، ومجموعة أكبر منها لا تؤيد هذه الادعاءات. فقد كان الكبار والأطفال من الذكور والإناث على حد سواء يمسكون بطائر الهدهد. وقد أمسك به أبناء كبار وصغار بأعدادٍ متساوية تقريبًا، بل وفي أغلب الأحيان، عندما يظهر الابن الأصغر ممسكًا بطائر الهدهد، نجد الابن الأكبر حاضرًا في نفس المنظر وهو غير ممسك بطائر الهدهد. يبدو أن طيور الهدهد هي مجرد طيور جذابة كان يمسك بها الكبار والأطفال على حد سواء على غرار الإمساك بالأوز والبط والحمام وطيور الصفير الذهبي وطيور صغيرة أخرى.

The hoopoe (*Upupa epops*) is a resident breeding bird in Egypt and is one of many birds shown in Egyptian art. In his 1930's article, Ludwig Keimer asserted that hoopoes had a special link to children.[1] In her 2015 article, Amandine Marshall stated that no adult is ever seen with this bird and concluded that in the Old Kingdom, when a child held a hoopoe, it indicated that they were the eldest son and the heir.[2] However, her data was limited and a more thorough examination of Old Kingdom material reveals that adults do hold hoopoes, as do daughters and both eldest sons and younger sons in almost equal numbers. Hence, the holding of a hoopoe by a child does not indicate that they are the eldest son and heir.

The hoopoe can be easily identified in the decoration of the elite tombs by their large fanned crests on their head, long curved beak and the square shape of its tail.[3] (figs. 1–2) Arlette David states that hoopoes appear in tombs mainly in three contexts: bird trapping scenes, perched on a tree, and in the hands of children.[4] However,

---

[1] L. Keimer, "Quelques remarques sur la huppe (Upupa epops) dans l'Égypte ancienne," *BIFAO* 30 (1930), 308.

[2] A. Marshall, "The Child and the Hoopoe in Ancient Egypt," *KMT* 26/2 (2015), 62.

[3] C. Roselaar, "*Upupa epops* Hoopoe," in S. Camp (ed.), *Handbook of the Birds of Europe the Middle East and North Africa: The Birds of the Western Palearctic*, Volume 4: *Terns to Woodpeckers* (Oxford-New York, 1985), 791.

[4] A. David, "Hoopoes and Acacias: Decoding an Ancient Egyptian Funerary Scene," *JNES* 73/2 (2014), 249.

Journal of the American Research Center in Egypt 56 (2020), 101–114
doi: http://dx.doi.org/10.5913/jarce.56.2020.a007

Fig. 1. Hoopoe with large curved beak, crest folded, and square tail. Photograph by author.

Fig. 2. Hoopoe with crest fanned. Photograph by author.

they also often appear in fishing, fowling, and marsh scenes. This is despite the fact that papyrus swamps are not their normal habitat, preferring instead bare or open ground on which to forage.[5]

Adults Who Hold Hoopoes in Old Kingdom Art

There are a substantial number of representations of Old Kingdom adults, both male and female, holding hoopoes that demonstrates to the contrary that they are not held just by children, as inferred by Keimer and asserted by Marshall. Keimer says that hoopoes have a special link to children, and he cites nine examples of boys holding hoopoes from the Old Kingdom.[6] Houlihan however, says "the species is routinely pictured in Old Kingdom art being clutched in the hands of children, who typically are shown standing at their parents' side holding the bird by its wings, just as Nefer's daughter does with her Lapwing."[7] Marshall, referring to the Old Kingdom, asserts that "the hoopoe is one of the most common birds associated with children—even though no adult is ever seen with this bird."[8] There are at least eleven instances, however, where adults are depicted holding hoopoes in Old Kingdom scenes.

Contrary to what Marshall states, there is evidence that demonstrates hoopoes are held by tomb owners, wives, and attendants. Take for example, the five male tomb owners who hold hoopoes by the legs as decoy birds in fowling scenes in the tombs of Akhethotep,[9] Niankhkhnum,[10] Meru/Tetisoneb,[11] Hesi[12] and Khenty[13] (fig. 3). There is also evidence for three adult females who hold hoopoes. They include the wives of Merefnebef[14] and

---

[5] M. Pforr and A. Limbrunner, *The Breeding Birds of Europe 2: A Photographic Handbook* (London, 1982), 82.

[6] Keimer, "Quelques remarques sur la huppe," 308.

[7] P. Houlihan, *The Birds of Ancient Egypt* (Cairo, 1988), 120.

[8] A. Marshall, "L'enfant et la huppe dans l'Égypte antique," *Archéologia* 531 (April 2015), 32.

[9] H. Petrie and M. Murray, *Seven Memphite Tomb Chapels* (London, 1952), pl. 21.

[10] A. Moussa and H. Altenmüller, *Das Grab des Nianchchnum und Chnumhotep*, AV 21 (Mainz am Rhein, 1977), fig. 6.

[11] A. Lloyd, A. Spencer and A. el-Khouli, *Saqqara Tombs II: The Mastabas of Meru, Semdenti, Khui and Others* (London, 1990), pl. 6.

[12] N. Kanawati and M. Abder-Raziq, *The Teti Cemetery at Saqqara*, Volume 5: *The Tomb of Hesi*, ACE Reports 13 (Warminster, 1999), pl. 16.

[13] M. Saleh, *Three Old Kingdom Tombs at Thebes: I the Tomb of Unasankh No. 413, II the Tomb of Khenty No. 405, III the Tomb of Ihy No. 186*, AV 14 (Mainz am Rhein, 1977), pl. 12.

[14] K. Myśliwiec, K. Kuraszkiewicz, D. Czerwik et. al., *Saqqara I The Tomb of Merefnebef* (Warsaw, 2004), pl. 21.

Fig. 3. Tomb owner with hoopoe, tomb of Khenty. After M. Salah, Three Old-Kingdom Tombs at Thebes, *pl. 12, redrawn by L. Donovan.*

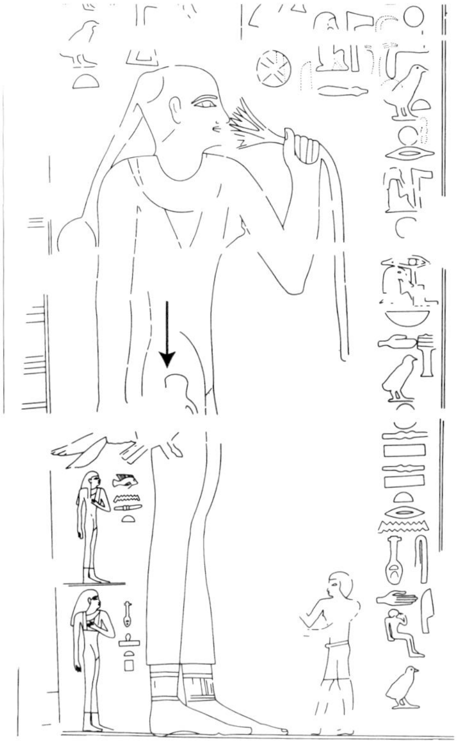

Fig. 4. Female with hoopoe, tomb of Idut. Kanawati and Abder-Raziq, The Unis Cemetery at Saqqara, Volume II: The Tombs of Iynefert and Ihy (reused by Idut), *pl. 62.*

Fig. 5. Attendant with hoopoe, tomb of Tjeti/Kaihep. Kanawati, The Rock Tombs of el-Hawawish: The Cemetery of Akhmim vol. 3, *fig. 13.*

Hewi/Tetiiker[15] who are depicted in fowling scenes, along with the female tomb owner, Idut/Seshseshet, in an inspection scene.[16] (fig. 4) Evidence of three attendants holding hoopoes in the fowling scenes are found in the

[15] Y. El-Masry, "Two Old Kingdom Rock-Tombs at Gohaina," *BACE* 15 (2004), fig. 2.

[16] N. Kanawati and M. Abder-Raziq, *The Unis Cemetery at Saqqara*, Volume II: *The Tombs of Iynefert and Ihy (reused by Idut)*, ACE Reports 19 (Oxford, 2003), pl. 62.

tombs of Mehu,[17] Niankhkhnum[18] and Tjeti/Kaihep[19] (fig. 5). Whilst Khuenre is another tomb owner who holds a hoopoe, he is shown as a young child in his tomb. He has his hand to his mother, Queen Kaemnebty's knee, and holds a hoopoe in his other hand.[20]

Girls Who Hold Hoopoes in Old Kingdom Art

Keimer and Marshall's findings can be challenged when a larger corpus, which includes both genders and considers all age brackets, is analysed. The evidence for young girls holding hoopoes will be considered first.-

Marshall concluded that the child-hoopoe association is almost exclusively male, and states that "the exceptional case of the two girls (or of the same girl figured twice) can be explained by the fact that they are on the walls of the mastaba of Meresankh III, at Giza, the only case of a tomb erected for a woman in this study."[21] The current survey found that while the majority of children holding hoopoes are male, there are five instances where four female children hold hoopoes (Table 1). Whilst there is only one image of a girl holding a hoopoe in the tomb of Meresankh, my research has identified four other examples:

- One girl holding a hoopoe, with no name and no stated relationship to the deceased, stands in the middle register behind the family scene in the tomb of Meresankh III.[22]
- A girl, similarly with no designation, holds a hoopoe in a group standing behind the fishing scene in the tomb of Hesi (fig. 6).[23]
- Merut, the daughter of Mehu, holds a hoopoe as she stands between her parents watching offering bearers, while the eldest son holds his father's staff.[24]

Fig. 6. Girl with hoopoe, tomb of Hesi. Kanawati and Abder-Raziq, The Teti Cemetery at Saqqara, Volume V: The Tomb of Hesi, *pl. 53.*

[17] Held by Iynefret, possibly Mehu's brother; H. Altenmüller, *Die Wanddarstellungen im Grab des Mehu in Saqqara,* AV 42 (Mainz am Rhein,1998), pl. 11.

[18] Held by hairdresser of the Great House Kaihersetef; Moussa and Altenmüller, *Das Grab des Nianchchnum und Chnumhotep*, fig. 6.

[19] Held by superintendent of painters Khewinptah, in N. Kanawati, *The Rock Tombs of El-Hawawish: The Cemetery of Akhmim,* vol. 3 (Sydney, 1982), fig. 13.

[20] G. Reisner, "The Servants of the Ka," *BMFA* 32/189 (1934), fig. 10.

[21] Marshall, "L'enfant et la huppe," 34–35.

[22] D. Dunham and W. Simpson, *The Mastaba of Queen Mersyankh III,* Giza Mastabas 1 (Boston, 1974), pl. 20d; Marshall records two naked girls with two arms lowered, right hand holding a hoopoe. There is only one naked girl recorded in the tomb, confirmed by personal inspection.

[23] Kanawati and Abder-Raziq, *The Tomb of Hesi*, pl. 15.

[24] Altenmüller, *Die Grab des Mehu,* pl. 53.

- Kedetes, the daughter of Insenefruishtef, holds a hoopoe in both the fishing and fowling scenes where she accompanies her parents and the eldest son (two scenes).[25]

The child-hoopoe association is not limited to sons, and in four of the five scenes where daughters hold hoopoes, the eldest son is present, but he does not hold a hoopoe as would be expected if the holding of a hoopoe designated the eldest son and heir.[26]

Boys Who Hold Hoopoes in Old Kingdom Art

It was important to identify the eldest son as his role varied from that of other children. In the Old Kingdom, the eldest son was the chronological eldest son and he was responsible for burying his parents and providing ongoing offerings.[27] He inherited all his parent's property unless an *jmyt-pr* document was signed and witnessed "to transfer property to someone other than the customary heir, namely the eldest (*smsw*) son."[28] He was also responsible for his siblings in the event of the death of his father.[29] These responsibilities and the proportion of property inherited changed over time.[30] Both men and women could own and bequeath property, and a child could inherit from both father and mother.[31] As divorce was not uncommon[32] and there was a high death rate amongst women in childbirth,[33] with the husbands often remarrying,[34] there was a need to identify eldest children from different wives. When more than one son is described as the eldest, it is as a result of the premature death of the eldest son with the next son taking over the responsibility,[35] the death or divorce of a wife and remarriage, polygamy,[36] or very rarely the sons being twins.[37]

---

[25] CG 1775; J. de Morgan, *Fouilles a Dahchour en 1894–1895* (Vienna, 1903), pl. 24.

[26] Scenes in the tombs of Meresankh, Insnefruishtef twice and Mehu. Mehu's eldest son holds a hoopoe in a different scene. Hesi's scene shows a son with a hoopoe but the inscription is a later addition.

[27] K. McCorquodale, "Reconsidering the Term 'Eldest Son/Eldest Daughter' and Inheritance in the Old Kingdom," *BACE* 23 (2012), 78–80.

[28] T. Logan, "The *Jmyt-pr* Document: Form, Function and Significance," *JARCE* 37 (2000), 67. Note the example of Nebsenet who transfers her land not to her son Metjen, but to her grandchildren; J. Johnson, "The Legal Status of Women in Ancient Egypt," in A. Capel and G. Markoe (eds.), *Mistress of the House, Mistress of Heaven: Women in Ancient Egypt* (New York, 1996), 177–78.

[29] By the Heracleopolitan Period the responsibility for orphans had passed to the nomarchs and by mid-Dynasty 12 it had passed to the community rather than the immediate family; K. Kóthay, "The Widow and Orphan in Egypt before the New Kingdom," *Acta antiqua Academiae scientiarium hungaricae* 46 (2006), 152.

[30] The roles of sons in funerary rites diminish in the Middle Kingdom see D. Franke, *Altägyptische Verwandtschaftsbezeichnungen im Mittleren Reich* (Hamburg, 1983), 175–76 and M. Nelson-Hurst, "The Increasing Emphasis on Collateral and Female Kin in the Late Middle Kingdom and Second Intermediate Period: The Vivification Formula as a Case Study," in M. Horn, J. Kramer, D. Soliman et al. (eds.), *Current Research in Egyptology 2010: Proceedings of the Eleventh Annual Symposium* (Oxford, 2011), 116.

[31] G. Robins, *Women in Ancient Egypt* (London, 1996), 127; Johnson, "The Legal Status of Women," 184.

[32] Robins, *Women in Ancient Egypt*, 62; Johnson, "The Legal Status of Women," 182. Note the example of Seshemnefer II's mother; K. McCorquodale, "Multiple Marriages and Polygamy in the Old Kingdom," in P. Piacentini and A. Castelli (eds.), *Old Kingdom Art and Archaeology 7 Proceedings of the International Conference Università Degli Studi di Milano 3–7 July 2017,* Edal 7 (Milan, 2019), 277.

[33] C. Graves-Brown, *Dancing for Hathor Women in Ancient Egypt* (London, 2010), 61–62, 69; Watterson compares the maternal death rate to that of rural England between the Sixteenth and Eighteenth centuries, where it has been calculated that for every thousand baptisms, twenty-five mothers died; B. Watterson, *Women in Ancient Egypt* (New York, 1991), 85.

[34] Note the example of Henqu/Iy[...]f at Deir el-Gebrawi; McCorquodale, "Multiple Marriages and Polygamy," 276. Women also remarried. Note the example of Senti who married Khuwi after the death of her husband Tjeti. She is shown with her four children described as "her son/daughter" in the tomb of her second husband. Both husbands travelled to Byblos and Punt on an expedition. She and her eldest daughter are also shown in the tomb of her first husband; K. McCorquodale, *Representations of the Family in the Egyptian Old Kingdom: Women and Marriage* (Oxford, 2013), 116.

[35] Note the examples of the two eldest sons of Henu and Ty; McCorquodale, "Multiple Marriages and Polygamy," 278; McCorquodale, *Representations of the Family,* 96–97.

[36] Note the example of Niankhre; McCorquodale, "Multiple Marriages and Polygamy," 275–76; N. Kanawati, "The Mentioning of more than one 'eldest' child in Old Kingdom inscriptions," *CdE* 51 (1976), 248–51.

[37] Note the possible example of the two eldest sons of Bawi, CG 20504; McCorquodale, "Reconsidering Eldest Son/Eldest Daughter," 83; McCorquodale, "Multiple Marriages and Polygamy," 278, n39.

Table 1. Children who hold hoopoes

Tomb Owner	Eldest Son/s	Younger Son/s	No Position Son/s	Not a Son	Inscription	Iconography	Daughter	P & M Reference
Meresankh III		✓				✓	✓	III1 197-9
Nebemakhti			✓					III1 230-2
G 5030			✓					III1 145
Seshathetep/Heti			✓					III1 149-50
Nikaure		✓			✓			III2 697
Khenukai			✓					IV 133
Ptahshepses		✓✓			✓			III2 340-2
Khufukhufuf [II]	✓				✓			III1 190-1
Niankhkhnum	✓				✓			III2 641-4
Khnumhotep	✓✓				✓			III2 641-4
Hetepherakhti	✓✓✓ / ✓?				✓			III2 593-5
Ankhemkai		✓			✓			III2 481
Raemkai	✓	✓				✓		III2 487-8
Kaiemankh	✓				✓			III1 131-3
Kaisabi			✓					Abusir
Akhethotep D 64	× / ✓				✓			III2 598-600
Ptahhotep D 64	✓ / ✓				✓			III2 600-5
Neferiretnef		✓ / ✓				✓		III2 583-4
Akhethotep E 17		✓			✓			III2 633-4
Hetepniptah	✓					✓		III1 94-5
Senedjemib/ Mehi		✓			✓			III1 87-9
Nikauhor	✓	✓			✓			III2 498
Hetepka			✓					III2 447-8
Sekhemka		✓	✓ / ✓			✓		III1 221-2
Ankhmasaef		✓			✓			III1 246
Hemminu			✓					V 19
Mereruka/Meri / Waatetkhethor	× / ✓✓✓✓✓✓			✓	✓	✓		III2 525-35
Hesi			✓✓				✓	Saqqara
Mereri	×✓	✓			✓			III2 518
Insenefruishtef							✓✓	III2 891-2
Mehu	✓				✓		✓	III2 619-22
Niankhnefertem/ Temi		✓			✓			Saqqara
Akhetmehu	✓				✓			III1 87
Bia/Ireri		✓			✓			III2 623
Hermeru/Mereri		✓				✓		III2 626

When Marshall looked at young children who hold hoopoes in the Old Kingdom, she concluded that "the image of a child holding a hoopoe is an iconographic code that conveyed symbolism linked to succession."[38] That is, "a hoopoe firmly held in hand implicitly designates the father's successor."[39] However, my wider survey and analysis of the results does not support this assertion.

Marshall's study looked at forty-six scenes on the walls of twenty-seven mastabas, but only considered very young, naked children holding hoopoes, with two exceptions.[40] In contrast, the current study which surveyed all descendants of the tomb owner, not just those shown as very young children, has identified fifty-seven scenes of children holding hoopoes in thirty-four tombs and reveals very different results (see Table 1).[41] Ten of Marshall's examples were excluded from this study as they either showed lapwings or golden orioles, the birds were unable to be clearly identified or scenes were duplications which later publications clarified, one showed the tomb owner as a child.[42]

The relationship between the hoopoe and young boys has been associated with the paternal relationship between the father and his eldest son,[43] however, this is not correct in every instance. While most children who hold hoopoes are the children of the tomb owner, in the tomb of Mereruka, a scene of catching songbirds (golden orioles) with hand-set traps, shows naked boys walking away with birds in hand, the second one holds a golden oriole and a hoopoe. He is not a son of Mereruka (fig. 7).[44]

Marshall asserted that holding a hoopoe designated the child as the eldest son who was the heir; while noting that her sample is quite small she says that of 148 boys with a filial designation, forty-eight are referred to as "eldest son" and of these eleven held a hoopoe, which is nearly one child out of four.[45] A previous, broader study of Old Kingdom tombs by the author, recorded 789 boys with a filial designation, 200 were referred to as eldest and of these only fifteen held a hoopoe.[46] This is a much smaller proportion of just over one in thirteen eldest sons holding a hoopoe. In sixty-eight other instances, the eldest son held another type of bird, in twenty-six instances it was a goose, far more frequent than the fifteen who hold a hoopoe.

Of the fifty-seven recorded scenes of children holding hoopoes in this study, one is not a child of the tomb owner and five are females. This leaves fifty-one scenes where sons hold hoopoes but only forty-one individual sons hold hoopoes, as some are shown more than once with the bird.[47] To test whether the holding of a hoopoe symbolises that they are the eldest and therefore the one to inherit, it is important to establish the chronological position of these forty-one individual boys amongst the sons of the tomb owners.

It is possible to identify whether a child is the eldest by either the inscription "his eldest son" (*sꜣ=f smsw*) or the iconography. In a former study of sixty-four Old Kingdom scenes where only one child in a group of children was described as "eldest":

- the eldest was always depicted as larger or of equal size, never smaller;
- the eldest was always shown wearing a kilt when other children wore kilts;
- the eldest was only shown as a naked child when all other children were naked;
- the eldest was in the most prominent position, being first in a line of children and

[38] Marshall, "L'enfant et la huppe," 35; Marshall, "The Child and the Hoopoe in Ancient Egypt," 6.

[39] Marshall, "The Child and the Hoopoe in Ancient Egypt," 63.

[40] One depiction of Mereruka's son and the boy in Hesi's tomb, both of whom wear kilts.

[41] Another possible instance is a relief from the tomb of Weta at Giza which shows him standing with his son Weta behind him. He is described as "Knab mit Wiedehopf (?)" but as this could not be confirmed it was not included in the data; CG 1479; Borchardt, *CG 1294-1803*, 166.

[42] I would like to thank Dr. Marshall who graciously supplied a list of the scenes she examined.

[43] Marshall ("The Child and the Hoopoe in Ancient Egypt," 60), states, "Let us consider the identity of the children. That they are the mastaba owner's son or daughter can be inferred by the context and possibly confirmed by the designation "his son/daughter."" See also, Marshall, "L'enfant et la huppe," 34.

[44] N. Kanawati, A. Woods, S. Shafik et al., *Mereruka and His Family, Part III:2 The Tomb of Mereruka*, ACE Reports 30 (Oxford, 2011), pl. 76.

[45] Marshall, "The Child and the Hoopoe in Ancient Egypt," 62.

[46] K. McCorquodale, *Representations of the Family*, 87, Table A.

[47] Ptahshepses shows the same son twice, Khnumhotep shows the same son twice, Hetepherakhty shows the same son three times, and Mereruka shows the same son twice in his chapel and four times in his wife's chapel. Hesi shows a boy behind both the fishing and the fowling scenes, he is possibly the same son.

Fig. 7. Child not of tomb owner with hoopoe, tomb of Mereruka. Kanawati, Woods, Shafik et al., Mereruka and His Family Part III: 2 The Tomb of Mereruka, *pl. 76.*

- the eldest held higher or equal titles than the other children, never lesser ones.[48]

Using either the inscription "eldest son" or the above iconographic criteria, it was possible to determine the chronological position of thirty-one of the sons who hold hoopoes. (See Table 1: columns labelled Inscription and Iconography) In ten instances it was not possible to determine the position of the son in the family hierarchy.[49]

Where it was not possible to establish the position of the son, it remains unclear if the son who holds the hoopoe was the eldest son or a younger son. This is the case in the scenes in the tombs of Nebemakhti,[50] G 5030,[51] Seshathetep/Heti,[52] Khenukai,[53] Kaisabi,[54] Hetepka,[55] Shekhemka (two sons),[56] Hemminu[57] and Hesi (two scenes).[58]

Examination of the chronological position of the remaining thirty-one individual sons revealed that in fifteen instances the son who holds the hoopoe was the eldest son and in sixteen instances the son who holds the hoopoe was a younger son, i.e., not the eldest son. The placement of scenes in which sons did and did not hold hoopoes was also revealing.

---

[48] McCorquodale, "Reconsidering the Term 'Eldest Son/Eldest Daughter,'" 78–80.

[49] This was due to lack of inscription, lack of comparable depictions or due to the son being shown alone rather than with siblings.

[50] S. Hassan, *Excavations at Giza The Mastabas of the Sixth Season and Their Decoration, vol. 4-part 3, 1934–1935* (Cairo, 1950), fig. 95.

[51] C. Lepsius, *Denkmäler aus Aegypten und Aethiopien: Ergänzungsband* (Leipzig, 1913), 29; Giza Archives Photo No A7179_NS.jpg (accessed 30/07/2018).

[52] While Junker says holding a hoopoe and Keimer says the hoopoe's crest is folded and the beak too short, recent publication by Kanawati shows what may be a lapwing. H. Junker, *Giza 2 Grabungen auf dem Friedhof des Alten Reiches: Die Mastabas der beginnenden V. Dynastie auf dem Westfriedhof* (Vienna-Leipzig, 1934), 184, pl. 15a, fig. 28; Keimer, "Quelques remarques sur la huppe," 309; N. Kanawati, *Tombs at Giza, Volume II: Seshathetep/Heti (G5150), Nesutnefer (G4970) and Seshemnefer (G5080),* ACE Reports 18 (Warminster, 2002), pls. 8, 45.

[53] This scene has now disappeared; G. Fraser, "The Early Tombs at Tehnah," *ASAE* 3 (1902), 75.

[54] V. Duliková, L. Jirásková, H. Vymazalová et al., "The Tombs of Kaisebi (AS 76) and Ptahwer (AS 76b)," *Prague Egyptological Studies* 19 (2017), fig. 4.

[55] G. Martin, *The Tomb of Hetepka and Other Reliefs and Inscriptions from the Sacred Animal Necropolis North Saqqara 1964–73* (London, 1979), pl. 7 [2].

[56] H. Junker, *Giza 11 Grabungen auf dem Friedhof des Alten Reiches: Der Friedhof südlich der Cheopspyramide* (Vienna, 1953), figs. 18, 19; Giza Archives Photo No: o-neg-nr_0135, AEOS 1150971.jpg (accessed 30/07/2018).

[57] N. Kanawati, *The Rock Tombs of el-Hawawish: The Cemetery of Akhmim,* vol. 5 (Sydney, 1985), fig. 9.

[58] Kanawati and Abder-Raziq, *The Tomb of Hesi,* pls. 15, 16, 53, 54. The first boy in the bottom register behind the fishing scene holds two geese and a hoopoe, he is named as his son Khewi but this is a later addition. The first boy in the middle register behind the fowling scene holds three geese and a hoopoe. There is no inscription, but this is probably the same individual as in both instances he is the first in a line of figures wearing sidelocks.

Younger Sons Who Hold Hoopoes

The recent analysis demonstrated that thirteen of the sixteen younger sons who hold hoopoes do so while the eldest son is shown without a hoopoe in the same scene (nine examples) or in a complementary scene, such as fishing and fowling or left and right jambs of the entrance door (four examples). Nine younger sons hold hoopoes, while the eldest son in the same scene does not. These are listed below and directly contradict the assertion that a child who holds a hoopoe is the eldest son.

- In a family scene, Meresankh III's younger son Kheterka holds a hoopoe and a lotus while her eldest son Nebemakhet does not.[59]
- On the false door of Nikaure's wife Ihat, a younger son Ptahshepses holds a hoopoe aloft on the bottom of the left inner jamb while the eldest son Sekhemka holds a pigeon on the left panel and a golden oriole on the right outer jamb.[60]
- On Ankhemkai's false door, his younger son Inkaef holds his father's staff and a hoopoe on the left outer jamb, while his eldest son Seshemnefer holds only his father's staff on the right outer jamb.[61]
- Standing between Senedjemib/Mehi and his wife, a younger son Mehi holds a hoopoe and a duck, while the eldest son Senedjemib stands in front and holds only his father's staff. They are viewing marsh and agricultural pursuits.[62]
- Niankhnefertem/Temi has a series of images of himself with various family members. One of his younger sons Mereri holds his father's staff and a hoopoe while his eldest son Meruka holds only his father's staff.[63]
- In Mereri's fishing scene he is followed by his younger son Haishtef who holds a hoopoe and lotus and his eldest son Mereri who holds two ducks.[64]
- A block from the tomb of Bia/Ireri shows a younger son Khai who stands in front of his parents and holds a hoopoe and a duck while the eldest son faces them censing.[65]
- Similarly, a young naked son touches Hermeru/Mereri's waist and holds a hoopoe while two older brothers face the family and one censes and the other presents a goose.[66]
- In an inspection scene Ptahshepses's younger son Hemakhty holds a hoopoe and lotus, while his eldest son Ptahshepses holds his father's staff and a lapwing.[67] On the opposite wall in another inspection scene, again it is the younger son who holds a hoopoe and also the staff, while the eldest son holds the staff and a lapwing (two scenes) (fig. 8).[68]

In three complementary scenes, four younger sons hold hoopoes, while the eldest son does not.

- Akhethetep's younger son Pehernefer holds a hoopoe in the fowling scene while in the fishing scene his eldest son Khure does not.[69]

---

[59] Dunham and Simpson, *Queen Mersyankh III*, pls. 7c, 20d, fig. 7; See Y. Harpur, *Decoration in Egyptian Tombs of the Old Kingdom: Studies in Orientation and Scene Content*, Stud Egypt 14 (London-New York, 1987), 249–50 for a discussion of Khenterka's identification as her son.

[60] CG 1414; A. el Shahawy and F. Atiya, *The Egyptian Museum in Cairo: A Walk Through the Alleys of Ancient Egypt* (Cairo, 2005), No. 56, 88–91.

[61] CG 1485; Borchardt, vol. 1, *CG 1295–1808*, pl. 40.

[62] E. Brovarski, *The Senedjemib Complex, Part I The Mastabas of Senedjemib Inti (G 2370), Khnumenti (G 2374) and Senedjemib Mehi (G 2378)*, Giza Mastabas 7 (Boston, 2000), pl. 115, fig. 115.

[63] K. Myśliwiec, "Father's and Eldest Son's Overlapping Feet: An Iconographic Message," in Z. Hawass, P. Der Manuelian and R. Hussein (eds.), *Studies in Honor of Edward Brovarski* (Cairo, 2010), fig. 3.

[64] The eldest son Mereri holds his father's staff and a hoopoe on the east wall of room 1; W. Davies, A. el-Khouli, A. Lloyd et al., *Saqqâra Tombs 1: The Mastabas of Mereri and Wernu* (London, 1984), pls. 5, 8.

[65] J. Wilson, "A Group of Sixth Dynasty Inscriptions," *JNES* 13 (1954), pl. 18a.

[66] Lintel of the façade; S. Hassan, *Mastabas of Princess Hemet-Re and Others Excavations at Saqqara, 1937–1938* vol. 3 (Cairo, 1975), pl. 56a.

[67] M. Verner, *Abusir I The Mastaba of Ptahshepses* (Prague, 1977), photos 49, 51, pl. 31.

[68] Verner, *Abusir I The Mastaba of Ptahshepses*, photo 64, pl. 38.

[69] E 17; Petrie and Murray, *Memphite Tomb Chapels*, pl. 6.

Fig. 8. Younger son with hoopoe, eldest son without, in the same scene, tomb of Ptahshepses. After Verner, Abusir I: The Mastaba of Ptahshepses, *pl. 38. Redrawn by L. Donovan.*

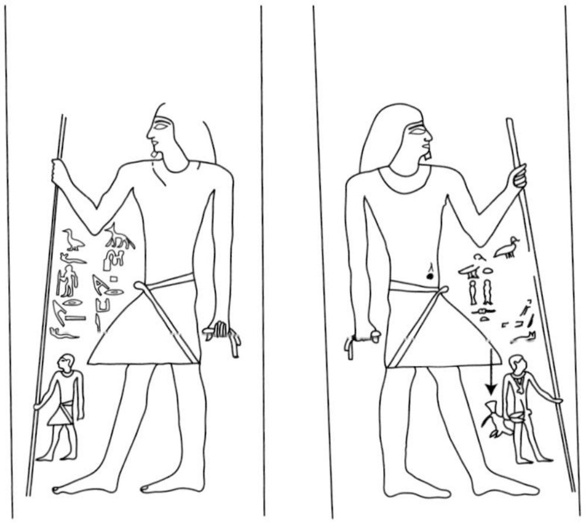

Fig. 9. Younger son with hoopoe, eldest son without, complimentary scenes, tomb of Ankhmasaf. After S. Hassan, Excavations at Giza: The Mastabas of the Sixth Season and their Decoration, *Vol. 6, Part 3. 1934–1935 (Cairo, 1950), figs. 144, 145. Redrawn by L. Donovan.*

- In the fishing scene, Neferirtenef's third and fourth sons both hold hoopoes, while in the fowling scene his eldest son and second son do not.[70]
- On the right entrance thickness, Ankhmasaef's younger son Hesetakhti holds his father's staff and a hoopoe, while on the opposite thickness his eldest son Merkai holds his father's staff but has no hoopoe (fig. 9).[71]

If the holding of a hoopoe designates the child as the eldest as Marshall states, these younger sons should not be holding hoopoes. It should be the eldest sons who hold them, but they appear in the scenes yet do not hold hoopoes. Of the sixteen individual younger sons holding hoopoes, thirteen of them are shown in scenes where the eldest son is present but does not hold a hoopoe.[72]

Eldest Sons Who Hold Hoopoes

To determine whether the holding of a hoopoe indicates that the son is the eldest, the scenes where eldest sons do hold hoopoes also need to be analyzed. While eldest sons hold hoopoes in twenty-three scenes, they are held by only fifteen individual eldest sons (some are shown multiple times).[73] Of these fifteen eldest sons who hold hoopoes, in three instances other younger sons also hold hoopoes. In five instances, the eldest son is one of two eldest sons shown in the tomb. In only seven instances does only one eldest son hold a hoopoe and no younger son holds a hoopoe (See Table 1).

Both eldest and younger sons hold hoopoes in the following three tombs:

[70] B. van de Walle, *La chapelle funéraire de Neferirtenef aux Musées Royaux d'Art et d'Histoire à Bruxelles (Brussels, 1978)*, pl. 1.

[71] Hassan, *Excavations at Giza* vol. 4, part 3, figs. 144, 145, pl. 64b.

[72] The younger son Hemakhi is shown twice in the tomb of Ptahshepses at Abusir.

[73] Knumhotep's eldest son holds a hoopoe twice; Hetepherahkti's eldest son holds a hoopoe three times; Mereruka's eldest son holds a hoopoe six times.

Fig. 10. Eldest and younger son both with hoopoes, tomb of Nikauhor. After Quibell, Excavations at Saqqara (1907–1908), *pl. 63, redrawn by L. Donovan.*

- Nikauhor's eldest son Kainefer holds his father's staff and a hoopoe on the left jamb of the false door as does the younger son Nikauhor on the right jamb (fig. 10).[74]
- Raemkai's eldest son stands in front of him and holds his father's staff and a hoopoe, while a younger, smaller son stands behind him and holds his father's leg and a hoopoe.[75]
- In an offering scene Mereri's eldest son holds a hoopoe but in the fishing scene (already discussed) the younger son holds a hoopoe while the eldest son does not.[76]
- Additionally, Sekhemka is shown three separate times standing with a naked child who holds his staff and a hoopoe. Two of the sons are named as Ini and Kaiemnefer.[77] While it is not possible to determine whether either of these sons was the eldest, the third child (with no inscription), who also holds his father's staff and a hoopoe, is probably younger than the other two because he wears the sidelock of youth while his two older brothers have short hair.

In five instances where the eldest son holds a hoopoe, there is more than one son designated as the "eldest." This occurs in four chapels, and these scenes warrant closer examination to determine if holding a hoopoe indicates that one eldest son is chronologically older than the other eldest son.

- On both the left and right entrance façade, Hetepherakhti's eldest son, Niankhptah is shown as a naked child who holds his father's staff and a hoopoe.[78] According to Mohr, he is shown twice in the fishing scene, both in front and behind his father.[79] However, it is very unusual for a child to be shown twice in the same scene. The fact that the child behind the tomb owner is smaller, reaching only to the first child's shoulder, seems to indicate that that these are different eldest sons with the same name: this is attested in several tombs in the Old Kingdom.[80] The first child holds a bird and a hoopoe, while the second smaller son holds a bird and second bird whose head is damaged, but its tail, legs, and body

74 Southern false door; J. Quibell, *Excavations at Saqqara (1907–1908)* (Cairo, 1909), pl. 63; https://www.metmuseum.org/art/collection/search/543914 (accessed 20/07/2018).

75 East wall; www.metmuseum.org/art/collection/search/590874 (accessed 20/07/2018).

76 Davies, el-Khouli, Lloyd et al., *Mereri and Wernu*, pls. 8, 9.

77 Junker, *Giza 11*, figs. 18, 19; Giza Archives Photo No: o-neg-nr_0135 and AEOS_11_5097_1.jpg (accessed 25/07/2018).

78 H. Mohr, *The Mastaba of Hetep-her-akhti: Study on an Egyptian Tomb Chapel in the Museum of Antiquities Leiden* (Leiden, 1943), figs. on 34–35; N. van de Beek, "Herta Mohr and the Mastaba of Hetepherakhty," in V. Verschoor, A. Stuart, and C. Demarée (eds.), *Imaging and Imagining the Memphite Necropolis Liber Amicorum René van Walsem* (Leiden, 2017), figs. 1, 3.

79 Mohr, *The Mastaba of Hetep-her-akhti*, 64–65, fig. 34.

80 Nikauisesi has three sons named Nikauisesi; Mery-aa at el-Hargarsa has three sons named Nenu born to different wives and five daughters named Shemat born to three different wives; Ankhmahor has probably three sons named Ishfi.

shape are the same as the first son's hoopoe. It is possible that there are two boys with the same name who are shown separately on either side of the entrance façade, as well as in the fishing scene, both holding hoopoes.

- Akhethotep's eldest son Ptahhotep holds his father's staff and a hoopoe as they view the works in the field.[81] This son has the title "Royal Chamberlain." Kanawati analysed the images of the eldest son and the associated titles and concluded that there were two eldest sons with the name Ptahhotep, but that they had different titles.[82] According to his titles, the eldest son who holds the hoopoe is Thefew with the good name Ptahhotep. Twice he is placed behind the other eldest son Ptahhotep, who holds the higher title of "Juridicial Overseer of Scribes." The Ptahhotep who holds the hoopoe is probably a younger son from a different wife.[83] The adjacent chapel belongs to the older of the sons named Ptahhotep, not the one holding the hoopoe.
- In the adjacent chapel of Ptahhotep on the northern half of the east wall, Ptahhotep stands viewing boats and the netting of birds. In front of him, holding his father's staff and a hoopoe is his eldest son Ptahhotep.[84] On the southern half of the same wall, Ptahhotep stands viewing the bringing of cattle and birds. In front holding his father's staff and a hoopoe and a pigeon, stands his other eldest son Akhethotep.[85] While both sons are referred to as "his eldest son" and they bear the same title "Inspector of Canals," Akhethotep appears on the southern half of the wall, that is behind the image of his father and Ptahhotep. Both sons are naked with the sidelock of youth but the son Ptahhotep has a locket in addition to the collars they both wear. This may indicate that Ptahhotep was the first born of the two eldest sons, probably to different wives, but they both hold hoopoes.
- The chapels of Mereruka and his second wife, princess Waatethethor/Seshseshet, have six representations of their son Meryteti where he holds a hoopoe.[86] Mereruka had another eldest son from his earlier marriage, and this son, Memi, who later changed his name to Pepyankh, is shown supporting his father.[87] He was the older of the two eldest sons but he is not shown holding a hoopoe.

Examination of the four tombs where more than one eldest son is shown in the tomb, does not support the idea that holding a hoopoe designated the chronological eldest son. The eldest son in Hetepherakhti's chapel holds a hoopoe, but a younger eldest son of the same name may also hold a hoopoe; Akhethotep's eldest son holds a hoopoe, but he is the younger of the two eldest sons; both eldest sons of Ptahhotep hold hoopoes; Mereruka's eldest son holds hoopoes, but he is the younger of the two eldest sons. The holding of a hoopoe does not seem to favor one eldest son over another, particularly as Akhethotep's eldest son who holds the hoopoe is not only younger but also has a lesser title.

This only leaves seven eldest sons from thirty-one sons holding hoopoes where the holding of a hoopoe could indicate that they were the eldest son and should inherit. This occurred in the following tombs.

- Khufukhuf [II]'s eldest son holds his father's staff and a hoopoe as they observe the bringing of cattle, wild beasts, offering bearers and dancers.[88]
- Kaiemankh's eldest son holds a harpoon and a hoopoe in the fishing scene (fig. 11).[89]

---

[81] West wall of the corridor D 64; N. de G. Davies, *The Mastaba of Ptahhetep and Akhethetep at Saqqara Part 2: The Mastaba. The Sculptures of Akhethetep* (London, 1901), pls. 6 and 26; https://osirisnet.net/popupImage.php?img=/mastabas/akhethtp_ptahhtp/photo/akhethtp_02_jb.jpg&lang=en&sw=1920&sh=1080 (accessed 3/03/2019).

[82] Kanawati, "The Mentioning of More Than One 'Eldest' Child," 235–37.

[83] Kanawati, "The Mentioning of More Than One 'Eldest' Child," 237. Both sons also hold the titles "Overseer of the Pyramid Town of Izezi" and "Staff of the Rekhyet People."

[84] R. Paget, A. Pirie and F. L. Griffith, *The Tomb of Ptah-hetep* (London, 1896), pl. 31.

[85] Paget, Pirie and Griffith, *Ptah-hetep*, pl. 30.

[86] N. Kanawati, A. Woods, S. Shafik, et al., *Mereruka and His Family, Part 3:1: The Tomb of Mereruka*, ACE Reports 29 (Oxford, 2010), pls. 35b, 29a; N. Kanawati, M. Abder-Raziq, *Mereruka and His Family, Part 2: The Tomb of Waatetkhethor*, ACE Reports 26 (Oxford, 2008), pls. 3, 4a, 20, 21a, 32a, 50.

[87] North wall of room A13; Kanawati, Woods, Shafik et al., *Mereruka and His Family, Part 3:2: The Tomb of Mereruka*, 75, pl. 13.

[88] W. Simpson, *Kawab, Khafkhufu I and II*, Giza Mastabas 3 (Boston, 1978), pl. 38a, fig. 48.

[89] N. Kanawati, *Tombs at Giza*, Volume I: *Kaiemankh (G4562) and Seshemnefer (G4940)*, ACE Reports 16 (Warminster, 2001), pl. 7b, fig. 31.

Fig. 11. Only the eldest son with hoopoe, tomb of Kaiemankh. Kanawati, Tombs at Giza, Volume I: Kaiemankh (G4562) and Seshemnefer (G4940)*, ACE Reports 16, fig. 31.*

- Hetepniptah's eldest son holds his father's staff and a hoopoe in a presentation scene.[90]
- Akhetmehu's eldest son holds his father's staff and a hoopoe in a family scene.[91]
- Mehu's eldest son holds his father's staff and a hoopoe in a boat in the papyrus thicket.[92]
- Niankhkhnum's eldest son holds a hoopoe and has a finger to his mouth in the fowling scene in the pillared portico.[93]
- Khnumhotep's eldest son holds a hoopoe and his father's staff on the southern wall of the second vestibule,[94] and he holds a hoopoe and his father's leg in the fishing scene on the west wall of the outer hall (two scenes).[95]

Conclusion

A close examination of the chronological position of sons who hold hoopoes in a larger corpus of Old Kingdom scenes does not support the assertion that a child holding a hoopoe indicated that they were the eldest son and therefore the heir of their deceased father. A more detailed examination of all sons who hold hoopoes revealed

[90] H. Altenmüller, "Das Grab des Hetepniptah (G 2430) auf dem Westfriedhof von Giza," *SAK* 9 (1981), fig. 6; Giza Archives photo no. A7722_NS (accessed 3/03/2019).

[91] Giza Archives photo no. A8402_NS (accessed 25/07/2018).

[92] Altenmüller, *Grab des Mehu*, pls. 9, 53. However, in another scene already discussed, his sister holds a hoopoe while he does not.

[93] Moussa and Altenmüller, *Nianchchnum und Chnumhotep*, fig. 6, pl. 5.

[94] Moussa and Altenmüller, *Nianchchnum und Chnumhotep*, fig. 21, pl. 51a.

[95] Moussa and Altenmüller, *Nianchchnum und Chnumhotep*, pl. 74.

that of the forty-one individual sons who hold hoopoes, the chronological position of thirty-one could be determined and of these, sixteen were younger sons and fifteen were eldest sons. Of the sixteen younger sons who hold hoopoes, thirteen of them are shown in scenes where the eldest son is present but does not hold a hoopoe. Of the fifteen eldest sons who hold hoopoes, in three cases other younger sons also hold hoopoes. In five cases, there is more than one eldest son present, and the holding of a hoopoe does not seem to indicate a hierarchy amongst them. Thus there are only seven individual eldest sons, from the thirty-one individual sons who hold hoopoes, where the holding of a hoopoe could possibly indicate that they are the eldest and heir. This small proportion, less than 23%, does not support the assertion.

The analysis of a larger database does not support Keimer's generalisation that children had a special link to hoopoes, as they more frequently hold geese. The results of Marshall's limited study of young naked children holding hoopoes is not supported by the broader study of all children of the tomb owner and a larger corpus. A thorough examination of the Old Kingdom evidence does not support the assertion that a son holding a hoopoe designates him as the eldest son and therefore the heir. In contrast, the review of Old Kingdom wall scenes demonstrates that hoopoes are held by adults as well as boys and girls. Girls often hold hoopoes when the eldest son does not. Moreover, in many instances it is the younger son who holds the hoopoe while the eldest son in the same scene does not. Clearly, a son holding a hoopoe in hand does not mean that he is the eldest son and therefore the heir. Eldest sons hold a variety of birds and often do not hold a hoopoe while a younger son does. This study highlights that a child holding a hoopoe is not symbolic as children hold many types of birds. Children hold all manner of birds—ducks,[96] geese,[97] pigeons,[98] golden orioles,[99] lapwings,[100] turtle doves[101] and kingfishers,[102] as well as hoopoes.

This study did not find any special symbolism associated with the holding of the hoopoe. Hoopoes are just distinctive, attractive birds that are among the large variety of birds that ancient Egyptians depict being held by both men and women and male and female children in the Old Kingdom (see Table 1).

---

[96] G. Steindorff, *Das Grab des Ti* (Leipzig, 1913), pl. 88, 94, 100.

[97] Davies, el-Khouli, Lloyd et al., *Mereri and Wernu*, pl. 31; N. Kanawati and M. Abder-Raziq, *Mereruka and His Family Part I: The Tomb of Meryteti*, ACE Reports 21 (Oxford, 2004), pls. 4, 45.

[98] Shahawy and Atiya, *The Egyptian Museum in Cairo*, No. 56, 88–91.

[99] Shahawy and Atiya, *The Egyptian Museum in Cairo*, No. 56, 88–91; Kanawati and Abder-Raziq, *The Tomb of Waatetkhethor*, 23, pl. 58; Kanawati says the bird is difficult to identify and may be a white wagtail or a dove.

[100] Y. Harpur and P. Scremin, *The Chapel of Nefer and Kahay Scene Details*, OEE 5 (Oxford, 2015), pls. 4, 277; N. Kanawati, *Tombs at Giza*, Volume 2: *Seshathetep/Heti (G5150), Nesutnefer (G4970) and Seshemnefer II (G5080)*, ACE Reports 18 (Warminster, 2002), pls. 20, 45.

[101] Steindorff, *Das Grab des Ti*, pls. 115, 130.

[102] Kanawati and Abder-Raziq, *The Tomb of Waatetkhethor*, pls. 47, 69; P. Kaplony, *Studien zum Grab des Methethi* (Bern, 1976), pls. 5, 6.

On the Pairs of Shafts in the Pyramid of Khufu as Means for the Ascent to the Akhet

LUCA MIATELLO
Como, Italy

Abstract

The shafts in the pyramid of Khufu have been investigated by robots in several projects. Mason's marks in red ink at the end of the southern shaft of the "Queen's Chamber" can be read as the hieratic number 121 (cubits), which would indicate the shaft's length. Precise measurements were planned for the pyramid superstructure and its architectural elements. This paper shows that the shafts represent paths of the solar circuit, which would have led the king's immaterial components to the akhet. The model is highly coherent, and all of its features are discussed, as the shape of the inner step pyramid, the sharp turns of 45° in the northern shafts, and the two metal pins inserted into a blocking slab at the end of each lower shaft.

ملخص

خضعت الممرات الضيقة داخل هرم خوفو للدراسة والفحص باستخدام روبوتات في مشاريع عدة. ويمكن قراءة العلامات المعمارية المسجلة بالحبر الأحمر في نهاية الممر الجنوبي بالغرفة المعروفة باسم «غرفة الملكة» باعتبارها تمثل الرقم 121 (ذراعًا) بالكتابة الهيراطيقية، وهو ما قد يشير إلى طول الممر. وأُجريت قياساتٌ دقيقةٌ للبناء العلوي للهرم ولعناصره المعمارية. تُبين هذه المقالة أن هذه الممرات تمثل مسارات مدار الشمس التي كانت تقود العناصر غير المادية للملك إلى الأفق «آخت». وهذا النموذج مترابطٌ للغاية وتُناقش معالمه كافة هنا، مثل شكل الهرم المدرج الداخلي، والمنعطفات الحادة عند 45 درجة في الممرات الشمالية، والوتدين المعدنيين المدخلين في كتلة حجرية حاجزة عند نهاية كل ممر سفلي.

The two pairs of shafts in the pyramid of Khufu, whose horizontal sections are carved in the northern and southern walls of the "Queen's Chamber" and the King's Chamber, have been investigated by robots in three projects: Upuaut (1992–1993); Pyramid Rover (2001); Djedi (2010).[1] Each shaft is very narrow, only about 22 cm (= 3 palms) in height and 22 cm in width.

Clearly, the term "air shafts," with which these ducts are occasionally identified, is incorrect, as the inlets to the Queen's Chamber were closed by a stone, and their upper ends are located within the superstructure, several meters from the pyramid's faces. Furthermore, the upper ends of the shafts of the King's chamber were probably covered by the original limestone casing.

The Upuaut project was the result of a collaboration between the Egyptian Supreme Council of Antiquities (SCA) and the German Institute of Archaeology in Cairo (DAIK), to study and clear the shafts. In 1992, the robot Upuaut 1, equipped with remote control and video camera, was able to travel only about 9 meters inside

[1] On these projects: Zahi Hawass, Shaun Whitehead, TC Ng, Robert Richardson, Andrew Pickering, Stephen Rhodes, Ron Grieve, Adrian Hildred, Mehdi Tayoubi and Richard Breitner, "First Report: Video Survey of the Southern Shaft of the Queen's Chamber in the Great Pyramid," *ASAE* 84 (2010), 203–16.

Journal of the American Research Center in Egypt 56 (2020), 115–141
doi: http://dx.doi.org/10.5913/jarce.56.2020.a008

each of the shafts of the Queen's Chamber. In 1993, a second robot with remote control, Upuaut 2, performed video inspections of the shafts of the King's Chamber, whose outlets are located nowadays at the 102th course of the south face, and at the 101th course of the north face. [2] At about 6 meters from the present exit point of the south shaft, the camera revealed a peculiar feature: two niches are carved on the shaft's walls.[3] Stadelmann suggested that they could have hosted a blocking slab.[4] This hypothesis is unlikely, as the niche in the western wall is longer, extending to the end of the block. It is more likely that this block was originally constructed as the final section of the shaft, to host a blocking slab, but it was installed in the wrong place. The master builder noticed the error and ordered the removal of the slab, which was performed by enlarging one recess on the wall.

The robot traveled about 19 meters along the north shaft of the Queen's Chamber; it could not advance further, hampered by a sharp turn of 45 degrees. Its exploration of the south shaft was initially blocked after about 57 meters by a small step. After several attempts, the robot could pass over it, reaching a blocking stone. Images revealed the presence of two metal pins inserted into the stone and bent down vertically against its face.[5]

In 2001, a collaboration of the SCA with National Geographic led to the building of the robot Pyramid Rover, equipped with video cameras and echo-impactor, rubber tracks to grip the floor and ceiling of the channels, and linked to the controller computer with a cable. Its aim was to acquire information on the purpose of the blocking slab with metal pins in the south shaft of the Queen's Chamber, and to explore entirely the north shaft.

In the first phase, the robot traveled up to the blocking slab of the southern shaft. The camera revealed the smooth face of the slab, whose color is lighter than the shaft's walls, and traces of mortar at its base. Exploring the northern shaft, the robot could manage the westward turn of 45 degrees, after which it followed two turns in the opposite direction, at 22 and 25 meters from the entrance. At 27 meters, it was blocked by two metal rods.

In a second stage, a small hole was drilled into the blocking slab of the south shaft, which is about 6 cm thick, in order to insert a camera with light. The camera revealed the presence of a second blocking stone, at about 18 cm from the first one. Resuming the exploration of the northern shaft of the Queen's Chamber, the robot reached, at about 63 meters from the entrance, a blocking stone with two pins, similar to the one at the end of the southern shaft.

A later collaboration of the SCA with the Leeds University resulted in the construction of the robot Djedi, which in 2010 was able to inspect carefully the space beyond the blocking stone of the southern lower shaft, measuring 19 cm in length, 23 cm in width, and 23 cm in height. [6] Photos of the floor taken with a snake camera were assembled in composite pictures.[7]

A 3D drawing of the end of the shaft, with the blocking slab and the final blocking stone, is shown in figure 1a. Each shaft was built in its oblique section by aligning one after another inverted-U elements on top of flat base blocks.[8] The opposite arrangement characterizes the horizontal sections of the shafts, carved across the limestone walls of the Queen's Chamber and the granite walls of the King's Chamber. Crevices are made on the upper surface of the blocks, on top of which are normal blocks with flat faces (fig. 2).[9]

Important discoveries were made by the Djedi project:

---

[2] See Rainer Stadelmann and Rudolf Gantenbrink, "Die sogenannten Luftkanäle der Cheopspyramide Modelkorridore für den Aufstieg des Königs zum Himmel," *MDAIK* 50 (1994), 285–94.

[3] See Stadelmann and Gantenbrink, "Die sogenannten Luftkanäle der Cheopspyramide Modelkorridore für den Aufstieg des Königs zum Himmel," 285, 287, fig. 2.

[4] Stadelmann and Gantenbrink, "Die sogenannten Luftkanäle der Cheopspyramide Modelkorridore für den Aufstieg des Königs zum Himmel," 289.

[5] The green color of the pins indicates that they are probably made of copper.

[6] On these measures: Hawass, Whitehead et al., "First Report: Video Survey of the Southern Shaft of the Queen's Chamber in the Great Pyramid," 208.

[7] Hawass, Whitehead et al., "First Report: Video Survey of the Southern Shaft of the Queen's Chamber in the Great Pyramid," 203 fig. 1.

[8] Hawass, Whitehead et al., "First Report: Video Survey of the Southern Shaft of the Queen's Chamber in the Great Pyramid," 207 fig. 3.

[9] See Stadelmann and Gantenbrink, "Die sogenannten Luftkanäle der Cheopspyramide Modelkorridore für den Aufstieg des Königs zum Himmel," 287–289, figs. 3, 4.

a. b.

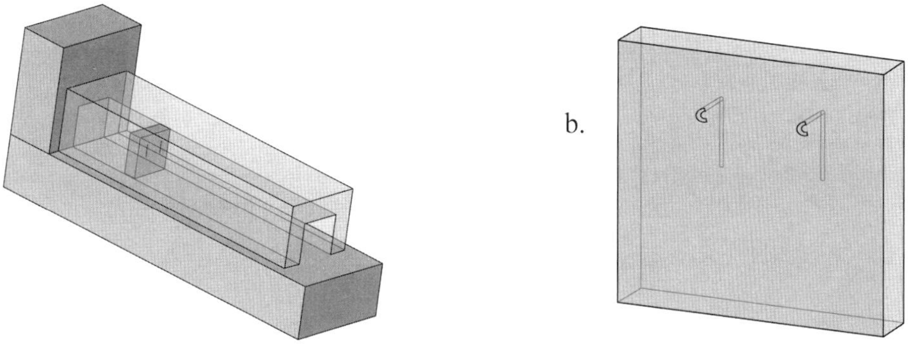

Fig. 1. a. Inverted-U element with blocking slab and final blocking stone. b. Blocking slab with two metal pins.

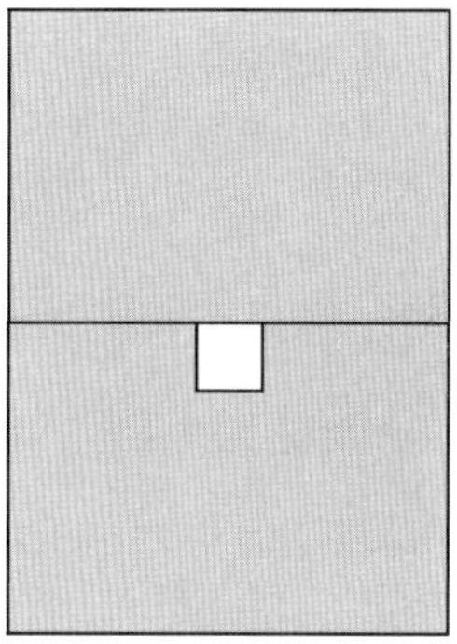

Fig 2. Diagram of the blocks at the entrance point of each shaft, on the walls of the chambers.

1. The two metal pins inserted into the blocking slab are curved on the back face, to form small semi-rings, whose inner diameter is approximately 3 mm (fig. 1b).[10]
2. On the floor beyond the blocking slab is a mason's mark in red ink, beside a red line (fig. 3).[11]

Probably the mason's mark is the number 121, written in hieratic.[12] In fact, the second sign is similar to the number 20 in a Fifth Dynasty papyrus fragment from Abusir.[13] The three signs should read: .

Usually in the Old Kingdom the lunette on top of the hieratic number 20, which represents a 10, is joined to the 10 below, and this ligature appears as a dot under the lunette.

An example of mason's mark in the cemetery of Giza is the number 1 cubit 5 palms, written beside a red line, in the Mastaba G 4560.[14]

This paper aims to address questions such as the following:

- What exactly is the symbolic purpose of the narrow shafts?
- Why do the lower shafts end within the superstructure, several meters from the pyramid's faces, unlike the upper ones, which reach the northern and southern face of the pyramid?
- What is the reason for the turns in the northern shafts?
- Why were two copper pins inserted into the blocking slab at the end of each of the lower shafts?

Both pairs of shafts are south-north oriented, and an explanation that has been often proposed is that they were created as means for the ascent to the stars.[15] On the other hand, the architectural program of the pyra-

---

[10] Composite image: Hawass, Whitehead et al., "First Report: Video Survey of the Southern Shaft of the Queen's Chamber in the Great Pyramid," 211 fig. 11.

[11] Composite images: Hawass, Whitehead et al., "First Report: Video Survey of the Southern Shaft of the Queen's Chamber in the Great Pyramid," 211 fig. 12 and 13. Color image of the mason's mark: www.nbcnews.com/id/43314221/ns/technology_and_science-science/t/mystery-pyramid-hieroglyphs-it-all-adds/

[12] On the similarity of two signs with the hieratic number 21: Hawass, Whitehead et al., "First Report: Video Survey of the Southern Shaft of the Queen's Chamber in the Great Pyramid," 211.

[13] Möller, *Paläographie* 1, 60 (no. 624).

[14] Hermann Junker, *Giza I, Die mastabas der IV. Dynastie auf dem Westfriedhof* (Vienna-Leipzig, 1929), 210.

[15] See, for example: Mark Lehner, *The Complete Pyramids* (London, 1997), 114; John J. Wall, "The Star Alignment Hypothesis for the Great Pyramid Shafts," *JHA* 38 (2007), 199–206. On the hypothesis that they were built to point to the sky, conceived as "Winding Waterway:" Anthony P. Sakovich, "Explaining the Shafts in Khufu's Pyramid at Giza," *JARCE* 42 (2005-2006), 1–12.

mid complex is largely inspired by solar concepts, with the king paralleled to Horus and Ra.[16] As suggested by Stadelmann, Khufu probably spread the concept of his merging with the sun god during his reign.[17] Indications of this merging are the name of the pyramid as a representation of the solar horizon (*3ḫ.t ḫwfw*); the placement of the burial chamber and the chamber for the *ka* in the pyramid's superstructure; the use by his son Djedefra of the title "son of Ra," which, in its original formulation, would have meant literally "son of Ra (= Khufu)."[18]

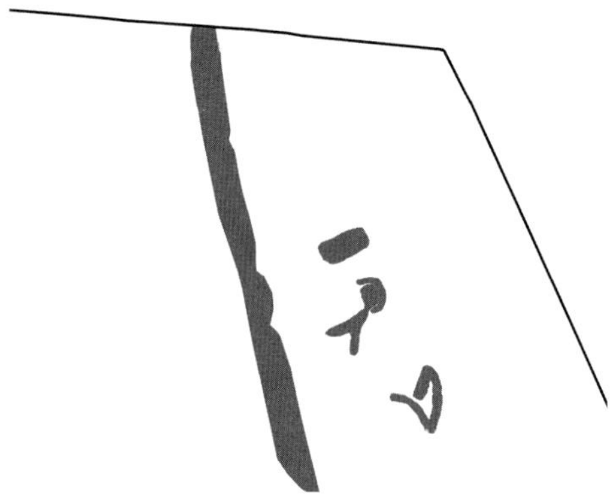

Fig. 3. Facsimile of the signs on the floor beyond the blocking slab at the end of the southern shaft.

In the Pyramid Texts there are numerous references to the king's encounter with the southern "Unwearying stars" and the northern "Imperishable stars," but the main objective is the king's emergence in the *akhet* with the solar boat. As we will see, this emergence could occur also in the north, not only in the east, as the travel of the solar boat was originally paralleled to the navigation along the Nile, with its outflow in the sea. There is probably a stellar symbolism in the pyramid architecture, in particular with the Descending Corridor pointing to the circumpolar stars: the king, as an eternal *akh*-spirit, could be transfigured in the light of the stars and the light of the sun. However, probably already in the early Old Kingdom stellar concepts were incorporated into the solar religion, and the king's merging with the sun in the *akhet* became the primary purpose of his burial in the pyramid.

The mason's marks at the end of the southern shaft of the Queen's Chamber are evidence of architectural planning. The difficulty of execution of the shafts occasionally resulted in imprecisions of angular and linear measures, but the intentions of the builders can be plausibly identified.

Base and Height of the Pyramid

The precision in the construction of the base sides of the Great Pyramid was known already at the end of the nineteenth century when Petrie made his excellent scientific surveys.[19] Other surveys of the sides were made later by Dorner,[20] and recently by Dash.[21] Measures of the sides at the casing's base from these surveys are shown in Table 1. Assuming a cubit of 52.36 cm, which is a generally accepted equivalence,[22] the average error in Dash's survey is only 2.6 cm, with a maximum deviation of 5 cm for the north and east side. Each side is 440 cubits. Errors in percentage are indicated in the last column of Table 1.

[16] See Zahi Hawass, "The Programs of the Royal Funerary Complexes of the Fourth Dynasty," in D. O'Connor and D. P. Silverman (eds.), *Ancient Egyptian Kingship* (Leiden-New York-Köln, 1995), 221–55.

[17] Stadelmann, *Die ägyptischen Pyramiden. Vom Ziegelbau zum Weltwunder* (Mainz, 1985), 110–26.

[18] See Stadelmann, *Die ägyptischen Pyramiden,* 125–126; Hawass, "The Programs of the Royal Funerary Complexes of the Fourth Dynasty," 227–28.

[19] William M. Flinders Petrie, *The Pyramids and Temples of Gizeh* (London, 1883), 39–43.

[20] Joseph Dorner, *Die Absteckung und astronomische Orienterung ägyptischer Pyramiden.* (PhD dissertation, Universität Innsbruck, 1981), 77.

[21] Glen Dash, "The Great Pyramid's Footprint: Results from Our 2015 Survey," *AERAGRAM* 16–2 (2015), 8–14.

[22] Measures in cubits vary from 52.3 cm to 52.5 cm, with an average of 52.36 cm. See Oswald A. W. Dilke. *Mathematics and Measurement* (Berkeley, London, 1987), 9. The latter value is obtainable also dividing the mean length of the sides at the casing's base (= 230.4 m) by 440 cubits. For a value of about 52.4 cm in the Red Pyramid: Josef Dorner, "Neue Messungen an der Roten Pyramide," in H. Guksch and D. Polz (eds.), *Stationen, Beiträge zur Kulturgeschichte Ägyptens* (Mainz, 1998), 26.

Table 1. Lengths of the sides of the pyramid at the casing's base

	Petrie's survey (meters)	Dorner's survey (meters)	Dash's survey (meters)	Dash's survey (cubits)	Design (cubits)	Err.%
N. side	230.25	230.33	230.33	439.90	440	- 0.022
E. side	230.39	230.37	230.33	439.90	440	- 0.022
S. side	230.45	230.37	230.38	440.00	440	0.000
W. side	230.36	230.37	230.41	440.05	440	+ 0.011
Mean	230.36	230.36	230.36	439.95	440	- 0.011

Table 2 shows estimations of the angle of the pyramid's faces made by Petrie.[23] An angle of 51°50'40 was estimated for the northern face, which is very close to the theoretical angle corresponding to a *seqed* of 5½ palms.[24] With a side of base of 440 cubits, these measures of the angles result in the pyramid's height of 280 cubits.[25]

Table 2. Angle of the pyramid's faces

	Mean angle	Gradient (design)	*Seqed* (design)	Theoretical angle	Err.
North face	51°50'40"	7:5.5	5.5 palms	51°50'34"	+ 0°0'
Mean angle	51°52'	7:5.5	5.5 palms	51°50'34"	+ 0°1'

King's Chamber and Upper Shafts

The floor of the King's Chamber is located at about 82 cubits from the pyramid's base.[26] Its south wall is 26 cubits distant from the pyramid's center.[27] The width of the chamber is 10 cubits,[28] hence its north wall is 16 cubits from the pyramid's center.[29] Each wall is about 11 cubits in height.[30] Measurements and deviations in percentage from theoretical values are shown in Table 3.

Table 3. Position and measures of the King's Chamber

	Meters	Cubits	Design (cubits)	Err.%
Floor from the pyramid's base	42.99	82.10	82	+ 0.1%
S. wall from the pyramid's center	13.64	26.05	26	+ 0.2%
N. wall from the pyramid's center	8.40	16.04	16	+ 0.2%
Width at the base	5.23	9.99	10	- 0.1%
Height of the walls	5.84	11.15	11	+ 1.4%

[23] Petrie, *Pyramids and Temples*, 42–43. See also Vito Maragioglio and Celeste A. Rinaldi, *L'architettura delle piramidi Menfite, Parte IV – Testo* (Rapallo, 1965), 18.

[24] In the Rhind Mathematical Papyrus, dated to the Hyksos period, the *seqed* is defined as the horizontal length corresponding to the height of 7 palms.

[25] Maragioglio and Rinaldi, *L'architettura delle piramidi Menfite, Parte IV – Testo*, 18.

[26] Petrie, *The Pyramids and Temples*, 83, 95; Vito Maragioglio and Celeste A. Rinaldi, *L'architettura delle piramidi Menfite, Parte IV – Tavole*, Tav. 3 fig. 1, Tav. 7 fig. 1.

[27] Petrie, *The Pyramids and Temples*, 83; Maragioglio and Rinaldi, *L'architettura delle piramidi Menfite, Parte IV – Tavole*, Tav. 3 fig. 1.

[28] Petrie, *The Pyramids and Temples*, 80; Maragioglio and Rinaldi, *L'architettura delle piramidi Menfite, Parte IV – Tavole*, Tav. 3 fig. 1.

[29] Petrie, *The Pyramids and Temples*, 83; Maragioglio and Rinaldi, *L'architettura delle piramidi Menfite, Parte IV – Tavole*, Tav. 3 fig. 1, Tav. 7 fig. 1.

[30] Petrie, *The Pyramids and Temples*, 83; Maragioglio and Rinaldi, *L'architettura delle piramidi Menfite, Parte IV – Tavole*, Tav. 3 fig. 1.

Estimations for the angles of the shafts of the King's Chamber were provided by the Upuaut project.[31] They indicate that the south shaft was designed with a *seqed* of 7 palms, and the north shaft with a *seqed* of 11 palms. These measures are shown in Table 4.

Table 4. Angles of the shafts of the King's Chamber

	Mean angle	Gradient (design)	*Seqed* (design)	Theoretical angle	Err.
S. shaft, angle	45°00'00"	7:7	7 palms	45°00'	0°00'
N. shaft, angle	32°36'08"	7:11	11 palms	32°28'	+ 0°08'

The inlets of the shafts in their middle is about 2 cubits from the chamber's floor (Table 5).[32] According to Maragioglio and Rinaldi, the horizontal section of the south shaft is 1.5 m (= 2.86 cubits).[33] There is a difference of 22 cm from the measure of 1.72 m (= 3.28 cubits) provided by Gantenbrink, which is probably referred to the length of the section as it is nowadays, with its inner opening badly damaged. Treasures hunters made a tunnel and enlarged the shaft, whose initial inclined part is almost round in section.[34] The horizontal section of the north channel is close to 5 cubits.[35] After this section, the shaft angles simultaneously 32° upward and 45° westward, before resuming its normal direction perpendicular to the Grand Gallery, right after the tunnel made by Caviglia.

Table 5. Measurements of the horizontal sections of the shafts of the King's Chamber

	Meters	Cubits	Design (cubits)	Err.%
S. shaft (middle), height of the inlet from floor	1.03	1.97	2	- 1.5%
N. shaft (middle), height of the inlet from floor	1.04	1.99	2	- 0.5%
S. shaft, horizontal length	1.5–1.72	2.86–3.28*	3, 3.07*	n.a.
N. shaft, horizontal length	2.63	5.02*	5, 5.07*	- 1.0%

The measurements in the tables above indicate that the upper shafts were designed by means of two oblique lines meeting in a point at 77 cubits from the pyramid's base: one with gradient 77:77 cubits; the other with gradient 77:121 cubits (fig. 4).[36]

Figure 5 shows the design of the shafts of the King's Chamber in their horizontal sections. They were presumably constructed as an application of the concept of *seqed* of 7 and 11 palms. Two horizontal lines of 7 and 11 units (= cubits) were drawn at 7 units from the meeting point of the two oblique lines, 2 units above the chamber's floor.

[31] Stadelmann and Gantenbrink, "Die sogenannten Luftkanäle der Cheopspyramide Modelkorridore für den Aufstieg des Königs zum Himmel," 293.

[32] See Maragioglio and Rinaldi, *L'architettura delle piramidi Menfite, Parte IV – Tavole*, Tav. 7 fig. 1.

[33] Maragioglio and Rinaldi, *L'architettura delle piramidi Menfite, Parte IV – Testo*, 134; *Tavole*, Tav. 7 fig. 1.

[34] Maragioglio and Rinaldi, *L'architettura delle piramidi Menfite, Parte IV – Testo*, 50; Rudolf Gantenbrink, "The findings," in: www.cheops.org. Petrie preferred not to provide a measure.

[35] Gantenbrink, "The findings," in: www.cheops.org. The values in cubits with the asterisk in Table 5 indicate horizontal lengths at the base of the shafts.

[36] It is plausible to assume that elements of the pyramid were drawn in cross-section, or with orthographic projection. In the Third Dynasty tomb of Hesira at Saqqara, cylindrical objects are drawn in profile, and there is an example of cross-section in the middle of the cylinders: see Luca Miatello, "Inferring the Construction Process of Two Geometric Algorithms," *GM* 256 (2018), 129–135, fig. 5–7.

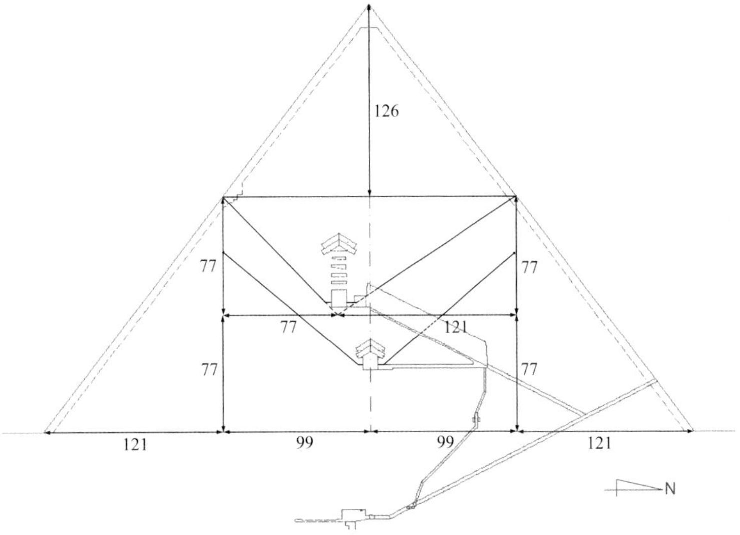

Fig. 4. Design of the oblique section of the shafts of the King's Chamber.

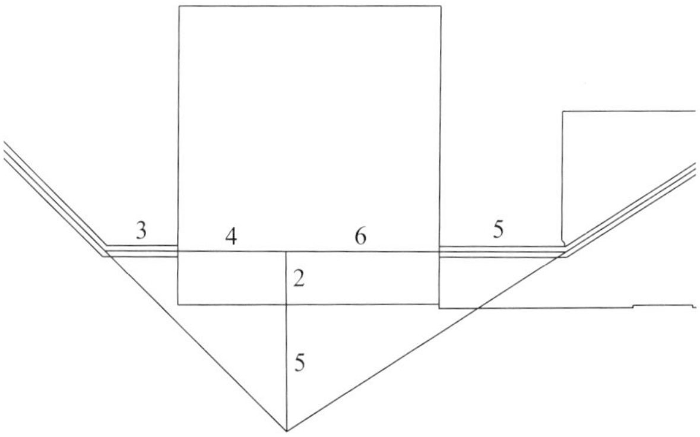

Fig. 5. Design of the horizontal section of the shafts of the King's Chamber.

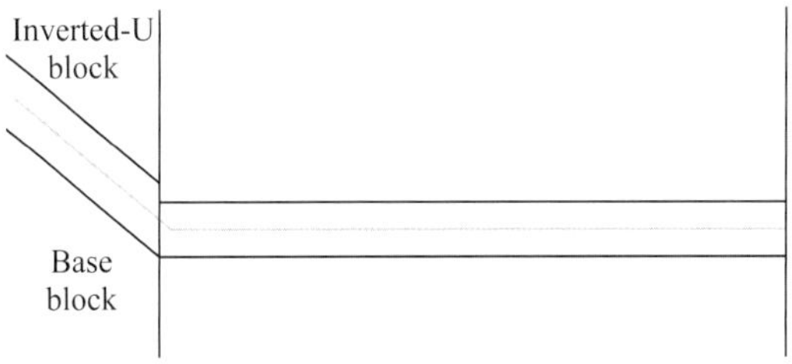

Fig. 6. Diagram of the horizontal part of the south shaft at the intersection point.

The theoretical value of 3 cubits is referred to the length in the middle of the south shaft, while the length at the base is 3.07 cubits (= 3 cubits and 2 fingers),[37] or 1.61 m (fig. 6). There is a difference of – 11 cm from the measure by Gantenbrink; + 11 cm from the measure by Maragioglio and Rinaldi.

Since the inner opening of the shaft is badly damaged, its exact original length is difficult to ascertain, but it seems evident that the builders intended to create horizontal lengths in accordance with a gradient of 7:7 for the south shaft, and 11:7 for the north shaft. After initial fluctuations in the angle, from 39°20' to 50°54', the south shaft maintains a constant slope of about 45°.[38]

[37] Measures in palms and fingers are attested already in Second Dynasty inscriptions on vessels from the pyramid complex of Djoser: Pierre Lacau and Jean-Philippe Lauer, *Inscriptions à L'encre sur les vases. La pyramide à degrés, vol. 5* (Cairo, 1965), 25–27.

[38] Gantenbrink, "The findings," in: www.cheops.org.

Queen's Chamber and Lower Shafts

The pyramids of Khufu and Menkaura were certainly constructed with a stepped core, surrounded by courses with the casing stones. Observation on the breach of the north face in the pyramid of Menkaura attests that the core probably consisted of 6 steps.[39] That the pyramid of Khufu had also a stepped core, made of piles of stones of various size that do not follow the alignment of the outermost courses, is indicated by observations of the breach more than 9m deep opened by Vyse in the south face, and of the tunnel made by tomb robbers on the north face.[40]

Recent observations of the "cave," in correspondence with a "notch" located on the 104th course of the northeast corner of the pyramid, provide further evidence of the existence of a stepped core, with stones of different sizes from those on the outside.[41] As we will see, the 104th course lies at 154 cubits from the pyramid's base, which will be identified as the "level of the *akhet*." This void is presumably an ancient artificial structure, unlike the breach in the south face.[42]

The reconstruction of the present paper is in accordance with Müller-Römer's proposal of 12 steps.[43] The steps would have had a mean height of about 20 cubits (ca. 10.5 m).[44] In total, the height of the inner step pyramid would have been 238 (= 7 x 34) cubits. As we will see, the design of the inner step pyramid is strictly related to the symbolism of the Queen's Chamber and its shafts.

Table 6 shows the position and measurements of the Queen's Chamber. Its floor lies about 40 cubits from the pyramid's base, while the apex of its roof is almost exactly aligned to the pyramid's center.

Table 6. Position and measures of the Queen's Chamber

	Meters	Cubits	Design (cubits)	Err.%
Floor from the pyramid's base	21.19	40.47	40	+ 1.2%
Apex from the pyramid's center	0.008	0.0015	0	-
N. wall from pyramid's center	2.60	4.97	5	- 0.6%
Width at the base	5.23	9.99	10	- 0.1%
Height of the walls	4.69	8.96	9	- 0.4%

The width of the chamber at its base is 10 cubits, and its walls reach the height of 9 cubits.[45]

The angles of the lower shafts have been measured by the Upuaut project.[46] Both are consistent with a theoretical gradient of 9:11, corresponding to a *seqed* of $8\frac{1}{2}\ \frac{1}{18}$ (=8.55 palms) (Table 7).

[39] See Frank Müller-Römer, "Eine neue Hypothese zum Pyradenbaum im alten Ägypten," *MDAIK* 65 (2009), 330, 331 fig. 6, 336, 337 fig. 7.

[40] See Müller-Römer, "Eine neue Hypothese zum Pyradenbaum im alten Ägypten," 330, 350, 352 fig. 16; Maragioglio and Rinaldi, *L'architettura delle piramidi Menfite, Parte IV – Testo*, 14.

[41] Yukinori Kawae, Yoshihiro Yasumuro, Ichiroh Kanaya, Fumito Chiba, "3D reconstruction of the 'cave' of the great pyramid from video footage," *Proceedings of the 2013 Digital Heritage International Congress, 28 Oct.-1 Nov. 2013* (Marseille, 2014), 227–30. DOI: 10.1109/DigitalHeritage.2013.6743739.

[42] Kawae, Yasumuro et al., "3D reconstruction of the 'cave' of the great pyramid from video footage," 230.

[43] Müller-Römer, "Eine neue Hypothese zum Pyradenbaum im alten Ägypten," 353 fig 16.

[44] Müller-Römer proposes a height of about 11 m: Müller-Römer, "Eine neue Hypothese zum Pyradenbaum im alten Ägypten," 350, 352 fig. 16.

[45] Petrie, *Pyramids and Temples*, 66; Maragioglio and Rinaldi, *L'architettura delle piramidi Menfite, Parte IV – Tavole*, Tav. 6 fig. 1.

[46] Stadelmann and Gantenbrink, "Die sogenannten Luftkanäle der Cheopspyramide Modelkorridore für den Aufstieg des Königs zum Himmel," 293–94. The values in cubits with the asterisk in Table 8 indicate horizontal lenghts at the base of the shafts.

Table 7. Angles of the shafts of the Queen's Chamber

	Mean angle	Gradient (design)	*Seqed* (design)	Theoretical angle	Err.
S. shaft, angle	39°36'28"	9:11	8.55 palms	39°17'	+ 0°19'
N. shaft, angle	39°07'28"	9:11	8.55 palms	39°17'	- 0°10'

Measurements of the shafts of the Queen's Chamber are shown in Table 8. The height of their inlets from the chamber's floor is about 3 cubits.[47] The horizontal section of the shafts is 1.93 and 1.96 m,[48] while the theoretical value is 3 cubits, 4 palms, and 2 fingers (1.90m). Slight differences from the theoretical values can be ascribed to the normal variation in the cutting of the blocks across which these sections are carved. Deviations from the theoretical values occur also with reference to the angles in both pairs of shafts, but the intentions of the builders can be plausibly identified.

Table 8. Measurements of the horizontal sections of the shafts of the Queen's Chamber

	Meters	Cubits	Design (cubits)	Err.%
S. shaft (middle), height of the inlet from floor	1.60	3.06	3	+ 2.0%
N. shaft (middle), height of the inlet from floor	1.60	3.06	3	+ 2.0%
S. shaft, horizontal length	1.96	3.74*	3.55, 3.62*	+ 3.3%
N. shaft, horizontal length	1.93	3.69*	3.55, 3.62*	+ 1.9%
S. shaft, total length	63.6	121.47	≈ 121	-
N. shaft, total length	≈ 63	≈ 121	≈ 121?	-

All the measurements in the tables above indicate that the lower shafts were designed by means of two oblique lines meeting in a point at 36 cubits from the pyramid's base, both with a gradient of 81:99 cubits (fig. 7).

Figure 8 shows the proposed design of the shafts of the Queen's Chamber in their horizontal sections. Both were presumably constructed as a direct derivation from the concept of *seqed* of 8½ 1/18 (= 8.55 palms). Two horizontal lines of 8.55 units (= cubits) were drawn at 7 units from the meeting point of the two oblique lines, 3 units above the chamber's floor.

The measurments in cubits of the horizontal sections of both pairs of shafts and the width of the two chambers were presumably defined by direct derivation from the concept of *seqed*, by drawing two oblique lines meeting at a point. All the measurements are in agreement with the values in the proposed design, and the hypothesis of mere coincidences should be ruled out.

From a symbolic point of view, each pair of shafts was conceived as a simulation of the nightly path of the sun. Their upper ends symbolize the point of intersection in the *akhet* between the lower and upper sky. The solar circuit is described by the rectilinear paths of the shafts and the lines of the pyramid's faces above them, but there is also the possibility that these lines were conceived as components of circular circuits.

[47] Maragioglio and Rinaldi, *L'architettura delle piramidi Menfite, Parte IV – Tavole*, Tav. 6 fig. 1.

[48] See Gantenbrink, "The findings," in: www.cheops.org. Petrie (*Pyramids and Temples*, 70) gives a measure in inches corresponding to 1.93 cm for the north channel, and 2.03 m for the south one.

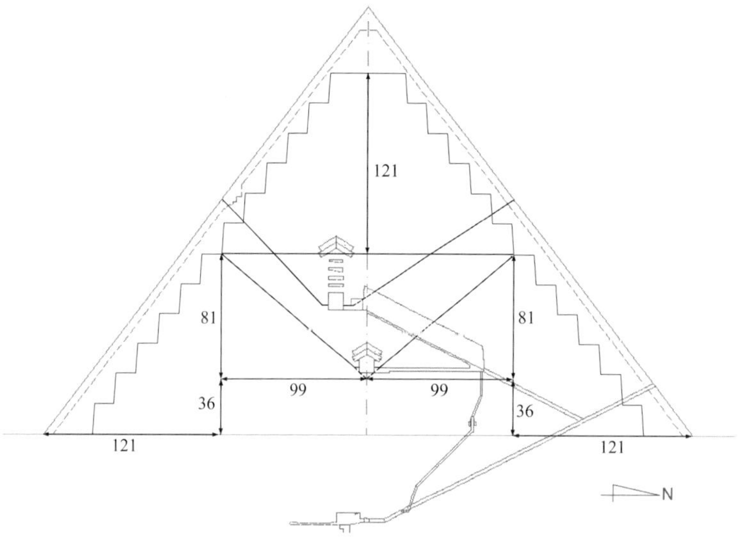

Fig. 7. Design of the oblique section of the shafts of the Queen's Chamber.

The Shafts as Components of Circular Circuits:
Coincidences or Intention of Plan?

Both pairs of lines meeting in a point under the chambers and the pyramids apex are inscribable in a circle (fig. 9).

The solar paths represented by the shafts are rectilinear, but they could have been conceived as being circular, to simulate the "real" circuit of the sun. Since the hypotheses of coincidences seems unlikely,[49] question arises on how these circular circuits could have been found.

The formal definition of the two circles, which could have occurred before the pyramid design, would imply a mathematical rule that could be ascertained experimentally. Figure 10 shows a circle, whose inscribed oblique lines are characterized by the equivalences: $u = a^2/q$; $q = a^2/u$. For example:

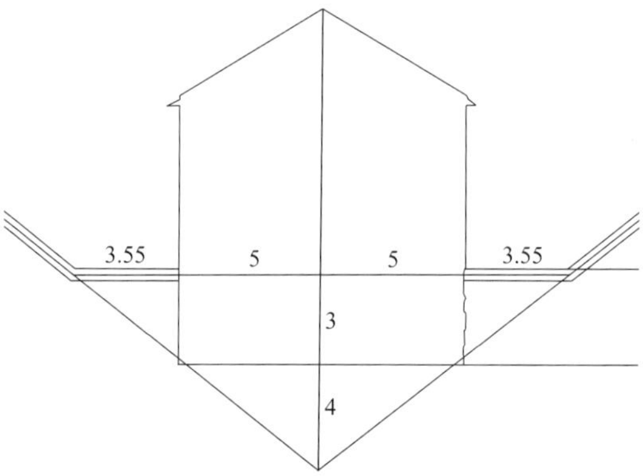

Fig. 8. Design of the horizontal section of the shafts of the Queen's Chamber.

When $a = 2$ and $q = 1$, then $u = 4$.
When $a = 5\frac{1}{2}$ and $u = 7$, then $q \approx 4\frac{1}{3}$.

The first circle (fig. 9, right) intersects the ends of the upper shafts at 154 cubits from the base. If a circle of diameter of 204 units is drawn, defined by $u = 126$, and $a = 99$, one obtains $q = 99^2 / 126 \approx 78$, and it is possible to ascertain that two oblique lines defined by the lengths 77 (= 7 x 11), and 121 (= 11 x 11), are practically

[49] It is sufficient to draw at random two lines meeting in a point in the pyramid design and try to inscribe them in a circle, to realize that the hypothesis of two coincidences is unlikely. However, the interpretation of the shafts as parts of linear circuits of the sun is independent from the hypothesis that these lines were formally conceived as components of circular circuits.

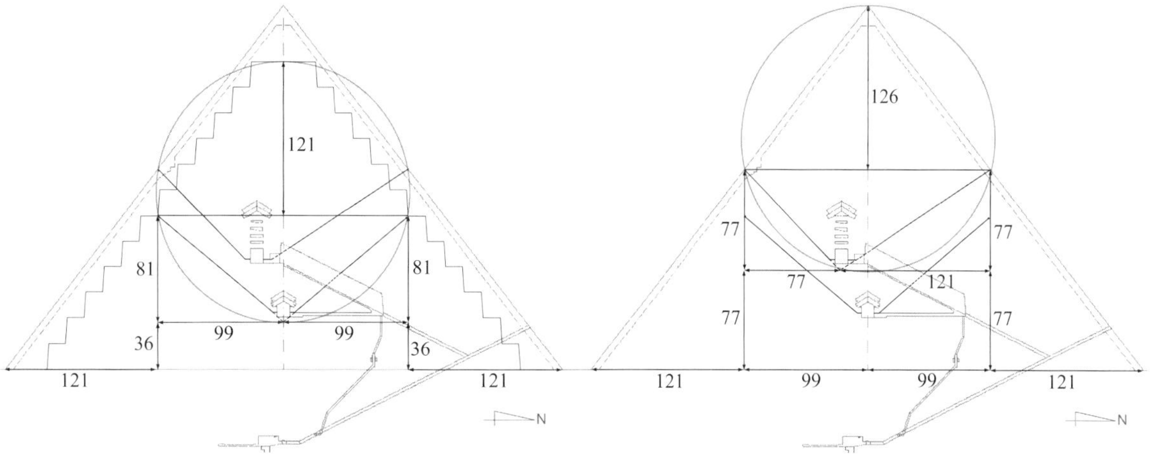

Fig. 9a–b. The upper and lower shafts as components of a circular circuit.

inscribable in the circle. There is a relatively small deviation of about 1 cubit,[50] but in a drawing not very large, the gap is hardly noticeable.[51]

In the case of the second circle (fig. 9, left), the rule of figure 10 can be used with a = 99, q = 81, obtaining u = 99^2 / 81 = 121. This gives a diameter of 202 = 81 + 121.

Diagrams with these circles could have been made on papyri or stones with the aid of grids in projects preceding the plan of the Khufu's pyramid, for example in studies identifying areas of circular lands.[52] The two circles are almost identical: their diameter is 204 and 202 cubits. Their formal definition could be made by finding experimentally the relationships between horizontal and vertical lengths that define them. Similar relationships between lengths in *seqed*-triangles ("Pythagorean triples") were probably discovered experimentally and intuitively.

Rules of Proportion and Sloping Distances

Problems dealing with the calculation of pyramids in the Rhind mathematical papyrus indicate how the architects of the Old Kingdom would have used rules of proportion. For example, to calculate the horizontal line corresponding to the pyramid's height of 154 cubits, the latter value would have been divided by 7, and the result then multiplied by the *seqed* of 5½, obtaining the value of 121 cubits.[53]

Obviously, no modern mathematical concept was used in the design of the pyramids. Scholars of the 19th century, including Petrie, believed that the use of the numbers 11 and 7 in the pyramid design implied the knowledge of a 22:7 circumference-to-diameter ratio as approximation of π,[54] but there is simply no connection between the pyramid design and the calculation of a circumference.[55]

---

[50] With modern instruments, it is possible to ascertain that the circle intersects the oblique lines at about 78 cubits from the pyramid's base: $(y - 178)^2 + x^2 = 102^2$ (equation of circle with center (0; 178), radius 102); $y = 7/11\ x + 91$ (equation of the line of the north shaft); solutions y1 = 153.87, y2 = 78.05.

[51] The error of intersection is 0.5% of the diameter.

[52] Problem 48 of the Rhind mathematical papyrus deals with the calculation of a large circular land (diameter about 470 m) inscribed in a square; Problems no. 37 and 38 of the Demotic papyrus Cairo JE 89127–30, 89137–43 identify areas of circular lands in which a square and a triangle are inscribed: Richard A. Parker, *Demotic Mathematical Papyri* (Providence, 1972), 44–49.

[53] See Problems no. 57 and 59b, in which the height of a pyramid is calculated, knowing the base side and the *seqed*: Annette Imhausen, *Ägyptische Algorithmen* (Wiesbaden, 2003), 167–68, 260–61, 264.

[54] Petrie, *Pyramids and Temples*, 220.

[55] In addition, such an interpretation is anachronistic. The algorithm to calculate a semi-circumference of diameter 4½ in problem

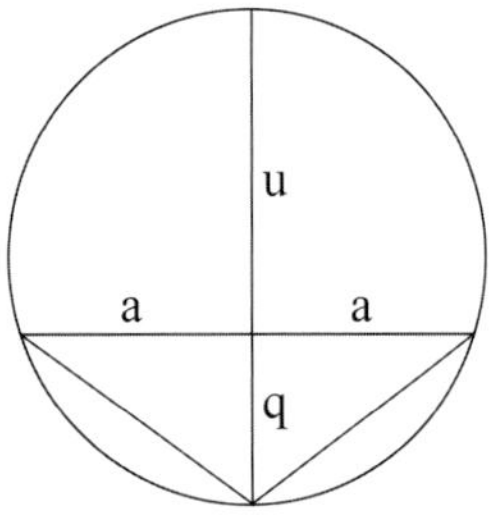

Fig. 10. Lengths in a circle with inscribed oblique lines.

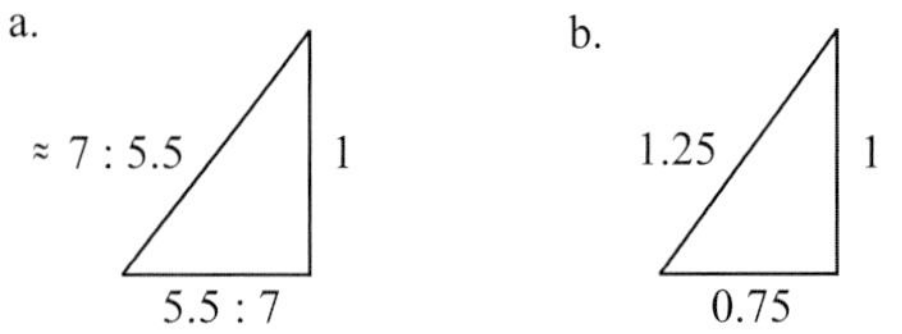

Fig. 11. Sloping distance at the height of 1 cubit in the pyramid of Khufu (a), and Khafra (b).

A *seqed* of $5\frac{1}{2}$ palms (= 5 palms and 2 fingers) was probably chosen for practical and symbolic reasons. In fact, in a right-angled triangle with the height of 1 cubit and the base that is equal to the division of $5\frac{1}{2}$ cubits by 7 cubits, the sloping distance can be approximated by the result of the division of 7 cubits by $5\frac{1}{2}$ cubits, with an error of 0.08% only. This rule would have allowed measuring the pyramid's height at a certain level by multiplying the sloping distance by $5\frac{1}{2}$ and dividing it by 7. A similar rule can be identified in the pyramid of Khafra, where the *seqed* of 5 palms and 1 finger corresponds to a "3-4-5 triangle" (fig. 11b).[56]

Pyramid levels could be measured directly during the construction of the inner step pyramid, whose walls were almost vertical. During the construction of the outer courses with the casing, planned levels could be monitored by measuring sloping distances. A rope with intervals in cubits marked on it could be placed at the bisection of each face of the pyramid with its end fixed at the base of the casing stones in the first course. Segments of rope would have been covered course after course by working platforms, which, as indicated by Müller-Römer, presumably enveloped the casing, allowing its top-down dressing after the placement of the pyramidion.[57] Elevations above the pyramid's base of some courses, as surveyed by Petrie, are shown in Table 9.[58] Levels above the pyramid's base were carefully monitored to avoid distortions.[59] Target levels were apparently planned at 50, 100, and 150 cubits. The level of the 104th course, where the upper shafts would have met the casing, is 154 cubits from the pyramid's base.[60] At the 104th course, the builders would have measured a sloping distance of about 196 (= 7 x 28) cubits, which, divided by 7 and multiplied by $5\frac{1}{2}$, gives the height of 154 cubits.[61] Both this course and the one above it have a thickness of about 1.28 cubits (1 cubit and 2 palms), which is equal to 7 divided by $5\frac{1}{2}$.

Table 9. Elevation above the base and thickness of courses in the pyramid of Khufu (Petrie's survey)

Course number	N-E corner, level in meters	N-E corner, level in cubits	N-E corner, thickness in cubits	S-W corner, level in meters	S-W corner, level in cubits	S-W corner, thickness in cubits
1	1.49	2.84	2.84	1.46	2.79	2.79
2	2.74	5.22	2.38	2.80	5.34	2.55

10 of the Moscow Mathematical Papyrus does not involve the ratio 22:7 in the calculations: see Luca Miatello, "The *nb.t* in the Moscow Mathematical Papyrus, and a Tomb Model from Beni Hasan," *JEA* 96 (2010), 228–32.

[56] On triangles associated to different *seqed*-slopes, see also: Corinna Rossi, *Architecture and Mathematics in Ancient Egypt* (Cambridge, 2004), 216–21.

[57] See Müller-Römer's model of pyramid construction in the Old Kingdom: Frank Müller-Römer, *Der Bau der Pyramiden im Alten Ägypten* (München, 2011), 355–412.

[58] Petrie, *Pyramids and Temples*, pl. 8.

[59] Already at the 2nd course there was a difference of thickness (2.38 and 2.55 cubits), which was corrected with the 3rd course.

[60] On the 104th course as theoretical meeting point of the southern upper shaft with the casing, see also: Maragioglio and Rinaldi, *L'architettura delle piramidi Menfite, Parte IV – Testo*, 50.

[61] Miatello, "Examining the Grand Gallery in the Pyramid of Khufu and its features," 8, fig. 5.

3	3.96	7.56	2.34	3.95	7.54	2.20
…	…	…	…	…	…	…
30	26.19	50.01	1.37	26.18	50.01	1.35
…	…	…	…	…	…	…
64	52.37	100.03	1.24	52.40	100.08	1.27
…	…	…	…	…	…	…
101	78.53	149.98	1.63	78.52	149.96	1.57
102	79.23	151.31	1.33	79.26	151.38	1.42
103	79.97	152.73	1.42	80.00	152.78	1.40
104	80.64	154.01	1.28	80,67	154.07	1.29
105	81.31	155.29	1.28	81,35	155.36	1.29
106	81.94	156.50	1.21	81,97	156.55	1.19
…	…	…	…		…	…

Pyramid Design

Lengths that are multiples of 7, 9, and 11, were certainly chosen for symbolic reasons.[62] The numbers 7 and 11 appear in the design of other Old Kingdom pyramids.[63]

The Westcar papyrus seems to indicate that Khufu was looking for a "magical" design. In a famous tale, the king seeks to know the secret of the chambers of the sanctuary of Thoth, "in order to make something similar for him, for his Horizon (= pyramid)."[64] This secret, *tnw* (*pl.*) *nꜣ n jp.wt*, generally translated "the number of chambers" (of the sanctuary of Thoth), is kept in a chest in a room called the Inventory (*sjp.ty*) at Heliopolis. The term  *tnw* (*pl.*) is written with the plural stokes, and the sentence should be read correctly "*the numbers* of the chambers." "Numbers" would be synonymous of measures in an architectural plan.

Evidence that the building of the pyramid, and in particular the shafts, was preceded by a process of planning, is provided by the hieratic number 121 inscribed at the end of the southern shaft of the Queen's Chamber beside a red line, to indicate its total length. The value of 121 cubits for the total length of the south shaft must have been calculated in an architectural plan.

Probably the lower shafts were drawn by means of grids, with horizontal lines at intervals of 9, and vertical lines at intervals of 11. In fact, the oblique lines meeting in a point are defined by measures that are multiples of 9 and 11, and using a ruler marked at intervals of 9, the oblique line of the shaft can be ascertained to be close to 117 (= 9 x 13).[65] This 117, added up to the horizontal length of the shaft, would yield the value 120.55, which can be considered the total length of the lower south shaft up to the blocking slab. Then there is a distance of about half cubit from the final blocking stone. Even if the geometrical diagram that has been previously proposed does not contain all the information for the builders, additional data can be derived from it.

On the other hand, grids with horizontal lines at intervals of 7, and vertical lines at intervals of 11, could be used in the design of the upper shafts. In fact, the main measures are defined by multiples of 7 (see fig. 4): 77 = 7 x 11; 126 = 7 x 18; 154 = 7 x 22. Measures of width, instead, are defined by multiples of 11, namely: 440 = 11 x 40; 99 = 11 x 9; 121 = 11 x 11.

---

[62] On the numerical symbolism: Richard H. Wilkinson, *Symbol and Magic in Egyptian Art* (London, 1994), 126–47.

[63] See Miatello, "Examining the Grand Gallery in the Pyramid of Khufu and its features," 6–7.

[64] See Aylward M. Blackman, *The Story of King Kheops and the Magicians* (Kent, 1988), 9.1–9.5.

[65] Using the Pythagorean theorem: $sqr(81^2 + 99^2) - sqr(7^2 + 8.55^2) = 116.9$.

In the Mastaba 17 at Meidum (Third to Fourth Dynasty), horizontal, vertical and oblique lines were drawn on walls under the ground level, as a guide for the slope of the tomb's walls.[66] A diagram representing the vertical section of a pyramid and its courses appears on the north wall of the chapel of Pyramid 8 at Meroe.[67] It is made with grids of horizontal and vertical lines drawn at regular intervals, with longer intervals for the vertical lines. These relatively small pyramids were built from 250 B.C. to A.D. 350, and the design method was handed down through the millennia.

Drawings of buildings and architectural elements, usually sketched on materials like ostraca or paving slabs, provide further indications on the stage of planning.[68]

A Third Dynasty ostracon, found at Saqqara in the area of the step pyramid of Djoser, shows a series of vertical measures—in cubits, palms and fingers—of a curve, probably representing an arch or vault.[69] The identification of points of a curve at intervals reminds the sketch of an elliptical vault from the Twentieth Dynasty, discovered in the Valley of the Kings.[70]

A drawing of the Middle Kingdom temple of Qasr el-Sagha is a clear example of a plan with the aid of a superimposed 1-cubit grid,[71] while several ground plans drawn on stone, as that of a garden from the temple of Mentuhotep at Deir el-Bahari, or the sketch of a temple from the quarries of Sheikh Said, are presumably preliminary drafts.[72]

The plan on papyrus of the tomb of Ramesses IV (Turin Cat. 1885) is carefully executed and provided with measurements and descriptions of wall decorations, but it is probably an "advertisement" for the king, more than a source of information for the builders.[73]

In general, plans of architectural elements that have survived are sketchy and not to scale, similarly to geometrical diagrams in mathematical texts. A large number of them are drawn on ostraca, as quick sketches with essential information, to be thrown away after their use, and not to be kept as permanent records.

Plans of royal buildings from the Old and Middle Kingdoms have not survived, therefore it is impossible to draw conclusions on the process of planning of the pyramid of Khufu. However, some considerations can be expressed:

1. It is likely that plans of Old Kingdom pyramids contained only essential information.
2. Quantitative information could be distributed on multiple levels: geometrical diagrams drawn with the aid of grids could be followed by plans of separate architectural elements, for example chambers, corridors, and the shafts, always containing essential information and not necessarily drawn to scale or with the aid of grids.

With regard to the symbolism of the shafts, it is plausible to assume that they simulate the nightly path of the sun, as both pairs of channels describe a circuit with the outer lines of both pyramids.

The model of the solar cycle is fundamental in the Pyramid Texts and later funerary texts.

---

66 See Rossi, *Architecture and Mathematics in Ancient Egypt*, 188–92, fig. 87.

67 See Rossi, *Architecture and Mathematics in Ancient Egypt*, 190–92, 8; Friedrich W. Hinkel, "The Royal Pyramids of Meroe, Construction and Reconstruction of a Sacred Landscape," *Sudan & Nubia* 4 (2000), 18–19, fig. 5.

68 For a list of plans, especially from the New Kingdom: Dieter Arnold, *Building in Egypt. Pharaonic Stone Masonry* (Oxford, 1991), 8, table 1.1.

69 Rossi, *Architecture and Mathematics in Ancient Egypt*, 115–16, fig. 58.

70 Rossi, *Architecture and Mathematics in Ancient Egypt*, 113–15, fig. 57.

71 Dieter Arnold and Dorothea Arnold, *Der Temple Qasr el-Sagha*, 18, pl. 22; Rossi, *Architecture and Mathematics in Ancient Egypt*, 124, fig. 62.

72 Arnold, *Building in Egypt. Pharaonic Stone Masonry*, 9–10, figs. 1.3,1.4.

73 Arnold, *Building in Egypt. Pharaonic Stone Masonry*, 9–10, fig. 1.5.

Fig. 12. Circular offering table in alabaster, Cairo EM CG 1304, from the Fifth Dynasty tomb of Hetepherakhet in Saqqara. Facsimile by Murray (1905).

The Model of the Solar Cycle and the Solar Barques

At least as early as the Third Dynasty the ring sign (𓍶) and the cartouche (𓍷) acquired a solar connotation, as representations of the solar circuit.[74]

Round offering tables inscribed around their rim appear in the early Old Kingdom, with a probable solar connotation.[75] An example from the Fifth Dynasty is shown in figure 12.[76] A text written in a loop implies its eternal recitation, as eternal is the circuit of the sun (*šn*).

In the Pyramid Texts, the reference to the solar circuit is frequent, in particular by means of the expression *dbn p.t* "go around the sky (in a circle)."[77] For example, in PT 210 (Unis's Spell 143):

> §130d *dbn wnjs p.t mr rˁ ẖns p.t mr ḏḥwty.*
> "Unis will go around the sky like the Sun; Unis will traverse the sky like Thoth."[78]

In PT 274 (Unis's Spell 180b):

> §406c *jw dbn.n=f pt.j tm.tj jw pẖr.n=f jdb.wy.*
> "For he has gone around the two skies entirely; for he has turned around the two banks."[79]

---

[74] See Alan Gardiner, *Egyptian Grammar* (Oxford, 1957), 74; Andrey O. Bolshakov, *Man and His Double*, *AAT* 37 (Wiesbaden, 1997), 179–82.

[75] See Ludwig Borchardt, *Catalogue Général des Antiquites Égyptiennes du Musée du Caire, Nos. 1295–1808. Denkmäler des Alten Reiches (ausser den statuen), Teil I* (Berlin, 1937), pl. 1.

[76] Margaret A. Murray, *Saqqara Mastabas, Part I* (London, 1905), 4, pl. 3 (4); Borchardt, *Catalogue Général des Antiquites Égyptiennes du Musée du Caire, Nos. 1295–1808*, 4–5, pl. 1.

[77] The frequent parallel reference to Horus and Seth suggests that the concept of circuit was probably created in early Dynastic times: *dbn=k j3t.w(=k) ḥr.t dbn=k j3t.w(=k) stš*, "You go around (your) places of Horus, you go around (your) places of Seth" (PT §1735c, §1928b, §2099a). See Jean Vercoutter, "Les Haou-nebout," *BIFAO* 46 (1947), 142–43.

[78] Kurt Sethe, *Die Altaegyptischen Pyramidentexte I* (Leipzig, 1908), §130d; translation after James P. Allen, *The Ancient Egyptian Pyramid Texts* (Atlanta, 2005), 30.

[79] After Katja Goebs, "The Cannibal Spell: Continuity and Change in the Pyramid Texts and Coffin Texts Versions," *BdE* 139 (2004),

There is obviously a close relationship between the solar circuit and the grave boats, which were usually set in pairs, prow to prow, to symbolize the solar boats of night and day.[80] The two grave boats of Khufu on the east side of the pyramid have a south-north direction, while those on the south side show a west-east direction.[81] It is possible that the boats with a west-east direction, as those of the actual circuit of the sun, were added by Khufu's son Djedefra.[82] Probably Khufu intended to use solar boats that would have led him to northern and southern doors of the *akhet*, not only to the eastern and western side of the sky, as suggested also by the two pairs of shafts, which are south-north oriented.

Altenmüller parallels Khufu's pairs of boats to the *ḥn.t* and *š3b.t* boats painted in tombs of the nobles at Giza. In scenes of private tombs of the early Old Kingdom, the hedgehog-headed *ḥn.t*-boat represents the night boat, and the *š3b.t*-boat is the day boat.[83] The *ḥn.t* was a sailing boat, used in upstream navigation of the Nile, from north to south, while the *š3b.t* was a rowing boat, used in downstream navigation, from south to north. In tomb inscriptions, however, the *ḥn.t*-boat sails in the night sky from west to east (from the "Canal of the West" to the "Marsh of Offering"), while the *š3b.t*-boat is rowed in the day sky from east to west (to the "beautiful west"), respecting the (apparent) motion of the sun.[84]

Khufu's pair of boats on the east side of the pyramid and other royal solar boats also follow a south-north direction, as in navigation along the Nile. This can be explained with the king's intention to dominate the cosmos from all the cardinal points, his solar boats reaching the Imperishable and Unwearying stars, and not only the eastern and western *akhet*. Such an absolute dominion of the sky is highlighted also in spells of the Pyramid Texts.

There were two models of the solar cycle: one postulating a direction of the night boat from south to north (or vice-versa); the other from west to east (see fig. 13).[85] Even in later representations of boats prow to prow and inscriptions, in several cases the night boat sails from south to north, and the day boat from north to south.[86]

In Spell 44 of the Coffin Texts, the night boat goes from north to south, and the day boat from south to north:

> "You sail (south) in the Night boat (*ẖnt=k m (m)skt.t*), and you row (north) in the Day boat (*ḫdy=k m (m)ʿnḏ.t*)." [87]

That the king dominated the sky and the *akhet* in all four directions is confirmed by spells of the Pyramid Texts. For example, in PT 529, §1252a-1252f (Pepi I's Spell 477):"Ho, you doorkeeper of the sky! Apply yourself toward that messenger who emerges. If he emerges from the western gate of the sky, get the southern gate of the sky for him. If he emerges from the eastern gate of the sky, get the northern gate of the sky for him."[88]

Even if the king's night boat normally emerged from the *duat* in the eastern *akhet* like that of the Sun, it could emerge in any of the four directions.

During the reigns of Snefru and Khufu, stellar concepts were incorporated into the solar religion, and Khufu's desire to ascend also to the northern sky is attested by two of his solar boats and the pairs of shafts, which are south-north oriented. A feature of the shafts, however, is difficult to explain.

165, 171. The concept of solar circuit is found also in the Coffin Texts and in the Book of the Dead. See, for example, BD 147: T. G. Allen, *The Book of the Dead or Going Forth by Day*, *SAOC* 37 (Chicago, 1974), 139 (S1–S3).

80 See Elizabeth Thomas, "Solar Barks Prow to Prow," *JEA* 42 (1956), 65–79; Hartwig Altenmüller, "Funerary Boats and Boat Pits of the Old Kingdom," *ArOr* 70 (2002), 283–84.

81 The purpose of the third boat on the east side, parallel to the causeway, is certainly peculiar: see Altenmüller, "Funerary Boats and Boat Pits of the Old Kingdom," 274. It could be the funeral boat. The arrangement of five boats is found also in the pyramid of Khafra.

82 Mason's inscriptions with dates inscribed on one pit stone are not easily interpretable. See: Miroslav Verner, "Archaeological Remarks on the 4th and 5th Dynasty Chronology," *ArOr* 69 (2001), 375; Anthony Spalinger, "Dated Texts of the Old Kingdom," *SAK* 21 (1994), 284–85.

83 Altenmüller, "Funerary Boats and Boat Pits of the Old Kingdom," 275–81, 287 fig. 3, 288 figs. 4–5.

84 Altenmüller, "Funerary Boats and Boat Pits of the Old Kingdom," 278–79.

85 On the scheme of the solar cycle: Jan Assmann, "Sonnengott," in *LÄ* 5, 1087–90.

86 Thomas, "Solar Barks Prow to Prow," 77–78.

87 See Adriaan De Buck, *The Egyptian Coffin Texts I* (Chicago, 1935), 184g; Thomas, "Solar Barks Prow to Prow," 77; Altenmüller, "Funerary Boats and Boat Pits of the Old Kingdom," 279.

88 See Allen, *The Ancient Egyptian Pyramid Texts*, 164.

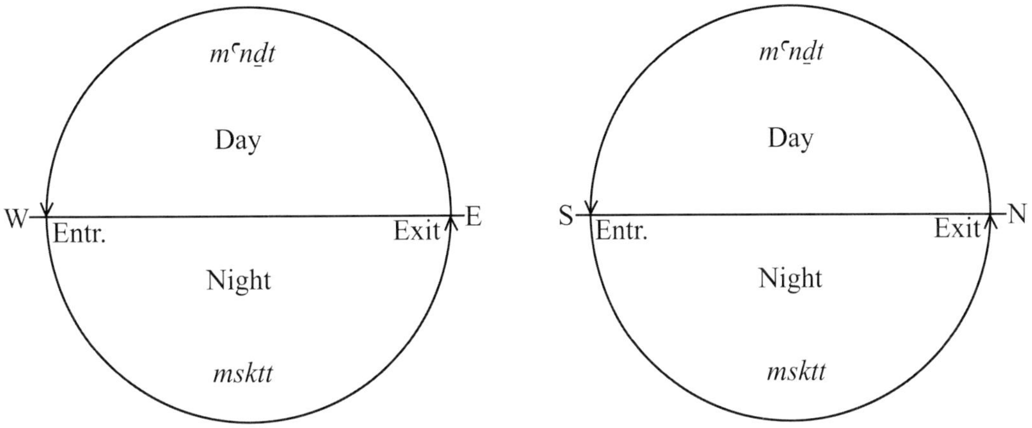

Fig. 13. Alternative directions of the solar boats in the model of the solar cycle.

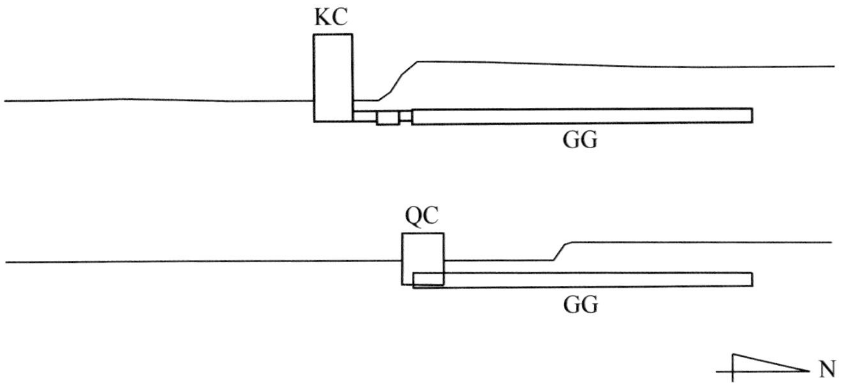

Fig. 14. Orthographic projection (top view) of Grand Gallery (GG), King's Chamber (KC), Queen's Chamber (QC), and their shafts.

The Sharp Westward Turn of the Northern Shafts

Both northern shafts turn about 45° westward for a short distance, then go straight again, as indicated in figure 14, where the shafts of the King's Chamber (KC) and Queen's Chamber (QC) are drawn in top views. It can be seen (fig. 14, lower diagram) that the northern shaft of the Queen's Chamber runs straight for about 19 meters below the Grand Gallery (GG), then it makes a sudden turn to avoid the static structure of the gallery, at about 2 meters from the interior of its western wall. After some meters, the shaft turns again twice to resume its normal direction, perpendicular to the Grand Gallery.[89]

The builders apparently respected anyway the planned length of 121 cubits for the northern shaft of the Queen's Chamber, as both shafts have a length of about 63m.[90] It would seem that they considered initially that the installation of the northern shaft could be made close to the Grand Gallery's wall, without considering that both constructions required operational maneuver space.

[89] See Hawass, Whitehead et al., "First Report: Video Survey of the Southern Shaft of the Queen's Chamber in the Great Pyramid," 205.
[90] Hawass, Whitehead et al., "First Report: Video Survey of the Southern Shaft of the Queen's Chamber in the Great Pyramid," 206.

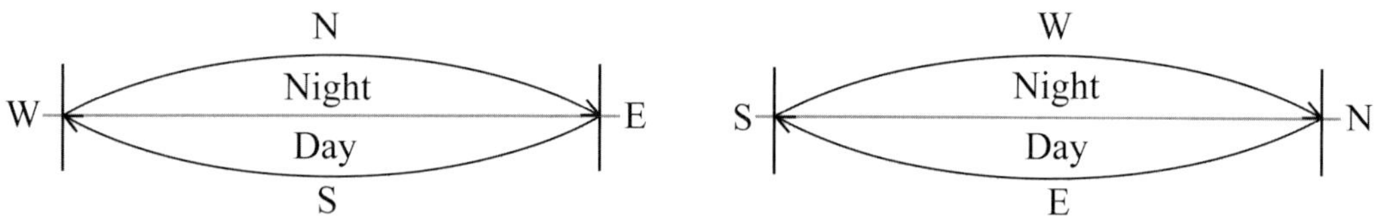

Fig. 15. Diagram from above of the apparent motion of the sun with its normal rise in the east (left), and with the night boat emergent in the north (right).

A similar bend was made for the northern shaft of the King's Chamber, before the shaft could reach the uppermost structure of the Grand Gallery (see fig. 14, top diagram).[91]

If an unforeseen circumstance led to the decision of making turns for the lower northern shaft, however, it is very odd that the builders repeated the error with the upper northern shaft, instead of positioning the horizontal sections of the shafts toward the middle of the King's Chamber.

However, there is a solar feature that could explain these bends. In its apparent motion, the sun makes an arc in the sky shifting toward the south by day, and toward the north by night (fig. 15, left).[92] A night boat emerging in the north would make a westward turn (fig. 15, right). As will be argued, it is possible that the turns of the northern shafts represented this "twisted" path.

Before dealing with this hypothesis, it is necessary to explain the reason for the arrangement of two chambers in the superstructure, each with a pair of shafts, which doubtless was conceived as a coherent system.[93]

The Pairs of Shafts as Solar Paths for the *Ba* and the *Ka*

The pyramid superstructure, in its original formulation of the pyramid of Netjerikhet, was presumably associated to the primeval mound (*bnbn*), and the subterranean burial chamber to the netherworld. The reign of Snefru marks the passage from the layer pyramid to the "true pyramid"—the casing is associated with the sky, with the sun in the zenith symbolized by the pyramidion (*bnbn.t*).[94] Other concepts inspired by the solar religion are introduced in the architectural program for the first time, such as the temples east of the tomb, and the burial chamber in the superstructure.[95]

In the pyramid of Khufu, the lower part of the superstructure with the two pairs of shafts represents the lower sky, with its exit and entrance symbolized by the blocking slabs at the ends of the shafts.

The upper part of the superstructure, above the level of the *akhet*, represents the earth and the day sky. This logical division could have been conceived already with the Bent Pyramid, and can be identified also in the pyramid of Menkaura where the casing in the lower part was made of dark granite.[96]

The burial chamber and the chamber for the *ka* (the Queen's Chamber),[97] are the places where the king had to be regenerated in the lower sky like the sun. The two pairs of shafts suggest that both the *ba* and the *ka* were destined to the *akhet* through the night sky. In Spell 268 of the Pyramid Texts (Unis's Spell 175), the *ka* is led from the *duat* to the king in the *akhet*:[98]

---

91 Diagram made on the basis of 3D drawings by Gantenbrink in www.cheops.org.

92 Thomas suggested that the apparent motion of the sun from north to south by day could explain the alternative motion of the solar boats across the south-north direction: Thomas, "Solar Barks Prow to Prow," 77–78.

93 See also: Rainer Stadelmann, "Das Dreikammersystem der Königsgräber der Frühzeit und des Alten Reiches," *MDAIK* 47 (1991), 373–87.

94 See also the probable etymological derivation of *mr* "pyramid" from *m-ḥr qr m-ʿr*, as instrument for the solar ascent to the sky: Wolfhart Westendorf, "Nachwort: Pyramiden und Sonnenbahn," *GM* 209 (2006), 101–3.

95 See Andrzej Ćwiek, *Relief Decoration in the Royal Funerary Complex of the Old Kingdom* (PhD Dissertation, Warsaw, 2003), 83.

96 Petrie, *Pyramids and Temples*, 110.

97 A *ka*-statue was inserted into the niche on the east wall of the Queen's chamber, which was conceived as a *serdab*: cf. Lehner, *The Complete Pyramids*, 111.

98 Allen, *The Ancient Egyptian Pyramid Texts*, 49.

> Isis will nurture him, Nephthys will suckle him. Horus will receive him at his two fingers, cleanse this Unis in the Jackal Lake, and release the ka of this Unis from the *Duat* Lake. He will purge the flesh of the ka of this Unis and of his body with that which is on the Sun's shoulders in the Akhet, which he receives when the Two Lands shine and he opens the gods' faces. He will conduct the ka of this Unis to his body at the Big Enclosure. The portals will act for him, the (Red Crown's) coil will be tied on for him, and this Unis will lead the Imperishable Stars. He will cross to the Marshes of Reeds with those in the Akhet rowing him and those in the Cool Waters sailing him. This Unis will become truly functional, and his arms will not go off. This Unis will become truly foremost, and his ka will reach him.

That the *ka* ascends to the *akhet*, reaching the king as a completely effective entity, is indicated also in PT 301, §455a–456e (Unis's Spell 206):

> Stand up, great one of the reedfloat, as Paths-Parter, filled with your effectiveness and emergent from the Akhet. Acquire for yourself the crown from the elder and great foreigners, foremost of Libya, (as) Sobek, lord of Bakhu. When you travel to your marshes and course the interior of your mangroves and your nose smells the fumes of Shezmet, you should make the ka of Unis ascend for him beside him just like that coursing of yours ascends for you.[99]

The rebirth of the king in the *akhet*, caused by the union of the individual components of the deceased with the rising sun, generates the new mode of existence of the *akh*.

Khufu wanted to be buried in a pyramid that represented the circuit of the sun, like the cartouche that contained his name. Curved paths were too difficult to be built, and they could be substituted by linear representations of it. The shafts were not constructed in later pyramids only because of the difficulty of their execution, as indicated by the pyramid of Khafra, in which their presence is alluded to by two rectangles carved in the south and north wall.[100]

The idea of the shafts representing the circular path of the sun was inspired by ideas about the sky and the solar barques of the Old Kingdom. Some concepts of the Pyramid Texts, inscribed in royal pyramids more than two centuries later, are certainly related to the symbolism of the shafts.

The Canal of the *ḫ3* in the Pyramid Texts

A particularly recurrent cosmographic concept in the Pyramid Texts is that of the "Canal of the *ḫ3*" (), crossed by the solar night boat in its travel to the *akhet*.

Frequently *mr-n-ḫ3* is translated "Winding Canal," in consideration of the occasional presence of the determinative of the twisted channel, and the mention of its "bends" (*ḳ3b.w*) in §2061c of the Pyramid Texts.[101] Definitions of this celestial channel make reference often to the hypothesis formulated by Krauss that it represented the ecliptic.[102] Allen provides the following explanation:[103]

> (...) The sky was seen as the surface of the cosmic ocean where it met the atmosphere, and the sun's daily journey through the sky therefore required a boat, known as the Dayboat. The sun's apparent path across the sky throughout the year follows a 12°-wide arc from east to west, known as the ecliptic:[104] the

---

[99] See Allen, *The Ancient Egyptian Pyramid Texts*, 56.

[100] See Iorwerth E. S. Edwards, "The Air-Channels of Chephren's Pyramid," In William Kelly Simpson and Whitney M. Davis (eds.), *Studies in Ancient Egypt, the Aegean, and the Sudan: Essays in Honor of Dows Dunham on the Occasion of His 90th Birthday, June 1, 1980* (Boston, 1981), 55–57.

[101] See Kurt Sethe, *Übersetzung und Kommentar zu den altägyptischen Pyramidtexten II* (Glückstadt, 1936), 44; Kurt Sethe, *Die Altaegyptischen Pyramidentexte II* (Leipzig, 1910), §2061c.

[102] Rolf Krauss, *Astronomische Konzepte und Jenseitsvorstellungen in den Pyramidentexten* (Wiesbaden, 1997), 56–66.

[103] Allen, *The Ancient Egyptian Pyramid Texts*, 9.

[104] More precisely, the angle of the ecliptic plane in relation to the celestial equator is nowadays about 23°27'. Its obliquity varies of about 5' per century, from a maximum of 24°35' to a minimum of 21°58'.

> Egyptians saw this as a distinct feature of the sky, which they called the Winding Canal. The region of the sky to its south was known as the Marsh of Reeds and that to its north as the Marsh of Rest or Marsh of Offerings. These names reflect the Egyptians' experience of their own country, where the marshes of the Delta gradually gave way to the Mediterranean Sea.

The Canal of the *ḫꜣ* in the Pyramid Texts is typically a feature of the night sky (lower sky), connecting the west with the east,[105] although obviously there was also a water path in the day sky (upper sky). A diagram of the sky is proposed in figure 16, with the Canal of the *ḫꜣ*, traversed by the night boat.[106] Between the upper and lower sky is the rectangle of the earth, with the *akhet* at the sides. Before the eastern *akhet* is the Marsh of Rushes (*sḫ.t-jꜣr.w*) and the Marsh of Offerings (*sḫ.t-ḥtp*), corresponding to the marshes of the Nile Delta.[107]

A plausible translation of *mr-n-ḫꜣ* is "Canal of the Knife."[108] This expression is modified in the New Kingdom to *mr-nḫꜣ*.[109] Pyramid Texts §1016b shows the variants *mr<-n>-ḫꜣ.w* and *mr<-n>-ḫꜣ.wj*,[110] which may be a plural and a dual referred to the double representation of the channel, whose shape reminds that of predynastic flint knives. The dual form *mr-nḫꜣ.wy* is attested in the New Kingdom.[111] The occasional use of the determinative of the twisted channel, written horizontally or diagonally (),[112] can be explained with the curved shape of this celestial canal.[113] It does not seem correct to explain such a shape with the concept of ecliptic,[114] which probably originated in the Ptolemaic period, with the introduction of the zodiac. In fact, the Pyramid Texts mention the Canal of the *ḫꜣ* with reference to the daily cycle of the sun (the solar boats).

It is possible, however, that the turns of the Canal of the *ḫꜣ* represented the shift toward south/north of the arc followed by the sun in its daily apparent motion (fig. 15). This shift could be perceived by the Egyptians simply by observing the shadows of objects during the hours of the day. The previously described turn toward the west of the northern shafts in the pyramid of Khufu could represent the bends of the Canal of the *ḫꜣ*. PT 684 relates:

> §2061a *jr.j nfr sṯz kꜣ jnn wꜣḥwꜣḥ.w*
> §2061b *mn ppy nfr-kꜣ-rꜥ jr=k r ẖr(.w) ẖ.t p.t m sb(ꜣ).t nfr.t*
> §2061c *ḥr kꜣb.w mr-n-ḫꜣ.*
> "Good companion, *ka*-raiser, returner, perpetual one (?): Pepi Neferkare will remain more than you beneath the sky's belly, as the beautiful constellation on the bends of the Canal of the *ḫꜣ*."[115]

---

[105] See James P. Allen, "The Cosmology of the Pyramid Texts," in William Kelly Simpson (ed.), *Religion and Philosophy in Ancient Egypt*, *YES* 3 (New Haven, 1989), 24; Allen, *The Ancient Egyptian Pyramid Texts*, 444.

[106] Usually the Egyptians represented the curved shape of two sides of the sky (the recumbent body of Nut). In §1094c of the Pyramid Texts, the king is paralleled to Swentju, "the sky's (round topped) chaste" (*dbn p.t*). The *dbn* (*Wb* 5, 437.16) was a rectangular wooden chaste with a curved lid.

[107] On the position of the Marsh of Rushes: Harold M. Hays, "Transformation of Context: The Field of Rushes in Old and Middle Kingdom Mortuary Literature," in Susanne Bickel and Bernard Mathieu (eds.), *D'un monde à l'autre. Textes des Pyramides & Textes des Sarcophages*, BdE 139 (Cairo, 2004), 177 n. 14.

[108] See the translation "Messercanal" in Thesaurus Lingue Aegyptiae (http://aaew.bbaw.de/tla/). Altenmüller proposes "Canal of the annihilation (of demons)," from *ḫꜣ.yt* "massacre" (*Wb* 3, 224): see Hartwig Altenmüller "'Messersee', 'gewundener Wasserlauf' und 'Flammensee'. Eine Untersuchung zur Lesung und Gleichsetzung der drei Bereiche," *ZÄS* 92 (1966), 87–95.

[109] On *nḫꜣ* "blade" (of flint knife): *Wb* 2, 306.5.

[110] See Sethe, *Die Altaegyptischen Pyramidentexte I*, §1016b.

[111] See Altenmüller, " 'Messersee', 'gewundener Wasserlauf' und 'Flammensee'," 93.

[112] See *DZA* 27.616.050; Krauss, *Astronomische Konzepte und Jenseitsvorstellungen in den Pyramidentexten*, 23.

[113] The sign of the twisted canal appears also in the Old Kingdom title *ḫrp mr.wy pr-wr*: Dilwin Jones, *An Index of Ancient Egyptian Titles, Epithets and Phrases of the Old Kingdom I*, BAR 866 (Oxford, 2000), 717–18.

[114] See also the doubts on Krauss's interpretation expressed in Kurt Locher, "The Ecliptic in Ancient Egypt. (Review of) Astronomische Konzepte und Jenseitsvorstellungen in den Pyramidentexten, by Rolf Krauss," *Journal of the History of Astronomy* 30, 75–76.

[115] The good companion could be Ra or Osiris. Allen translates "as the young girl's helmsman on the bends of the Winding Canal": Allen, *The Ancient Egyptian Pyramid Texts*, 291 (N 514). For the reading "constellation" of the term *sb.t*, which is written with the star determinative: *Wb* 4, 83.6.

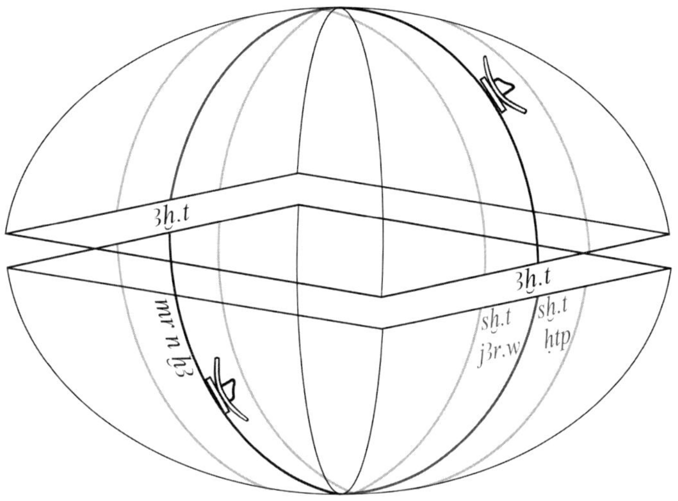

Fig. 16. Diagram of the upper and lower sky, with the Canal of the ḫꜣ.

The king lingers where the canal makes turns, as a "beautiful constellation" does. Could this part of the sky be associated to the cosmic symbolism of the Grand Gallery,[116] beside which the turns of the lower northern shaft would represent the bends of the Canal of the *ḫꜣ*? This hypothesis might even account for the large void recently detected by cosmic ray muons above the Grand Gallery, which could have been replicated beside the turns of the upper northern shaft.[117] On the other hand, the double execution of architectural elements, for the king's corpse and his *ka*, dates back to the pyramid of Netjerikhet, when the pyramid's substructure, with a maze of corridors and chambers, was replicated in the South Tomb.

At the edge of the eastern and western *akhet* (fig. 16) there is the cusp of the solar circuit. PT 613 mentions the "two lips" (*sp.ty*), or lips-shaped shores, of the Canal of the *ḫꜣ*, conjuring the ominous event that the two solar boats can be marooned in the west, in a point corresponding to the cusp between upper and lower sky:[118]

> §1736b *jn-n[.tt] ppy pn jwi.y ḥr sp.ty mr-n-ḫꜣj sšꜣ.y n=f dp(w).ty rꜥ m jmnt n pẖ.n=f [j]r jꜣb[.t n p]sḏ.n [rꜥ] m ꜣḫ.t n mꜣ[ꜣ sw nṯr nb].*
> "In case Pepi is marooned on the two lips of the Canal of the *ḫꜣ*, the Sun's two boats having been beached for him in the west, and he cannot return to the east, [the Sun cannot] shine forth in the *akhet* and no [god] will see [him]."[119]

In PT 1069, line P/V/E 75 (Pepi I):

> *di n=k tp=k ḥr r(m)ny=k zwr=k mw bꜥḥ.w jm(y).w mr-šnwnw ḥr sp.ty š-n-ḫꜣj (…).*
> "Your head has been placed on your shoulders, that you may drink the waters of the inundation that

---

[116] The Grand Gallery with its corbelled ceiling was doubtless a representation of (part of) the sky. See also Miatello, "Examining the Grand Gallery in the Pyramid of Khufu and its features," 20–21. The long oblong layout of the gallery reminds the rectangular shape of several constellations.

[117] Voids caused by pockets of sand are not infrequent in pyramids, but this is apparently a large void. See Kunihiro Morishima, Mitsuaki Kuno et al., "Discovery of a Big Void in Khufu's Pyramid by Observation of Cosmic-ray Muons," *Nature* 552 (2017), 386–90.

[118] The concept of cusp is present also in religious texts of the New Kingdom:. see John C. Darnell, *The Enigmatic Netherworld Books of the Solar-Osirian Unity* (Fribourg, Gottingen, 2004), 426–48.

[119] Jean Leclant, Catherine Berger-El Naggar, Bernard Mathieu, Isabelle Pierre-Croisiau, *Les textes de la pyramide de Pépy Ier*, MIFAO 118 (Cairo, 2001), fig. 47, pl. 12; translation after Allen, *The Ancient Egyptian Pyramid Texts*, 193 (P 551).

are in the circular canal on the lips of the Canal of the *ḫ3* (…)."[120]

That the Canal of the *ḫ3* was symbolic of the solar circuit is indicated also by spells mentioning a ferryman of the canal, Swentju, who encircles the sky.[121] In PT 483 (Pepi I):

§1019b *dbn=k p.t mj zwnṯ.*
"May you go around the sky like Swentju."[122]

In PT 1023, line P/F-A/S 18 (Pepi I):

[*w…*]*n=k dbn=k p.t m ḏbꜥ=k mj zwnṯ.*
"You shall [row] and go around the sky with your finger (on the tiller) like Swentju."[123]

As pointed out by Sakovich,[124] even if usually the Canal of the *ḫ3* is traversed by the night boat from west to east, PT 437 §802 (Pepi I) mentions a northern path:

§801c *snsn jb n stš jr=k wr js n jwn.w*
§802a *nm.n=k mr-n-ḫ3 mḥ.t nw.t*
§802b *m sb3 d3i w3ḏ-wr ḫr.y ẖ.t nw.t.*
"The heart of Seth shall be fraternal toward you as the great one of Heliopolis, when you have traveled the Canal of the *ḫ3* north of Nut, as a star that crosses the Great Green that is under Nut's belly."[125]

It is uncertain whether the northern end of the canal is mentioned here: "north of Nut" could be the northern part of the sky crossed by the sun in its nocturnal path from west to east (see fig. 15). However, as previously mentioned, the daily solar path could imply also a nightly path from south to north. The northward direction of the night boat is accounted for by the original model of the solar boats which follow the course of Nile. With his solar boats prow to prow, showing a south–north and west–east direction, Khufu intended to embrace the entire limits of the sky, in the four directions. In PT 697 (Pepi II), the solar boat meets the southern "Unwearying stars" and the northern "Imperishable stars:"

§2172c *h3i.y ppy nfr-k3-rꜥ m wj3 mj rꜥ ḥr jdb.w n.w š-n-*[*ḫ*]*3*
§2173a *ḫni.t ppy nfr-k3-rꜥ jn jḫm.w-wrḏ*
§2173b [*wḏ*] *ppy nfr-k3-rꜥ mdw n jḫm.w-sk*
§2173c *ḫni.t ppy nfr-k3-rꜥ m ḥn.tj.*
"Pepi Neferkare will descend into a boat like the Sun on the shores of the Canal of the *ḫ3*, so that Pepi Neferkare may be rowed by the Unwearying ones. Pepi Neferkare will govern the Imperishable stars, so that Pepi Neferkare may be rowed in the limit (of the sky)."[126]

---

120 Leclant, Berger-El Naggar et al., *Les textes de la pyramide de Pépy Ier*, fig. 47, pl. 12; translation after Allen, *The Ancient Egyptian Pyramid Texts*, 194 (P 553).

121 On Swentju as ferryman of the canal, see Krauss, *Astronomische Konzepte und Jenseitsvorstellungen in den Pyramidentexten*, 79–84. Other ferrymen, mentioned often, are *ḥr=f-ḥ3=f* "His face is behind him" (Christian Leitz (ed.), *Lexikon der ägyptischen Götter und Götterbezeichnungen*, vol. 5 (Leuven, Paris, Dudley, 2002), 303), and *m3-ḥr=f* (Leitz (ed.), *Lexikon der ägyptischen Götter und Götterbezeichnungen*, vol. 3, 201–2).

122 After Allen, *The Ancient Egyptian Pyramid Texts*, 132 (P 334).

123 Leclant, Berger-El Naggar et al., *Les textes de la pyramide de Pépy Ier*, fig. 14, pl. 5; Allen, *The Ancient Egyptian Pyramid Texts*, 121 (P 311). See also Spell 724 of the Coffin Texts: Adriaan De Buck, *The Egyptian Coffin Texts VI* (Chicago, 1956), 354k.

124 Sakovich, "Explaining the Shafts in Khufu's Pyramid at Giza," 9.

125 After Allen, *The Ancient Egyptian Pyramid Texts*, 105 (P 31).

126 Allen, *The Ancient Egyptian Pyramid Texts*, 298–99 (N 564). A similar concept is expressed in PT 513 (Pepi I's Spell 453): see Allen, *The Ancient Egyptian Pyramid Texts*, 155. In PT 481 (Pepi II's Spell 432), the king emerges in the northern part of the eastern side of the sky, among the imperishable stars: see Allen, *The Ancient Egyptian Pyramid Texts*, 282. The sun rises in this part of the sky during the summer solstice.

Originally, the boat of the dead traveled the nightly sky along a channel oriented from south to north, as in the navigation along the Nile, and a plausible hypothesis is that each pair of shafts in the pyramid of Khufu represented the Canal of the *ẖꜣ*. However, another concept of the Pyramid Texts that may contribute to explain the symbolism of the shafts is that of the two *zẖn.w* of the sky.

The Two *zẖn.w* of the Sky in the Pyramid Texts

In the Pyramid Texts, the dual noun  *zẖn.wy*, referred to the sky, is frequently mentioned, in spells dealing with the ascent of the king to the *akhet*. The term *zxn* is usually translated "reed-float,"[127] but it means literally "embracer," from *zẖn* "to embrace."[128]

The determinative of *zẖn* is a cigar-shaped object (), an elongated rectangle (), or an object similar to the mouth sign ().[129] In the Third Dynasty tomb of Sekerkhabau at Saqqara, the determinative of *zẖn* is a very elongated reed-float: .[130]

These rudimentary boats were made of reeds tied together with ropes, and their elongated shape suggests that they were used in early dynastic times along narrow canals. The literal meaning of the word *zẖn*, "embracer," could derive from the elongated shape of the float, which recalls an arm, but probably also from the custom of using them in pairs, bound together.[131]

In PT 519 (Pepi I), four young gods who stand on the eastern side of the sky bind two reed-floats together for the king, so that he can go on them to the *akhet*:

> §1205b *wbꜣ pꜣꜥ.t mḥi pꜣꜥ.t m mw*
> §1205c *jꜣẖi r=s sẖ.t-jꜣr.w*
> §1205d *mḥi r=f sẖ.t-ḥtp m mw*
> §1206a *šmi=sn js n fd jpw ḏꜣn.w*
> §1206b *ꜥḥꜥ.jw ḥr gs jꜣb(.j) n.j p.t*
> §1206c *spi=sn zẖn.wy n rꜥ*
> §1206d *šmi rꜥ jm jr ꜣẖ.t=f*
> §1206e *spi=sn zẖn.wy n ppy pn*
> §1206f *šmi ppy pn jm jr ꜣẖ.t ḫr rꜥ*
> "The *pꜣꜥt*-canal has been opened up, the *pꜣꜥt*-canal has filled with water. So, the Marsh of Reeds has flooded and the Marsh of Offering has filled with water, and where they go is to those four youths who stand on the eastern side of the sky, who bind two reed-floats together for the Sun, so that the Sun goes on them to the *akhet*. They bind two reed-floats together for this Pepi, so that Pepi goes on them to the *akhet*, to the Sun."[132]

In this spell, the two *zẖn.w* are means of transport along canals, leading the sun and the king to the *akhet*. In PT 263 (Unis):

> §337a *ḏ(d)-mdw di zẖn.wy p.t n rꜥ ḏꜣi=f jm jr ꜣẖ.t*
> §337b *di sẖn.wy p.t n ḥr-ꜣẖ.tj ḏꜣi ḥr-ꜣẖ.tj jm ḫr rꜥ*
> §337c *di sẖn.wy p.t n wnjs ḏꜣi=f jm jr ꜣẖ.t ḫr rꜥ*
> §337d *di sẖn.wy p.t n wnjs ḏꜣi=f jm ḫr ḥr-ꜣẖ.tj ḫr rꜥ*.

---

[127] James H. Breasted, "The Earliest Boats of the Nile," *JEA* 4 (1917), 174–76, pls. 33–34; Selim Hassan, *Excavations at Giza, Vol. VI – Part I* (Cairo, 1946), 1–29; *Wb* 3, 471.3–8.

[128] *Wb* 3, 468.14–469.18.

[129] See Hassan, *Excavations at Giza, Vol. VI – Part I*, 2; *DZA* 28.717.430–440.

[130] See Murray, *Saqqara Mastabas, Part I*, pl. 1 (right column), pl. 39 (no. 67).

[131] See a modern example from Nubia in: Breasted, "The Earliest Boats of the Nile," pl. 34 fig. 1.

[132] After Allen, *The Ancient Egyptian Pyramid Texts*, 160 (P 467).

> Words recited. The two reed-floats of the sky have been set for the Sun, that he might cross on them to the *akhet*. The two reed-floats of the sky have been set for Horakhty, that Horakhty might cross on them to the Sun. The two reed-floats of the sky have been set for Unis, that he might cross on them to the *akhet* and to the Sun. The two reed-floats of the sky have been set for Unis, that he might cross on them to Horakhty and to the Sun.[133]

Usually the reed-floats are two, but in PT 303, Osiris and the king are led to the *akhet* by four reed-floats, which are set by the gods of the four directions.[134]

In PT 473, the two reed-floats are set by the night boat and the day boat for the sun and the king, in order that they can reach the *akhet*.[135] The function of the reed-floats is to connect the sun with the *akhet*. They are set either from the sun (the solar boat) to the *akhet*, or from the *akhet* to the sun.

Noticeably, the epithet *zẖn-wr*, for example in PT 301 (Unis), can be translated both "The great reed-float" and "The great embracer," to indicate that the sun has encircled the sky. In the Middle Kingdom tomb of Sebakhsuwer, at Kom el-Hisn, this concept is clearly enunciated:

> *šm m ḥtp n rꜥ*
> *jw(j) m ḥtp r=k n rꜥ*
> *pẖr=k p.t ḥnꜥ rꜥ*
> *dbn=k s(j) ḥnꜥ zẖn-wr*
> "Come in piece to the Sun! Welcome in piece to the Sun! You go around the sky together with the Sun, you encircle it (the sky), together with The great embracer."[136]

The two *zẖn.w*, originally intended as "reed-floats," seem to have later acquired the metaphorical meaning of "embracers" of the sky, connecting the sun with the *akhet*.[137] This may have been inspired by the model of the shafts in the pyramid of Khufu. In fact, observing their design, the shafts are similar to two long arms (the *zẖn* sign set upside down, ()), which "embrace" the two horizons. If each pair of shafts in the pyramid of Khufu originally represented the Canal of the *ẖꜣ*, they could have been identified later also as "two embracers of the sky" (*zẖn.wy p.t*).

As mentioned in the introduction of this paper, a feature of great relevance is constituted by the two metal pins inserted into the blocking slab at the end of the southern shaft of the Queen's Chamber. In 2010, the Djedi project revealed their shape on the back face.

The Two Metal Pins Inserted into the Blocking Slab

Certainly the two metal pins inserted into the blocking slab at the end of the lower shafts had a symbolic purpose. On the back face of the slab, they have the shape of small semi-rings (fig. 17a). As previously argued, the end of the shafts was symbolic of the level of the two horizons. Originally the end of each upper shaft reached the casing stone at the level of 154 cubits, presumably preceded by a blocking slab with two metal pins. These pins can be interpreted as guides for a door bolt, or handles of a double leaf door. Examples of door bolts (fig. 17b) are found in Tutankhamun's small shrine: they run through two guides inserted into the double leaf doors.[138] The insertion of the metal pins into the blocking slab could signify that the bolt had been magically removed, and that the doors of the *akhet* are open to the king.

---

[133] After Allen, *The Ancient Egyptian Pyramid Texts*, 48 (W 173).

[134] Allen, *The Ancient Egyptian Pyramid Texts*, 56 (W 208).

[135] Allen, *The Ancient Egyptian Pyramid Texts*, 127 (P 324).

[136] Hieroglyphic transcription in: Olivier Perdu, "Zekhen-wr," *BIFAO* 82 (1982), 320.

[137] Hassan, *Excavations at Giza, Vol. VI – Part I*, 3; Perdu, "Zekhen-wr," 319–24; Leitz (ed.), *Lexikon der ägyptischen Götter und Götterbezeichnungen*, vol. 6, 570.

[138] See Carter 108, Burton photo no. P0316: www.griffith.ox.ac.uk/gri/carter/gallery/p0316.html.

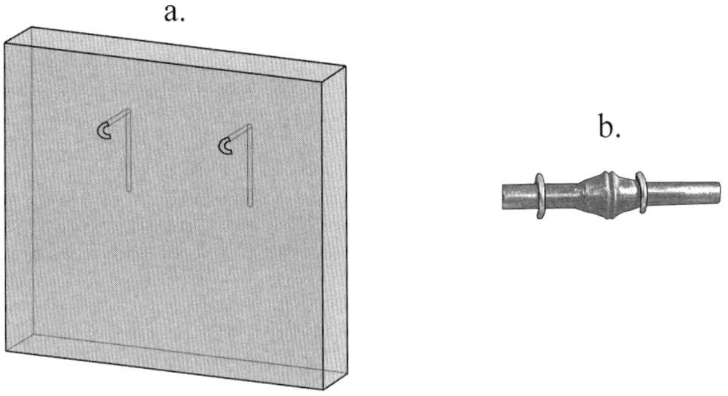

Fig. 17. a. The two metal pins on the blocking slab. b. Bolt with two guides.

Spells of the Pyramid Texts and Coffin Texts often mention the opening of the double door of the *akhet* by drawing back its bolts. For example, in PT 220 (Unis):

> §194a *wn ꜥꜣ.wj ꜣẖ.t nẖbẖb ḳꜣnst=s*
> "The double door of the *akhet* has been opened, its door-bolts have drawn back." [139]

In PT 355 (Teti):

> §572d *wn n=k ꜥꜣ.wy p.t snẖbẖb n=k s.w wr.w*
> §572e *sṯꜣ n=k ḏb.t m ḥꜣ.t ꜥꜣ.t.*
> "The double door of the sky has been opened for you, the great door-bolts have been drawn back for you; the brick has been pulled for you from the great tomb."[140]

The small size of the pins complies with the proportions of a bolt in a door, symbolized by the slab, or the handles of a double leaf door.

A second hypothesis is that the two pins represented hieroglyphs.[141] As we have seen, PT 613 and 1069 mention "the two lips" (*sp.ty*) of the Canal of the *ẖꜣ*. These lips, or lip-shaped shores, indicated the cusp of the solar circuit at the two ends of the channel, where the sun passes from the night boat to the day boat and vice-versa.[142] In the Old Kingdom, the dual determinative in the word *sp.ty* was commonly written as two lunettes (, or),[143] and the two metal pins could indicate the "two lips" of the Canal of the *ẖꜣ*. These lips are related to the symbolism of Nut, who swallows the Sun at sunset to deliver it from her vulva at dawn.[144] In the vignette of Spell 466 of the Coffin Texts, representing the Marsh of Offerings, the solar boat is depicted in the lowermost register beside a bifurcating canal.[145] In vignettes of Spell 110 of the Book of the Dead, in which the toponym is renamed as the Marsh of Reeds, this bifurcation is rounded.[146] Frequently, instead of the bifurcation there are two semi-circles.[147] In the papyrus of Ani and later vignettes, beside two semi-rings is the label *jsh/jsh.t*,[148]

---

139 Allen, *The Ancient Egyptian Pyramid Texts*, 38 (W 153).

140 After Allen, *The Ancient Egyptian Pyramid Texts*, 72 (T 144).

141 The hypothesis that the pins represented magical hieroglyphs was proposed by Stadelmann when their shape on the rear face of the slab was still unknown: Rainer Stadelmann, "The Pyramids of the Fourth Dynasty," in Zahi Hawass (ed.), *The Treasures of the Pyramids* (Cairo, Vercelli, 2003), 125.

142 See also the expression "lip of horizon:" Raymond O. Faulkner, *A Concise Dictionary of Middle Egyptian* (Oxford, 1991), 222.

143 See *Wb* 4, 99.13–100.16.

144 On the term *sp.ty* referred to the vulva: Faulkner, *A Concise Dictionary of Middle Egyptian*, 222.

145 See Adriaan De Buck, *The Egyptian Coffin Texts V* (Chicago, 1954), V359–V362.

146 E.g., Judith S. Gesellensetter, *Sechet-Iaru.* (PhD dissertation, Julius-Maximillians-Universität Würzburg, 1997), pl. 2.2.

147 E.g., Gesellensetter, *Sechet-Iaru*, pl. 10.1–2.

148 See Gyula Priskin, "A Map of Egypt Reconstructed from the Description of the Country at Edfu," *BEJ* 2 (2014), 29 fig. 3.

"sleeve" (?),[149] with water determinative, which substitutes for the term *spꜣ.t* of the Coffin Texts.[150] The terms *spꜣ.t* and *ḏfꜣ.t* ("provisions"), each written with the water determinative within an oval, probably identify two celestial shores, in the middle of which stands the solar boat. Occasionally in vignettes of Spell 110 of the Book of the Dead in this point of the canals there are two solar boats, as this is the cusp of the solar circuit where the sun god passes from the night boat to the day boat.

The two proposed hypotheses on the meaning of the metal pins are not necessarily alternative, as the Egyptians frequently constructed syncretistic associations. In the vignette of Spell 110 of the Book of the Dead in the tomb of Osorkon II,[151] beside two semi-rings of water and the solar boat is the inscription:

> *ꜥꜣ.wy r pr.w pw n.ty wḏꜣ.y (j)tm ḥr=f ḫft wḏꜣ.y=f r ꜣḫ.tj jꜣb.tt n.t p.t.*
> "This is the double leaf of the door of the temples which Atum passed (lit. 'went on it') when he went to the eastern *akhet* of the sky."[152]

One of the two semi-rings in the vignette in the papyrus of Ani resembles the sign of the door leaf (Gardiner's signs list O31).[153]

Conclusions

In the early Old Kingdom, stellar concepts were incorporated into the solar religion, and even in much later representations of the solar cycle, the solar boat could emerge both in the east and in the north.

The name of the Great Pyramid was *ꜣḫ.t(y) ḫwfw*,[154] and the level of the two horizons corresponded to the ends of each pair of shafts, as evidenced in the following points of discussion.

- Mason's mark in red ink on the floor after a blocking slab at the end of the lower southern shaft are interpretable as the hieratic number 121 (cubits). This number corresponds to the approximate length of the shaft, and also to key measures that define the pairs of shafts. The *akhet* was an actual level of the pyramid: 154 (= 7 x 22) cubits for the true pyramid; 117 (= 9 x 13) cubits for the inner step pyramid. Probably grids with intervals of 7 and 9 for horizontal lines, and intervals of 11 for vertical lines, were used as aid in geometrical diagrams, which would have allowed to define the main measures and positions of the chambers with their shafts.
- Plans in Egyptian architecture are often preliminary sketches, but there are also indications of the use of grids. The realization of plans of the Khufu pyramid with the *seqed* of the shafts could have benefited of previous geometrical studies.
- The pyramid superstructure was symbolically divided into two parts: a lower one representing the lower sky, and an upper one symbolic of the earth and the upper sky. This symbolic division is indicated also by the dark granite casing on the lower part of the pyramid of Menkaura, and probably this concept was inaugurated with the Bent Pyramid of Snefru.
- Previous attempts to explain the shafts do not take into consideration that the ends of the lower ones are far from the pyramid's faces. This can be explained with the presence of the inner step pyramid, symbolically associated with the chamber for the *ka*. Spells of the Pyramid Texts attest that the *ka* traveled to the *akhet*: the union of the individual components of the deceased with the rising sun generated the fully effective mode of existence of the *akh*.
- Two hypotheses have been formulated: 1) that the shafts represented the Canal of the *ḫꜣ*, that is, the

[149] On this term, see Leonard H. Lesko and Barbara Switalski Lesko (eds.), *A Dictionary of Late Egyptian I* (Providence RI, 2002), 47.

[150] See Gesellensetter, *Sechet-Iaru*, 135–94.

[151] Facsimile: Gesellensetter, *Sechet-Iaru*, pl. 8.3.

[152] This sentence is commonly found in BD 17. See Richard Lepsius, *Das Todtenbuch der Ägypter nach dem Hieroglyphischen Papyrus in Turin* (Leipzig, 1842), pl. 8 (col. 2); Allen, *The Book of the Dead or Going Forth by Day*, 28 (9).

[153] Priskin, "A Map of Egypt Reconstructed from the Description of the Country at Edfu," 29, fig. 3.

[154] On the name of the pyramid in titles: Jones, *An Index of Ancient Egyptian Titles, Epithets and Phrases of the Old Kingdom I*, 710.

solar circuit in the lower sky; 2) that they contributed to a metaphoric reinterpretation of the ancient concept of *zẖn.w*, "reed-floats," as "embracers of the sky." The turns of the northern shafts may be symbolic of the bends (*ḳ3b.w*) of the Canal of the *ẖ3*.

- The pyramid of Khufu with its two upper chambers and pairs of oblique shafts is a representation of the sun's path in the nightly sky to the *akhet*, and its emergence into the day sky. Two copper adjuncts having the shape of semi-rings, inserted into the blocking slab, can be interpreted as guides for a bolt, installed on the door of the *akhet*, or handles of a double leaf door. A second hypothesis that has been proposed is that they are hieroglyphs identifying the "two lips" (*sp.ty*) of the Canal of the *ẖ3*.

A passage in Papyrus Westcar indicates that Khufu was remembered for his interest in the "numbers" of the pyramid design. This complies with the presence of a mathematical aesthetic in the design of his pyramid. In the early Old Kingdom, the increasing complexity in the construction of royal monuments led to the definition of rules of proportions, in which practical, aesthetic, and symbolic purposes converge.

The burial chamber and the chamber for the *ka* were the places where the king was regenerated in the lower sky to be reborn in the *akhet*, whose symbolic level was planned in the pyramid itself.

Only the interpretation of the shafts as elements of a circuit can explain the fact that the ends of the lower shafts are located far from the pyramid's faces.

A difficult problem concerns the large void recently detected by cosmic-ray muons above the Grand Gallery: if there is a large chamber there, even comparable in size with the Grand Gallery itself, its exploration by a robot does not appear to be an easy task. In any case, confirmation of the presence of such an important component would indicate that the builders intended to replicate all the main architectural elements of the superstructure, and that the turns of the northern shafts were not necessarily the result of unforeseen circumstances.

Virtuous or Wicked: New Occurrences and Perspectives on the Black Silhouette in Graeco-Roman Egypt

Wahid Omran
Fayoum University

Abstract

The present study explores the depictions, forms, and funerary role of the black silhouette figures of Graeco-Roman Egypt. These semi- or full skeletal silhouettes figures which appear on coffins, mummy shrouds, papyri, stelae, and in tombs, have various functions. This study compares the Egyptian, Greek, and Roman funerary conceptions of these silhouettes, offers new occurrences and depictions of them, and gives new interpretations for them, namely that they are mainly of two contrasting types; one being beneficial, as a blessed spirit who assists the deceased at the judgment, while the other is an enemy of the deceased who is destroyed at the judgment. The Roman tombs at el-Salamuni show new unpublished examples of these silhouettes that reflect an ambivalent function, and present their virtuous and guilty characteristics in the same scene.

ملخص

تتناول تلك الورقه البحثيه دراسة الدور الجنائزى للأشكال الهيكلية السوداء فى مصر خلال العصر اليونانى – الرومانى. تظهر تلك الأشكال السوداء على التوابيت ، لفائف المومياوات، البرديات ، اللوحات الجنائزيه أوالمقابر سواء بشكل هيكلى كامل أو شبة هيكلي ،حيث تقوم بأدوار جنائزية مختلفه. تقارن الدراسة بين الدور الجنائزى لتلك الأشكال فى العقيدة المصرية ،اليونانية، والرومانيه، وذلك من خلال نشر مناظر جديدة يمكن من خلالها التعرف بشكل كبير على المغزى الجنائزى لتلك الأشكال الهيكلية ، والذى يتمثل أساسا فى دورين متناقضين تماما، أحدهما يتمثل فى روح طيبه نقيه تساعد المتوفى أثناء المحاكمه ،بينما الأخر يمثل الوجه الشرير كأحد أعداء المتوفى الذى يجب التخلص منه أثناء المحاكمه. تبرز المقابر الرومانية بالسلامونى مناظر جديدة يمكن من خلالها التعرف على تلك الطبيعه المتناقضه سواء الإيجابه أوالسلبيه لتلك الأشكال الهيكلية، والتى تعكس طبيعتهم الفاضله والمذنبه فى نفس المنظر داخل قاعة المحاكمه.

I. Introduction

During the Graeco-Roman era in Egypt, the syncretism between Re and Osiris was still strongly attested.[1] Therefore, in the attempt for a transfigured posthumous state, the deceased wanted to join the solar-Osirian cycle[2] hoping to open the gates of the earth and the sky to rest in the underworld realm of Osiris and to share

[1] C. Manassa, *The Late Egyptian Underworld: Sarcophagi and Related Texts from the Nectanebid Period* (Wiesbaden, 2007), 386–87, pl. 280 A-B.

[2] For further information see, M. Smith, *Following Osiris, Perspectives on the Osirian Afterlife from Four Millennia* (Oxford, 2017); J. Darnell, *The Enigmatic Netherworld Books of the Solar-Osirian Unity: Cryptographic Compositions in the Tombs of Tutankhamun, Ramesses VI and Ramesses IX* (Fribourg-Göttingen, 2004).

Journal of the American Research Center in Egypt 56 (2020), 143–167
doi: http://dx.doi.org/10.5913/jarce.56.2020.a009

Re's rebirth each dawn and return to the tomb each night. The deceased himself, represented by his shadow (*šwt*) or his soul (*b3*), attended the judgment hopeful to be found innocent and jubilant overcoming all the demons who are ready to rip out his heart, cut off his head, crush him with knives, imprison him, and burn or devour him.

In that period, the idea of punishment after death according to the deceased's behavior during life continued to be important, and the judgment scene continued to be shown in tombs of the Roman period.[3] According to ancient Egyptian beliefs, the deceased asked the tribunal's gods to save his *šwt* from Ammit, variously labeled as the "soul-eater" or "swallower of the damned,"[4] the creature that guarded the *nsrt* (Lake of Fire).[5] The devourer's punishment didn't differentiate between the poor and rich dead, as related by the Roman-era demotic story of Setne II (P. BM EA 10822) that describes the visit of Setna Khaemwast and his son Siosiris to the underworld. There, Setne saw two men were being judged: one rich, the other poor. The judge found that the rich man's misdeeds outweighed his good deeds, while the poor man's good deeds outweighed his misdeeds. The judges placed the poor man, clad in the garments of the wealthy man, "among the noble spirits, as a man of god who serves Sokar-Osiris and stands near the spot where Osiris is…[while] It was ordered to imprison [the wealthy man] in the netherworld…" with the pivot of a door eternally fixed in his eye.[6]

II. The Silhouette: Origin and Role

The black shadow (*šwt*), one of the essential components of the deceased to survive after death,[7] was painted in a smaller scale than the deceased himself. The deceased desired that his *b3* and *šwt* follow him to his resurrection in the *duat*.[8] During the New Kingdom, the *šwt* appeared in private[9] and royal tombs (fig. 1),[10] and it also appeared in the vignettes of the Book of the Dead.[11] In Greek culture, the shadow is mainly connected to the soul

[3] M. Venit, *Visualizing the Afterlife in the Tombs of Graeco-Roman Egypt* (Cambridge, 2016), 110.

[4] In CT 335 and 336, the deceased pleads to Atum to save him and his *šwt* from the swallower. The earliest representation of the Ammit-Amemet dates to the end of the Eighteenth Dynasty: C. Seeber, *Untersuchungen zur Darstellung des Totengerichts im Alten Ägypten*, MÄS 35 (Munich, 1976), 163–84; C. Leitz, *Lexikon der ägyptischen Götter und Götterbezeichnungen*, vol. 2 (Leuven, 2002), 114; M. Gabolde Une interprétation alternative de la 'pesée du cœur' du Livre des Morts, Égypte," *Afrique & Orient* 43 (2006), 11–22.

[5] For the Lake of Fire, see, E. Abbas, *The Lake of Knives and the Lake of Fire, Studies in the Topography of Passage in Ancient Egyptian Religious Literature* (Oxford, 2010); D. Brewer, "Shadow," in D. B. Redford (ed.), *The Oxford Encyclopedia of Ancient Egypt*, vol. 3, 277; E. Hornung, *Altägyptische Hollenvorstellung* (Berlin, 1968), 29–30.

[6] M. Lichtheim, *Ancient Egyptian Literature. A Book of Readings, Volume III: The Late Period* (Berkeley-Los Angeles-London, 1980), 140–41; On the story of Setna, see F. Hoffmann and J. Quack, *Anthologie der demotischen Literature* (Berlin, 2007), 118–37, 340–43 and F. Dunand and C. Zivie-Coche, *Dieux et hommes en Égypte: 3000 av. J.-C. 395 apr. J.-C. Anthropologie religieuse* (Paris, 1991), 313; M. Smith, *Traversing the Afterlife, Texts for the Afterlife from Ptolemaic and Roman Egypt* (Oxford, 2009), 27–29; M. Smith, *Following Osiris*, 365, 369, 371. Scholars suggested that the author of the demotic Setna text is derived from the Greek mythology of Oknos and Tantalos which refer to the same torments: F. Hoffmann, "Seilflechter in der Unterwelt," *ZPE* 100 (1994), 339–46; G. Vittmann, "Tradition und Neuerung in der demotischen Literature," *ZÄS* 125 (1998), 68–69.

[7] On the shadow, see, B. George, *Zu den Altägyptischen Vorstellungen, vom Schatten als Seele* (Bonn, 1970); J. Zandee, *Death as an Enemy: According to Ancient Egyptian Conceptions*, Studies in the History of Religions, vol. 5 (Leiden, 1960), 20; G. Pinch, *Magic in Ancient Egypt* (London, 1994), 147; W. Schenkel, "Schatten," in W. Helck and E. Otto (eds.), *LÄ V* (1984). 535–36; G. Englund, *Människans Möjligheter* (Stockholm, 2007), 137.

[8] W. Budge, *Papyrus of Ani, II* (New York, 1913), chapters 79, 89.

[9] The shadow is depicted in tombs at Deir el-Medina including TT 2 of Khâbékhénet, reign of Ramesses II, in Saleh, *Das Totenbuch in den Thebanischen Beamtegräbern des Neuen Reiches*, AV 46 (Mainz, 1984), 37, fig. 41; George, *Vom Schatten Als Seele*, 80; TT 219 of Nenen-Maat, Ninteenth Dynasty, in; M. Saleh, *Das Totenbuch in den Thebanischen Beamtegräbern des Neuen Reiches*, 53, fig. 61; TT 290 of Irenefer, reign of Ramesses II, E. Naville, *Das Aegyptische Todtenbuch der 18. bis 20. Dynastie*, vol. 1 (Berlin, 1886), pl. 104; TT 291 of Nakht-Min, Eighteenth Dynasty, in G. Bruyère and C. Kuentz, *Tombes thébaines: la nécropole de Deir el-Médineh: la tombe de Nakht-Min et la tombe d'Ari-Nefer 'Nos 291 et 290'* (Cairo, 2015), pls. XLIV–XLVI; G. Bruyère and C. Kuentz, *La Tombe de Nakht- Min et la Tombe d'Ari-Nefer,*" MIFAO 54 (Cairo, 1926), 138.

[10] E. Lefébure, *Les hypogées royaux de Thèbes I. Le tombeau de Séti Ier*, MMAF II (Paris, 1886), pl. III; George, *vom Schatten Als Seele*, 88, fig. 8; F. W. von Bissing, "Tombeaux d'Epoque Romaine a Akhmim," *ASAE* 50 (1950), 571, fig. 14; E. Schiaparelli, *Libro dei Funerali degli antichi egiziani* (Rome, 1882), 66, pl. 3.

[11] It is widely depicted in the vignettes for spells 85, 89, and 92. See E. Naville, *Das Aegyptische Todtenbuch der XVIII. bis XX. Dynastie, vol. I* (Berlin, 1886), pls. XCVIIpc, CICc, CIVPc; P. Barquet, *Le Livre des Morts des Anciens Égyptiens* (Paris, 1967), 122–23, 126,128; S. Quirke, *Going Out into Daylight – prt m hrw: The Ancient Egyptian Book of the Dead, Translations, Sources, Meanings*, GHP Egyptology 20 (London, 2013), 199–200, 205–6, 210–11.

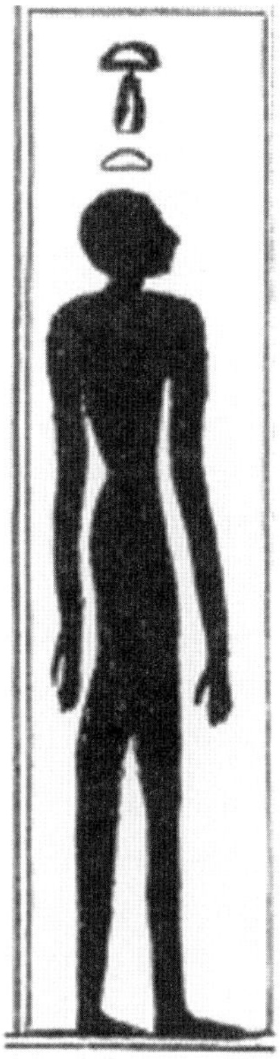

Fig. 1. The shadow in the tomb of Seti I. From Lefébure, Les hypogées royaux de Thèbes I. Le tombeau de Séti Ier, *pl. III.*

(*keres, eidola, psyche*, and *umbrae*), and sometimes also to the skeletal image of the deceased as a ghostly shadow that is found in Greek culture as a manifestation for the dead, both in Hades and when haunting the living.[12]

Skeletal silhouettes referred to in Greek as an *eidola* represented the spirit-image of a dead person. In Greek art, they personified the dead body, for the Greeks believed that the soul at this point either had ceased to exist or had assumed a figural form that closely mirrored the physical body of the deceased, but unlike the physical body, the *eidolon* could not be touched.[13] In Graeco-Roman Egypt, these desiccated skeletal, or near skeletal, figures appear first in funerary art in a Hellenistic form, substituting for the ancient traditional Egyptian black human *šwt* figure.[14] Von Bissing described these figures in his famous tomb at Akhmim (el-Salamuni tomb C1) as "silhouettes," and interpreted them as shadows,[15] while Brunner-Traut identified them as skeletons and considered them to be representations of the dead.[16]

Dunbabin[17] studied the silhouette in Greek art, while Régen[18] studied the depictions of these black shadows (*ombres*) in Egyptian art of the Graeco-Roman period. Dunbabin proposed that the Greek term *skeletos*, which means a dried up or mummified body, overlaps the Latin term *larva* which originally meant an evil or maleficent spirit of the wicked condemned dead, for in some contexts, *larva* also refers to a skeletal or near-skeletal figure. They are not exact equivalents; the *skeletos* represented the skeletal corpse, not the spirit of the dead, and it never had the spiritual sense of a specter. Dunbabin noted that these *skeletoi* are connected with the pleasures of life, because they can represent the deceased celebrating at banquets, symposium, and funerary ceremonies.[19]

The depiction of shadows in funerary iconography of Graeco-Roman Egypt was probably associated with the ancient Egyptian funerary practice, as accounted by Herodotus, of displaying a wood statue of a corpse in a coffin at banquets of rich men.[20] Plutarch refers twice to a similar Egyptian custom, once describing a figure as a *skeletos.*[21] Later, Silius Italicus and Lucian confirmed the custom.[22] These wooden skeletal statues are more likely to have been found in tombs, where they symbolize the *šwt* of the deceased. They were contained in a small box to protect them from the enemies of the evil spirits of the wicked dead. Examples of these small wooden figurines of desiccated near-skeletal corpses are known from Graeco-Roman Egypt, such as a late Ptolemaic figurine that was placed in a box shaped like an obelisk (Kestner-Museum Hanover 1955.153),[23] and

[12] Homer, *The Odyssey*, Book 11.

[13] N. Arrington, "Touch and Remembrance in Greek Funerary Art," *The Art Bulletin* 100:3 (2018), 16–17.

[14] George, *vom Schatten als Seele*, 106; R. S. Bianchi, "Skelett," *LÄ* V, 981–82.

[15] von Bissing, "Tombeaux d'Epoque Romaine à Akhmim," 557, 569 (as skeletons), 570 (as shadows).

[16] E. Brunner-Traut, H. Brunner and J. Zick-Nissen, *Osiris. Kreuz und Halbmond. Die Drei Religionen Ägyptens* (Mainz, 1984), 137; E. Brunner-Traut, *Gelebte Mythen: Beiträge zum altägyptischen Mythos* (Darmstadt, 1981), 76.

[17] K. Dunbabin, "*Sic erimus cuncit* :The Skeleton in Graeco-Roman Art," *JDAI* 101 (1986), 185–255.

[18] I. Régen, "Ombres, Une iconographie singulière du mort sur des « linceuls » d'époque romaine provenant de Saqqâra," in A. Gasse, F. Servajean, and Ch. Thiers (eds.), *Et in Ægypto et ad Ægyptum, Recueil d'études dédiées à Jean-Claude Grenier*, CENiM 5 (Montpellier 2012), 603–47.

[19] Régen, "Ombres, Une iconographie singulière," 188, 193–95; E. Otto, "Die biographischen Inschriften der ägyptischen Spätzeit," *Revue de l'histoire des religions* 50.1 (1956), 45–51, 70, 79–80.

[20] Herodotus, *The Histories*, Book II, 78.

[21] Plutarch, *De Iside et Osiride*, 17; G. Griffiths, *De Iside et Osiride* (Cambridge, 1970), 335, 336; Régen, "Ombres, Une iconographie singulière," 208.

[22] Sil. It. 13, 474–76; Lucien, *De Luctu*, 21; Petrone, *Satiricon*, 34.

[23] It dates to the second half of the 1st century BC and has no known provenance; I. Woldering, *Ausgewählte Werke der Ägyptischen Samm-*

a Roman-era skeletal figurine (Berlin ÄM 20472) that was wrapped in linen bands and placed in a shrine-like wooden box.[24] Both of them are more likely to have been found in tombs than in private houses.[25] A near skeletal figurine was also found at Tell Edfu,[26] and many examples of these small wooden figurines in small coffins were found in both tombs and private houses at Tanis.[27]

The silhouette figures were depicted on the walls of Graeco-Roman era tombs, on funerary papyri, and on mummy shrouds. Although Régen classified the various funerary roles of the silhouette in Egyptian beliefs, this paper offers new depictions of these figures and differentiates two groups; spirits beneficial to the deceased, and enemies of the dead.

The funerary banquet was a popular custom that could be celebrated at certain times of the year in Roman Egypt.[28] These banquets were held by family members who visited the tomb or may have dined near the tomb in the necropolis, as in Tuna El-Gebel.[29] Dunbabin assumed that it seems plausible that the practice of bringing shadow-skeletons to symposia and their representation in funerary art were transferred from Egypt to the Hellenistic and Roman world by way of Alexandria.[30] No evidence exists, at present, for the skeleton banquet-motif in Graeco-Roman art from Alexandria or elsewhere in Egypt. Adriani[31] argued strongly for an Alexandrian origin for the skeleton-motif theme,[32] citing the Roman-era Hermopolis paintings in House-tomb 21 as a source of the whole skeleton theme,[33] while other scholars[34] suggested that the appearance of the skeletal figures in Hermopolis and in Egyptian art was a sign of Graeco-Roman influence and the hybridization of Egyptian-Hellenistic funerary beliefs. In Graeco-Roman Egypt, the funerary characteristics of these skeletal figures remain firmly Egyptian. They are depicted in the funerary art of Graeco-Roman Egypt as a new variant of the ancient Egyptian traditional depiction of the shadow-soul with a Hellenistic influence. In contrast, the funerary skeletons in Hellenistic art stay firmly within the symposium context as an image of the dead with the association of entertainment and the urge to enjoy the pleasures in the afterlife. Paintings in Egyptian-Hellenistic style representing the fate of the dead are a real indicator of biculturalism in funerary iconography of the afterlife during that

lung. Bildkatalog des Kestner Museums (Hanover, 1958), 80, no. 80; D. Von Recklinghausen, "Man hat dir eine Bestattung mit salbe und Binden bereitet," in Anonymous (ed.), *Ägyptische Mumien. Unsterblichkeit im Land der Pharaonen, Stuttgart Landesmuseum Württemberg, Große Landesaustellung 6. Oktober 2007 bis 24. März 2008* (Stuttgart, 2007), 63; Régen,"Ombres,Une iconographie singulière," 616, fig.17; F. W. von Bissing,"Die älteste Darstellung eines Skeltts," *ZÄS* 50 (1912), 63–65.

[24] It dates to the 1st century AD, and has no known provenance; W. Seipel, *Ägypten: Götter, Gräber und die Kunst. 4000 Jahre Jenseitsglaube*, vol. 1 (Linz, 1989), 167–68; E. Brunner-Traut, H. Brunner and J. Zick-Nissen, *Osiris. Kreuz und Halbmond. Die Drei Religionen Ägyptens* (Mainz, 1984), 110; A. Herman and W. Schwan, *Ägyptische Kleinkunst* (Berlin, 1940), 101; Dunbabin, "*Sic erimus cuntci*," 209, 211, fig. 20; Régen, "Ombres, Une iconographie singulière," 615–16, figs. 16–19.

[25] Dunbabin, "*Sic erimus cuntci*," 210.

[26] K. Michalowski, et al, *Fouilles Franco-Pollonaises* : rapports / Wykopaliska Polsko-Francuskie: sprawozdania, Rapports II, *Tell Edfou 1938* (Cairo, 1938), 135, no. 741, pl. 46.

[27] A. Lloyd, Herodotus, *The Histories, Book II, Commentary 1–98*, EPRO 43 (Leiden, 1976), 336.

[28] K. Hopkins, *Death and Renewal* (Cambridge, 1983), 226–34. It was a typical custom in Rome itself, M. Caroll, *Spirits of the Dead: Roman Funerary Commemoration in Western Europe* (Oxford, 2006), 180–86.

[29] The funerary banquet was an important feature in Egypt and the elsewhere in the Roman Empire. These regular visits and funerary banquets confirm the close social connection between the dead and their relatives and friends to commemorate his or her death. See P. Tebt. I.118; P. Oxy.III. 494.22.5; P. Oxy. III. 494.24 cited in D. Montserrat, "The Kline of Serapis," *JEA* 78 (1992), 304. On funerary banquets in Roman Egypt, see H. Youtie, "The Kline of Serapis," *HTR* 41 (1948), 9–29 and J. Milne, "The Kline of Serapis," *JEA* 11 (1925), 6–9.

[30] Dunbabin, "Sic erimus cuntci," 208–11; Y. Abdelwahed, *Egyptian Cultural Identity in the Architecture of Roman Egypt (30 BC–AD 325)*, Archaeopress Roman Archaeology 6 (Oxford, 2015), 119.

[31] A. Adriani, *Gli Archeologie italiani in onore di Amedo Maiuri* (Rome, 1965), 37–62.

[32] Dunbabin ("Sic erimus cuncit," 211) assumed that the knowledge of the skeleton construction came from Alexandria which was a center for anatomical studies and experiments.

[33] Dunbabin, "Sic erimus cuntci," 247. On this scene, see S. Gabra, *Peintures à fresques et scènes peintes à Hermoupolis Ouest (Touna el-Gebel)* (Cairo, 1954), 13–15, pls. 25, 28; L. Castiglione, "Dualité du Style dans l'Art Sepulcral Egyptien a l'Epoque Romaine," in *Acta Antiqua Academiae Scientiarum* 9 (1954), fig. 2; L. Castiglione, "Kunst und Gesellschaftim Römischen Ägypten," in *Acta Antiqua Academiae Scientiarum* 15 (1967), 124, pl. 12.3.

[34] S. Gabra et. al, *Rapport sur les Fouilles d'Hermoupolis Ouest (Touna el-Gebel)* (Cairo, 1941), 46; von Bissing, "Tombeaux d'époque romaine à Akhmîm," 575; George, *Zu den Altägyptischen Vorstellungen*, 106.

period, which Venit described as "the Egyptian conception of perils of the afterlife journey and Greek conception of an ignoble death."[35]

Other Hellenistic funerary beliefs occur elsewhere than in Alexandria. For example, skeletons of men, children, and women were found underneath the tombs in Kom Abou Billou (Terenouthis) accompanied by thousands of bronze coins found most often in the left hand of the deceased or near the head, or on the chest or the abdomen, a practice which is related to the Greek custom of Charon's Obols, the ferryman of the dead who demanded payment for the voyage to the afterlife. This Greek religious observance is similar to the Egyptian conception of the transition to the fields of the gods (yaru) that was conceived of as a journey by boat across the Nile to the western regions where Osiris ruled and where traditionally Egypt's necropolises were located.[36]

In Roman Egypt, the silhouette figures are connected with scenes of a fire-cauldron shown in the court of judgment. There, the deceased is shown as a skeletal figure running to his judgment, in a sense naked. He may be shown either beneath the scale, or inside or beside the cauldron, hoping that the court's positive decree will help him to be reborn in his human form.[37] These silhouettes were initially regarded as bad characters and negative influences, and as sources of weakness and illness for the dead souls.[38] They met their end either through boiling in the Lake of Fire,[39] in the fire-cauldron of the Place of Annihilation,[40] or being relished as fatty meals for the devourer, as shown on a fragmentary shroud illustrated by Brunner-Traut.[41] Therefore, according to this interpretation, the deceased had to get rid of these wicked shadows that evidently represented the enemy against whom protection was sought by the deceased to secure his or her association with Osiris in the blessed afterlife.

Seeber argued for the negative aspect of these silhouettes being enemies of the blessed Osirian-deceased, or guilty ones who were victims and meals for the devouring monster.[42] Žabkar suggested a sexual power role for the silhouettes, related mainly to the black color of the shadow that referenced the black earth that makes seeds grow, the darkness of the night that gives life to the new sun, and the dark color of Osiris which the god assumed at his second birth.[43]

III. The Silhouette as a Beneficial Spirit

The beneficial silhouette is depicted in tombs and on mummy cases where it is shown mainly in the judgment court, depicted either standing or lying on one of the scale's pans acting as a counterweight to Maat, or standing near the court, its arms upheld in an orans-gesture of joy and happiness.[44] It also follows the deceased witness-

---

[35] M. Venit., "Referencing Isis in Tombs of Graeco-Roman Egypt: Tradition and Innovation," in L. Bricault and M. J. Versylus (eds.), *Isis on the Nile, Egyptian Gods in Hellenistic and Roman Egypt, Proceedings of the IVth International Conference of Isis Studies, November 27–29 2008* (Leiden, 2010), 118.

[36] K. Parlasca, "Zur Stellung der Terenuthis-Stelen," *MDAIK* 26 (1970), 181; S. El-Nassery and G. Wagner, "Nouvelles Stèles de Kom Abu Bellou," *BIFAO* 78 (1978), 231–32, fig. 2; A. El-Sawy, "More Light on the Necropolis of Ancient 'Terenouthis' (Kom Abou-Bellou)," in Z. Hawass (ed.), *The Realm of the Pharaohs (Treasures of Ancient Egypt): Essays in Honor of Tohfa Handoussa*, ASAE Cahier 37 (Cairo, 2008), 222; Z. Hawass, "Preliminary Report on the Excavations at Kom Abou Bellou," *SAK* 7 (1979), 82–83.

[37] D. Kurth, *Der Sarge der Teüris, Eine Studie zum Totenglabuen im Römerzeitlichen Ägypten,* AegTrev 6 (Mainz, 1990), 80.

[38] W. Wreszinki, *Der Grosse medizinische Papyrus des Berliner Museums* (Leipzig, 1909), 17, 19, 70, 73; M. Lichtheim, "The Songs of the Harpers," *JNES* 4 (1954), 195, fig. 7.

[39] S. Quirke, "Judgment of Dead," in D. Redford (ed.), *Oxford Encyclopedia of Ancient Egypt*, vol. 2 (Oxford, 2001), 211, 214; Zandee, *Death as an Enemy*, 176–77.

[40] Venit, "Referencing Isis," 114. The shadows were consigned to a cauldron in the Book of the Caverns alongside figures or other body parts including enemies, shadows, *bas*, decapitated figures, hearts and heads; A. Piankoff, "Le Livre des Quererts," *BIFAO* 42 (1944), 56–57, pl. LI; E. Hornung, *The Ancient Egyptian Books of the Afterlife* (Ithaca, 1999), 88, 89, fig. 45.

[41] Brunner-Traut, *Gelebte Mythen*, 76, 79.

[42] Seeber, *Untersuchungen zur Darstellung*, 101–2, 171–73; I. Kaplan, *Grabmalerei und Grabreliefs der Römerzeit, Wechselwirkung zwischen der ägyptischen und Griechisch-Alexandrinischen Kunst*, BzÄ 16 (Vienna, 1999), 11.

[43] L. Žabkar, *A Study of the Ba Concept in Ancient Egyptian Texts,* SAOC 34 (Chicago, 1968), 104.

[44] B. Dominicus, *Gesten und Gebärden in Darstellungen des Alten und Mittleren Reiches*, Studien zur Archäologie und Geschichte Altägyptens 10 (Heidelberg 1994), 59. Parlasca and Walker describe the position of the standing figure as being an *orans*; K. Parlasca, "Zur Stellung der Terenuthis-Stelen," *MDAIK* 26 (1970), 177 and S. Walker and M. L. Bierbrier, *Ancient Faces: Mummy Portraits from Roman Egypt* (London, 1997), 81, fig. 59.

Fig. 2. The deceased and his skeletal form in the judgment court on a shroud from Bahariya, Graeco-Roman Museum, Alexandria. From C. Riggs, The Beautiful Burial in Roman Egypt *(Oxford, 2002), 146, fig. 67.*

ing the purification's ritual, or appears independently receiving his own purification by the deities. Furthermore, numerous silhouette figures are depicted on Roman-era mummy shrouds from Saqqara, where they are shown scattered around the figures of the deceased, Osiris, and Anubis, and helping a peasant with the *shedouf* (see figs. 11–12).

The Orans-Silhouette

A Roman mummy shroud from Bahariya (fig. 2)[45] shows the silhouette in the court of judgment. There, the deceased male is depicted twice beneath the balance, once as a human figure wearing Hellenistic garb,[46] raising his arms in the orans-gesture symbolizing piety and purity,[47] reflecting the positive outcome of the judgment.[48] The second depiction shows him as a black near-skeletal figure with a life-like frontal face that is very similar to that of the deceased, recalling the shadow that accompanies the deceased. Osiris sits on a throne on the far left.[49] To the far right, Ammit, the devourer, waits upon a pylon-shaped pedestal. Behind her is a figure, perhaps Maat, who holds small scrawny human figure with upraised hands and skeletal feet and legs. It most likely represents a third silhouette figure because it assumes the same orans-gesture as the deceased human beneath the scale.

The silhouette is also depicted in the orans-attitude on a Roman mummy shroud from Akhmim (Berlin 22728, fig. 3).[50] It is shown on the lower left with upraised arms and with palm branches protruding from his skeletal corpse. The *psychopompos* Anubis[51] leads the silhouette to Osiris, acting in his role of guiding souls to the afterlife. The devourer crouches between Osiris and Anubis. In Roman Egypt, the palm branch was a symbol of

---

45 It is now in the Graeco-Roman Museum, Alexandria, and dates to the 1st century AD: E. Breccia, *Le Musée gréco-romain d'Alexandrie 1925–1931* (Rome, 1970), 59, pl. LVIII; C. Riggs, *The Beautiful Burial in Roman Egypt: Art, Identity and Funerary Religion* (Oxford, 2005), 146, fig. 67; Régen, "Ombres. Une iconographie singulière," 614, fig. 8.

46 The Hellenistic garb of the deceased most often supposes his Greek or Roman identity. Moreover, portraying a deceased Hellenized style within Egyptian funerary iconography is also following the "Egyptianizing manner" and the "double-style" which was familiar in Egyptian funerary art during that period. Venit, "Referencing Isis," 105; Castiglione, "Dualité du Style," 209–30.

47 The orans in Roman art refers to the pietas, or the prayer in early Christianity, the orans gesture of the dead was depicted on a wide scale in the sarcophagi in Rome during the imperial period as symbol of pietas: T. Klauser, *Studien zur Entstehungsgeschichte der christlichen Kunst III*, JbAC vol. 3 (Münster, 1960), 112, pl. 7b.

48 For the upraised hands as one of the gestures of justification, Seeber, *Untersuchungen zur Darstellung*, 98–101, fig. 34; F. Dunand, "Gestes symboliques," *CRIPEL* 9 (1987), 81–87. This joyful gesture of the deceased below the scale could be also similar to the dead figures from Kom Abou Bellou stelae. See, M. A. Abd el-Hafeez, J. C. Grenier, G. Wagner, *Stèles funéraires de Kom Abu Bellou* (Paris, 1985), fig. 2; A. H. Abdel-Al, "The Excavations of Abu Bellou's Mound," *ASAE* 65 (1983), 73–78, pl. IX A, B, C.

49 E. Breccia, *Le Musée gréco-romain d'Alexandrie 1925–1931*, 59, pl. LVIII; Riggs, *The Beautiful Burial in Roman Egypt*, 146, fig. 67; Régen, "Ombres. Une iconographie singulière," 614, fig. 8.

50 It dates to the second half of the 1st century AD. See D. Kurth, *Materialien zum Toten glauben im römerzeitlichen Ägypten* (Hützel, 2010), 77, fig. 5; Régen, "Ombres. Une iconographie singulière," 613, fig.13.

51 In Greek methodology, Anubis as psychopomos conducted the souls of the deceased to the shores of the river Styx and led the deceased to the afterlife. He is identified with Hermes as Anubis-Hermes or "Hermanubis." For Anubis as *psychopompos*, see J. Grenier, *Anubis Alexandrin et Romain*, EPRO 57 (Leiden, 1977); D. Doxey, "Anubis," in D. B. Redford (ed.), *The Oxford Encyclopedia of Ancient Egypt*, vol. I (Oxford, 2001), 98; Riggs, *The Beautiful Burial in Roman Egypt*, 126–28, figs. 53–54, 165–73. Hathor is also well attested leading the deceased to

Fig. 3. Anubis and a silhouette with palm fronds shown on a shroud, at lower left (Berlin 22728). From D. Kurth, Materialien zum Toten glauben im römerzeitlichen Ägypten, *77, fig. 5.*

victory over death, signaling the transfiguration and rebirth of the deceased. Moreover, the orans-attitude of this silhouette figure is also in anticipation and hope of a positive judgment. In ancient Egypt, the deceased, or his *ba,* was shown at the judgment.[52] But here, the orans-silhouette substitutes for the deceased.

Osiris, especially in funerary art created for woman, A. Abdalla, Graeco-Roman Funerary Stelae from Upper Egypt (Liverpool, 1992), 112, catalogue nos. 5, 62, 89, 117 (pl. 45), 166, 181.

[52] For the justification gesture of the *ba* of the deceased, Seeber, *Untersuchungen zur Darstellung*, 106–9, figs. 39, 40. In the tomb of Petosiris at el-Mazawaka, the *ba* attends the judgment in two forms, once as a *ba* bird standing on a podium, raising his hands rejoicing at the positive judgment, while the second shows Petosiris himself in the same gesture of his *ba*. See J. Osing et al., *Denkmäler der Oase Dachla, aus dem Nachlass von Ahmed Fakhry*, AV 28 (Berlin, 1982), pl. 25b; Venit, *Visualizing the Afterlife*, 166–67, 168, fig. 5.11, pl. XXVII. In other cases, the deceased

Fig. 4. Silhouette in orans-attitude (upper right). Philadelphia University Museum mummy shroud 326-2-1. From Kurth, Materialien zum Toten römerzeitlichen Ägypten, *95, fig. 7.*

Another orans silhouette of the deceased is depicted on a mummy shroud in the Philadelphia University Museum (no. 326-2-1; fig. 4).[53] Régen suggested that the shroud's provenance is Akhmim or Thebes. The shroud is damaged, but the second register from the top right shows another depiction of a black silhouette with upraised

himself attends the court without his *b3* or *šwt* and he raises his hands triumphantly as is depicted on the mummy coffin of a child from Maghagha el-Minya (first century A.D.). It is now in the Ägyptische Museum Berlin; see Riggs, *The Beautiful Burial in Roman Egypt*, 103–5, fig. 42.

[53] It dates to the second half of the first century AD. Its provenance is unknown. For this shroud, see Kurth, *Materialien zum Toten glauben*, 91–107, figs. 6a–b, 7.

Fig. 5a. Pushkin Museum mummy shroud I 1a, 5763. From Kurth, Materialien zum Toten römerzeitlichen Ägypten, *8, fig. 1.*

Fig. 5b. Detail of Pushkin Museum mummy shroud I 1a, 5763 (middle left), showing the deceased in a desiccated semi-skeletal form in orans-attitude. From Kurth, Materialien zum Toten römerzeitlichen Ägypten, *8, fig. 1.*

Fig. 6. The silhouette following the female deceased in the House-tomb 21 at Tuna el-Gebel. From Gabra, Peintures à fresques et scènes, *pl. 28.*

hands.[54] Another Roman-era shroud (Pushkin Museum I. 1a, 5763; figs. 5a–b)[55] shows a desiccated semi-skeletal figure in orans-attitude led by Anubis and Maat.[56]

An orans-skeletal figure is also depicted on Liverpool stela SAOS A647,[57] as well as in House-tomb 21 at Tuna el-Gebel where the skeletal figure follows the female deceased (fig. 6).[58] In the tomb, the skeleton has cropped red hair with knobby ends. The female deceased, dressed in Egyptian style, raises her right hand as she is led forward

---

[54] Régen, "Ombres. Une iconographie singulière," 613, fig. 11; Kurth, *Materialien zum Toten glauben*, 104, fig. 7.

[55] It dates to the second half of the first century AD and is of unknown provenance: Seeber, *Untersuchungen zur Darstellung*, 57, fig. 9; Kurth, *Materialien zum Toten glauben*, 8, fig. 1; Régen, "Ombres. Une iconographie singulière," 613, 624, fig. 12.

[56] Kurth (*Materialien zum Toten glauben*, 19) described the figure of the deceased as "eine auffälligen menschengeschtaltigen."

[57] A. Abdalla, *Graeco-Roman Funerary Steale from Upper Egypt* (Liverpool, 1992), 48, cat. no. 107, pl. 41b. It was formerly in the MacGregor Collection (Garstang 226G A07). Its location is now unknown, and its material and dimensions are not recorded in the School of Archaeology and Oriental Studies, University of Liverpool.

[58] S. Gabra, *Peintures à Frescques et Scènes peintes a Hermopolis–Ouest*, pl. 28.

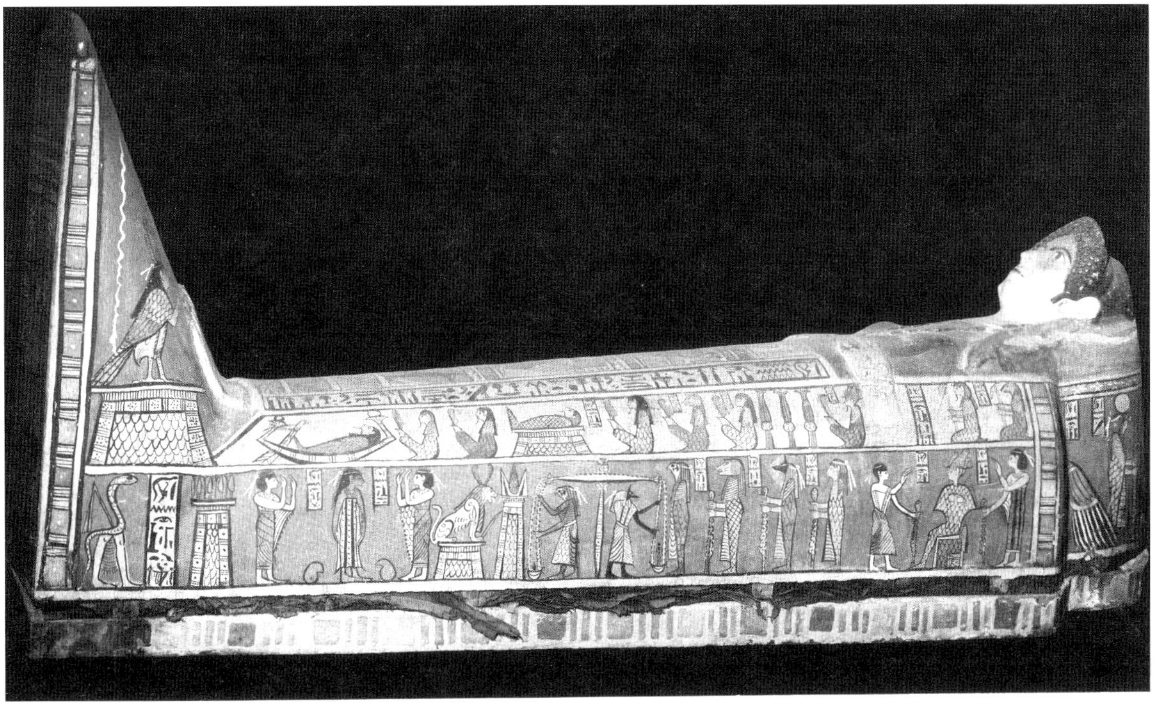

Fig. 7a. The coffin of Didyme, Mallawi Museum, el-Minya. From D. Kurth, Sarge de Teüris, *pl. 5.*

Fig. 7b. Detail of the coffin of Didyme showing the silhouette as a counterweight for the scale at the judgment. From Kurth, Sarge de Teüris, *pl. 5.*

by an only partially preserved goddess, certainly Hathor,[59] who holds the deceased woman by her left wrist.[60] Riggs assumed that the deceased woman was a goddess, or her near equal, because she is indistinguishable from the deities portrayed in the tomb.[61] The presence of a *seshed* band around her head assumes her transfiguration, symbolizing a "crown of justification."[62] These silhouette figures represent spirits beneficial to the dead.

[59] Hathor substitutes for Anubis and guides the female deceased to Osiris. See Riggs, *The Beautiful Burial in Roman Egypt*, 128, fig. 54. The deceased woman is closely associated with Hathor rather than Osiris in texts and funerary art in Ptolemaic-Roman Egypt: Riggs, *The Beautiful Burial in Roman Egypt*, 71–78; V. Rondot, "L'Empereur et le petit prince: les deux colosses d'Argo: iconographie, symbolique et datation," in V. Rondot, F. Alpi, and F. Villeneuve (eds.), *La pioche et la plume: autour du Soudan, du Liban et de la Jordanie. Hommages archéologiques à Patrice Lenoble* (Paris, 2011), 428–31; V. Rondot *Derniers visages des dieux d'Égypte: iconographies, panthéons et cultes dans le Fayoum hellénisé des IIe-IIIe siècles de notre ère. Passé présent* (Paris, 2013), 265, 355–56; Smith, *Following Osiris*, 385–89.

[60] S. Gabra et al., *Fouilles d'Hermoupolis Ouest*, pl.14.2; Venit, *Visualizing the Afterlife*, 124, fig. 4.16.

[61] Riggs, *The Beautiful Burial in Roman Egypt*, 136, fig. 61.

[62] The broad collars, ornamental wreaths, and *seshed* fillets that crown the heads of women and girls in funerary art in Roman period indicate that the deceased was pure, justified, and rejuvenated. See Riggs, *The Beautiful Burial in Roman Egypt*, 60–61, 81–82, 93, 94.

The Silhouette at the Judgment

Images of the silhouette at the judgment of the dead start to appear in Egyptian funerary art in the Roman period. A Roman-era mummy shroud from Meir (Louvre E 32634b)[63] shows a near skeletal figure standing on one the scale's pans being weighed against the heart of the deceased. Beneath the crossbar of the scale are two trees that may symbolize paradise. The adjacent scene shows the deceased wearing a traditional Egyptian kilt, purified by Horus and Thoth and being led to Osiris.

The silhouette functioning as a counterweight in a judgment scene is depicted on the coffin of Didyme (figs. 7a–b)[64] and also on a Roman-era coffin (Louvre AF 13027) from Antinoopolis.[65] On the latter, the silhouette lies in one of the scale's pans while being weighed against a heavy spherical object. House-tomb 20 at Tuna el-Gebel (fig. 8) shows a very poorly preserved judgment scene with a unique depiction of a near-skeletal figure in

Fig. 8. The silhouette in the pan of the judgment scale. House-tomb 20 at Tuna el-Gebel. I. Kaplan, Grabmalereinund Grabreliefs der Römerzeit, Wechselwirkung zwischen der ägyptischen und griechisch-Alexandrinischen Kunst, *pl. 78c.*

---

[63] It dates to the first half of the second century AD: D. Kurth, in K. Parlasca and H. Seemann (eds.), *Augenblicke: Mumienporträts Mumienporträtsund ägyptische Grabkunst aus römischer Zeit* (Munich, 1999), 92–94. Régen ("Ombres. Une iconographie singulière du mort," 623, fig. 9) suggested that Hermopolis Magna (Tuna El-Gebel) is the provenance of this shroud. See also C. Ziegler, H. Rutschowscaya, *Le Louvre. Les antiquités égyptiennes* (Paris, 2002), 87; M. Aubert and R. Cortopassi, *Portraits funéraires de l'Égypte Romaine, Cartonnages, linceuls et bois,* vol. 2 (Paris, 2008), 105.

[64] It is now in the Museum of Mallawi-Minya, and dates to the second century AD. It was found at Zaweit el –Meitin. See D. Kurth, *Der Sarge der Teüris*, pl. 5.

[65] It dates to the 2nd–3rd century AD. E. Brunner-Traut, *Gelebte Mythen,* 70; Seeber, *Untersuchungen zur Darstellung,* 77, fig. 23; Régen, "Ombres. Une iconographie singulière," 614, fig. 10; M.-Fr. Aubert, R. Cortopassi, *Portraits funéraires de l'agypte Romaine*, 219; M. Aubert and R. Cortopassi, *Portraits funéraires de l'Égypte romaine*, 219–20; Régen, "Ombres. Une iconographie singulière," 614, 623, fig. 10.

Fig. 9. Two silhouettes at the judgment, el-Salamuni Tomb F2, burial chamber, west wall. Photo: W. Omran.

the orans-gesture emerging from a vessel that is set on the scale's right pan. Unfortunately, the other pan is now lost. Anubis and Horus, crowned with a solar disc, stand below the crossbar attending each pan, while Thoth (partially damaged) stands in the middle of the beam.[66]

The silhouette figure is depicted multiple times in the judgment scenes in the tombs at el-Salamuni. In the burial chamber of Tomb F2 (fig. 9),[67] Anubis and a damaged deity, presumably Horus, are shown beneath the scale, and a baboon is perched on its cross beam. A large silhouette stands to the left of the scale (viewer's right), while another damaged silhouette possibly rests on the right pan being weighed against a seated figure of Maat on the left one. The artist depicts the judgment scene without the devourer and the cauldron, probably due to the lack of wall space.[68]

[66] S. Gabra et. al, *Fouilles d'Hermoupolis Ouest*, 102–3; Kaplan, *Grabmalerei und Grabreliefs der Römerzeit*, 161–62, pl. 78c, d; M. Venit, *Visualizing the Afterlife*, 112–13.

[67] It is located on terrace F at the south part of the mountain. This tomb was first recorded by J. Clédat during his visit to the mountain in 1903 when he visited three tombs and named them Tomb 1, 2, and 3. They were later recorded by C. Meurice (*Jean Clédat en Égypte et en Nubie (1900-1914)*, BdE 158 (Cairo, 2014), 69–70, 463, fig. 20). Tomb F2 is also briefly described by Kaplan as Tomb VII with a reference to the scene which Clédat recorded that depicts the god Tithoes in the bark with Isis and Nephthys: Kaplan, *Grabmalerei und Grabreliefs der Römerzeit*, 176, pl. 99a.

[68] This tomb could have been used earlier than the Roman period and was reused later because older paintings under the top layer of paint are still visible on its walls and ceilings. This tomb is located on the south section of the mountain. In 1903, it was one of three tombs that was visited by Clédat (*Couvents Rouge et Blanc, unpublished manuscript at the département des Antiquités égyptiennes du Musée du Louvre* (Paris, 1903), 192–74) who gave a very brief description of them in his notebook and photographed a scene in this tomb. See also C. Meurice, *Jean Clédat en Égypte et en Nubie (1900–1914)*, 69–70, 463, fig. 20.

Fig. 10. Silhouettes and the shedouf *on shroud Pushkin 4229/1 1a 5749. From I. Régen, "Ombres. Une iconographie singulière du mort…," fig. 2.*

The Silhouette and the Shadouf

Small silhouettes are depicted on four Roman mummy shrouds from Saqqara dating to the 1st century AD.[69] These shrouds are almost identical in their tempera technique, and each illustrates the deceased in Hellenistic

[69] They are registered as Berlin, Ägyptisches Museum, 11651; Moscow, Pushkin, Museum of Fine Arts, 4229/ I 1a 5749; Moscow, Pushkin, Museum of Fine Arts, 4301/I 1a 5747; and Paris, Louvre N 3076. Two lists of the scholars who studied these shrouds are presented by Riggs, *The Beautiful Burial the Roman Egypt*, 168–74, fig. 82, pls. 7–9, 277–78; Régen,"Ombres. Une iconographie singulière," 612–13, 621–22, 626–34, figs. 1–4. Parlasca paid great attention to these four shrouds: K. Parlasca, *Mumienporträts und verwandte Denkmäler* (Wiesbaden, 1966), pls. 12.1, 35.1, 61.2; K. Parlasca et al., *Repertorio d'arte dell'Egitto greco-romano* (Rome, 1977); K. Parlasca and H. Seemann, *Augenblicke: Mumienporträtsund ägyptische Grabkunst aus römischer Zeit* (Munich, 1999); K. Parlasca, "Osiris und Osirisglaube in der Kaiserzeit," in D. Françoise and P. Lévêque (eds.), *Les syncrétismes dans les religions grecque et romaine: Colloque de Strasbourg, 9–11 juin 1971* (Paris, 1973), 95–102.

Fig. 11. Silhouettes and the shedouf *on shroud (Pushkin shroud 4301/I 1a 5747). From I. Régen, "Ombres. Une iconographie singulière du mort…," fig. 4.*

costume standing between Anubis and Osiris. Osiris' face on the shrouds resembles that of the deceased, symbolizing the deceased's successful association with the god.[70]

Three of the shrouds (Berlin 11651, Pushkin 4229/1 1a 5749 (fig. 10), and Louvre N3076, depict a male deceased holding either a papyrus scroll, a bunch of wheat, or a garland in his left hand. The fourth one (Pushkin 4301/I 1a 5747 (fig. 11), commemorates the death of a women and her son. A figure, perhaps an Egyptian

[70] Smith (*Following Osiris*, 365) argued that the deceased depicted in his living contemporary dress in the presence of Osiris shows the end of the transfiguration process.

Fig. 12. The silhouette witnesses the purification of the female deceased. House-tomb 21, Tuna El-Gebel. From Gabra, Peintures à fresques et scènes, *pl. 25.*

peasant,[71] working a *shadouf,* appears on the left top of three of the shrouds (Berlin 11651, Pushkin 4229/1 1a 5749, and Louvre N 3076). Pushkin 4301/I 1a 5747 shows the deceased with Osiris and Anubis. The silhouettes at the bottom of the shroud stand on the *neshmet*-bark holding long sticks, perhaps paddles. On Pushkin shroud 4229/1 1a 5749, Anubis holds the keys to open the massive Egyptian-style gateway that represents the netherworld gate to Hades—the threshold between life and death over which the deceased has to pass for his transfiguration.[72]

Kákosy discussed the main scene on these shrouds that show the deceased between Osiris and Anubis, suggesting that the silhouettes represent the shadow-spirits that accompany the deceased in his journey to the netherworld, hoping that Anubis, with the keys of Hades, will permit him to traverse the gates of the afterlife.[73]

Riggs[74] assumed that these skeletal figures seem to represent the souls of the damned. Morenz however considered the silhouettes to be positive, as did Régen, who noted that they are engaged in activities related to the sustenance of the deceased. They are scattered around the figure of the deceased and around Anubis, Osiris, and the Four Sons of Horus in order to welcome and care for them. Some with long sticks act as sailors for the

[71] Morenz (*Das Werden zu Osiris,* 59) described the peasant as a *pileus* (*fellah*), or as a priest of Mithras because he wears a Phrygian cap.

[72] L. Corcoran, *Portrait Mummies from Roman Egypt, II–IV Centuries AD,* SAOC 56 (Chicago, 1994), 52–53; Parlasca and Seemann, *Augenblicke:Mumienporträts*, 25. In CT 491, 493, 494, and 500, the *bꜣ* and the *šwt* of the deceased are in danger of their free movement being restricted by the bad mysterious beings who try to constrain them. These guardians of the portals of the netherworld are called "trappers" (CT 494), and the "ones of pitchforks" (CT 500). CT 335 mentions that the name of the god who guards the portal is "the one who swallows millions."

[73] L. Kákosy, "Selige und Verdammte in der Spatägyptischen Religion," *ZÄS* 97 (1971), 96–98, figs. I–Ia.

[74] Riggs, *The Beautiful Burial in Roman Egypt*, 170.

Fig. 13. Mummification and purification of the shadow shown on the coffin of Mutirdis (Roemer-und Pelizaeus-Museum 1953). Photo by Sh. Shalchi, courtesy of the Roemer- und Pelizaeus-Museum, Hildesheim.

boat that will convey the deceased into the afterlife, and they are shown with the *shadouf*, helping to lift water, presumably for the benefit of the deceased.

The shrouds represent a synthesis of Egyptian-Roman funerary art and iconography. Here, the large numbers of silhouettes on each shroud do not represent the shadows of damned sinners who are punished by being swallowed by the devourer or being burned in the fire-cauldron, nor do they represent the *larva*, the evil and maleficent spirits, or the *skeletos* in the context of a symposium. The four shrouds present a new role for the silhouettes as blessed spirits who accompany the posthumous deceased in the netherworld and provide water for the deceased with the *shadouf*. They are not a subject of punishment—they are beneficial, serving the deceased in the afterlife, much like ushabtis.

The Silhouette and Purification

In House-tomb 21 at Tuna el-Gebel (fig. 12), a deceased woman is shown being purified by Horus and Thoth as a skeletal shadow figure looks on.[75] The woman is garbed in an Egyptian-Greek style costume and her face is

[75] It was uncovered in February 1935 by Sami Gabra. It dates to the second century AD and consists of four chambers. The anteroom and the burial chamber are on axis with one another, while to the east and west of the antechamber are two small undecorated chambers: S. Gabra, *Chez les Derniers Adorateurs du Trismegiste, la nécropole d'Hermopolis, Touna el Gebel (Souvenir d'un Archéologue)* (Cairo, 1971), 96; S. Gabra et al., *Fouilles d'Hermoupolis Ouest*, 39–50, pl. 9; Gabra, *Peintures à Frescques et Scènes peintes a Hermopolis–Ouest*, 13–15, figs. 25, 28; K. Lembke et al., *Ägyptens spat Blüte, Die Römer am Nile* (Mainz, 2004), 61, fig. 107; J. Corbelli, *The Art of Death in Graeco-Roman Egypt* (Princes

drawn in three-quarter view.[76] Her silhouette-form to the right is shown as a shriveled black corpse with closely cropped red hair, its surface delineated by knobs. The silhouette mimics the woman's gesture and posture, although it is shown in Egyptian profile view. A falcon hovering above the deceased's head may be serving the function of a *ba* bird.[77] This purification ritual is an intermediate stage between life and passing into the netherworld where the deceased is given new life.[78] Riggs assumed that the scene's location near the tomb's main entrance and the female's fashionable hair and jewelry indicated that the she was still connected with the earthly world, and the scene could be interpreted as showing a liminal stage—a transitory space and a threshold for entering the afterlife.[79] Smith disagreed, arguing that because "there is no distinction between mummy wrappings and clothing," garments cannot be used to indicate stages of the deceased's transformation.[80] After the purification process, the deceased was ready to undertake the voyage to the afterlife and to join with her silhouette spirit in the netherworld.[81]

The ablution of the deceased performed before preparing the finest clothes for his funeral was also a feature of Greek funerary practice.[82] In ancient Egypt, the lustration was an essential step of passing from death to rebirth and preparing the body for the spiritual journey towards the afterlife. It was conducted either on the mummy of the deceased, or on his *šwt*. Scenes of the purification of the shadow of the deceased by priests are shown on the Late Period-Ptolemaic mummy coffins of Mutirdis (Roemer-und Pelizaeus-Museum 1953; fig. 13), Djedbastetiouefankh (Roemer-und Pelizaeus-Museum 1954), and Paiuenhor (Kunsthistorisches Museum 7497).[83] All three coffins are from el-Hibeh, and they feature a similar scene of the mummification of the *šwt* on a lion-headed bier illustrating the theme of "becoming Osiris."

Risborough, 2006), 28, fig. 27; D. Kessler, *Histoire Topographie der Region zwischen Mallawi und Samalut* (Wiesbaden, 1981),109–19 ; Riggs, *The Beautiful Burial in Roman Egypt*, 134–35, fig. 60; Kaplan, *Grabmalerei und Grabreliefs der Römerzeit*, 162–65, pl. 83a; G. Grimm, *Die römischen Mumienmasken aus Ägypten* (Wiesbaden, 1974), pl. 132.2; Venit, *Visualizing the Afterlife*, 121–23, fig. 4.14.

[76] The House-tomb 21 reflects the Greek and Egyptian mix in art and architecture in masonry patterns. See G. Grimm, "Tuna El-Gebel 1913–1973," *MDAIK* 31 (1975), 229–30, pls. 68–69.

[77] The *ba* bird is one of the appropriations of royal imagery in private tombs in the Graeco-Roman period. The *ba* as a birdlike spirit normally hovers either near the deceased's body, as in Habachi Tomb A, B (L. Habachi, "Two Tombs of the Roman Epoch Recently discovered at Gabbary," *BSAA* 9 [1936], 275, fig. 4) and in Tomb 1 (Persephone Tomb) at Kom el-Schukafa (A. Guimier-Sorbets and M. Seif el-Din, "Life after Death," 139, fig. 7.3). In other cases, the *ba* bird flutters over the mummy, as is depicted twice in House-tomb 21, once as a ba-bird, and once as a falcon that hovers over the mummy lying on the goddess Nut's extended legs: Venit, *Visualizing the Afterlife*, 131–32, fig. 4.25. Kurth (*Der Sarge de Teüris*, 59) identified this falcon in the House-tomb 21 as a *ba* bird. The *ba* bird is also depicted in the Tomb of Petosiris, Osing et. al., *Denkmäler der Oase Dachla aus dem Nachlass von Ahmed Fakhry*, AV 28 (Mainz, 1982), pl. 32a.

[78] The earliest depiction of purification appears in the Twelfth Dynasty temple at Medinet Maadi where the king is purified by Horus and Thoth: A. Gardiner, "Addendum to 'The Baptism of Pharaoh,' *JEA* 36 (1950), 3–12," *JEA* 37 (1951), 111. A. Gardiner ("Baptism of Pharaoh," *JEA* 36 (1950), 10–12), suggested that Horus and Thoth were shown as two of the four gods of the cardinal points, while Corcoran, Portrait Mummies from Roman Egypt, 59 (citing G. Jécquier, *Considérations sur les religions* égyptiennes (Neuchâtel, 1946), 80–83, 133–36) notes that the choice of the two gods may have been influenced by their substitution for "Sia and Hu who journeyed with Re in the solar boat and who were responsible for the resurrection of the sun from the primeval waters." The rite was depicted on non-royal coffins and on tomb walls of the Ramesside period, as well as on cartonnage coffins of the Third Intermediate Period. See L. Corcoran, "Mysticism and the Mummy Portraits," in M. L. Bierbrier (ed.), *Portraits and Masks: Burial Customs in Roman Egypt* (London, 1997), 47 (revising her chronology given in *Portrait Mummies from Roman Egypt*, 59).

[79] Riggs, *The Beautiful Burial in Roman Egypt*, 135–36.

[80] Smith, *Following Osiris*, 365.

[81] On this scene, see Venit, *Visualizing the Afterlife*, 122–23, fig. 4.14.

[82] Euripides, *Alcestis*, 158–62, Sophocles, *Oedipus at Colonus*, 1598–599. In Greek funerary rituals, the lamenting woman of the family washed the dead body and laid it out in a coffin inside the house (*prosthesis*) for a day, then the deceased and the mourners were dressed in clothing specific to the funeral, identified as being a black or white *himatia* which varied according to sex, age, wealth, and status. Jewelry is also provided for the deceased, and there were workshops manufacturing jewelry specifically for funerary use. Finally, the deceased was transported on a wagon, a bier, or by hand to the place of burial (*ekphora*). See N. Dimakis, "Death, Burial and Ritual: Commemorating the Dead in Hellenistic and Roman Argos," in M. Dominique Nenna, S. Huber, and W. van Andringa (eds.), *Constituer la tombe, honorer les défunts en Méditerranée antique* (Alexandria, 2018), 356–57.

[83] S. Ikram and A. Dodson, *The Mummy in Ancient Egypt* (Cairo, 1998), 108, fig. 106. For the coffins of Mutirdis, Djedbastetiouefankh, and Paiuenhor, see, S. Chapman, *The Embalming Ritual of Late Period Through Ptolemaic Period* (PhD dissertation, University of Birmingham, 2016), figs. 1–7. Roeder dated them to the Twenty-Sixth Dynasty or later: G. Roeder, D*ie Denkmäler des Pelizaeus-Museums zu Hildesheim* (Hildesheim, 1921), 98–99, fig. 35. J. Taylor (*Death and the Afterlife in Ancient Egypt* [London, 2001], 49) dated the Hildesheim coffins to the Late Period (600–300 BC).

In Roman Egypt, the deceased's baptism was still depicted on the shrouds or stucco layer that covered the body of Roman-era portrait mummies.[84] But no scenes of the mummification and purification practices of silhouettes are yet documented in the tombs of the Ptolemaic and Roman period.

IV. The Silhouette as an Enemy

The silhouette could represent the hostile powers of the dead or of evil spirits.[85] Berlin coffin 11652 (fig. 14)[86] reflects the evil nature of the silhouette who would have to be suppressed and punished in the netherworld. The coffin shows three black silhouettes as victims of the Ammit beast. One is already in the mouth of the beast, while the two others are in panic at her feet, crying and begging for mercy. To my knowledge, in the funerary iconography of Graeco-Roman Egypt, this is the only known depiction of Ammit actually punishing and swallowing the silhouette. It emphasizes the negative character of these silhouettes as evil spirits and as enemies who face the deceased during his attempts to follow Osiris in the *duat*, therefore their destruction and elimination was essential for resurrection.

Fig. 14. Ammit swallowing silhouettes shown on Berlin coffin 11652. From D. Kurth, Der Sarge der Teüris, *66, fig. 24.*

V. The Ambivalent Nature of the Silhouette

All the previous examples show the silhouette expressing either their good or evil qualities. It may be a faithful companion of the deceased, substituting for him at the judgment or in purification scenes, and following the deceased into the realm of Osiris. The dead are still judged before Osiris who rewards the virtuous and accepts them as his followers and punishes the wicked as an enemy. The damned silhouette must be completely cursed, burned, or swallowed by the devourer before the tribunal of Osiris, showing the torments inflicted upon sinners in the underworld. However, in other cases, within the same court of the judgment, the silhouette may also play an ambivalent role—sometimes supportive, and sometimes not.

[84] The funerary conception of the baptism process was mainly the initiation of the deceased into the Isis cult. See V. von Gonzenbach, *Unterschunungen zu den knabenweihen im Isiskult der römischen Kaiserzeit, Antiquitas I; Abhandlungen zur alter Geschichte* (Bonn, 1957); Corcoran, "Mysticism and the Mummy Portraits," 47–48; Venit, "Referencing Isis in Tombs of Graeco-Roman Egypt," 94.

[85] A. Delatte and P. Derchain, *Les Intailles magiques gréco-égyptiennes* (Paris, 1964), 93.

[86] It dates to the Roman period (2nd century AD) from Saqqara: Parlasca, *Mumienporträts und verwandte Denkmäler* pl. 12 (2); S. Morenz, *Das Werden zu Osiris :Die Darstellungen auf einem Leichentuch der römischen Kaiserzeit, Berlin (II651) und verwandten Stücken, Forschungen und Berichte I* (Berlin, 1957), 64, fig. 7; Seeber, *Untersuchungen zur Darstellung*, 171 (fig. 69); Riggs, *The Beautiful Burial in Roman Egypt*, 168, fig. 80, 170, 226, 276; Kurth, *Der Sarg der Teüris*, 66, fig. 24; Brunner-Traut, *Gelebte Mythen*, 79.

Fig. 15. Four silhouettes shown at the judgment, el-Salamuni Tomb C1 (von Bissing's Tomb 1897), antechamber, north wall, upper register. Photo: W. Omran.

El-Salamuni Roman Tomb C1, the so-called " Tomb of von Bissing 1897" in Akhmim (fig. 15)[87] preserves a remarkable version of the judgment scene in its anteroom. In my opinion, it is the most important judgment scene of the Roman period, showing four silhouettes on trial, some of which play a positive role and others a negative role. One stands in frontal view beneath the beam of the scale. The second tiny one is in the right pan being weighed against a seated figure of Maat. The third, shown frontally, stands before the forelegs of the devourer, its feet placed irregularly and its arms dangling, while the last damned one bounces inside a fire-cauldron, its legs emerging from the sides of the cauldron which is shown as a white skyphos-shaped vase colored red inside in imitation of blood or fire.[88] The devourer sits on an Egyptian-style low shrine with a cornice as she licks her lips, awaiting her meal with relish. Osiris-Sokar supervises the court, while Maat stands to the far left, and Thoth strides to report to Osiris-Sokar.[89]

[87] El-Salamuni Mountain was the main cemetery of Akhmim during the Graeco-Roman period. It is located 6 km north of Akhmim. The Akhmim inspectorate divided the mountain into eight registers (A, B, C, D, E, F, G, H), The so-called von Bissing's Tomb 1897 is on the north section of the mountain. It is now registered it as Tomb C1. For more information, see W. von Bissing, "Aus Römischen Gräben zu Achmim," *JDAI* 61/62 (1946/1947), 1–16; von Bissing, "Tombeaux d'époque romaine à Akhmim," *ASAE* 50 (1950), 554–73, pl. 1; K. Kuhlmann, *Materialien zur Archäologie und Geschichte des Raumes von Achmim*, SDAIK 11 (Mainz, 1983), pl. 35c, d; Venit, "Referencing Isis," 117–19; Kurth, *Der Sarg der Teüris*, 67, fig. 25; Seeber, *Untersuchungen zur Darstellung*, 186 (fig. 79); G. Cartron, *L'architecture et les Pratiques funéraires dans L'Egypte romaine* (Oxford, 2012), 19.

[88] Von Bissing ("Tombeaux d'époque romaine à Akhmim," 573) interpreted the red interior of the vessel as the Lake of Fire. Seeber (*Untersuchungen zur Darstellung*, 186), called it a cauldron of fire, as did E. Brunner-Traut, *Gelebte Mythen*, 76.

[89] At the end of the 1980s, during his excavation in el-Hawawish necropolis, Kanawati visited von Bissing's Tomb 1897. He cleaned the interior of the tomb of heavy debris. Later in March 2015, I visited the tomb, and unfortunately found that its floor was again full of debris and suffering from environmental risks and bad activities including writing on the walls. Kanawati included three images of its walls in his monograph *Sohag in Upper Egypt: A Glorious History* (Giza, 1990), pls. 40–42. In March 2020, I had the concession from the Egyptian Ministry of Tourism and Antiquities to remove the heavy debris again, as well as to conduct restoration and to clean the bitumen from its walls and ceiling. Further investigation and publication of the tomb is forthcoming by the author.

George described these four silhouettes as shadows of the deceased.[90] Von Bissing noted that the Akhmim silhouettes, unusually for pharaonic depictions,[91] resemble a more Hellenistic-fashion deceased, fitting better stylistically with the Greek image of the soul. He differentiated the Egyptian and the Greek conception of the weighing of the soul, concluding that the Greek version lacked the ethical sense implicit in the Egyptian, that it determined only which one of the warriors whose souls are weighed would live and which would die.[92] Venit suggested that the silhouette figures and the drooling devourer in von Bissing's Tomb 1897 act like the images of the damned in the fire-cauldron depicted in the various books of the afterlife.[93] Though devouring the silhouette is depicted on Berlin coffin 11652, von Bissing's Tomb 1897 documents the only known scene in Graeco-Roman tombs that shows the silhouette being devoured. Boiling the shadows, as enemies of Osiris, either in the fire-cauldron or in the Lake of Fire, was previously depicted in pharaonic funerary art,[94] where the damned shadows were captured before being pressed and roasted according to the court's decree.[95]

In von Bissing's Tomb 1897, the two silhouettes beneath the scale and in the scale's pan are good followers, while the other two—the one boiled in the cauldron and the one waiting his destiny before the devourer—are damned and enemies of the deceased. This contrast in one scene is amazing, unique, and puzzling. If the deceased was so keen to prove his innocence at his judgment, one would not expect him to depict his shadow follower as a guilty being who receives his punishment in the fire cauldron or by being eaten by the wild devourer. Therefore, the deceased confirms his transfiguration twice in the tomb, first depicting himself in the orans-gesture before Osiris on the lower frieze below the judgment's scene, while a fascinating scene depicts a sexual encounter between Anubis and a woman atop of a classical *kline* on the southern wall of the chamber. Klotz concluded that this erotic scene is a proof of the transfiguration of the deceased, and his desire to remain sexually active in the afterlife.[96]

Six silhouettes, which again represent good and bad, are shown in another judgment scene in el-Salamuni Roman Tomb C3 (fig. 16).[97] The scene spans the north and east walls of the tomb's antechamber. On the north wall is the beginning of the judgment procession where the *psychopomp* Anubis, the divine messenger, leads the deceased to the court,[98] holding the left wrist of the deceased in his right hand, while the right hand of the deceased is raised in a gesture of adoration. A partially damaged silhouette—only its thin black legs are preserved—is shown between Anubis and a damaged female goddess, certainly Hathor. Anubis turns his head towards the silhouette, and holds it with his left hand, while Hathor holds the same silhouette with her right hand, and another silhouette with her left hand.

---

[90] George, *Vom Schatten als Seele*, 106.

[91] von Bissing,"Aus Römischen Gräben zu Achmim," 2.

[92] A. Baumeister, *Denkmäler des klassischen Altertums:zur Erläuterung des Lebens der Griechen und Römer in Religion, Kunst und Sitte* (Munich,1885), 921; C. Daremberg and E. Saglio, *Dictionnaire des antiquités grecques et romaines, d'après les textes et les monuments* (Paris, 1873), figs. 4263, 4947, 4957; von Bissing, "Tombeaux d'époque romaine à Akhmim," 571–72, no. 4; Seeber, *Untersuchungen zur Darstellung*, 77 (fig. 23).

[93] Venit, "Referencing Isis," 114.

[94] Boiling the shadows is depicted in the 11th hour of the Amduat in the Tomb of Thutmose III: S. Schott, "Das blutrünstige Keltergerät," *ZÄS* 74 (1938), pl. VIb; P. Bucher, *Les textes des tombes de Thoutmosis III et d'Aménophis II*, MIFAO 60 (Cairo, 1932), pl. 10). For the shadow in the Lake of Fire, see Louvre 3297 (Papyrus of Bakenmut) in A. Piankoff and N. Rambova, *Mythological Papyri* (New York, 1957), 127, pl. 12.

[95] Von Bissing, "Tombeaux d'époque romaine à Akhmim," 573.

[96] D. Klotz, "The Lecherous Pseudo-Anubis of Josephus and the 'Tomb of 1897' at Akhmim," in A. Gasse, F. Servajean, and C. Thiers (eds.), *Et in Ægypto et ad Ægyptum, Recueil d'études dédiées à Jean-Claude Grenier*, CENIM 5, vol. 2 (Montpellier 2012), 385–92, fig.1. Kaplan identified the two figures as Bes and Beset; Kaplan, *Grabmalerei und Grabreliefs der Römerzeit,* 87, pls. 88b, e. Bresciani also described it as an erotic scene: E. Bresciani, "Un' insolita figura di'concubina in terracotta: la suonatrice di tamburo," in P. Buzi, D. Picchi and M. Zecchi (eds.), *Aegyptiaca et Captica. Studi in onro di Sergio Pernigotti*, BAR-IS 2264 (Oxford, 2011), 28, 32, fig. 7.

[97] It lies on terrace C in the mountain at the southern part of the mountain near the modern village of el-Salamuni. It consists of two chambers with a western entrance and three burial niches (*kline*) cut in the burial chamber. According to Its architecture, artistic style, and zodiac, it appears to date to the Roman period. The publication is forthcoming by the author.

[98] Anubis in the court is assimilated with the Greek god Aiakos, the son of Zeus and Aigina, who was worshipped by the Greeks as the protector of the deceased in his afterlife, see S. Morenz, "Anubis mit dem Schlüssel," in S. Morenz (ed.), *Religion und Geschichte des alten Ägypten* (Vienna, 1975), 516–17.

Fig. 16. Anubis and Hathor lead silhouettes to the judgment, el-Salamuni Tomb C3, antechamber, north wall. Photo: W. Omran.

On the east wall (fig. 17), a third partially damaged silhouette (only his legs are still visible), stands beneath the center of the scale, while a fourth one is being weighed in the right pan of the scale. Unfortunately, the left pan is damaged. The fifth silhouette is awaiting his destiny before the devourer, while the last partially damaged one is submerged inside the fire-cauldron, similar to the one shown in von Bissing Tomb 1897. The next vignette shows Thoth recording the court's result, most probably before a seated figure of Osiris-Sokar, now lost.

Silhouettes are also depicted in the judgment of the deceased in el-Salamuni Roman Tomb C5 (fig. 18).[99] There, the scene is depicted in two friezes on the eastern wall of the burial chamber. Two silhouettes act in contrasting functions in the scene. The lower frieze shows the scale, with a partially preserved silhouette standing beneath it, in the role of the shadow as a beneficial follower of the deceased who attends the judgment on behalf of the deceased himself. The upper frieze shows a silhouette tortured in a fire-cauldron before the devourer. Just to the left of the judgment scene, the deceased, shown in a larger scale spanning the two friezes of the wall, is depicted in the orans-attitude, supposedly passing the judgment of the dead successfully and expressing his glorification and that he and his good silhouette will follow and serve Osiris in the underworld, while the damned silhouette enemy is burned.

VI. Conclusions

The ancient Egyptian concept of the *šwt* as a manifestation of the deceased continued to be an important iconographical aspect in Graeco-Roman Egypt, although its appearance and special funerary characteristics were modified. In Ptolemaic Egypt, the funerary concept of the silhouette was perhaps a Hellenistic variant of the ancient Egyptian tradition of the soul as a shadow. As a result of the merging of Egyptian and Hellenistic ideas, the concept of the shadow was influenced by Greek culture, and the skeletal figure in Egypt started to appear in the Ptolemaic period in the form of a black wooden skeletal statue that was associated with symposium

[99] It is located on terrace C on the mountain at the southern part of the mountain near the modern village of el-Salamuni adjacent to C3. It consists of two chambers with two burial niches in the burial chamber. Publication is forthcoming by the author.

Fig. 17. The silhouette in the court, el-Salamuni Tomb C3, east wall. Photo: W. Omran.

and banquet ceremonies of the wealthy. Although some of these little skeletal figurines of wood that were placed in small coffins were found in tombs, they are not depicted among the funerary motifs in tombs or on coffins during that period. Depicting the shadow in funerary art of Ptolemaic Egypt, either in the tombs or on mummy cases, was still rare. Though they still kept their ancient pharaonic *šwt* in appearance, embalming and purification rituals were performed directly on them instead of on the dead, as depicted on the coffins of Mutirdis, Djedbastetiouefankh, and Paiuenhor.

Roman Egypt was multi-cultural, and the afterlife too was characterized as a blend of Egyptian, Hellenistic, and Roman influence. The Egyptians, Greeks, and Romans all had a strong desire to enjoy a blessed afterlife. The harmonization of Egyptian, Greek, and Roman conceptions of the afterlife was facilitated by their shared cultures, but the Egyptian conception of the afterlife became universal. The people in Ptolemaic-Roman Egypt employed traditional Egyptian funerary iconography to proclaim the identification of the deceased with Osiris.[100] However, features of their own cultures continued to be expressed, especially in their style of dress.

In Roman Egypt, the shadows became more skeletal in appearance, and the representation of them became more common than in Ptolemaic Egypt. The silhouette in funerary iconography of Roman Egypt is a result of the hybridization and biculturalism in funerary art of that time. They are depicted in multiple attitudes and acting in various functions in tombs and on mummy cases and shrouds.

The use of skeletal figures in Egypt was completely different than in the Hellenistic-Roman world. In Egypt, the figures are associated mainly with the fate of the dead in the afterlife, denoting that the deceased made a safe passage to the afterlife, but also showing the negative consequences that awaited the unworthy dead. In contrast, the Hellenistic funerary silhouette was always a personification of the better fate of the soul and an image of the deceased who received pleasure and entertainment.

At the judgment, Osiris rewards the virtuous and punishes the wicked, therefore, the deceased had to get rid of his enemies and to be fully protected from all the hostile powers represented by these silhouettes.[101] Punishing the silhouette in a fiery cauldron starts to appear in Egyptian funerary iconography in the Roman era. Books of the afterlife were well-known in the *chora* of Roman Egypt as indicated by their pictorial references in Roman

---

[100] For the conception of afterlife in Ptolemaic Egypt, see Smith, *Following Osiris*, 358–60 and Venit, *Visualizing the Afterlife*, 196–201. The mask of Titus Flavius Demetrius, a Roman citizen in the late first century AD from Hawara, now kept in the Ipswich Borough Council Museum (R1921-89), suggests that he was mummified and buried in Egyptian style: Riggs, *The Beautiful Burial in Roman Egypt*, 21, fig. 4.

[101] E. Preisendanz, *Papyri Graecae Magicae. Die griechischen Zauberpapyri*, vol.1 (Stuttgart, 1973), 1885, 1930, 2006.

Fig 18. Two silhouettes in the judgment court, el-Salamuni Tomb C5, burial chamber, east wall. Photo: W. Omran.

tombs. To my knowledge, depictions of damned silhouettes in the fiery cauldron, and the devourer swallowing them, are not attested in funerary art in Egypt earlier than the Roman era.

The silhouette is a distinctive feature in the Roman tombs of el-Salamuni where it is characterized by a number of features, most important being that it is shown only in connection with the judgment of the deceased.

El-Salamuni is the only necropolis that records the ambivalent nature of the silhouette within a single judgment scene, where it plays a double role as a manifestation of the deceased and as a tortured victim and stubborn enemy who hinders the deceased's transfiguration. This contrasting role of the silhouette gives el-Salamuni a special funerary character, and it helps to create a more nuanced understanding of the role these black figures played in funerary beliefs in Roman Egypt.

The tombs at el-Salamuni preserve the only examples in any tombs of scenes of the punishment of the silhouette either by the devourer or the cauldron of fire at the judgment. In contrast, in the el-Mazawaka tomb of Petosiris, the devourer spits into a fiery cauldron that does not contain sinners. I assume that the hieroglyphic text next to Petosiris substituted for the visual depiction of the condemned silhouette and guaranteed a blessed transfiguration and eternity for the Osiris-Petosiris. It reads: "O Osiris-Petosiris…may your ba follow Sokar, may you follow Osiris every day…may your ka depart to the heaven towards the gods and goddesses who dwell there… without any obstruction for your ba in the underworld forever!"[102] The scenes in the tombs at el-Salamuni specifically included images of the silhouettes as enemies who had to be destroyed during the judgment, using the visual depiction of the destruction of the enemies instead of texts to declare his innocence and justification.

[102] Venit, *Visualizing the Afterlife*, 168, fig. 5.11, 170.

No depictions of the *ba,* either as a complete bird or as a human-headed bird, appear in the judgment scenes in the el-Salamuni tombs which suggests that the "good" silhouette acted in the role of the *ba* of the deceased, enjoying proximity to Osiris, and exiting and entering the tomb freely.

Although the silhouette appeared in the judgment scenes in the el-Salamuni tombs, it was not shown in contemporary Books of the Dead from the area.[103] The difference between the tomb scenes and the Book of the Dead could be a good future research question.

Unfortunately, the tombs of el-Salamuni have not yet been studied enough to allow them to be assigned a more precise date—although a Roman date is most probable—and it is hoped that with further research, more can be said about these fascinating images.

[103] P. BM EA 10479 in M. Mosher, *The Papyrus of Hor (BM EA 10479), with Papyrus McGregor. Late Period Tradition at Akhmim.* Catalogue of the Books of the Dead in the British Museum, vol. 2 (London, 2001); P. Nesmin in J. Clère, *Le papyrus de Nesmin. Un Livre des Morts hiéroglyphique de l'époque ptolémaïque*, BiGen 10 (Cairo, 1987); P. Twt in E. Bayer-Niemeir et al., *Ägyptische Bildwerke III. Skulptur, Malerei, Papyri und Särge* (Frankfurt, 1993), 254–92; P. Berlin P. 10477 and P. Hildesheim 5248 in B. Lüscher, *Die Totenbuch pBerlin 10477 aus Achmim (mit Photographien des verwandten pHildesheim 5248)*, HAT 6 (Wiesbaden, 2000); P. Berlin 3064 A-B in U. Kaplony-Heckel, *Aegyptische Handschriften, III* (Stuttgart, 1986), 33; Omar Pacha Pap. 408 in Collection Omar Pacha Sultan = (Anonymous), *Collection de feu Omar Pacha Sultan. Catalogue déscriptif, I. Art égyptien; II. Art musulman*, Paris Collection Omar Pacha Sultan (Paris, 1929), pl. 76.

A Lost *Dipinto* from the Tomb of Ramesses III and New Insights into the Nature of the Architectural Feature *nfr.w*

Dora Petrova
Heidelberg University

Abstract

This paper provides the editio princeps of a hieratic dipinto in corridor G of KV 11, where the Opening of the Mouth Ritual is situated. The text is of importance because it has a preserved date, which might shed more light on the question of how far the construction of the tomb proceeded during the reign of Sethnakht and depending upon whether the dipinto was written under his successor, Ramesses III. The inscription also gives insight into the nature of an architectural feature called nfr.w and how it was envisioned in the plan of the tomb. This research was carried out in the framework of The Ramesses III (KV 11) Publication and Conservation Project.

ملخص

تتناول هذه المقالة النسخة الأصلية من رسمٍ لنص هيراطيقي يقع في الممر G بالمقبرة KV11 بوادي الملوك، حيث يوجد طقس فتح الفم. يُعد هذا النص مهمًا لأنه يحتوي على تاريخ قد يلقي مزيدًا من الضوء على السؤال المتعلق بمدى استمرار أعمال بناء هذه المقبرة في عهد الملك "سِت نَخْت"، ومعتمدًا على ما إذا كان هذا الرسم قد نُفِّذ في عهد خليفته رمسيس الثالث. يُقدم النص كذلك معلوماتٍ حول طبيعة معلم معماري يعرف باسم "نِفِرو"، وكيف كان متصورًا في مخطط المقبرة. أُجري هذا البحث في إطار مشروع نشر وحفظ مقبرة الملك رمسيس الثالث (KV11).

I had the great opportunity of reconstructing the Opening of the Mouth Ritual depicted on the left (east) wall of corridor G in the tomb of Ramesses III, as part of my research within The Ramesses III (KV 11) Publication and Conservation project[1] (fig. 1) (see article by Weber et al., in this volume). While examining the third scene of the ritual, I noticed traces of a hieratic *dipinto* written across the depiction of the royal statue (fig. 2).[2]

My research on the reconstruction of the Opening of the Mouth Ritual in KV 11 was based primarily on an image enhancement technique called DStretch®[3] using the color-spaces LDS and LAB. I therefore decided to use the same method for enhancing the hieratic dipinto. It did not come as a surprise when the color-space LDS revealed much more of the text (fig. 3). From what is visible, it can be determined that the inscription consists of

[1] The height of the corridor is 3.07 m, and the width is 2.64m, while the length is 6.88m. See the preliminary results on the reconstruction of the wall in D. Petrova, "From Invisible Traces to Invincible Ritual. Reconstructing the Opening of the Mouth Ritual in the Tomb of Ramesses III," in A. Weber, M. Grünhagen, L. Rees, and J. Moje (eds.), *Achet Neheh, Publication in Honour of Willem Hovestreydt on Occasion of His 75th Birthday* (London, 2020).

[2] The beginning of the *dipinto* slightly touches scene four.

[3] For the successful application of DStretch® in the field of Egyptology see L. Evans, A. L. Mourad, "DStretch® and Egyptian tomb paintings: A case study from Beni Hassan," *JAS* 18 (2018), 78–84; P. Witkowski, J. M. Chyla, and W. Ejsmond, "Combination of RTI and Decorrelation: An Application to the Examination of Badly Preserved Rock Inscriptions and Rock Art at Gebelein (Egypt)," in S. Campana, R. Scopigno, and G. Carpentiero (eds.), *Keep the Revolution Going, Proceedings of the 43rd Annual Conference on Computer Applications and Quantitative Methods in Archaeology* (CAA2015; Oxford 2016), 939–44; R. Enmarch, "Writing in the 'Mansion of Gold': Texts from the Hatnub Quarries," *EA* 47 (2015), 10–12.

Journal of the American Research Center in Egypt 56 (2020), 169–174
doi: http://dx.doi.org/10.5913/jarce.56.2020.a010

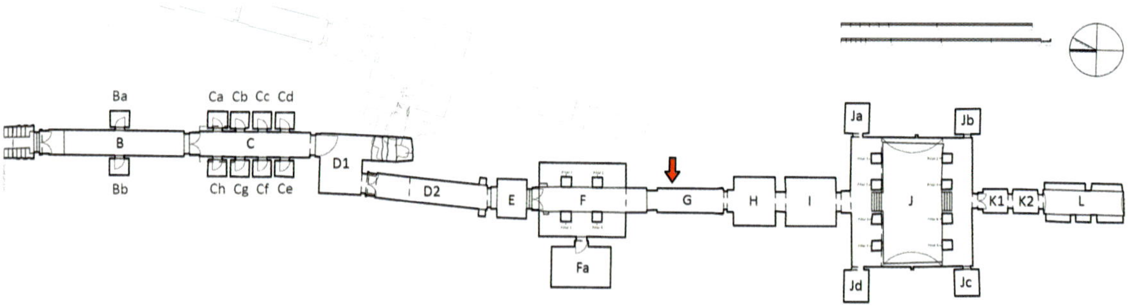

Fig. 1. Map of KV 11 indicating where the dipinto is situated.

Fig. 2. Left (east) wall of corridor G, KV 11 containing a hieratic dipinto. Photo: J. Kramer for The Ramesses III (KV 11) Publication and Conservation Project. © The Ministry of Tourism and Antiquities.

Fig. 3. Left (east) wall of corridor G, KV 11 after applying DStretch® color-space LDS. Photo: J. Kramer for The Ramesses III (KV 11) Publication and Conservation Project. © The Ministry of Tourism and Antiquities.

Fig. 4. Hieratic dipinto and the royal statue from scene three of the Opening of the Mouth Ritual, corridor G, left (east) wall, KV 11. Facsimile by D. Petrova.

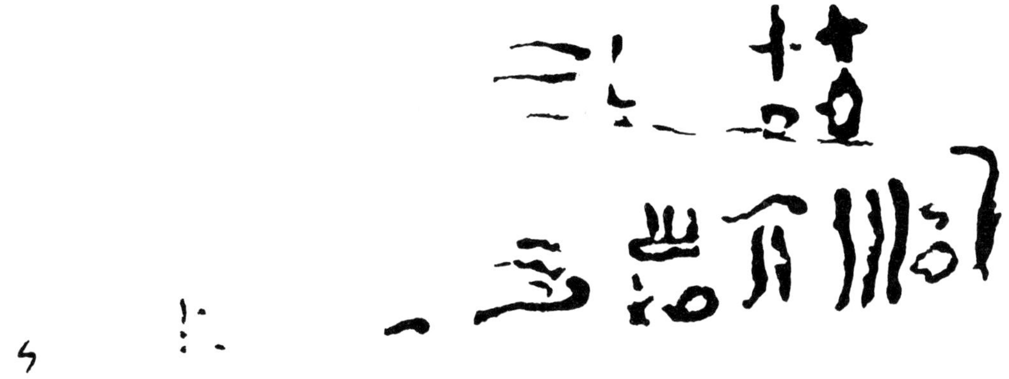

Fig. 5. Hieratic dipinto*, corridor G, left (east) wall, KV 11. Facsimile by D. Petrova.*

two lines (fig. 4). The text of the second line reads "regnal year 3, month 2 of Achet, (day) 13," but unfortunately the name of the king is not preserved.

Luckily, the line above the date of the *dipinto* is visible, providing a hint for interpretation and possible dating of the inscription. Nevertheless, the reader should keep in mind that the conclusions given below are far from definitive, and a close inspection of the *dipinto* may reveal additional information not available at the current state of the investigation. Furthermore, it is difficult to determine whether the inscription was written on top of or below the red contour of the depiction of the king's statue. On the enhanced image, it seems that the black ink of the text is on top of the red contour, but this might also be due to DStretch® enhancing the black more than the red.[4] This leaves a slight probability that the inscription might have been added later, after the reign of Ramesses III. However, at this early stage of investigation, this paper will consider primarily the idea that the *dipinto* is contemporary either with Ramesses III or with his father Sethnakht.

Transcription (fig. 5)

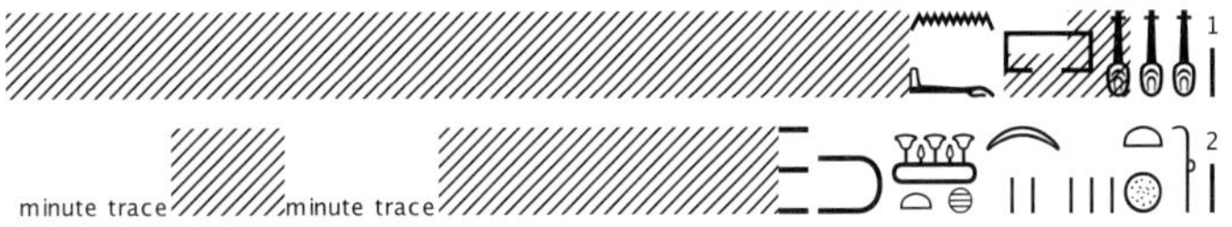

Transliteration and Translation

1. *nfr.w ꜥ n mḥ* [...	The innermost of [X] cubits [...
2. *ḥꜣ.t-zp 3 ꜣbd 2 ꜣḫ.t* (*sw*) 13[...	Year 3, month 2 of Achet, (day) 13 [...

a. According to the traces, the first line of the text seems to be separated from the second by a dividing line.

b. The traces corroborate the reading *n mḥ*—of [X] cubits. If the reading is valid, then the line probably continued by indicating the breadth and the height of the nfr.w as in: O. BM 8505, rto 1, *passim*, where *nfr.w* is followed by *n mḥ* and its dimensions.[5]

[4] I am thankful to Thomas Christiansen for his observations and sharing his knowledge on the very plausible connection between DStretch® and the chemistry of the ink with me.

[5] H. Carter, A. H. Gardiner "The Tomb of Ramesses IV and the Turin Plan of a Royal Tomb," *JEA* 4 (1917), 143, pl. 29.

The *nfr.w* of the Tomb

The word *nfr.w* is used to denote a particularly secluded architectural structure, such as the royal bedroom, the inner parts of the temple, the innermost part of the tomb, or even the inner parts of the Amduat.[6] According to the plan of the tomb of Ramesses IV, the *pr-ḥḏ* of the *nfr.w* was located in the back room of the burial chamber and contained the canopic jars and the funerary items.[7] As Gardiner observed, the *nfr.w* was not "the name of a specific room,"[8] but rather the innermost part of the tomb. The same is noted by Frandsen who collected the attestations of the term and concluded: "*nfr.w* does not refer to a single, specific room, but rather to the core of the tomb." Moreover, he added that it cannot designate the burial chamber itself, since this is already called *tꜣ s.t ḳrs.t*.[9]

Based on the preserved examples and the abovementioned interpretations, the word *nfr.w* seems to designate the innermost part of the tomb, which also happens to be the lowest part.[10] This is significant for the interpretation of the placement and the nature of the *dipinto* in KV 11, since corridor G indeed marks the end of the descent into the innermost/lowest part of the tomb. Thus, the placement of the inscription here does not come as a surprise. It is likely that it was meant to serve as a reminder of the dimensions of the *nfr.w* to the builders of this part of the tomb, which had yet to be carved.

Whether corridor G[11] was included in the *nfr.w* cannot be ascertained at this point of the investigation, but what seems to be evident is that all chambers situated further down the tomb, namely the antechambers and burial chamber, must have been subsumed under the term *nfr.w*. Another feature that suggests that corridor G was not included in the *nfr.w* is the presence of square holes in both walls next to the entrance to the antechamber. These might have been used to support a wooden beam that was used to seal a door between corridor G and the antechamber from left to right (see figs. 6–7). The depth of one of these holes decreases away from the door, which suggests that the bolt was pulled open in exactly this place.[12] The possibility of a barrier here raises the suggestion that the actual *nfr.w* started behind it, in the antechamber, and that the *dipinto* was situated before this area.

Sethnakht or Ramesses III?

It is important to mention the other seven *dipinti* in KV 11 which are written over the plaster above the entrances of the eight additional chambers in corridor C.[13] The inscriptions reveal the nature and purpose of these structures, among which are the treasury, the house of food, and the hall of two truths.[14] On paleographical grounds, it is difficult to ascertain whether the *dipinti* found in corridor C belong together with the one located in corridor G. However, when it comes to their purpose, they all share information regarding structural features of the tomb, and it merits consideration to assign them all to the same time period and perhaps the same king.

6 E. Hornung, *Das Amduat*, vol. 1 (Wiesbaden, 1963), 84; E. Hornung, *Das Amduat*, vol. 2 (Wiesbaden, 1967), 100, n. 8.

7 Carter, Gardiner, "The Tomb of Ramesses IV," 143.

8 J. Capart, A. H. Gardiner, and B. van de Walle, "New Light on the Ramesside Tomb-Robberies," *JEA* 22 (1936), 178.

9 P. J. Frandsen, "On the Root *nfr* and a 'Clever' Remark on Embalming," in J. Osing, E. K. Nielsen (eds), *The Heritage of Ancient Egypt. Studies in Honour of Erik Iversen*, CNI Publication 13 (Copenhagen, 1992), 53, 54. For the designation for the burial chamber, see P. Abbot, 3,4 and P. Leopold/Amherst 2,10.

10 Petrie translates *nfr.w* as "ground level," W. M. Flinders Petrie, *Medum* (London, 1892), 12–13. Gardiner, comments that *nfr* was used in opposition to *kꜣ* (height) as "bottom" or "level." See H. Carter, "A Tomb Prepared for Queen Hatshepsut and Other Recent Discoveries in Thebes," *JEA* 4 (1917), 110. In a footnote, Frandsen specifies that it was Gardiner in his capacity as an editor of *JEA* who added the footnote in Carter's article. See Frandsen, "On the Root *nfr*," 54, n. 75.

11 This is not to say that the *nfr.w* always started after corridor G, since the corridor was not always present in the architectural plan of the royal tomb. Corridor G is found only in the tombs of Seti I, Ramesses II, Merenptah, Tausret/Sethnakht, and Ramesses III.

12 O. Königsberger, *Die Konstruktion der* Ägyptischen Tür (Glückstadt, 1936), 28.

13 For the nature and purpose of the chambers see W. Hovestreydt, "Sideshow or Not? On the Side-Rooms of the First Two Corridors in the Tomb of Ramesses III," in B. J. J. Haring, O. E. Kaper, and R. van Walsen (eds.), *The Workman's Progress: Studies in the Village of Deir El-Medina and Other Documents from Western Thebes in Honour of Rob Demarée* (Leuven, 2014), 103–32.

14 J. Černý, *Valley of the Kings*, BdÉ 61 (Cairo, 1973), 32–33.

Figs. 6 and 7. Cavities (west and east) at the end of corridor G. The depth of the west cavity decreases away from the door, which suggests that the bolt was pulled open in this place. Photo: J. Kramer for The Ramesses III (KV 11) Publication and Conservation Project. © The Ministry of Tourism and Antiquities.

The question that remains is to which king this text can be assigned. Based on the available information, there are two working hypotheses regarding the *dipinto* in corridor G. The first is that the inscription, along with the others in corridor C, might have originated in Sethnakht's reign.[15] The reference to year 3 would then refer to

[15] Hornung has already suggested that the side chambers in corridor B and C might have been constructed under the reign of Sethnakht: E. Hornung, *Das Tal der Könige* (Munich, 2002), 51–52. See also A. Weber, "Der Eingang zum Reich des Sokar. Überlegungen zur antiken Interpretation der Bereiche D bis E in KV 11," in J. Moje, S.-W. Hsu, and V. Laisney (eds.), *Festschrift für Karl Jansen-Winkeln*, ÄAT 99 (Berlin, 2020), 404.

the last years of the rule of that pharaoh.[16] This would indicate that the king's construction activities reached at least corridor G and might have continued further, maybe even on to the burial chamber. It is known that Sethnakht had to change the axis of the tomb while constructing corridor D due to its collision (at D1a) with room Fa of KV 10 (Amenmesse).[17] The king, however, proceeded further with the construction and the decoration, as is evident from the presence of his cartouches at the entrance of corridor D2. Then, due to his death in year 4, his burial was instead accommodated in KV 14 (Tausret).[18] His son Ramesses III took over KV 11 and redecorated everything that was already finished by his father under his own name, as is evident at least up to corridor D, where he covered the cartouches of his father with his own.[19] Then he continued further on and decorated the empty walls already constructed by Sethnakht, reaching corridor G, drawing the outlines for the Opening of the Mouth Ritual, inscribing it, and coating the *dipinto* with plaster.[20]

The second plausible scenario is that the *dipinto* in corridor G refers to year 3 of Ramesses III, perhaps when he reached and started the constructions of the lower part of the tomb. It has already been suggested that the chambers in corridors B and C were added during the reign of this king, resulting in the destruction of parts of the texts of the Litany of Re.[21]

A future close investigation of all the *dipinti* as well as the traces of coating and recoating in the tomb might lead to more definitive answers pertaining the newly discovered inscription in corridor G and especially the significance of the mentioned year 3.

---

[16] The length of Sethnakht's reign was four years: H. Altenmüller, "Royal Tombs of the Nineteenth Dynasty" in R. H. Wilkinson, K. R. Weeks (eds.), *The Oxford Handbook of the Valley of the Kings* (Oxford, 2016), 203.

[17] A. Dodson, "Royal Tombs of the Twentieth Dynasty," in R. H. Wilkinson, K. R. Weeks (eds.), *The Oxford Handbook of the Valley of the Kings*, 218. For a ground plan of the tomb see Weber et al., "Second Report on the Publication and Conservation of the Tomb of Ramesses III in the Valley of the Kings (KV 11)," in this volume, fig. 1.

[18] Dodson, "Royal Tombs of the Twentieth Dynasty," 218.

[19] A. Weber, "Der Eingang zum Reich des Sokar," 346–47.

[20] For the stages of decoration of the royal tomb in the Valley of the Kings see Černý, *Valley of the Kings*, 35–41.

[21] Dodson, "Royal Tombs of the Twentieth Dynasty," 219. It will be interesting, however, to compare the side rooms in KV 11 to the side rooms from KV 17 (Seti I) and KV 14 (Tauseret/Setnakht), which also appear to be cut through the already existing decoration. See, Hornung, E., H. Burton, *The Tomb of Seti I. Das Grab Sethos'I.* (Zürich, 1991), pls. 136, 141 and 168. In KV 14 a side chamber is cut through the title and scenes one and two of the Opening of the Mouth Ritual in corridor G.

Did Akhenaten's Founding of Akhetaten Cause a Malaria Epidemic?

Lisa Sabbahy
American University in Cairo

Abstract

This paper presents and discusses evidence for changes in the environment that would have taken place at the site of Amarna, ancient Akhetaten, during the rapid building and populating of the city in the reign of King Akhenaten. The evidence suggests that the effect of the founding of this city, with all the consequences of a changed environment on both sides of the river, could have been responsible for a malaria epidemic. This scenario is backed up by the high prevalence of signs of malaria in the skeletal material from Amarna, as well as in the short-lived history of the city, which was deserted after about fifteen years.

ملخص

يقدم ويناقش هذا المقال أدلةً على تغيرات بيئية ربما قد حدثت بموقع العمارنة –آخت أتون قديمًا – في أثناء العملية السريعة لبناء وتعمير هذه المدينة في عهد الملك أخناتون. تُشير الأدلة إلى أن أثر تأسيس هذه المدينة مع كل ما نتج عنه من عواقب تغير البيئة على ضفتي النهر قد تسبب على الأرجح في تفشي وباء الملاريا. ويدعم هذا الرأي الانتشار الواسع لعلامات الإصابة بالملاريا في البقايا الآدمية القادمة من العمارنة، فضلًا عن التاريخ القصير لعمر المدينة التي صارت مهجورة بعد حوالي خمسة عشر عامًا من تاريخ تأسيسها.

In year 5 of his reign, Amenhotep IV, son of Amenhotep III, of the later Eighteenth Dynasty, changed his name to Akhenaten, closed the temple of Amun at Karnak, the repercussions of which are not really understood, and moved with his family and court officials to a virgin site in Middle Egypt, to build his new royal city for the Aten, called Akhetaten, "The Horizon of the Aten." The king set out his plans for the city in a decree, known as the "Early Proclamation" that was carved on two stelae, called M and X, cut into the rock on the northern and southern limits of the area that would become the city Akhetaten, now known by its modern name Amarna.[1]

The city of Akhetaten was located on the east bank of the Nile in an apparently empty and barren area, safely above the level of the Nile inundation. Across on the west side of the Nile was a large area of flood plain through which flowed the Bahr Yussef, the only tributary of the Nile in Egypt. In year 6, King Akhenaten set up eleven more stelae laying out the boundaries of his city on the east, and on the west side of the river stelae A, B, and F marked the edges of the fertile agricultural land that would feed the population of the city.[2] Because the Bahr Yussef bisected this two-hundred-kilometer-square area, it could be irrigated all year round, and thus could produce two crops of grain every year, rather than the traditional one crop that was dependent on the annual inundation.[3]

---

[1] William Murnane and Charles Van Siclen, *The Boundary Stelae of Akhenaten* (London-New York, 1993), 11; Barry Kemp, "The City of El-Amarna as a Source for the Study of Urban Society in Ancient Egypt," *World Archaeology* 9, no. 2 (1977), 124, fig. 1.

[2] Aidan Dodson, *Amarna Sunrise: Egypt from Golden Age to Age of Heresy* (Cairo, 2014), 11.

[3] Christian Tietze, "Amarna – The City and Surrounding Area," in F. Seyfried (ed.), *In the Light of Amarna: 100 Years of the Nefertiti Discovery* (Berlin, 2012), 58.

Journal of the American Research Center in Egypt 56 (2020), 175–179
doi: http://dx.doi.org/10.5913/jarce.56.2020.a011

Agriculture enhances the breeding of mosquitos and therefore also the intensity of malaria for people nearby agricultural land. Irrigation attracts mosquitos because it facilitates water accumulation and "crop cover," especially grain, provides mosquitoes with a favorable environment.[4] Studies show that there was "widespread endemic malaria in the Nile Valley"[5] throughout ancient Egyptian history, and specifically there was infection from *Plasmodium. falciparum,* which causes the most "severe malaria."[6] The year-round cultivation of the standard ancient Egyptian grains, emmer and barley, would have attracted mosquitoes and enhanced their ability to thrive.

On the other side of the river, the building of the city spread north to south about four miles along the east bank of the river from the North Riverside Palace to the Sun Temple of Nefertiti.[7] The king lived in the North Riverside Palace, and royal females were in the North Palace slightly south of it. The bulk of the city's population was in the two main suburbs of the north and the south, where there was a mixture of elite villas with clusters of small houses around or near them. In the southeast, in a more barren area, were two workmen's villages, now referred to as the Workmen's Village and the Stone Village. The population of the city has been estimated to have ranged from 20,000 to 50,000 people.[8]

Buildings for the living in ancient Egypt were constructed of mud brick, and Akhetaten was no exception. The palaces, all the administrative buildings, and all houses were mud brick covered with mud plaster, and that included floors and ceilings of both houses and palaces. The temples were built of rectangular blocks of limestone known as *talatat*, although the pylons of the largest two temples were mud brick, and all enclosure walls would have been mud brick, as well as other large structures, such as the massive pillars of the bridge from the King's House to the Great Palace.[9]

Mud brick at Akhetaten was of two basic types: alluvial or marl, and the typical inclusions, especially with marl mud brick, was gravel.[10] The best ancient Egyptian evidence of brick making is a scene in the Eighteenth Dynasty tomb of the vizier Rekhmire at Thebes.[11] There, men are shown filling pottery vessels with water from a square pool with trees,[12] and then mixing and working together the soil, water, and inclusions, forming the rectangular shape of the bricks with a mold, and then laying them out in the sun to dry.

The important point about bricking-making for this discussion is twofold. First, because there had to be water by any brick-making area, a pit was dug that was then filled with water from a well or brought from the Nile. Such pits, often referred to as borrow pits, are still dug for mud brick making in villages today. One could assume with the building of the city, particularly the private houses, there would have been bricks made at different sites throughout the city, each of which would have had a pit for water. "Various pits found beneath the floors and walls of houses at Amarna might have been dug for brick-making materials," so bricks seem to have been made at the building site where they were used.[13] Brick evidence from the Workmen's Village shows that the bricks used to build the substantial enclosure wall around the village were made from materials used in the construction of the main city, while the village houses themselves were built with bricks made from material from a huge pit dug right by the village.[14]

The second point is that houses of traditional materials, such as mud brick, attract mosquitoes because the cracks and spaces in mud bricks and mud plaster offer mosquitos not only ways into the house, but the cracks and

---

[4] Kwadwo Asenso-Okyere, Felix Asante, Jifar Tarekegn, et al., *The Linkages between Agriculture and Malaria,* International Food Policy Research Institute (2009), 16, 21.

[5] Nicole Smith-Guzmán, "Cribra orbitalia in the Ancient Nile Valley and Its Connection to Malaria," *International Journal of Paleopathology* 10 (2015), 1.

[6] Andreas Nerlich, Bettina Schraut, Sabine Dittrich, et al., "Plasmodium falciparum in Ancient Egypt," *Emerging Infectious Diseases* 14/8 (2008), 1317–18.

[7] Barry Kemp, *The City of Akhenaten and Nefertiti: Amarna and Its People* (Cairo, 2012), 46, fig. 2.1.

[8] Kemp, *City of Akhenaten and Nefertiti*, 272.

[9] Kemp, *City of Akhenaten and Nefertiti,* 132, fig. 4.7.

[10] Charles French, "A Sediment Analysis of Mud Brick and Natural Features at el-Amarna," in B. Kemp (ed.), *Amarna Reports I* (London, 1984), 191.

[11] Norman De Garis Davies, *The Tomb of Rekh-Mi-Rēʿ at Thebes* (New York, 1943), pl. 58.

[12] Undoubtedly showing an idealized pond for the afterlife, and not just a pit, Davies, *The Tomb of Rekh-Mi-Rēʿ*, 54.

[13] Kemp, *City of Akhenaten and Nefertiti,* 70.

[14] Kemp, *Amarna Reports I*, 4–5.

crannies offer them a micro-environment in which to live. Mud brick houses usually have a grass or reed roof as well, which also attracts mosquitoes and makes it easy for them to get into the house.[15] Particularly at the Workmen's Village, matting, loose grass, and reeds have been found with roof fragments, and these plant materials seem to have been used to fill the gaps between the poles and beams in the roofs.[16] The Workmen's Village also had animal pens on the its east side, and keeping animals is "associated with greater exposure to mosquitos."[17]

It has been estimated that there must have been about three thousand houses at Akhetaten, ranging from small tri-partite houses to large villas, all built of mud brick.[18] Adding to that all the other administrative and royal buildings made of mud brick, the construction and the repair and upkeep of Akhetaten's buildings, along with the large fields of irrigated land just across the river, this newly established city provided an excellent environment for mosquitos to live and breed.

Borrow pits were not the only standing bodies of water that would have allowed mosquitos to thrive. For a barren desert area, the city of Akhetaten had numerous wells, pools, and water gardens, as well as irrigated plots for trees and other plants. The royal palaces and every elite villa had their own well, and wells were also dug in public places for occupants of smaller houses to use. In fact, King Akhenaten's city "is the location of the earliest wells in the Nile Valley."[19] Only a few of these wells have been excavated; in particular, there is a large well in excavation square Q48.4, Area 23, on the east side of the main city, in the beginning of the wadi leading to the Workmen's Village.[20] The Workmen's Village did not have a well, but water was brought from well Q48.4 to a "zir area" near the village, a plot of land with large vessels that would be filled with water, and set into stones to keep them upright.[21] The Workmen's Village was too far into the desert to dig a well, and any water reached would have been brackish because of the "naturally high salt content of the desert."[22]

The Q48.4 well was formed of two parts. First, a staircase or ramp led down to a square platform, and then a shaft cut in the platform dropped down to water level that varied with the height of the Nile.[23] A *shadouf* on the platform was used to bring water up to that level, and then the water could be poured into vessels and carried up the stairs or ramp. This type of large well with *shadouf* is depicted in the midst of an orchard in the rock cut tomb of the High Priest Meryra at Amarna.[24] Smaller wells, found with houses or in public areas, had a spiral staircase that descended down far enough that pottery vessels could be filled with water and carried back up.[25] In the North Suburb, there seems to have been at least two public wells that were associated with a well-house for a guard that was reached by a long, straight, flight of steps.[26]

The palaces and many of the villas at Akhetaten also had pools, although the largest pool, probably better referred to as a lake, was the one found at the Maru-Aten, the sun temple, or Sunshade of Ra, belonging to Akhenaten's daughter Meretaten, south of the city. There was also a second, but very much smaller enclosure on its south side.[27] The lake of the Maru-aten was almost four hundred feet long, two hundred feet wide and

---

15 London School of Hygiene and Tropical Medicine, *Malaria Centre Report* (London, 2014–2016), 48.

16 Barry Kemp, "Report on the 1985 Excavations, Work inside the Walled Village," in B. Kemp (ed.), *Amarna Reports 3* (London, 1986), 24; Barry Kemp, "Work inside the Walled Village (1): south-west corner," in B. Kemp (ed.), *Amarna Reports 4* (London, 1987), 7, fig. 1.4.

17 Hassan Bassiouny, "Bioenvironmental and meteorological factors related to the persistence of malaria in Fayoum Governorate: a retrospective study," *Eastern Mediterranean Health Journal* 7, no. 6 (2001), 904.

18 Kemp, *City of Akhenaten and Nefertiti*, 272.

19 Henning Franzmeier, "Wells and Cisterns in Pharaonic Egypt: The Development of a Technology as a Process of Adaption to Environmental Situations and Consumers' Demands," in K. Griffin (ed.), *Current* Research *in Egyptology 2007* (Oxford, 2008), 41.

20 Pamela Rose, "The pottery survey," in B. Kemp (ed.), *Amarna Reports 4*, 124–25 and fig. 9.6.

21 Kemp, *City of Akhenaten and Nefertiti*, 194.

22 Kemp, *City of Akhenaten and Nefertiti*, 55.

23 Barry Kemp, "Report on the 1987 Excavations, A Large Well beside Building Q48.4," in B. Kemp (ed.), *Amarna Reports 5* (London, 1989), 1–14.

24 Alex Wilkinson, *The Garden in Ancient Egypt* (London, 1998), 160, fig. 84; Kemp, "A Large Well beside Building Q48.4," 13; Cathie Spieser, "Eau et lumière dans les monuments amarniens – Le disque solaire, le miroir et l'oeuf solaire," *CENiM* 20 (2018), 130–32; Kemp, *City of Akhenaten and Nefertiti*, 51, figs 2.4 and 2.5.

25 Franzmeier, "Wells and Cisterns in Pharaonic Egypt," 42, fig. 5.

26 Henri Frankfort and John Pendlebury, *The City of Akhenaten, Part II* (London, 1933), 61, and pl. 9.

27 Thomas Peet and Charles Woolley, *The City of Akhenaten, Part I* (London, 1923), pl. 29

three feet deep, and surrounded by a garden of trees and flowers.[28] In the northeast corner of the Maru-Aten's enclosure were also eleven T-shaped offering pools twenty feet long, more than ten feet wide, and 3 feet deep.[29] There is no evidence of a channel to bring water in from the Nile for the lake or garden of the Maru-Aten and its smaller southern enclosure, so "deep and large wells within the enclosures" were the sources of water.[30]

The need for water in everyday life does not seem to have been the only reason for such an emphasis on wells, ponds, and water gardens. Water, and animals and plants in and near water, were also depicted on the painted mud plaster of the walls and floors of royal palaces and the sun temples in the south of the city. This type of decoration may have been purposely used to reflect fertility and abundance, as well as to represent the Aten's creation of every aspect of the living world, as put forth in the Great Hymn to the Aten.[31] Kemp's idea that Akhenaten might have issued a decree requiring the digging of wells because of this symbolic purpose would make sense in this light.[32]

Since the mid-2000s excavation of two non-elite cemeteries at Amarna that seem to have been the "main public burial grounds,"[33] have produced extensive evidence of death and disease, which possibly substantiates some kind of epidemic at the city. Excavation at the South Tombs Cemetery for six seasons shows that it probably contains burials for 6,000 individuals, of whom 417 were excavated and their skeletons studied for indications of malaria; 50% showed signs of recent malarial infection.[34]

The North Tombs Cemetery began to be excavated in 2015. It contains an estimated 4,000–5,000 burials.[35] Of the 150 individuals who had been studied by 2017, 85.7% have bone lesions "that have been previously identified as indicators of malarial infection."[36] The latest report from the 2017–2018 seasons suggests 92% have these bone lesions.[37] The report on these findings suggests the individuals buried in this cemetery belonged to a workforce "subject to working/living conditions that saw their immune responses compromised."[38] In both cemeteries, but particularly in the North Tombs Cemetery, as well as malarial infection, skeletal remains produced evidence of stunting, nutritional insufficiencies, and a high rate of bone fractures and trauma. Granted, all the publications on these human remains so far are preliminary, but they all point to a very high malaria rate among the non-elite population of Akhetaten.

It is not a surprise that with intensive agriculture, the making of mud brick, living in mud brick houses, as well as all the pits and pools of water, that the human remains found at Amarna reflect the existence of extensive malarial infection. In fact, it appears that Egypt, in general, suffered from malaria in ancient times.[39] But, could the extent of the suffering from malaria at Akhetaten have been intensified by the fact that the city was probably built in no more than seven years, beginning in year 5 and completed by the *durbar* in year 12?[40] During that time,

---

28 Wilkinson, *Garden in Ancient Egypt*, 148–49.

29 Wilkinson, *Garden in Ancient Egypt*, 151. For a detailed plan, see Fran Weatherhead, *Amarna Palace Paintings* (London, 2007), 276–78, and figs. 139a–139b.

30 Kemp, *City of Akhenaten and Nefertiti*, 54.

31 Weatherhead, *Amarna Palace Paintings*, 28–29; Kate Spence, "Royal Power in New Kingdom Egypt: The Palaces and Gardens of Amarna," in J. Ganzert and I. Nielsen (eds.), *Herrschaftsverhäitnisse und Herrschaftslegitimation: Bau- und Gartenkulturals historisch Quellengattung hinsichtlich Manifestation und Legitimation von Herrschaft* (Hamburg, 2014), 26; Patrick Sallard, *Palatial Paintings and Programs: The Symbolic World of the Egyptian Palace in the New Kingdom (c. 1550–1069 BCE)*, PhD dissertation (Institute of Fine Arts, New York University, 2015), 208. For the Great Hymn see William Murnane, "The Great Hymn to the Aten," *Texts from the Amarna Period in Egypt* (Atlanta, 1995), 113–15.

32 Kemp, "Report on the 1987 Excavations," 14.

33 Anna Stevens, "Death and the City: The Cemeteries of Amarna in Their Urban Context," *Cambridge Archaeological Journal* 28.1 (2017), 103.

34 Nicole Smith-Guzmán, Jerome Rose and Kathleen Kuckens, "Beyond the Differential Diagnosis: New Approaches to the Bioarchaeology of the Hittite Plague," in M. Zuckermen and D. Martin (eds.), *New Directions in Biocultural Anthropology* (Hoboken, 2016), 309–10.

35 Stevens, "Death and the City, 111–12.

36 Anna Stevens and Gretchen Dabbs, "Tell el-Amarna, Spring 2017," *JEA* 103.2 (2017), 146.

37 Anna Stevens, Gretchen Dabbs, Corina Rogge, et. al., "Tell el-Amarna, Autumn 2017 and Spring 2018," *JEA* 104.2 (2018), 133.

38 Stevens and Dabbs, "Tell el-Amarna, spring 2017," 148.

39 Nicole Smith-Guzmán, "Cribra orbitalia in the Ancient Nile Valley and Its Connection to Malaria," *International Journal of Paleopathology* 10 (2015), 11; Andreas Nerlich, Bettina Schraut, Sabine Dittrich, et al., "Plasmodium falciparum in Ancient Egypt," *Emerging Infectious Diseases* 14.8 (2008), 1317–18.

40 Dodson, *Amarna Sunset*, 10, 13. It has been suggested that the foreign emissaries coming to Akhetaten for the *durbar* brought plague

all the mud brick buildings had been completed, the agricultural fields established, and the entire population of the city brought in from other parts of Egypt. The building of Akhetaten was not the normal slow growth of a settlement from a small village to a city; it was a relatively swift transformation of the environment of that area of Middle Egypt.

A study of land reclamation and settlement in the Fayum from 800 BCE to Roman times, a much more extended time than the settlement and cultivation at Amarna, has shown high frequencies of malaria brought about by the intensified irrigation, cultivation, and human crowding.[41] The situation in the Fayum was exacerbated by co-infection with tuberculosis, which has not been found at Amarna, although the human remains from the non-elite cemeteries show extensive trauma from hard labor, as well as nutritional deficiencies, that must have made the burden of malaria more deadly.

Within three to four years after Akhenaten's death, the few members remaining of the royal family and their entourage left the city. The rest of the population chose to move away as well, abandoning a place where so many of their family, friends, and neighbors had been buried. Only the southernmost part of the site has evidence that people remained on into the late Ramesside Period.[42] The reason for the desertion of the city of Akhetaten has never really been satisfactorily addressed; maybe it was simply an unhealthy place to live.

---

with them, and this might have caused the apparent deaths of several royal females. See Donald Redford, *Akhenaten: The Heretic King* (Princeton, 1984), 186–87, and Dodson, *Amarna Sunset*, 17–18.

[41] Albert Lalremruata, Markus Bell, Raffaella Bianucci, et. al., "Molecular Identification of Falciparum Malaria and Human Tuberculosis Co-infection in Mummies from the Fayum Depression (Lower Egypt), *PLoS ONE* 8/4 (April 2013), e60307, 4–5.

[42] Kemp, *City of Akhenaten and Nefertiti*, 301.

The Myth of the Mundane: The Symbolism of Mud Brick and Its Architectural Implications

Luiza Osorio G. Silva
University of Chicago

Abstract

The Egyptological truism that mud brick was simply mundane limits our understanding of the material and how it functioned in architecture. In order to explore the possible meanings of the brick medium beyond its tie to the mundane and its practical functions, this study focuses on the symbolism of brick objects. This can be seen in the presence of model bricks and brick molds in foundation deposits, in the molding of bricks by the king in foundation rituals, in the personification of bricks as a goddess of birth and the use of ritual birth bricks, and in the placement of magical bricks in tomb walls. Together with textual references that speak of the connection of mud to the inundation and the creation of the world, this symbolism suggests an association of the mud-brick architectural medium with creation and life cycles, and thus neheh *time, as well as archaic architecture. This reinterpretation will be used to re-evaluate the employment of bricks in the specific contexts of the Middle Kingdom pyramids, temple annexes, and royal palaces. The architectural use of bricks will also be contextualized in matters of materials choice more generally, highlighting the need for both brick and stone in cosmologically significant architecture.*

ملخص

يُحد المعتقد السائد عند علماء المصريات أن الطوب اللبن كان ببساطة أمرًا دنيويًا من إدراكنا لمادته ووظيفته في العمارة. ومن أجل استكشاف المعاني المحتملة لمادة الطوب، بعيدًا عن ربطه بالعالم الدنيوي، ولمعرفة وظائفه العملية، تُركز هذه الدراسة على رمزية الآثار المصنوعة من الطوب. ويمكن رؤية ذلك في وجود الطوب النموذجي وقوالب الطوب في ودائع الأثاث، وفي صب الملك لقوالب الطوب في طقوس التأسيس، وفي تجسيد الطوب كإلهة للولادة، وفي استخدام طوب الولادة الشعائري، وفي وضع الطوب السحري في جدران المقبرة. وإلى جانب النصوص التي تتحدث عن الصلة بين الطين والفيضان وخلق الكون، تُرجح هذه الرمزية وجود علاقة بين الطوب اللبن بوصفه مادة معمارية وبين عملية الخلق ودورات الحياة، ومن ثم زمن «نِحِح» والعمارة العتيقة. سيُستخدم هذا التفسير الجديد في إعادة تقييم توظيف الطوب في سياقات محددة بالأهرامات وملاحق المعابد والقصور الملكية في عصر الدولة الوسطى. وسيوضع كذلك الاستخدام المعماري للطوب في سياقه فيما يتعلق بمسائل اختيار المواد بصورة أعم، مع تسليط الضوء على الحاجة إلى كلٍ من الطوب والأحجار في العمارة ذات الأهمية الكونية.

The meaning of stone in ancient Egyptian architecture and cosmology has been discussed nearly *ad nauseum* by modern scholars, but the significance of mud brick (*djebet*) as a building material has rarely been explored.[1] In studies of ancient Egyptian architecture, stone in general is associated with royal and divine buildings, as well as

[1] I am happy to thank Candy Rui, Nadine Moeller, and especially Laurel Bestock for editing assistance, and Laurel in particular for her guidance and support throughout this project. Of course, any errors remain my own.

Journal of the American Research Center in Egypt 56 (2020), 181–197
doi: http://dx.doi.org/10.5913/jarce.56.2020.a012

(perhaps consequently) with power and permanence.[2] Brick was the most common building material in ancient Egypt. Despite its common use in royal and divine constructions, brick as a medium is usually simplistically tied to the mundane realm, as well as ephemerality, when it is discussed at all.[3] However, just because it was the material most frequently used in day-to-day architecture does not mean that its meaning was solely tied to that sphere, or that its use was merely for practical reasons. Considering ancient Egyptian multivalent logic, that would in fact be surprising.

The Egyptian idealized form of temporality was dualistic: it consisted of *neheh*, an incessantly cyclical conception of time, tied to motion and change, the repetition of events, and the life cycle of living things; and *djet*, a lasting, stable, and linear progression that extended from the primeval time.[4] Stone as a building material is generally tied to continuous existence (*djet*) and the Egyptian desire to return the world to its sacred origins and the association between bricks and ephemerality arises out of a comparison with stone.[5] The instinct to compare brick and stone is not unwarranted; they are very different materials, and it is not unreasonable to think that they would have meant and accomplished very different things. The problem lies in the framing of this comparison as a straightforward dichotomy: because one is divine and eternal, the other has to be mundane and ephemeral. Studies that comment on the use of mud bricks in architecture often make it seem as if the building material is somehow inferior to stone, in particular due to its assumed lack of divine connotations and its perceived impermanence.[6] Despite the baggage associated with the term "polluting" in modern scholarship,[7] and the lack of use of that specific word in previous interpretations of the use of mud bricks in ancient Egypt, I choose to employ it here precisely for its harshness, in hopes that it will draw attention to the necessity for a re-consideration of mud brick.[8] Herodotus wrote of a personified brick pyramid who berates those who think it inferior to its stone counterparts, therefore demonstrating the precedent for considering brick more than a meaningless substance when compared to stone: "Do not look down on me in comparison to the stone pyramids: for I am preeminent over them as Zeus is over the other gods. For with a pole they struck down into a lake, and gathering whatever they could get from the lake-mud with the pole they made bricks and in this way completed me."[9] There is in fact

[2] For example, S. Aufrère, "L'univers minéral dans la pensée égyptienne: essai de synthèse et perspectives (autour de l'univers minéral X)," *Archéo-Nil* 7 (1997), 113–44; D. Klemm and R. Klemm, "The Building Stones of Ancient Egypt - A Gift of Its Geology," *Journal of African Earth Sciences* 33.3–4 (2001), 631–42; J. Baines, "Stone and Other Materials: Usages and Values," in *Visual and Written Culture in Ancient Egypt* (Oxford, 2007), 263–80; R. Bianchi, "The Stones of Egypt and Nubia," in Z. Hawass and J. Richards (eds.), *The Archaeology and Art of Ancient Egypt: Essays in Honor of David B. O'Connor*, vol. 1 (Cairo, 2007), 109–17.

[3] E.g., J. Weinstein, "Foundation Deposits in Ancient Egypt" (PhD dissertation, University of Pennsylvania, 1973), 12–13; A. Spencer, *Brick Architecture in Ancient Egypt* (Warminster, 1979); J. Assmann, "Ancient Egypt and the Materiality of the Sign," in Hans Ulrich Gumbrecht and K. Ludwig Pfeiffer (eds.), *Materialities of Communication* (Stanford, 1994), 26; B. Kemp, "Bricks and Metaphor," *Cambridge Archaeological Journal* 10.2 (2000), 335–46; Klemm and Klemm, "The Building Stones of Ancient Egypt," 631. For a previous acknowledgement of the symbolism of brick objects, see V. Emery, "Mud-Brick," *UCLA Encyclopedia of Egyptology* (2009), 5–6 (https://escholarship.org/uc/item/7v84d6rh). Also see notes 53 and 68 below, which are associated with the Step Pyramid complex and royal palaces.

[4] J. Assmann, "La notion d'éternité dans l'Égypte ancienne," in V. Pirenne-Delforge and Ö. Tunca (eds.), *Représentations du temps dans les religions. Actes du colloque organisé par le Centre d'Histoire des Religions de l'Université de Liège* (Geneva, 2003), 111–22. This is one of the most recent and useful sources on the topic, but it has been treated extensively in Egyptological scholarship.

[5] For example, J. Leclant, "Espace et temps, ordre et chaos dans l'Égypte pharaonique," *Revue de Synthèse* 90 (1969), 233; Assmann, "Ancient Egypt and the Materiality of the Sign"; J. Assmann, *The Mind of Egypt: History and Meaning in the Time of the Pharaohs*, A. Jenkins, trans. (Cambridge, 2003), 63, 73; P. Vernus, "Modelling the Relationship between Reproduction and Production of 'Sacralized' Texts in Pharaonic Egypt," in T. Gillen (ed.) *(Re)productive Traditions in Ancient Egypt: Proceedings of the Conference Held at the University of Liège, 6th-8th February 2013*, Aegyptiaca Leodiensia 10 (Liège, 2017), 475–509; J. Thum and A.-C. Salmas, "Narrating Temporality: Three Short Stories about Egyptian Royal Living-Rock Stelae," in J. Ben-Dov and F. Rojas (eds.), *Carvings In and Out of Time* (Leiden, forthcoming).

[6] For examples, see sources cited in notes 3, 53, and 68.

[7] Cross-cultural conceptions of pollution and purity have most famously been explored by M. Douglas, *Purity and Danger: An Analysis of Concepts of Pollution and Taboo* (London, 1966). For rare examples of their consideration in ancient Egypt, see: J. Quack, "Conceptions of Purity in Egyptian Religion," in C. Frevel and C. Nihan (eds.), *Purity and the Forming of Religious Traditions in the Ancient Mediterranean World and Ancient Judaism* (Leiden, 2013), 115–58; M. Maitland, "Dirt, Purity, and Spatial Control: Anthropological Perspectives on Ancient Egyptian Society and Culture during the Middle Kingdom," *Journal of Ancient Egyptian Interconnections* 17 (2018), 47–72, and their sources.

[8] Such a reconsideration is necessary in studies of other cultures where archaeologists also concentrate on stone, consequently missing the ancient valuation of different substances. Felipe Rojas and I are working on a comparative study that will address these gaps and highlight diverse understandings of this material not only in the ancient world, but also in contexts with anthropological and ethnographic data.

[9] Herodotus 2.136.4. Translation by F. Rojas, "Mudbrick as gold" (unpublished manuscript). I thank Felipe Rojas for bringing this pas-

Fig. 1. This recent photograph of the Ramesseum illustrates how bricks generally survive less well than their stone counterparts, leading to modern misrepresentations of the two materials. Photo by the author.

no straightforward dichotomy between the two materials, other than the one manufactured in modern scholarship due to their relative conditions after millennia of differential decay (fig. 1), and their functions were by no means entirely opposed.

The impossibility of this opposition becomes difficult to ignore when considering cosmologically symbolic architectural forms that include both brick and stone in their construction. Rather than "polluting," bricks in contexts traditionally considered more closely associated with the divine and generally predominantly built of stone—such as temples and tombs—added to their meaning in different ways, and in fact seem to have been necessary for their functioning. The idea that bricks are divorced from divinity has also led to the widespread association of royal palaces, which were built in brick, with the mundane realm. This is a perplexing conclusion considering the nature of kings, who were both human and divine. Those two sides of kingship were manifest in different ways and measures at different times, but it certainly cannot be claimed that one was ever divorced from the other. Just like the dual nature of kingship cannot be set up as a straightforward dichotomy, neither can the two strands of time. Bricks and stone in architecture similarly worked in complementary ways to support beings and interactions that were both cyclical and enduring, and the amount of each material used is tied directly to the function of the architectural context. A closer look at the materiality of brick, therefore, has the potential to add to our understanding of Egyptian architecture as a whole, particularly cosmologically charged architecture.

sage to my attention.

The term materiality in archaeology generally refers to how manmade and natural materials interact and are understood in human society.[10] I will focus here on the less apparent, symbolic meanings of brick, since its physical properties have been discussed extensively by others.[11] They will, however, also inform the discussion when appropriate. The symbolic importance of bricks is clear from their multiple uses as ritual objects in foundation ceremonies as well as birthing and funerary rituals, and in visual depictions of the king molding bricks. This clear symbolism of brick objects, as well as textual references to mud and brick,[12] can be used to elucidate possible meanings of the symbolic materiality of brick as an architectural medium, which—at least in the royal and divine spheres—went beyond its tie to the mundane and its practical functions. The evidence discussed here will demonstrate that mud brick as a construction material in specific contexts, perhaps particularly when used alongside stone, was deeply associated with creation and life cycles, and thus much more *neheh* than *djet*, as well as evocative of archaic brick-built architecture fundamental to the definition of kingship.

The Symbolism of Ritual Brick Objects

Mud bricks were often involved in the ritual of founding a new structure. These foundation rituals are well documented in texts, reliefs, and archaeological evidence mainly from the Middle Kingdom onwards, but the ceremony is mentioned as early as the First Dynasty on the Palermo Stone.[13] In their fully developed form, foundation rituals consisted of ten steps that included both the construction and sanctifying of temples. The burying of foundation deposits in temples can be traced at least as early as the Fifth Dynasty, as attested by a relief from Niuserre's temple at Abu Ghurob.[14] Extensively present in the archaeological record, foundation deposits are usually understood to have sanctified or protected the building under construction, among other functions. Foundation deposit pits were sometimes lined with mud bricks when dug into soft material, clearly a practical use.[15] However, model bricks also remained standard components of foundation deposits for over two thousand years, from at least the Eleventh Dynasty to the Ptolemaic Period, with a brief interlude in the Nineteenth Dynasty.[16] Brick molds started appearing in deposits in the Eighteenth Dynasty, including in the royal tomb deposits of Hatshepsut, Thutmose IV, and Amenhotep III in the Valley of the Kings.[17] The royal tombs did not feature bricks in their construction (other than to temporarily close entrances), and foundation deposits more generally were often associated with stone buildings; thus, the presence of bricks and brick molds requires explanation. Foundation deposits have also been found in what Weinstein refers to as "royal secular" structures: two palaces (Malqata and Medinet Habu), fortress and town walls, and gateways. Though it would be unwise to draw conclusions from this small a corpus, it is perhaps of note that none of the deposits listed by Weinstein under the

[10] For studies of materiality in Egypt specifically, see: J. Thum, "Words in the Landscape: The Mechanics of Egyptian Royal Living-Rock Stelae" (PhD dissertation, Brown University, 2018), chapter 2 and sources therein. For thoughts on materiality in general, see the following: D. Miller, "Materiality: An Introduction," in D. Miller (ed.), *Materiality* (Durham, 2005), 1–50; L. Meskell, "Introduction: Object Orientations," in L. Meskell (ed.), *Archaeologies of Materiality* (Oxford, 2008), 1–17; C. Conneller, *An Archaeology of Materials: Substantial Transformations in Early Prehistoric Europe*, Routledge Studies in Archaeology (London, 2010); I. Hodder, *Entangled: An Archaeology of the Relationships between Humans and Things* (West Sussex, 2012).

[11] E.g., Spencer, *Brick Architecture in Ancient Egypt*; B. Kemp, "Soil (Including Mud-brick Architecture)," in P. Nicholson and I. Shaw (eds.), *Ancient Egyptian Materials and Technology* (Cambridge, 2000), 78–103 and sources therein.

[12] Texts do not often consider the brick material itself, and mentions of it are generally restricted to discussions of construction processes and techniques. Sources that have discussed bricks in texts include A. Badawy, "Philological Evidence about Methods of Construction in Ancient Egypt," *ASAE* 54 (1957), 43–51; W. Simpson, *Papyrus Reisner I. The Records of a Building Project in the Reign of Sesostris I* (Boston, 1963), 56–58; Spencer, *Brick Architecture in Ancient Egypt*, 3–4; Kemp, "Soil," 78.

[13] Weinstein, "Foundation Deposits in Ancient Egypt," 1–3, 24.

[14] L. Borchardt and H. Schäfer, "Vorläufiger Bericht über die Ausgrabungen bei Abusir im Winter 1899/1900," *ZÄS* 38 (1900), pl. 5.

[15] For example, at Hatshepsut's temple at Deir el-Bahri: C. Roehrig, "The Foundation Deposits of Hatshepsut's Mortuary Temple at Deir el-Bahri," in J. Galán, B. Bryan, and P. Dorman (eds.), *Creativity and Innovation in the Reign of Hatshepsut: Papers from the Theban Workshop 2010* (Chicago, 2014), 139–55. For other examples, see: Weinstein, "Foundation Deposits in Ancient Egypt."

[16] Weinstein, "Foundation Deposits in Ancient Egypt," lxxiii–lxxiv, 241.

[17] Weinstein, "Foundation Deposits in Ancient Egypt," 98–99.

Fig. 2. Relief of king molding a brick during the foundation ritual, Temple of Efdu. Photo by the author.

secular building category (except for a couple from the Late and Ptolemaic periods) included mud bricks.[18] Since these so-called secular structures were built of brick, it is tempting to hypothesize whether bricks and brick molds in the deposits in stone temples and tombs served a similar function to those used to construct predominantly brick buildings. Rather than "polluting," mud bricks were symbolically necessary to any significant architectural structure. If they were not present in the construction itself, they needed to be added.

This necessity is reinforced by the fifth step of the foundation ritual, which featured the molding of mud bricks by the king, depicted in a relief from the Ptolemaic Temple of Edfu (fig. 2). The ritualization of brick molding, as well as the later placement of bricks in the four corners of the temple before any stone blocks could be put in place, suggest that the material was an essential part of the temple creation process. This is further implied by one of the inscriptions accompanying the Edfu foundation ritual reliefs, in which the king says: "I

[18] Weinstein, "Foundation Deposits in Ancient Egypt," 430–32.

Fig. 3. Khnum creating the divine child Ihy on his potter's wheel, Temple of Dendera. Photo courtesy of Aidan McRae Thomson.

make a brick in order to build your sanctuary."[19] Though the Temple of Edfu proper was constructed entirely of stone, the molding of a brick was necessary in order to build it. The fact that reliefs also depict the king moving the first stone block into place during the eighth stage of the ritual does not detract from the importance of brick molding, but instead highlights it by emphasizing that both actions were of equal importance.

The making of bricks by the king in the foundation ritual mimics the creation of children by Khnum on his potter's wheel (fig. 3), demonstrating that the founding of a temple was parallel to the birth of a living being.[20] Though a more refined material than the mud used to make bricks, the similarity between the ritual of brick molding and the creation of children from clay is inescapable. Inscriptions that accompany the royal brick-molding relief refer to the king as the heir of Khnum, making it clear that the two actions were parallel, as already

[19] É. Chassinat, *Le temple d'Edfou*, vol. 2, MMAF 11 (Paris, 1897), 61; Spencer, *Brick Architecture in Ancient Egypt*, 3.

[20] That temple foundation is parallel to birth has been previously argued by S. el-Adly, "Das Gründungs- und Weiheritual des Ägyptischen Tempels von der frühgeschichtlichen Zeit bis zum Ende des Neuen Reiches" (PhD dissertation, Universität Tübingen, 1950). For a Mesopotamian parallel to the symbolic aspects of brick temple construction, see translations of Gudea's cylinders A and B, specifically dealing with the use of personified bricks in the building of Ningirsu's temple.

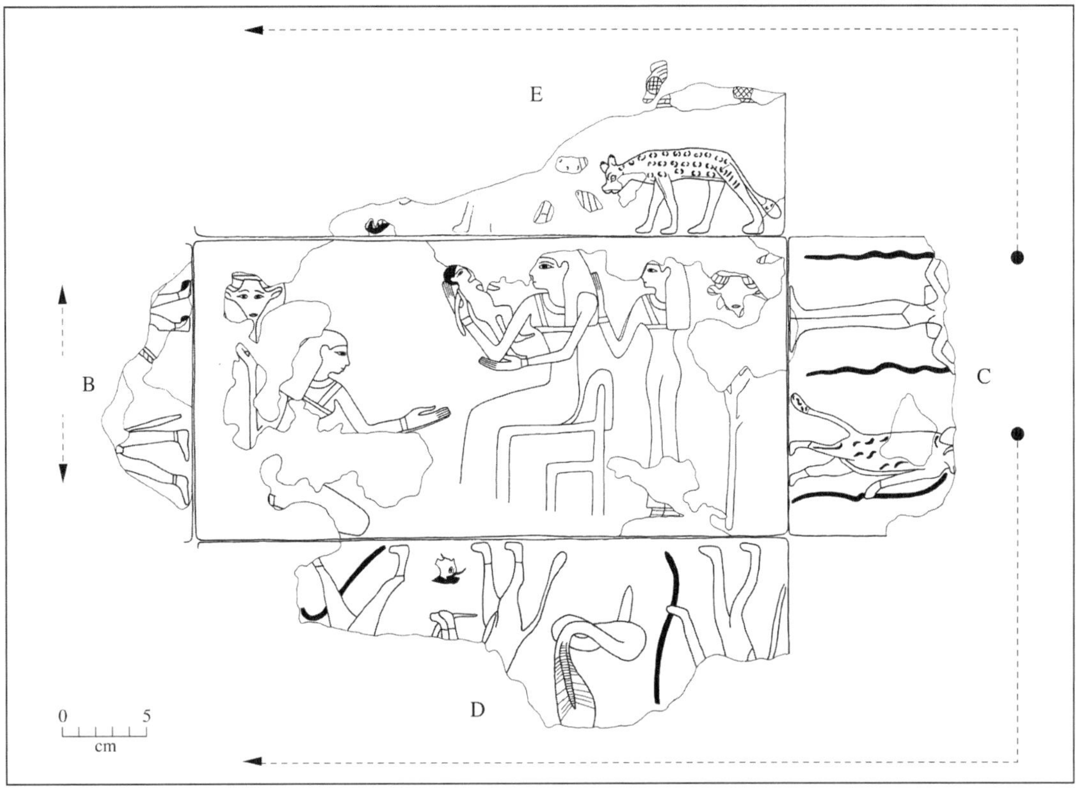

Fig. 4. The imagery on the Abydos birth brick, which includes a childbirth-related scene and protective figures. From J. Wegner, "A Decorated Birth-Brick from South Abydos: New Evidence on Childbirth and Birth Magic in the Middle Kingdom," in D. Silverman, W. Simpson, and J. Wegner (eds.), Archaism and Innovation: Studies in the Culture of Middle Kingdom Egypt *(New Haven, 2009), fig. 6. Image courtesy of Josef Wegner.*

suggested by the formal similarities between the Edfu relief and more traditional representations of the potter god. In these depictions, both king and god stand or sit before a table or wheel and create bricks, and life. The placement of bricks at the four corners of the temple and the connection of that part of the ritual to Khnum suggest that bricks were necessary for the creation of the divine structure, and the similarity between temples and living beings is supported by New Kingdom reliefs of personified temples.[21]

Bricks were also symbolically critical in birthing and funerary rituals of living beings. Women crouched on top of four bricks stacked in pairs to assist them in childbirth. Brick was most likely initially chosen as the material for these birthing platforms both in Egypt and elsewhere in the Near East because it was easily acquired and manufactured, but it remained in use through the Coptic Period and Islamic times and is still used today. Beyond their functional use in childbirth, bricks very quickly became imbued with more symbolic associations. Indeed, there is abundant evidence that bricks used in birthing rituals also served a protective function.[22] A late Middle Kingdom decorated birth brick found at the mayoral residence of Wah-Sut (Abydos) further strengthens the connection between bricks and childbirth, as well as unarguably highlights the significance of ritual brick objects (fig. 4). The only one of its kind so far discovered, this object is beautifully decorated with painted scenes of a mother and newborn child, as well as apotropaic imagery in line with that found on other types of ritual arti-

[21] For example, from Medinet Habu and Sety I's mortuary temple at Qurna: G. Haeny, "New Kingdom 'Mortuary Temples' and 'Mansions of Millions of Years,'" in B. Shafer (ed.), *Temples of Ancient Egypt* (Ithaca, 1997), 108–9.

[22] A. Roth and C. Roehrig, "Magical Bricks and the Bricks of Birth," *JEA* 88 (2002), 132–33.

Fig. 5. The goddess Meskhenet from Hatshepsut's Deir el-Bahri mortuary temple. Drawing by the author after Roth, "The psš-kf and the 'Opening of the Mouth' Ceremony: A Ritual of Birth and Rebirth," fig. 11.

facts related to the protection of children and mothers, such as the so-called magic wands. It is not clear how representative of other birth bricks this object should be considered, particularly due to its elite context and elaborate decoration, and it is impossible to determine for certain whether it would have functioned as part of a birthing stand and/or as more of an amuletic object.[23] However, the use of bricks during childbirth can be dated to as early as the Sixth Dynasty based on an inscription from a Saqqara tomb, where they are referred to as "O four" and represented by four rectangles.[24] The fact that they were already personified to this extent at this point perhaps suggests that the use of birth bricks began even earlier.

Starting in the Middle Kingdom, birth bricks were further personified as a goddess of birth, Meskhenet (fig. 5), whose name has been translated as "the place of alighting"[25] and "that which is in the front of birthing,"[26] further tying bricks to the beginning of life in a parallel to the creation of temples. The goddess was often represented as a brick with the head of a woman (fig. 6), clearly giving this material an existence apart from its inanimate materiality. Meskhenet was not only the goddess of childbirth, but also the one who often determined the fate and social status of the newborn child. She announces that the newborn baby is destined for kingship both in Papyrus Westcar and in the divine birth scenes of Hatshepsut at Deir el-Bahri and Amenhotep III at Luxor.[27] In Westcar, the proclamation that the newborns are worthy of kingship immediately follows their placement on bricks that the goddess herself embodies. Shai and Renenutet, gods of fate and nourishment respectively, were sometimes also depicted as personified bricks.[28] In later periods, Meskhenet took on four different forms, all of which were associated with the female goddesses of the Ennead.[29] Meskhenet, and thus bricks, were therefore not only associated with childbirth (including of kings), but also with the overall cosmological creation.

Furthermore, Roth has suggested that the headdress used by Meskhenet in the divine birth scenes was a *psš-kf*, traditionally used in the Opening of the Mouth ceremony.[30] Though this ritual is usually associated with

---

[23] J. Wegner, "A Decorated Birth-Brick from South Abydos: New Evidence on Childbirth and Birth Magic in the Middle Kingdom," in D. Silverman, W. Simpson, and J. Wegner (eds.), *Archaism and Innovation: Studies in the Culture of Middle Kingdom Egypt* (New Haven, 2009), 447–96, and especially 471–80 for different potential functions.

[24] Roth and Roehrig, "Magical Bricks and the Bricks of Birth," 129–33, 138.

[25] Roth and Roehrig, "Magical Bricks and the Bricks of Birth," 130; Roth, "The *psš-kf* and the 'Opening of the Mouth' Ceremony: A Ritual of Birth and Rebirth," *JEA* 78 (1992), 145–46.

[26] Wegner, "A Decorated Birth-Brick from South Abydos," 471.

[27] Roth and Roehrig, "Magical Bricks and the Bricks of Birth," 136. For the scene from Deir el-Bahri, see É. Naville, *The XIth Dynasty Temple at Deir el-Bahari*, part II (London, 1910), pl. 51.

[28] G. Pinch, *Egyptian Mythology: A Guide to the Gods, Goddesses, and Traditions of Ancient Egypt* (Oxford, 2004), 194; Roth and Roehrig, "Magical Bricks and the Bricks of Birth," 136.

[29] Roth and Roehrig, "Magical Bricks and the Bricks of Birth," 131, 136.

[30] Roth, "The *psš-kf* and the 'Opening of the Mouth' Ceremony," 144–46; A. Roth, "Fingers, Stars, and the 'Opening of the Mouth':

rebirth after death, Roth has argued that it was primarily a ritual of birth mimicked after death to enable rebirth. Roth and Roehrig have also suggested that four objects termed *abet* and offered in the New Kingdom version of the Opening of the Mouth ritual were birth bricks.[31] This is significant because the offering of these four objects is accompanied by the verbs *snṯ* and *sk*. The verb *sk* in this context likely means "to wipe the mouth," which would be a clear reference to the ritual.[32] Even more important is the meaning of *snṯ*, which can either refer to Khnum's fashioning of children and men from clay or to the laying of foundations for architectural structures.[33] Several scholars have pointed out that the ritual of founding a temple consists of a version of the Opening of the Mouth ritual.[34] The use of these verbs with regards to the presentation of *abet* not only supports the interpretation that *abet* were birth bricks, but also and more importantly again connects bricks to both birth and the founding of temples.

Fig. 6. The goddess Meskhenet pictured as a brick with a woman's head (indicated by arrow), Papyrus of Ani, Nineteenth Dynasty. © Trustees of the British Museum.

Brick's relation to death and rebirth is further supported by the presence of bricks as ritual objects in mortuary contexts, already mentioned with regards to brick molds found in royal funerary foundation deposits. In the New Kingdom, four so-called "magical bricks" were often placed in niches cut into tomb walls, perhaps a parallel to the four bricks placed at the corners of temples in foundation rituals. Niches that would have been prepared for magical bricks are found in most royal tombs from the middle of the Eighteenth Dynasty through at least the middle of the Nineteenth Dynasty,[35] and published magical bricks themselves range from the mid-Eighteenth through the Thirtieth Dynasty.[36] Niches for magical bricks are sometimes also found in tombs of the Apis bull and in private tombs, which shows that their meaning was not relegated solely to the royal sphere and was instead relevant also in divine and private funerary contexts. These magical bricks were associated with the four traditional amuletic figures (Anubis, the flame, the *djed* pillar, and a mummiform image) and thus served a protective function in the tomb. They were usually inscribed with texts from Chapter 151 of the Book of the Dead which provided extremely detailed instructions including the exact wall in which each brick should go, and that they should remain unbaked.[37] While these instructions seem to have rarely been followed in their entirety, it is clear that the insertion of these bricks into tomb walls was extremely ritualized, and one wonders whether the specification to leave them unbaked aimed to preserve their potency as Nile mud.

The Nature and Function of the nTrwj-Blades," *JEA* 79 (1993), 57–79. This emblem had been previously identified as a cow uterus, which would also be a connection to birth, and other interpretations have also been proposed: H. Frankfort, "A Note on the Lady of Birth," *JNES* 3.3 (1944), 198–200.

31 Roth and Roehrig, "Magical Bricks and the Bricks of Birth," 134-5. For a previous interpretation, see: E. Otto, *Das ägyptische Mundöffnungsritual*, vol. 1 (Wiesbaden, 1960), 88–90; E. Otto, *Das ägyptische Mundöffnungsritual*, vol. 2 (Wiesbaden, 1960), 96–97.

32 For sources for this interpretation, see Roth and Roehrig, "Magical Bricks and the Bricks of Birth," 135, n76.

33 For sources for this interpretation, see Roth and Roehrig, "Magical Bricks and the Bricks of Birth," 135, ns 74–75.

34 A. Blackman and H. Fairman, "The Consecration of an Egyptian Temple According to the Use of Edfu," *JEA* 32 (1946), 75–91; P. Barguet, "Les dimensions du temple d'Edfou et leur signification," *BSFE* 72 (1975), 23–30; Roth and Roehrig, "Magical Bricks and the Bricks of Birth," 135–36; J. Karkowski, "'A Temple Comes to Being': A Few Comments on the Temple Foundation Ritual," *ET* 29 (2016), 112.

35 For their locations inside the tombs, see: Roth and Roehrig, "Magical Bricks and the Bricks of Birth," 124.

36 F. Scalf, "Magical Bricks in the Oriental Institute Museum of the University of Chicago," *SAK* 38 (2009), 275.

37 Roth and Roehrig, "Magical Bricks and the Bricks of Birth," 121–22, 136.

From the Symbolism of Brick Objects to the Symbolism of Mud and Mud Bricks

Ritual mud-brick objects have been shown to be connected to the beginning of life, as well as life cycles, in a variety of ways. Mud itself was a substance intimately associated both with the creation of the world and the Nile inundation, as evidenced by the following Pyramid Text:

Atum Beetle!
You became high, as the hill;
You rose as the *benben* in the
Benben Enclosure in Heliopolis.[38]

This Pyramid Text recounts the moment when the universe was created, and it refers to both earth and stone. From the chaotic waters of Nu, the universal ocean, rose the primordial mound on which the creator god Atum stood to engender the rest of the world in the so-called Heliopolitan cosmogony. Translated here as "hill," the mound of creation was composed of earth. In this particular Pyramid Text, the *benben*, a stone, is said to have risen out of the water together with the earth mound. The *benben*-stone, associated with the concept of the primeval mound, was thought to have been kept in a shrine at Heliopolis, the Benben Enclosure.[39] Here, Atum rises as both the earth hill and the *benben*-stone, signaling that *both* earth and stone were critical, and critical together, in the cosmic beginnings of the world.[40]

The cosmological story of the appearance of the primeval mound could have conceivably derived from the real event of the annual Nile flood; high mounds of fertile earth would have also seemed to rise out of the water once it receded. The earth of the primeval mound (or at least of the real annual inundation) was therefore equivalent to the mud that is the principal component of mud bricks, and the essence of the latter was inextricably tied to that of the former.[41] This fertile soil came with the inundation, was covered by water and invisible for part of the year, and was later renewed and refreshed when the cycle began anew. Soil has a life cycle and a life, and it is also the medium by which plants and animals are sustained in their own life cycles. Soil—mud—was not only vital to the creation of the world, but it was also essential for the continued functioning of it. Particularly given the instruction on the funerary bricks that they should remain unbaked, it is reasonable to suggest that their mud composition is the property of bricks that makes them suited to associations with birth and rebirth.

This potential significance of mud also has implications for how it might be interpreted in relation to the ancient Egyptian conception of time. As mentioned above, stone is associated with *djet*. Like brick, the material was mythologized and deified and was deeply meaningful in several contexts including architecture, statuary, and funerary beliefs,[42] but its ultimate function was quite different. This is effectively demonstrated by the physical desert cliffs that flanked the Nile floodplain on either side, which would have served as constant reminders of stone's perennial nature. Stone did not have a life cycle; it rose up out of the water just like earth, but it immediately became a constant. Cliffs were an unmoving and unmissable part of the landscape: they did not visibly change during one's lifetime, being divorced from the cyclicality of living things. Mud, on the other hand, was

38 Pepy II Pyramid Text Recitation 369, Response to the Offering Ritual. Translation: J. Allen, *The Ancient Egyptian Pyramid Texts* (Atlanta, 2005), 269.

39 S. Quirke, *Ancient Egyptian Religion* (London, 1992), 27.

40 Thum ("Words in the Landscape," chapter 3) has interpreted this Pyramid Text as equating the primeval mound with the *benben*-stone, and it is quite possible that both readings are valid.

41 C. Reader ("On Pyramid Causeways," *JEA* 90 (2004), 63–71) and W. Wood ("The Archaic Stone Tombs at Helwan," *JEA* 73 (1987), 70) have previously associated bricks used in construction with the inundation. Sinusoidal brick walls have also been tied to the cosmological creation, but there has been much debate about their potential religious vs. functional purposes: R. Pirelli, "Once More on Undulating Walls in Ancient Egypt: Mythological Reasons or Technical Requirements?," in R. Pirelli (ed.), *Egyptological Studies for Claudio Barocas* (Naples, 1999), 55–94; O. Siegel, "The Development and Function of Serpentine/Sinusoidal Walls," *JARCE* 52 (2016), 53–89.

42 For example, a recent study conducted by U. Rummel ("Gräber, Feste, Prozessionen: Der Ritualraum Theben-West in Der Ramessidenzeit," in G. Neunert, K. Gabler, and A. Verbovsek (eds.), *Nekropolen: Grab – Bild – Ritual: Beiträge Des Zweiten Münchner Arbeitskreises Junge Aegyptologie (MAJA 2) 2. Bis 4.12.2011* (Wiesbaden, 2013), 207–32) on the basis of iconographic and textual evidence demonstrated that the Theban mountain, which was considered an embodiment of several goddesses, was associated with continued existence after death.

intimately tied to that cyclicality, making objects made of mud eminently suited to foundation ceremonies and birthing and funerary rituals. Brick, therefore, seems to have been much more closely tied to *neheh*, which denotes cyclicality rather than ephemerality or banality.

It has also been proposed, for example by Weinstein, that the significance of bricks in foundation ceremonies is due to their potential to represent archaic architecture.[43] Brick was the material in which the first monumental Egyptian royal constructions were built, monuments that were immortalized in the *serekh* symbol. The *serekh* concretized the link between kingship and early architecture in its inclusion of the royal Horus name in association with the two-dimensional representation of the niched façade of a building, generally thought of as a palace. The *serekh* symbol itself seems to have served as a connection to archaic architecture in New Kingdom palaces and temples: *serekh* dadoes were often paired with the torus molding, another decorative feature linked to architectural archaism because it mimicked braces that stabilized corners of buildings made with reed mats tied to wooden posts.[44] In fact, several canonical architectural forms, such as the *kheker* frieze, are clear emulations in stone of ephemeral plant materials used in earlier periods, often in ritually significant buildings.[45] Reed mats are also sometimes found in foundation deposits, making it possible that they were similarly used to evoke early architectural traditions in those contexts.[46] In inscriptions at the Temple of Edfu, the divine structure is referred to as the "brick-built seat of Horus."[47] References to early architectural traditions exist elsewhere in this temple, and this could be another nod to archaic architecture besides a tie between temple and creation as discussed above.

A Reevaluation of the Use of Mud Bricks in Architecture

Given that bricks as objects could clearly be symbolic in ways that relied on their mud composition, can we expect the same symbolism to have been present when bricks were used not as individual objects but en masse to build architecture? Since brick was the most common building material in all periods of ancient Egypt, it would be unreasonable to argue that every architectural use of it was symbolic. Rather, it is its use in specifically cosmologically significant architecture, and perhaps particularly the way in which brick was used alongside stone, that can be interpreted as symbolically meaningful. In this section, the use of bricks in the Middle Kingdom pyramids, in temple annexes, and in royal palaces will be discussed.

The symbolic use of brick in architecture is not necessarily mutually exclusive with practical considerations. Mud bricks can be produced from a variety of different types of soils, though regional variations and inclusions (often sand and straw) sometimes resulted in different types of brick—in terms of color or strength, among other factors.[48] Evidence from ancient Egypt pertaining to the actual manufacturing process of mud bricks is scarce,but what we do have suggests that the ancient techniques were identical to those used in modern Egypt:[49] moist Nile mud was placed into the brick mold and smoothed by hand, and bricks were left to dry in the sun. Bricks are thus relatively simple to make and would have been easier to attain than stone, as well as cheaper. Mud bricks have also been lauded for their thermal insulating properties.[50] However, opinions seem to differ on whether bricks would have been more suitable for domestic architecture due to their temperature regulation

---

43 Weinstein, "Foundation Deposits in Ancient Egypt," 13. This seems to be the case elsewhere as well. For example, in Lydian Sardis bricks may have also served as a connection to the city's "glorious past" (F. Rojas, "Mudbrick as Gold," unpublished manuscript).

44 P. Lacovara, *The New Kingdom Royal City*, Studies in Egyptology (New York, 2016), 413; L. Osorio G. Silva, "The Myth of the Mundane: Situating Mudbrick Royal Palaces in Ancient Egyptian Cosmology" (Undergraduate thesis, Brown University, 2018), chapter 4.

45 This phenomenon of architectural petrification has been extensively discussed with regards to Djoser's Third Dynasty Step Pyramid complex at Saqqara. For example, G. Porta, *L'architettura egizia delle origini in legno e materiali leggeri* (Milan, 1989), 135–48; M. Baud, *Djéser et la IIIe dynastie* (Paris, 2002), 100.

46 E.g, Weinstein, "Foundation Deposits in Ancient Egypt," 57, 101–12, 156–58, 269.

47 Chassinat, *Le temple d'Edfou*, vol. 2, 61. I thank Inês Torres for help with this translation.

48 For a detailed analysis of different soil types, see Kemp, "Soil," 79–81.

49 Kemp, "Soil," 83.

50 E.g., G. Austin, "Adobe as a Building Material," *New Mexico Geology* 6, no. 4 (1984), 69–71; F. El Fgaier, Z. Lafhaj, F. Brachelet, E. Antczak, and C. Chapiseau, "Thermal Performance of Unfired Clay Bricks Used in Construction in the North of France: Case Study," *Case Studies in Construction Materials* 3 (2015), 102–11.

potential,[51] and it is quite likely that other architectural considerations would have come into play.[52] Nevertheless, it is important to keep in mind that their physical properties may have had something to do with the decision to use them in construction, particularly of royal palaces and perhaps of temple storage annexes.

The long-standing expectation in Egyptological scholarship that an opposition between supposedly permanent stone and ephemeral brick existed in ancient Egypt should not be given much weight. While clear that it would have often required more frequent maintenance and upkeep than stone, brick was a key building material for structures—such as enclosure walls of both temples and cities—that had to, by definition, endure, and it was not feeble. The use of stone in Djoser's Third Dynasty Step Pyramid complex has tended to make the relationship between brick and stone in early architecture seem simpler than it is. That monument has suggested an evolution from brick to stone as a technological achievement and a replacement of formerly brick forms with stone forms where supposedly eternal properties were desired.[53] Particularly the opposition of permanence and ephemerality has been quite overblown, as alluded to above. This can be demonstrated on the ground by the mud-brick monuments of Djoser's Second Dynasty predecessor, Khasekhemwy, at Abydos and Hierakonpolis—unlike other funerary enclosures, they were not purposefully destroyed and so still stand today.[54] That the Egyptians themselves knew full well that human action rather than building material was the chief threat to longevity of a building can be shown by the following Sixth Dynasty Giza *mastaba* inscription: "As for any man who will take possession of (or) destroy the stone (or) brick in this tomb…"[55] The fact that stone and brick are equated here as materials that could have been moved from their locations in the tomb shows that both were on equal footing in certain contexts, and that the assumption that one was seen as eternal while the other was ephemeral is insupportable.

Middle Kingdom Pyramids

Bricks were used to build several of the Twelfth Dynasty pyramids, a dramatic shift from the use of stone in the construction of pyramids since Djoser's reign in the Third Dynasty. The core of Senwosret II's pyramid at Lahun consisted of a stone framework that was filled with bricks, while the pyramid cores of Senwosret III at Dashur and Amenemhat III at Dashur and Hawara were built entirely of bricks. Two brick pyramids at Mazghuna have also been tentatively identified as belonging to Amenemhat IV and Queen Sobeknefru, the last two rulers of the Dynasty.[56] Even if these monuments were cased in stone, it is useful to hypothesize why kings at this time might have chosen to build predominantly brick pyramids.

Practical considerations may have certainly been in play. Bricks would normally have been easier to procure than stone, possibly even more so in the Twelfth Dynasty. Senwosret II's pyramid at Lahun and Amenemhat

---

[51] For example, Kemp ("Soil," 88) claims that brick architecture would have been uncomfortable in different temperatures; M. Dabaieh ("Earth Vernacular Architecture in the Western Desert of Egypt," in M. Markku (ed.), *VERNADOC RWW 2002* (Lund, 2013), 24–30) claims the opposite.

[52] The placement of windows and wind-catchers, for instance. For discussions of such architectural adaptations, see: K. Spence, "The Three-Dimensional Form of the Amarna House," *JEA* 90 (2004), 123–52; and for later periods, G. Marouard, "Rues et habitats dans les villages de la chôra égyptienne à la période gréco-romaine (IIIe s. av–IVe s. apr. J.-C.): quelques exemples du fayoum," in P. Ballet, N. Dieudonné-Glad, C. Saliou (eds.), *La rue dans l'Antiquité définition, aménagement et devenir de l'Orient méditerranéen à la Gaule; actes du colloque de Poitiers, 7–9 septembre 2006 organisé par l'Équipe d'Accueil EA 3811 (HeRMA), Université de Poitiers* (Rennes, 2008), 117–28.

[53] E.g., J. Baines, "Palaces and Temples of Ancient Egypt," in J. Sasson, J. Baines, G. Beckman, K. Rubinson (eds.), *Civilizations of the Ancient Near East*, vol. 1 (New York, 1995), 305; Baud, *Djéser et la IIIe dynastie*, 104; D. O'Connor, *Abydos: Egypt's First Pharaohs and the Cult of Osiris* (London, 2009), 177. Evidence that shows how erroneous this expectation is can be seen, for example, in the use of mud bricks to coat walls built of finely cut stones at a few mastabas in the cemetery of Abusir: K. Kytnarová et al., "Záhady hrobky AS 67. Jedna hrobka pro dvě generace?" *Pražské Egyptologické Studie* 10 (2013), fig. 1.

[54] L. Bestock, *The Development of Royal Funerary Cult at Abydos: Two Funerary Enclosures from the Reign of Aha*, Menes 6 (Wiesbaden, 2009), 56–57; O'Connor, *Abydos*, 175–77. There are doubts regarding the function and purpose of Khasekhemwy's enclosure in Hierakonpolis. See R. Friedman, "Investigations in the Fort of Khasekhemwy," *Nekhen News* 11 (1999), 9–12.

[55] Thum, "Words in the Landscape," chapter 3, citing Simpson, *Mastabas of the Western Cemetery, Part I, Giza Mastabas*, vol. 4 (Boston, 1980), 4:8, 13, XV, XVI–XVII, figs. 12–15.

[56] Spencer, *Brick Architecture in Ancient Egypt*, 37–39.

III's at Hawara are thought to have been located there because kings of the Twelfth Dynasty and perhaps a bit earlier were prioritizing the Fayum for the creation of new agricultural land,[57] which would have been a mud-centric project. Perhaps the access of these kings to stone was limited, though the fact that they were casing the monuments in stone, and, in Senwosret II's case, using stone as a structure frame for the bricks, suggests that the material could have been procured. It is also possible that these kings prioritized pursuits other than pyramid-building during their reigns. Senwosret III, for example, expended significant resources in constructing many of the Nubian fortresses. Senwosret I also built several fortresses and commissioned a pyramid at Lisht with an interior structure of stone walls filled with rubble, sand, and mortar,[58] which perhaps adds credence to the lack of resources argument. Furthermore, it is unlikely that every use of brick in the context of the Twelfth Dynasty pyramids would have been associated with a symbolic meaning; it is more probable that the brick sub-foundations discovered in the construction of all stone structures in Senwosret III's complex at Dashur, for example, were used predominantly for practical purposes.[59]

However, there are also several reasons to entertain the possibility that the use of brick in pyramid cores was connected to the symbolism of the medium. Statuary from the reigns of Senwosret III and Amenemhat III often showed both kings with lined faces, sometimes interpreted as manifestations of their aging humanity, or of their purposeful emulation of kings "of the old age."[60] This is perhaps evidence that the conception of kingship was in flux in this period, also suggested by literary texts such as *The Teaching of Amenemhat*. Additionally, the architectural style of the Twelfth Dynasty pyramid complexes was largely unstandardized in comparison to Old Kingdom complexes, a fact that Arnold has linked to "shifting conceptions of kingship and the relationships between royal and divine authority."[61] The association between mud brick, life cycles, and creation makes it plausible that its use in the pyramids was connected to this potential reinterpretation of kingship. It is also possible that this particular symbolism of bricks was tied to other changing funerary traditions at this time; burials and sarcophagi of this period seem to have sometimes been surrounded by soil, perhaps in an allusion to the earth mound of the cosmological creation.[62]

In analyzing Senwosret III's funerary complex at Abydos, Wegner convincingly argued that the unusual design of the tomb manifested a changing understanding of the afterlife of the king,[63] emphasizing how architecture might reflect a redefinition of kingship at this time. The complex, which was located at the site of the first Egyptian kings' burials, included archaizing architectural decorative elements, namely carved masonry in the form of wooden pole roofing that was characteristically found in those same Early Dynastic royal tombs. Several archaizing elements are also found in Senwosret III's Dashur funerary complex.[64] This evidently conscious return to archaic funerary architecture in Senwosret III's reign may have been paralleled in the use of brick, which might have also been tied to archaic architecture, in the royal pyramids in this period.

The diversity of materials employed in the construction of the Twelfth Dynasty pyramids, as well as the fact that even the brick ones would have been cased in stone and thus would not have looked different from their predecessors, brings to the fore questions of materials choice as related to the appearance of monuments and their meanings. It also highlights the impossibility of placing these monuments and their compositions in strict

---

[57] N. Moeller, *The Archaeology of Urbanism in Ancient Egypt: From the Predynastic Period to the End of the Middle Kingdom* (New York, 2016), 249–52.

[58] Dieter Arnold, *The Pyramid of Senwosret I*, Publications of the Metropolitan Museum of Art Egyptian Expedition 22; The South Cemeteries of Lisht, vol. 1 (New York, 1988), 66.

[59] Some of these brick sub-foundations have been published by Dieter Arnold, *The Pyramid Complex of Senwosret III at Dahshur* (New York, 2000). I thank Adela Oppenheim for discussing this with me.

[60] Arnold, *The Pyramid Complex of Senwosret III at Dahshur*, 122; G. Andreu, *Egypt in the Age of the Pyramids* (Ithaca, 1997), 15–16. Alternative interpretations have also been proposed, for example: D. Laboury, "Senwosret III and the Issue of Portraiture in Ancient Egyptian Art," in G. Andreu-Lanoë and F. Morfoisse (eds.), *Sésostris III et la fin du Moyen Empire, CRIPEL 31* (Lille, 2016–2017), 71–84.

[61] Quoted from J. Wegner, "The Tomb of Senwosret III at Abydos: Considerations on the Origins and Development of the Royal Amduat-Tomb," in Silverman, Simpson, and Wegner, *Archaism and Innovation: Studies in the Culture of Middle Kingdom Egypt*, 136; original work: D. Arnold, "Vom Pyramidenbezirk zum 'Haus für Millionen Jahre," *MDAIK* 34 (1978), 1–9.

[62] Arnold, *The Pyramid Complex of Senwosret III at Dahshur*, 112.

[63] Wegner, "The Tomb of Senwosret III at Abydos," 103–68.

[64] Arnold, *The Pyramid Complex of Senwosret III at Dahshur*, 121–22.

categories. The use of bricks instead of, and in addition to, stone demonstrates the danger of imposing modern classifications onto ancient Egyptian practices and beliefs: the dividing line between mundane and divine as reflected in these materials did not exist in such cosmologically significant contexts, and bricks were anything but "polluting" substances.

Temple Annexes

This lack of a strict separation between the meanings of brick and stone is further demonstrated by the use of bricks in temples. While major temples were usually built in stone, particularly from the Middle Kingdom onwards,[65] minor temples were often built in brick. This should certainly not be taken as indication that they were any less divine or meant to last for a shorter period of time than major temples, and it is perhaps related to brick being cheaper and easier to procure than stone. The same argument can be made for the brick composition of temple annexes attached to both stone and brick temples, such as storage magazines and temple palaces. Nevertheless, it is also possible to consider the use of the brick medium in annexes in light of its symbolic interpretation.

Temple annexes, which were essential for the operation of the temple, were always brick-built structures, regardless of the main building material used for the construction of the temple core. The fact that these brick buildings that surrounded the temple proper were necessary for it to function is a parallel to the addition of bricks and brick molds to temple foundations and foundation deposits, also in order to ensure their effectiveness as divine spaces. While brick annexes would certainly have had to be cared for more regularly than the stone temples they were attached to, since brick as a building material requires frequent repairing and re-plastering, stone temples themselves were never fully complete either. Divine temples such as Karnak received constant additions by different kings, and even mortuary temples of specific rulers that would not have been modified as often would likely have been refurbished as necessary while cult was still performed. However, the need to fix the brick annexes more often might have even been part of the point—it would have emphasized the cyclicality of the medium in contrast to the stone temple proper.

This inherent cyclicality of the brick medium, both physical and symbolic, is particularly linked to two types of temple annexes: storage magazines and temple palaces. Grain is bound to the inundation of the Nile and to the sustenance necessary to support life. The grain of temples, particularly in the New Kingdom, was used both for cultic purposes and to feed large parts of the population, and the fact that bricks were the medium suited for their storage can perhaps be associated with its own life-giving properties. Besides that symbolic link, it is also likely that the traditional use of mud brick to build granaries was tied to its physical properties; modern parallels in Africa suggest that brick is well-suited for grain storage in dry environments.[66]

Temple palaces, characteristic parts of New Kingdom royal mortuary temples, were usually attached to the first courtyard of the temple proper, their front walls in stone while the rest of the building was brick (fig. 7). Because of their location and their material connection to the temple, temple palaces were inextricably linked to the domain of the king and god. However, they were also unarguably disconnected from it—the difference in materials between the two, a clear and deliberate choice, ensured that they remained attached to the divine abode of stone while at the same time separate. It is unclear whether temple palaces would have actually been functional buildings or mainly ceremonial.[67] Even if ceremonial, it is clear that they were meant to emulate

[65] D. Warburton, "Karnak and the Kings: Architecture, Religion, Ideology and Political History," in R. Gundlach and K. Spence (eds.), *Palace and Temple: Architecture – Decoration – Ritual* (Wiesbaden, 2011), 155–79.

[66] Food and Agriculture Organization of the United Nations (FAO) and Information on Post-Harvest Operations (INPhO), *African Experience in the Improvement of Post-Harvest Techniques. Based on the Workshop Held in ACCRA, Ghana 4–8 July 1994* (Rome, 1998), chapter 4 (http://www.fao.org/3/w1544e/w1544e00.htm).

[67] It has been said that temple palaces were created when kings no longer lived permanently in Upper Egypt, leading some to believe that they served as temporary residences for the king when he visited Thebes: U. Hölscher, *The Excavation of Medinet Habu, Volume III: The Mortuary Temple of Ramses III, Part I*, Oriental Institute Publications 54 (Chicago, 1941), 40–43; S. Snape, *The Complete Cities of Ancient Egypt* (Cairo, 2014), 46. However, the fact that these palaces seem to have been abbreviated versions of other palaces and that false doors sometimes survive behind throne bases suggests to others a mostly ceremonial and symbolic function: R. Stadelmann, "Royal Palaces of the Late

Fig. 7. A back view of the stone front wall of Ramses III's Medinet Habu temple palace, also showing the bricks that made up the majority of the palace and the connection between the two. The stone door socket visible on the left was inside the palace. Photo by the author.

lived-in royal palaces, and so the meaning of their brick composition needs to be discussed in light of that architectural context.

Royal Palaces

An exploration of the symbolic brick medium in architecture is particularly relevant for our understanding of royal palaces, which have been the focus of relatively little scholarship largely due to the poor preservation and rarity of excavated examples. They were predominantly built in brick, and though scholars have discussed the positionality of palaces in both Egyptian society and cosmology,[68] none have explicitly addressed their material composition and what it reveals about these buildings, as well as the king who lived and ruled in them. Most assume that palaces relate to the terrestrial duties of the king, and that their brick composition sets them apart

---

New Kingdom in Thebes," in B. Bryan and D. Lorton (eds.), *Essays in Egyptology in Honor of Hans Goedicke* (San Antonio, 1994), 311–12; R. Stadelmann, "Temple Palace and Residential Palace," in M. Bietak (ed.), *Haus und Palast im Alten Ägypten/House and Palace in Ancient Egypt* (Vienna, 1996), 228; P. Lacovara, *The New Kingdom Royal City*, Studies in Egyptology (New York, 1997), 33.

[68] E.g., D. O'Connor, "City and Palace in New Kingdom Egypt," *Cahiers de Recherches de l'Institut de Papyrologie et d'Égyptologie de Lille* 11 (1989), 73–87; J. Baines, "Trône et dieu: aspects du symbolisme royal et divin des temps archaïques," *BSFE* 118 (1990), 5–37; D. O'Connor, "Mirror of the Cosmos: The Palace of Merenptah," in E. Bleiberg and R. Freed (eds.), *Fragments of a Shattered Visage: The Proceedings of the International Symposium of Ramesses the Great* (Memphis 1991), 168, 184; Baines, "Palaces and Temples of Ancient Egypt," 303–17; R. Gundlach, "'Horus in the Palace': The Centre of State and Culture in Pharaonic Egypt," in R. Gundlach and J. Taylor (eds.), *Egyptian Royal Residences: 4. Symposium zur ägyptischen Königsideologie* (Wiesbaden, 2009), 45–67; Snape, *The Complete Cities of Ancient Egypt*, 47.

from temples as mundane buildings—a conclusion that arises from the pitting of stone against brick, which as discussed above is not supportable.

Practical considerations should again not be disregarded, and in this case the thermal properties of brick may well have played a part. But the symbolism of the medium, and particularly its ties to life cycles rather than continuous existence, provide a satisfying explanation for the use of brick in palatial construction. The human, cyclical part of kingship has been largely neglected in modern scholarship, with some important exceptions;[69] one way to access it is through a consideration of brick palaces, where the king resided during life.[70] Mud brick in the context of royal palaces can be tied to *neheh* and the finite lives of the kings who built them. They were architectural expressions of primarily incarnate kingship, which like the brick medium was itself not mundane. That does not mean, however, that they were completely divorced from continuous kingship; such stifling dichotomies do not sit well with Egyptian ideology. Instead, bricks also tied them to the royal institution through their connection to the *serekh* and archaic architecture.

Furthermore, though stone was less suitable as the main building material of palaces because of its connection to *djet*, it was also necessary for their functioning, just as bricks were needed in predominantly stone temples and tombs. Stone was used for practical reasons, such as window gratings, door frames, and water installations. But it was likely also used for symbolic ones, such as the carving of reliefs of the king smiting enemies and interacting with the gods—elements perhaps more closely tied to the royal institution than the king's human life.[71] Exceptions to this general rule that bricks were needed as the main building material of palaces, including the so-called Great Palace of Akhenaten and a Ramses II temple palace recently discovered at Abydos, support rather than weaken the validity of the rule due to their unusual contexts, both locational and temporal.[72] Bricks in palaces played a cosmological role in allowing the building to support the king and his movements in a body that was born, aged, and would die; brick's connections to soil and creation shaped the building's purpose and enabled it to fulfill it effectively.

Conclusion

The cosmological importance of dualities in ancient Egypt is evidenced by their dualistic conception of time and the two facets of kingship, as well as by the Pyramid Text that mentions both stone and brick rising out of the waters at the moment of creation. To say that such a thing as a "brick palace" or a "stone temple" existed would be an unwise simplification of a highly complex architectural symbology—because they were cosmologically charged buildings, they needed to access the two strands of time manifested by brick and stone in order to fulfill

[69] A. Moret, *Du caractère religieux de la royauté pharaonique* (Paris, 1902); H. Frankfort, *Kingship and the Gods: A Study of Ancient Near Eastern Religion as the Integration of Society & Nature* (Chicago, 1948); G. Posener, *De la divinité du Pharaon*, Cahiers de la Société Asiatique 15 (Paris, 1960); H. Goedicke, *Die Stellung des Königs im Alten Reich* (Wiesbaden, 1960); D. Lorton, "Review: Towards a Constitutional Approach to Ancient Egyptian Kingship," *JAOS* 99, no. 3 (1979), 460–65; A. Morales, "Los dos cuerpos del rey: cosmos y política de la monarquía egipcia," *ARYS: Antigüedad, Religiones y Sociedades* 12 (2014), 47–86.

[70] While the function of most palaces would have likely been at least partly domestic, some prefer to think that different categories of palaces (domestic, ceremonial, and administrative) would have been much more rigid: O'Connor, "City and Palace in New Kingdom Egypt," 76.

[71] For example, reliefs from Merenptah's palace in Memphis (Penn Museum E17527, E13575E, E13575C). Not much is known about palatial decoration due to the rarity of preserved remains, so any conclusions on this front are highly conjectural: Osorio G. Silva, "The Myth of the Mundane," chapter 4. For a survey of palatial decoration, see: P. Salland, "Palatial Paintings and Programs: The Symbolic World of the Egyptian Palace in the New Kingdom (c. 1550–1069 BCE)" (PhD dissertation, New York University, 2015).

[72] There is debate about whether the Great Palace was a palace at all: E. Uphill, "The Per Aten at Amarna," *JNES* 29, no. 3 (1970), 151–66; J. Assmann, "Palast oder Tempel? Überlegungen zur Architektur und Topographie von Amarna," *JNES* 31, no. 3 (1972), 143–55; B. Kemp, "The Window of Appearance at el-Amarna and the Basic Structure of this City," *JEA* 62 (1976), 99; O'Connor, "City and Palace in New Kingdom Egypt," 85; B. Kemp, *The City of Akhenaten and Nefertiti. Amarna and Its People* (London, 2012), 123, 140–41. Even if it was, the status of Akhenaten and Nefertiti as members of the divine triad during the Amarna Period make it plausible that the use of stone in this building is tied precisely to that increased divinity: Osorio G. Silva, "The Myth of the Mundane," chapter 4. The Ramses II palace, attached to his temple at Abydos, has walls of both limestone and mud brick. This mixing of materials implies that bricks were needed in that context, but in this case (perhaps due to its Abydene location or the nature of the temple) a more considerable use of stone than was usual in palaces was also warranted. I thank Sameh Iskander for bringing this find to my attention at the 2019 ARCE Annual Meeting.

their purposes of supporting beings and interactions that similarly cannot be placed in restrictive categories. While the current visibility of building materials has left a considerable mark in modern interpretations of these ancient monuments, it is fairly certain that they would not have been very visible anciently due to the plastering and painting of walls, and that visibility did not play much of a role in determining how these materials functioned. However, materials predominantly found in each building were the best suited to fulfill each one's particular purpose, and the combining of brick and stone was itself significant and necessary. The Twelfth Dynasty pyramids are excellent examples of this intermingling of materials: predominantly built of brick but cased in stone, they are not simply of one material or the other. Stone tombs had bricks inserted into their walls and brick molds deposited in their foundation deposits; stone temples had brick-built annexes, and bricks were placed both in their four corners and in foundation deposits. Palaces were built in brick but also relied on stone to fulfill their functions effectively. This blending of construction media can be documented and is considered significant from the First Dynasty on, when stone first appears in the brick tombs of kings at Abydos.

Rather than either brick or stone, rather than either practical or symbolic, Egyptian architecture for 3,000 years shows meaningful combinations of materials to achieve complex ends. That stone has been so extensively considered in scholarship is perhaps a testament to how well it survives in the archaeological record as compared to brick, but that should certainly not be cause to disregard the latter. The evidence discussed here, which demonstrates that brick objects were certainly symbolic and allows for suggestions of how the construction medium itself could have functioned symbolically, shows how looking at brick is a necessary balance to looking at stone. There is much left to explore regarding materials choice in ancient Egypt and this first foray into discussing primarily the meaning of brick in architecture and cosmology, but also how it functioned alongside stone, demonstrates the relevance of such questions and their answers.

The Dating of Heneni's False Door at Hildesheim

Saleh Soleiman
Faculty of Archaeology, Damietta University

Abstract

This article deals with dating the false door of Heneni which was found at Giza and is now preserved in the Roemer-und Pelizaeus-Museum, Hildesheim. The false door is dated from late in the reign of Pepy II to the Eighth Dynasty on the basis of its place of its discovery in the cemetery, the name of its owner, the titles and epithets of the deceased, the prt-ḫrw *formula, and its form and decoration. The small size and location of Heneni's tomb are discussed. His rank and status are determined, the short offering formula on the false door is explicated, and a new reading and translation are suggested for the* prt-ḫrw *formula.*

ملخص

تتعامل هذه المقالة مع تأريخ الباب الوهمى الخاص بـ حننى الذى عُثر عليه جنوب شرق الهرم الأكبر بالجيزة ومحفوظ الآن بمتحف رومير و بلوزيوس بهليدشتايم. أرخ بعض الباحثين هذا الباب بالأسرة السادسة بصفة عامة وبعضهم الأخر اقترح أواخر هذه الأسرة. يقترح الباحث تأريخه بالفترة الزمنية الممتدة من آواخر عهد ببى الثانى وحتى الأسرة الثامنة وذلك بناء على مكان اكتشافه واسم صاحب القبر وألقابه وطريقة كتابة اسم أنوبيس وصيغة قربان برت خرو والعناصر المعمارية للباب وزخرفته. ونتج عن هذا التاريخ المقترح معرفة متى تم تشييد مقبرة حننى بالجبانة وسبب صغر حجمها وسبب اختياره لموقع مقبرته وسبب غياب اسم الملك المعاصر ومعرفة ما اضطره لاختصار صيغة القربان. وتمكنت الدراسة من تأريخ 13 مقبرة علاوة على مقبرة حننى. توجد هذه المقابر بهليوبوليس والجيزة ودشاشة وأبيدوس ودندرة.

Introduction

The tomb of Heneni is an unnumbered stone built mastaba located in the GIS cemetery located to the south of the Khufu pyramid at Giza. The tomb was excavated by Junker in 1929. It included a false door now preserved as no. 3179 in the Roemer-und Pelizaeus-Museum, Hildesheim (figs. 1–2). The false door measures 169.5 x 95 x 14 cm and is carved from one block of fine white limestone. It has a cavetto cornice, a torus molding, two lintels, a central panel, two side apertures, four jambs, a drum and central niche. There is a frame consisting of a lintel and two jambs outside the cavetto cornice and the false door proper.

The scenes and inscriptions of the false door are executed in sunk relief. The owner of the tomb is depicted on the central panel. He is shown seated on a lion-legged chair, with his right hand extended towards the offering table and the other folded across his breast. He wears a shoulder-length wig. On top of the offering table are loaves of bread. The deceased is also depicted at the end of the vertical texts on the four jambs of the false door and two jambs of the frame, facing the central niche. He wears a shoulder-length wig in three of the representations

---

I would like to thank Annette Gray and Waleed Alkalla who reviewed the English of this article.

Journal of the American Research Center in Egypt 56 (2020), 199–211
doi: http://dx.doi.org/10.5913/jarce.56.2020.a013

Fig. 1. False Door of Heneni (Roemer-und Pelizaeus-Museum, 3197). From http://giza.fas.harvard.edu/objects/54746/full/.

Fig. 2. False Door of Heneni (Roemer-und Pelizaeus-Museum, 3197). After Junker, Gîza, *vol. 11 (1953), fig. 40.*

and a short wig in the other three. He wears a pointed kilt in all representations. In two, he holds a scepter and staff; the staff only in two others, and he has empty hands in the last two.

The supplementary frame, upper lintel, central panel, lower lintel and jambs are inscribed, while the drum and central niche are blank. These inscriptions are the offering formula, the thousand offering list, titles, epithets, and the name of the deceased.[1]

Dating of Heneni's False Door

The tomb of Heneni is dated by Porter and Moss to the Sixth Dynasty.[2] Martin suggested the late Sixth Dynasty.[3] Brovarski dated it to the end of the Sixth Dynasty or later depending on four features of the false door.[4] We suggest dating it from late in Pepy II's reign to the Eighth Dynasty for a number of criteria that are listed below:

1. Location of the Tomb

The tomb of Heneni is located south of the Great Pyramid at Giza, GIS.[5] This cemetery includes tombs dated to the reign of Menkaure and from the end of the Fifth Dynasty to the Sixth Dynasty, from the reign of Teti to Pepy II.[6]

2. Personal Name

The name of the tomb owner *Ḥnni* is attested in tombs dated from late in Teti's reign to early in Pepy I's reign (Nikauisesi[7]); Pepy I's reign and Merenre's reign (Mehu[8]); Merenre's to Pepy II's reign (Pepyankh[9] and Khesu[10]); Pepy II's reign (his funerary temple,[11] Pepyankh[12] and Pepyankhheriib[13]); late Sixth Dynasty (Heneni[14] and Khewenwekh[15]) and the late Old Kingdom (Nyankhpepy,[16] and three more persons named Heneni[17]).

---

[1] http://giza.fas.harvard.edu/objects/54746/full/

[2] PM 3², 222.

[3] K. Martin, *Reliefs des Alten Reiches*, vol. 2 Corpus Antiquitatum Aegyptiacarum 7 (Mainz, 1979), 107–13.

[4] E. Brovarski, "False Doors and History: The Sixth Dynasty," in M. Bárta (ed.), *The Old Kingdom Art and Archaeology, Proceedings of the Conference held in Prague, May 31–June 4, 2004* (Prague, 2006), 111.

[5] PM 3², pls. 3, 19; http://giza.fas.harvard.edu/sites/4103/full/.

[6] PM 3², 216–28.

[7] N. Kanawati and M. Abder-Raziq, *The Tomb of Nikauisesi* (Warminster, 2000), pl. 54.

[8] H. Altenmüller, *Die Wanddarstellungen im Grab des Mehu in Saqqara* (Mainz, 1998), pl. 85; N. Strudwick, *The Administration of Egypt in the Old Kingdom, The Highest Titles and their Holders* (London, 1985), 101–2; Y. Harpur, *Decoration in Egyptian Tombs of the Old Kingdom* (London-New York, 1987), 274; N. Cherpion, *Mastabas et hypogées d'Ancien Empire – Le probléme de la datation* (Brussels, 1989), 233.

[9] PM 4, 125; W. Schenkel and F. Gomaà, *Scharuna I: der Grabungsplatz, die Nekropole, Gräber aus der Alten-Reichs-Nekropole, Text* (Mainz, 2004), 199.

[10] H. Schäfer, *Aegyptische Inschriften aus den Königlichen Museen zu Berlin* (Wiesbaden, 1913), 42.

[11] G. Jéquier, *Le Monument Funeraire de Pepi II. Tome 2, Le temple* (Cairo, 1938), pl. 89.

[12] A. Blackman and M. Apted, *The Rock Tombs of Meir*, vol. 5 (London, 1953), pls. 25, 28.

[13] A. Blackman, *The Rock Tombs of Meir*, vol. 4 (London, 1924), pl. 8; PM 4, 254; N. Kanawati, *The Egyptian Administration in the Old Kingdom, Evidence on its Economic Decline* (Warminster, 1977), 91; Harpur, *Decoration*, 280; Cherpion, *Mastabas*, 234; N. Kanawati, *The Cemetery of Meir*, vol. 1 (Oxford, 2012), 24–26.

[14] PM 3², 681; G. Jéquier, *Tombeaux de particuliers contemporains de Pepy II. Fouilles à Saqqarah* (Cairo, 1929), 28; K. Dawood, "Animate decoration and burial chambers of private tombs during the Old Kingdom: New evidence from the tomb of Kairer at Saqqara," in L. Pantalacci and C. Berger-El-Naggar (eds.), *Des Néferkarê aux Montouhotep. Travaux archéologiques en cours sur la fin de la VIe dynastie et la première période intermédiaire. Actes du Colloque CNRS – Université Lumière-Lyon 2, tenu le 5–7 juillet 2001* (Lyon, 2005), 118.

[15] A. El-Khouli and N. Kanawati, *Quseir el-Amarna, the Tombs of Pepy-ankh and Khewen-wekh* (Sydney, 1989), pls. 37, 41.

[16] S. Hassan, *Excavations at Saqqara 1937–1938*, vol. 2, *Mastabas of Ny-ʿankh-Pepy and Others* (Cairo, 1975), pl. 3; Harpur, *Decoration*, 274.

[17] PM 3², 543, 545; C. Firth and B. Gunn, *Excavations at Saqqara, Teti Pyramid Cemeteries*, vol. 1 (Cairo, 1926), 211; V. Dobrev and J. Laclant, "Les tables d'offrandes de particuliers décou- vertes aux complexes funéraires des reines près de la pyramide de Pépi I," in N. Grimal (ed.), *Les Critères de Datation Stylistiques à l'Ancien Empire* (Cairo, 1998), 156, fig. 16; A. Kamal, "Rapport sur les fouilles de Said Bey Khachaba au Déîr-el-Gabraouî," *ASAE* 13 (1914), 177.

It is noticeable that this name appeared from late in Teti's reign to the late Old Kingdom. It was common from the reign of Pepy II to the end of the Old Kingdom and is more connected to the reign of Pepy II.

The way his name is written also provides dating criterion. The name of the Heneni is written using the hoe without the rope connecting the two pieces of the hoe. This is found only on this false door and in the funerary temple of Pepy II at South Saqqara,[18] so this writing can be dated to the reign of Pepy II.

3. Titles and Epithets

Heneni had ten titles and three epithets. The first of his titles is *imy-r ꜥrrwt,* "overseer of the approach to a building/approach area to temple precinct." *ꜥrrwt* is translated as "gates," "vestibules," "judicial departments," or a type of portico or area which may have been roofed for protection.[19] This title is only found in Heneni's tomb in the Old Kingdom. It is also found later in the tomb of Initef at Naga ed-Dêr, which is dated to the Ninth Dynasty.[20] The tomb of Heneni is near this tomb, which most probably is of the Eighth Dynasty.

The second of Heneni's titles is *imy-r ꜥrrwt m prwy,* "overseer of the approach to a building/approach area to temple precinct in the two houses."[21] This title is only found on the false door of Heneni.

The third title of Heneni is *ꜥḏ mr ṯnw,* "administrator" or "boundary official of a frontier district (the boundary area, oasis)."[22] This title is rare, and is dated to the second half of the Old Kingdom. It is attested in the Fifth Dynasty (tombs of Nesutnefer[23] and Kawedjankh[24]) and in the late Fifth Dynasty to early Sixth Dynasty (tomb of Nekhetsaes[25]).

The fourth title of Heneni is *ḥḳꜣ ḥwt*, "estate manager/property administrator/chief of the estate/chief of the field district." This title is attested as early as the Fourth Dynasty. It continued in use in the Fifth Dynasty and became widespread during the Sixth Dynasty in both the residence and the provinces.[26] This title was most commen in the reign of Pepy II (tombs of Ibi,[27] Uha,[28] Djau,[29] and Pepyankhheriib[30]).

The fifth title of Heneni is *ẖry-ḥb*, "the lector priest" "he who carries the ritual-book"[31] indicating that Heneni was responsible for reciting spells and rites in temples and at funerals. The title "lector priest" was attested since the Second Dynasty onwards. The lector priest is usually shown with an unrolled papyrus scroll in his hand and wears a linen strap from his shoulder across his chest.[32] It was early held by members of the royal family, and then by different categories of officials. The lector priest was considered to be a wise man and sage who could foresee coming events. He was among the principal practitioners of magic and medicine.[33]

The sixth title of Heneni is *ẖry-tp nzwt,* "royal chamberlain" or "he who is under king's head/the one upon royal property."[34] The title was known from the early Old Kingdom[35] and it was held by officials who owned tombs in the necropolis of the capital and provincial cemeteries, and by persons who participated in the expedi-

---

[18] Jequier, *Monument*, vol. 2, pl. 89.

[19] D. Jones, *An Index of Ancient Egyptian Titles, Epithets and Phrases of the Old Kingdom* (Oxford, 2000), 79 [344].

[20] D. Dunham, *Naga-ed-Dêr Stelae of the First Intermediate Period* (Boston, 1937), 62.

[21] Jones, *Titles*, 79 [345].

[22] Jones, *Titles*, 363–64 [1346].

[23] PM 3^2, 143; H. Junker, *Grabungen auf dem Friedhof des Alten Reiches bei den Pyramiden von Gîza*, vol. 3 (Vienna-Leipzig, 1938), figs. 27–30; N. Kanawati, *Tombs at Giza*, vol. 2 (Warminster, 2002), 36–41, pls. 1a, 12–15, 52, 54.

[24] PM 3^2, 894; T. James, *Hieroglyphic Texts from Egyptian Stelae etc. in the British Museum*, vol. 1 (London, 1961), 8, pl. viii.

[25] J. Cooney, "Three Egyptian Families of the Old Kingdom," *BMB* 13.3 (1952), 15–18, fig. 10.

[26] Jones, *Titles*, 670–71 [2453]; K. Dawood, *The Inscribed Stelae of the Herakleopolitan Period from the Memphite Necropolis*, vol. 1 (Liverpool, 1998), 109.

[27] PM 4, 243–44; N. Kanawati, *Deir el-Gebrawi*, vol. 2 (Oxford, 2007), pls. 4–12, 19–33, 46, 47, 51, 53–56, 67, 68, 71, 72; Harpur, *Decoration*, 280.

[28] PM 4, 246; Kanawati, *Deir el-Gebrawi*, vol. 2, 79–81, pl. 61, 75b (14).

[29] PM 4, 244–46; N. Davies, *The Rock Tombs of Deir el-Gebrâwi*, vol. 2 (London, 1902), pls. 3–6, 9–12; Harpur, *Decoration*, 280.

[30] Blackmann, *Meir*, vol. 4, pl. 15; Kanawati, *Meir*, vol. 1, 47, pls. 83, 84.

[31] Jones, *Titles*, 781 [2848].

[32] R. Forshaw, *The Role of the Lector in Ancient Egyptian Society* (Oxford, 2014), 7, 10.

[33] D. Doxey, "Priesthood," in D. Redford (ed.), *The Oxford Encyclopedia of Ancient Egypt*, vol. 3 (Oxford, 2001), 69.

[34] Jones *Titles*, 788 [2874].

[35] H. Goedicke, "Title for Titles," in S. Allam (ed.), *Grund and Bodenim Altägypten* (Tübingen, 1994), 231.

tions to the quarries. The duties of this title are unknown. The holder of this title could care for the king in his bedroom[36] or he acted on behalf of the king to perform short-term management of the royal property, so he was an assistant or deputy of the king.[37] This title could be granted by the king himself, as Nekhebu mentioned in his autobiography.[38]

This title was known from the Third Dynasty onwards[39] and it was attested in tombs, quarries, and on papyrus.[40] The title was rare in the Third and Fourth Dynasties, but it became more common in the Fifth Dynasty and was even more prevalent in the Sixth Dynasty. It became rare in the late Old Kingdom (end of the Sixth Dynasty to the Eighth Dynasty). This title was more common in the reign of Pepy II, and more than twenty-five examples of it are known.[41]

The seventh title of Heneni is *smr,* "companion/courtier."[42] If we study examples of this title,[43] we notice that it too provides dating criterion. It appears from the reign of Sekhemkhet in the Third Dynasty and continued to be used in inscriptions in tombs, quarries, and on papyrus in the Old Kingdom until the end of the Eighth Dynasty. It was very rare in the Third and Fourth Dynasties, but it became more common in the Fifth and Sixth Dynasties. It was most common in the reign of Pepy II, when the title appears in tombs (Pepyankhheriib,[44] Kaheb,[45] Nehuet-desher,[46] Sefekhu,[47] Iy,[48] Shepsipumin,[49] and Harkhuf[50]), in quarries (Graffito 06 at Hatnub[51]), and on papyrus (a letter of complaint over farming (Turin CG 54002[52]). The title *smr* became rare again from the end of the Sixth Dynasty to the Eighth Dynasty.

The eighth title of Heneni is *smr wꜥty* "the sole companion."[53] This title is mentioned more than any other, being attested nine times on his false door. It precedes all his titles, except *ḥḳꜣ ḥwt*. This title was bestowed on the person by the king himself, as was mentioned in the autobiography of Nekhebu.[54] It was an important title,

---

[36] Jones, *Titles*, 788 [2874].

[37] Goedicke "Title for Titles," 227–34.

[38] PM 3², 90; *Urk.* 1, 215–19; M. Lichtheim, *Ancient Egyptian Autobiographies Chiefly of the Middle Kingdom* (Freiburg-Göttingen, 1988), 12–14; S. Soleiman, *The Self Talks and Appeal to the Living in the Old Kingdom Private Tombs at Memphis Necropolis, Cultural-Analyzing Study*, PhD diss., Archaeology and Culture Department, Faculty of Arts, Helwan University (Cairo, 2014), 52–57, fig. 17.

[39] Goedicke, "Title for Titles," 231.

[40] Jones, *Titles*, 788 [2874].

[41] For these examples see: "Thesaurus Linguae Aegyptiae,"lemma no. 450367 (version October 31, 2014, accessed January 20, 2020, http://aaew.bbaw.de/tla/index.html)

[42] Jones, *Titles*, 891 [3263].

[43] "Thesaurus Linguae Aegyptiae," lemma no. 135420, version October 31, 2014, accessed January 20, 2020, http://aaew.bbaw.de/tla/index.html.

[44] Blackmann, *Meir*, vol. 4, pl. 15; Kanawati, *Meir,* vol. 1, 47, pl. 83.

[45] N. Kanawati, *The Rock Tombs of El-Hawawish, The Cemetery of Akhmim*, vol. 1 (Sydney, 1980), 32, 37, pls. 9, 13, figs. 5, 13, 18; P. Newberry, "The Inscribed Tombs of Ekhmîm," *AAA* 4 (1912), 118; N. Kanawati, *Akhmim in the Old Kingdom, I: Chronology and Administration* (Sydney, 1992), 313.

[46] N. Kanawati, *The Rock Tombs of El-Hawawish, The Cemetery of Akhmim*, vol. 8 (Sydney, 1988), 11–13, pls. 4, 13, figs. 1, 4; Kanawati, *Akhmim*, 311.

[47] N. Kanawati, *The Rock Tombs of El-Hawawish, The Cemetery of Akhmim,* vol. 6 (Sydney, 1986), 31–33, pls. 2, 6, figs. 10, 11; Kanawati, *Akhmim*, 250–51, 312.

[48] N. Kanawati, *The Rock Tombs of El-Hawawish, The Cemetery of Akhmim*, vol. 7 (Sydney, 1987), 16, 17, figs. 7, 8; Newberry, "Ekhmîm," 107; *Urk.* 1, 264; Kanawati, *Akhmim*, 309.

[49] N. Kanawati, *The Rock Tombs of El-Hawawish, The Cemetery of Akhmim*, vol. 2 (Sydney, 1981), pls. 5, 8, figs. 1, 25; Newberry, "Ekhmîm," 119; Kanawati, *Akhmim*, 267, 312.

[50] E. Schiaparelli, *Una tomba egiziana inedita della VIa dinastia, con inscrizioni storiche e geografiche* (Rome, 1892), 10–11; K. Sethe, *Documents of the Old Kingdom* (Leipzig, 1933), 128.3–131.7; E. Eichler, "Investigations on the royal letters of the Old Kingdom," *SAK* 18 (1991), 152–55; E. Wente, *Letters from Ancient Egypt* (Atlanta, 1990), 20; Harpur, *Decoration*, 282.

[51] R. Anthes, *Die Felsinschriften von Hatnub: Untersuchungen zur Geschichte und Altertumskunde Ägyptens* (Leipzig, 1928), 21–22, pl. 11; E. Eichler, *Untersuchungen zum Expeditionswesen des ägyptischen Alten Reiches* (Wiesbaden, 1993), 44.

[52] A. Roccati, "Una lettera inedita dell'Antico Regno," *JEA* 54 (1968), 14–22; Wente, *Letters*, 57; N. Strudwick, *Texts from the Pyramid Age* (Atlanta, 2005), 179.

[53] Jones, *Titles*, 892 [3268].

[54] D. Dunham, "The Biographical Inscriptions of Nekhebu in Boston and in Cairo," *JEA* 24 (1928), 4.

as indicated by the princes and viziers who were among the persons who held it.[55] The frequency of this title on Heneni's false door suggests he was proud of holding this title that expressed the special status that the king had given to him.

This title provides further dating criterion. It is dated to the Third Dynasty and it is widely attested during the Fourth Dynasty.[56] After the late Fifth Dynasty, it was common (about ninety examples are known), associated with all categories of officials, and it became a title of rank.[57] It was most prevalent from the reign of Pepy II to the Eighth Dynasty, and more than fifty-five of the ninety examples date from that period.[58]

Heneni had both titles *ẖry-tp nzwt* and *smr wꜥty*. The first title appears to have been held almost always in conjunction with *smr wꜥty*. These two titles appear sporadically in the early Sixth Dynasty and then more frequently later. A man holding *ẖry-tp nzwt* was granted *smr wꜥty*, especially in the reign of Pepy II.[59]

The ninth title of Heneni is *zꜣb imy-r zš(w)*: "juridical overseer of the scribes," "overseer of the scribes of the judiciary,"[60] or "judge and overseer of the scribes."

This title too can be used as a dating criterion. It was known from the Fourth Dynasty onwards and held mainly by persons who were buried in the Memphis necropolis and more rarely those buried in the provincial cemeteries. It was also attested in the quarries.[61] This title was very rare in the Fourth Dynasty, but it increased in use in the Fifth Dynasty, and it was most prevalent in the Sixth Dynasty. It became rare from the end of the Sixth Dynasty to the Eighth Dynasty. This title was most commonly attested in the reigns of Unas, Teti, and Pepy II.[62]

The last title of Heneni is *zš ꜥ(w) nzwt ḫft-ḥr,* "scribe of the royal records in the presence"/ "king's document scribe in the presence"/ "personal scribe of the royal records."[63] This title first appears in the quarries from the Fourth Dynasty in Wadi Hammamat (G 37 and C-M 265).[64] It appears in tombs from the reign of Neuserre including in the tomb of Rawer (G 5270), in the West Field at Giza[65] onwards till the end of the Old Kingdom in the tomb of Twau (N 359), which is dated from end of the Sixth Dynasty to the Eighth Dynasty.[66] So this title makes its appearance in the middle or later Fifth Dynasty but is principally a Sixth Dynasty title.[67]

This title was most common in the reign of Pepy II and the end of the Sixth Dynasty (tombs of Meru, Neferseshemseshat, Irenakheti/Irenptah, Senedjemib/Inti, Seshemnefer/Ifi, Idu, Qar, Ankhuza/Ithi, Idu II, Nisuptah, Theteti, Pepysonb, Biu, Nenkheftek, Hesymin, and Pepyankhheriib).[68]

---

[55] M. Baud, *Famille royale et pouvoir sous l'Ancien Empire égyptien* (Cairo, 1999), 259–63.

[56] M. Bárta et al., *The Cemeteries at Abusir South I* (Prague, 2001), 12.

[57] W. Helck, *Untersuchungenzu den Beamtentiteln des ägyptischen Alten Reiches* (Glückstadt, 1954), 25, 111; Strudwick, *Administration*, 224–25.

[58] Jones, *Titles*, 892 [3268].

[59] Strudwick, *Administration*, 182.

[60] Jones, *Titles*, 803 [2933].

[61] Jones, *Titles*, 803 [2933].

[62] For these examples see: "Thesaurus Linguae Aegyptiae," lemma no. 450596, version October 31, 2014, accessed January 20, 2020, http://aaew.bbaw.de/tla/index.html.

[63] Jones, *Titles*, 839 [3063].

[64] J. Couyat and P. Montet, *Les inscriptions hieroglyphiques et hieratiques du Ouadi Hammama*t (Cairo, 1912), 117; G. Goyon, *Nouvelles inscriptions rupestres du Wadi Hammamat* (Paris, 1957), 67, pl. 13; Eichler, *Expeditionswesen*, 63, 81.

[65] PM 3^2, 158; Junker, *Gîza*, vol. 3, 119–22, 217–23, figs. 11, 40, 42 [a], pl. 13; Harpur, *Decoration*, 268.

[66] C. N. Peck, *Some Decorated Tombs of the First Intermediate Period at Naga Ed-Dêr* (Providence, 1958), 13, pl. 2; Harpur, *Decoration*, 281.

[67] Strudwick, *Administration*, 211.

[68] Meru: PM 4, 62; G. Daressy, "La nécropole des grands prêtres d'Héliopolis sousl'Ancien Empire," *ASAE* 16 (1916), 195, 198; N. Strudwick, review of *Excavations at Saqqara North-West of Teti's Pyramid*, vol. 1 by N. Kanawati, A. El-Khouli, A. McFarlane, and N. V. Maksoud, *JEA* 73 (1987), 277; Neferseshemseshat: Daressy, "Héliopolis," 211–12; M. Kuentz, *CG 1308–13151 and CG 17001–17036*, 7–10, pl. 3. Irenakheti/Irenptah: S. Hassan, *Excavations at Gîza 1934–1935*, vol. 6.3 (Cairo, 1950), 9–17, figs. 5, 8, 9, pls. 3–5. It is dated to the Sixth Dynasty (PM 3^2, 250; Harpur, *Decoration*, 265 [28]). We think it could be dated to the late Sixth Dynasty because of writing of the *tꜣ*-sign with two pellets underneath, as shown on his lintel and false door. According to Dawood's study this is more common from the end of the Sixth Dynasty (Dawood, *Inscribed Stelae*, 38); Senedjemib/Inti: H. Junker, *Grabungen auf dem Friedhof des Alten Reiches bei den Pyramiden von Gîza,* vol. 7 (Vienna-Leipzig, 1944), fig. 104. It is dated by Porter and Moss to the Sixth Dynasty (PM 3^2, 161). We prefer to date it from Pepy II's reign to the latter part of the end of the Old Kingdom because of the panel of Senedjemib's false door is T-shaped. This type appeared from the middle of the Sixth Dynasty onwards, particularly in the reign of Pepy II (Strudwick, *Administration*, 36). Anubis is written on the false door with the unilateral signs but without the figure of the jackal. This feature indicates to the very end of the Old Kingdom (Brovarski, "False Doors," 108). The offering table on the panel of the false door is uncompleted and has only outlines (without details). This indicates a quick

These two titles, *z3b imy-r zš(w)* and *zš ꜥ(w) nzwt ḫft-ḥr* indicate that Heneni was involved with scribal functions.

Heneni had three different expressions connected with *im3ḫw.* This title is derived from the root *im3ḫ* which means being revered, honored or equipped. The word *im3ḫ* could be written alone as a self-contained qualification of the person, as Heneni does or with reference to a prepositional phrase describing additional conditions of the state of *im3ḫw ḫr/n* (by/of a god, a king, or a private person). Heneni was *im3ḫw* by the great god and by Osiris. There was a close relationship between the status of *im3ḫw* and possessing a tomb and *prt-ḫrw* offerings. Heneni was *im3ḫw,* so he owned a tomb and the ceremonies and offerings were carried out for him.

The word *im3ḫw* designated a person who could establish his own funerary cult, so he was in need of a cult place, a person who would perform the cult, and the material resources. These could be performed by the king,

---

and economic work, which appeared rarely in the reign of Teti onwards and increasingly in the reign of Pepy II (Cherpion, *Mastabas*, 49, 171, fig. 33); Seshemnefer/Ifi: Hassan, *Gîza*, vol. 6.3, fig. 220. It is dated to the Sixth Dynasty (PM 3[2], 250; Harpur, *Decoration*, 270). We prefer to date it from the reign of Pepy II to the end of the Sixth Dynasty because of the panel of the two false doors of Ifi and his son Iqueri is T-shaped. This type appeared from the middle of the Sixth Dynasty onwards, particularly in the reign of Pepy II. The rectangular form of the bread of the offering table on the panel of the false doors is uncompleted and has only outlines, which appeared rarely in the reign of Teti onwards and increasingly in the reign of Pepy II. The use of *prt-ḫrw nt* in the offering formula of a male probably indicates a date of the Sixth Dynasty and is more frequent from the middle of the reign of Pepy II according to Postel (L. Postel, "Une variante septentrionale de la formule d'offrande invocatoire à la Première Période Intermédiaire : *prt-ḫrw nt*," in L. Pantalacci and C. Berger-El-Naggar (eds.), *Des Néferkarê auxMontouhotep. Travaux archéologiques en cours sur la fin de la VIe dynastie et la première période intermédiaire. Actes du Colloque CNRS – Université Lumière-Lyon 2, tenu le 5–7 juillet 2001* (Lyon, 2005), 256–61). According to Brovarski (Brovarski, "False Doors," 111), it is dated to the end of the Sixth Dynasty and later, and to the very end of the Old Kingdom (Eighth Dynasty) according to Dawood (Dawood, *Inscribed Stelae*, 287). The deceased and his son wear patterned kilts of a type that do not appear in relief before the second half of the reign of Pepy II (Brovarski, "False Doors," 115); Idu: W. Simpson, *The Mastabas of Qar and Idu* (Boston, 1976), figs. 12, 33–41; K. Baer, *Rank and Title in the Old Kingdom, The Structure of the Egyptian Administration in the Fifth and Sixth Dynasty* (Chicago, 1960), 240, 288 [77]; Strudwick, *Administration*, 69–70 [23]; Harpur, *Decoration*, 312, 319, 323, 332 =; Cherpion, *Mastabas*, 230, 236; Qar: PM 3[2], 184; Simpson, *Qar*, pl. 5a, figs.15, 18b; Ankhuza/Ithi: PM 3[2], 167; H. Junker, *Grabungen auf dem Friedhof des Alten Reiches bei den Pyramiden von Gîza*, vol. 8 (Vienna, 1947), figs. 58, 59; R. Hölzl, *Reliefs und Inschriftensteine des Alten Reiches I* (Mainz, 1999), 114–18. It is dated to the Sixth Dynasty (Harpur, *Decoration*, 265; Hölzl, *Reliefs*, 62–69; N. Kloth, *Die (auto-) biographischen Inschriften des ägyptischen Alten Reiches: Untersuchngen zu Phraseologie und Entwicklung* (Hamburg, 2002), 10; Strudwick, *Texts*, 218). We think it could be dated to the reign of Pepy II because of the figures of deceased on the outer jambs are taller than those on the inner jambs. This feature is dated to the reign of Merenra or Pepy II (Brovarski, "False Doors," 100–103). In the second half of the reign of Pepy II, jambs became very narrow, usually with only one column of text (Strudwick, *Administration*, 36; Brovarski, "False Doors," 99). This false door has three narrow jambs with one column of text, which is a feature of the second half of the reign of Pepy II; Idu II: PM 3[2], 166; Junker, *Gîza*, vol. 8, figs. 40–46. It is dated by Kanawati to the reign of Pepy I (N. Kanawati, "Decoration of the burial chambers, sarcophagi and coffins in the Old Kingdom," *CASAE* 34 (2005), 61). Late Sixth Dynasty is preferred here because of the arrangement of  as mentioned on the coffin of Idu II, indicates that this coffin belongs to the end of the Sixth Dynasty (Brovarski, ""False Doors," 108). The writing of the *t3*-sign with two pellets underneath, as it is shown on his coffin, is more common from the end of the Sixth Dynasty onwards (Dawood, *Inscribed Stelae*, 38). The dangerous reptile (the viper ) is mutilated and written in this form . These are the characteristic features of the late phase of burial chamber decorations that occur in the reign of Pepy II and in the late Old Kingdom (N. Kanawati, *Decorated Burial Chambers of the Old Kingdom* (Cairo, 2010), 55); Nisuptah: Junker, *Gîza*, vol. 8, figs. 88, 89. The end of the Sixth Dynasty or later is preferred here to date this tomb because of there are two figures of the deceased holding the staff alone. This posture was connected to tombs of late Sixth Dynasty (Harpur, *Decoration*, 127). The writing of the offering formula *ḥtp di nzwt in* + name of god is dated to the end of the Sixth Dynasty or later (H. Fischer, "Some Early Monuments from Busiris, in the Egyptian Delta," *MMJ* 11 [1976], 15); Theteti: PM 3[2], 566–67; Strudwick, *Administration*, 160 [159]; Pepysonb: Borchardt, *CG 1295–1541*, 77–78. Late Sixth Dynasty is preferred here (Pepy II) to date this false door because of the panel of Pepysonb's false door is T-shaped, which appeared from the middle of the Sixth Dynasty onwards, particularly in the reign of Pepy II as mentioned before; Biu: PM 3[2], 677; Jéquier, *Particuliers*, figs. 114–15; G. Maspero, "Trois années de fouilles dans les tombeaux de Thèbes et de Memphis," *MIFAO* 1 [2] (1885), 192; Nenkheftek: W. Petrie, *Deshasheh 1897* (London, 1898), pl. 29; Lacau, *CG 28087–28126*, 135. It is dated by Porter and Moss to the late Fifth Dynasty or the Sixth Dynasty (PM 4, 123). Late Sixth Dynasty is preferred because of the writing of the *t3*-sign with two pellets underneath is more common from the end of the Sixth Dynasty onwards. The use of *prt-ḫrw nt* in the offering formula of a male is most probably common from the early reign of Pepy II onwards; Hesymin: Kanawati, *El-Hawawish*, vol. 6, 12, figs. 1–3; A. Mcfarlane, *The God Min to the End of the Old Kingdom* (Sydney, 1995), 65 (105); Pepyankhheriib: Blackmann, *Meir*, vol. 4, pl. 4; Kanawati, *Meir*, vol. 1, 47, pls. 75, 76.

another person, or a god.[69] As for Heneni, the "great god" and Osiris were the grantors of his cult. This great god could be Ra, Osiris, or the living or dead king. He was lord of the sky, the West and burial.[70]

The epithet *imꜣẖw* inscribed on Heneni's false door can also provide dating criteria. It is written in its complete form, with the reed leaf, sickle, back-bone, placenta, and the quail chick. This unabbreviated form is of the Old Kingdom, predating the First Intermediate Period examples.[71] In that period the word *imꜣẖw* was abbreviated and usually written with the back-bone and the placenta.[72]

Heneni had the epithet *imꜣẖw ẖr Wsir,* "revered by Osiris."[73] It is attested in late Fifth Dynasty (tombs of Meruka, Seshemnefer, Gegi, Idu and Iynefert), the late Fifth and early Sixth Dynasty (tombs of Sneferunefer and Ptahshepses), and in the Sixth Dynasty from Teti's reign to late of the Dynasty (tombs of Irenakhet, Idu I, Seshemnefer/Ifi, Khnumenti, Nikauisesi, Shepsipuptah, Mereruka, Kagemni, Merefnebef, Meru/Tetiseneb, Meryteti, Inumin, Methethi, Ishefi, Pehenptah and Nypepy, Thetu, Pepyankhheriib, Ipi, Herimeru, and Iri[74]).

This epithet appeared in the Old Kingdom from the late Fifth Dynasty to late Sixth Dynasty. So the false door of Heneni could be dated within that period.

Heneni had the epithet *imꜣẖw ẖr nṯr ꜥꜣ nb pt* "revered by the great god, lord of the heaven."[75]

This epithet is attested in tombs dated from late Teti to early Pepi I (Nikauisesi[76]), the reigns of Pepy I to Merenre (Mehu[77]), Pepy II's reign (Khabaukhnum, Hesymin, Sefekhu, Qar, Zau, Ibi, Mekhu and Sabni, Sebeky, Meni, Neferseshempepy, Ty, Neferseshemptah/Seankhptahmeryre, Seankhenptah, Iri, and Irenes[78]), end of the

[69] K. Kuraszkiewicz, "Remarks on the meaning of the word *imꜣẖw*," in J. Popielska-Grzybowska et al. (eds.), *ACTA Archaologica Pultuskiensia,* vol. I, *Proceedings of the Third Central European Conference of Young Egyptologists*, *Egypt 2004, Perspectives of Research, Warsaw 12–14 May 2004* (Pultusk, 2009), 117–18.

[70] For more details of the great god see: H. Junker, *Grabungen auf dem Friedhof des Alten Reiches bei den Pyramiden von Gîza*, vol. 2 (Vienna-Leipzig, 1934), 52–59; J. Baines, "Greatest God or Category of Gods," *GM* 67 (1983), 13–25.

[71] R. Leprohon, "The Sixth Dynasty False Door of the Priestess of Hathor Irti," *JARCE* 31 (1994), 45.

[72] Dawood, *Inscribed Stelae*, 23.

[73] Jones, *Titles*, 19–20 [89].

[74] Meruka: PM 3², 270; S. Hassan, *Excavations at Gîza 1929-1930*, vol. 1 (Oxford, 1932), 62–63; Seshemnefer: PM 3², 595; A. Mariette, *Les mastabas de l'Ancien Empire* (Paris, 1889), 400; Gegi: Bárta et al., *Abusir South,* 128, 140; Idu: M. Verner and V. Callender, *Djedkare's Family Cemetery* (Prague, 2002), 63–69; Iynefert: N. Kanawati and M. Abder-Raziq, *The Tombs of Iynefert and Ihy (reused by Idut)* (Oxford, 2003), pl. 37; Harpur, *Decoration*, 272 [345]; Kanawati and Abder-Raziq, *Iynefert*, 12–13; Strudwick, *Administration*, 58–59 [6]; Sneferunefer: PM 3², 145; Junker, *Gîza*, vol. 7, 34; Ptahshepses: S. Soleiman and A. El-Batal, *The Tomb of Ptahshepses,* Part I, *The Tomb owner, Architecture and Dating of the Tomb* (Cairo, 2015), 22, 77; Irenakhet: PM 3², 250; Hassan, *Gîza*, vol. 6.3, 9; Idu I: Junker, *Gîza*, vol. 8, 70, 76, 90, 91, fig. 34; PM 3², 165; Seshemnefer/Ifi: S. Hassan, *Excavations at Gîza 1935-1936,* vol. 7 (Cairo, 1953), 57, fig. 49; PM 3², 250; Baer, *Rank*, 133 [481]; Khnumenti: E. Brovarski, *The Senedjemib Complex*, Part 1 (Boston, 2000), fig. 90; Baer, *Rank*, 293 [402]; Harpur, *Decoration*, 269; Nikauisesi: Kanawati and Abder-Raziq, *Nikauisesi*, pls. 45, 46; Shepsipuptah: N. Kanawati and M. Abder-Raziq, *The Tombs of Shepsipuptah, Mereri (Merinebti), Hefi and Others* (Warminster, 2001), 14–15, pl. 38; Mereruka: N. Kanawati et al., *The Tomb of Mereruka*, vol. 1 (Oxford, 2010), 18, 32–33; Kagemni: Baer, *Rank*, 295 [548]; Kanawati, *Administration*, 155 [361]; Strudwick, *Administration*, 154–55 [151]; Harpur, *Decoration*, 276 [534]; Cherpion, *Mastabas,* 230; S. Soleiman, *The Tomb of Kagemni/Mmi* (Cairo, 2013), 13; Merefnebef: K. Myśliwiec et al., *The Tomb of Merefnebef* (Warsaw, 2004), 53, 246–50, pls. 14, 17, 18, 23; Meru/Tetiseneb: PM 3², 520; A. Lloyd et al., *The Mastabas of Meru, Semdenti, Khui and Others* (London, 1990), pl. 9; Strudwick, *Administration*, 97–98 [64]; Harpur, *Decoration*, 322; Meryteti: N. Kanawati et al., *The Tomb of Meryteti* (Oxford, 2003), pls. 49, 50; N. Kanawati, *Governmental Reforms in the Old Kingdom Egypt* (Warminster, 1980), 35; Strudwick, *Administration*, 97 [63]; Harpur, *Decoration*, 274 [415]; Cherpion, *Mastabas*, 184, 230; Inumin: N. Kanawati, *The Tomb of Inumin* (Oxford, 2006), pl. 50; Methethi: J. Harvey, *A Typological Study of Egyptian Wooden Statues of the Old Kingdom* (London, 1994), 187; Baer, *Rank*, 291; Harpur, *Decoration*, 274; Ishefi: Baer, *Rank*, 64 [94]; Strudwick, *Administration*, 75 [30]; Harpur, *Decoration*, 273 [374]; Cherpion, *Mastabas*, 153, 232; N. Kanawati and A. Hassan, *The Tomb of Ankhmahor* (Sydney, 1997), 18, pl. 62; Pehenptah and Nypepy: K. Kuraszkiewic, "Inscribed Objects from the Old Kingdom Necropolis West of the Step Pyramid," *ArOr* 70 (2002), 351–76, figs. 5, 7; Thetu: W. Simpson, *Mastabas of the Western Cemetery*, part 1 (Boston, 1980), figs. 12, 23; Brovarski, "False Doors," 95; Pepyankhheriib: N. Kanawati, *The Tomb of Pepyankh the Middle* (Oxford, 2012), 24–26, 86; Ipi: C. Ziegler, *Catalogue des stèles, peintures et reliefs égyptiens de l'Ancien Empire et de la Première Période Intermédiaire vers 2686–2040 avant J.-C* (Paris, 1990), 66–69; Herimeru: S. Hassan, *Excavations at Saqqara 1937-1938*, vol. 3 (Cairo, 1975), 69–70, 81, fig. 38, pl. 57 [c]; Iri: PM 3², 117; http://www.museivaticani.va/content/museivaticani/en/collezioni/musei/museo-gregoriano-egizio/sala-i--reperti-epigrafici/stele-a-falsa-porta-di-iri.html#&gid=1&pid=1. The arrangement of  as mentioned on the upper lintel of the false door, indicates that this false door dates to the end of the Sixth Dynasty.

[75] Jones, *Titles*, 31 [146].

[76] Kanawati and Abder-Raziq, *Nikauisesi*, pl. 45.

[77] Altenmüller, *Mehu*, 37.

[78] Khabaukhnum: G. Jéquier, *Le Monument Funeraire de Pepi II, Tome 3, Les approches du temple* (Cairo, 1940), 64; PM 3², 684; Hesymin,

Sixth Dynasty (Weha and Idu II[79]), end of the Old Kingdom (late Sixth Dynasty-Eighth Dynasty) (Khai[80]), late Old Kingdom or FIP (Shedabed[81]).

It is noticeable that this epithet appeared rarely late in Teti's reign and early Pepy I. Its use increased and became more common in the reign of Pepy II onwards. So the false door of Heneni could be dated to that period.

The tomb of Heneni is not dated by Baer in his study *Rank and Title in the Old Kingdom*. However, the sequence of the tomb owner's titles probably fits into the sequencing of Baer's period VI G (i.e., late Pepy II to the end of the Eighth Dynasty).[82]

4. The Funerary Formula

The funerary formula inscribed on Heneni's false door also provides dating criteria because it includes a reference to Osiris. Osiris occurs in private funerary texts from the reign of Isesi onwards.[83] In the offering formula, "Anubis" is written with the unilateral signs without the figure of the jackal, a feature of the very end of the Old Kingdom.[84]

On Heneni's false door, *prt-ḫrw* is written with the determinative consisting of only three items: bread, beer, and cake which is a characteristic of the Old Kingdom, predating the Herakleopolitan Period.[85]

Sefekhu, and Qar: Kanawati, *El-Hawawish*, vol. 6, 10, 12, figs. 2, 11, 16; Kanawati, *Akhmim*, 296; Zau: Davies, *Deir el-Gebrâwi*, vol. 2, pls. 9, 11, 12; Ibi: N. Davies, *The Rock Tombs of Deir el-Gebrâwi*, vol. 1 (London, 1902), pl. 23; Mekhu and Sabni: U. Bouriant, "Les tombeaux d'Assouan, " *RT* 10 (1888), 184; Harpur, *Decoration*, 282; Sebeky: Daressy, "Héliopolis," 201, 204; PM 4, 61. The use of *prt-ḫrw nt* in the offering formula of a male most probably common from the early reign of Pepy II onwards; Meni and Neferseshempepy: W. F. Petrie, *Dendereh* (London, 1898), pls. 1, 13; PM 5, 110, 112. The deceased and his son are each shown with a patterned kilt, which does not appear in relief before the second half of the reign of Pepy II as mentioned before; Ty: Borchardt, *CG 1295–1541,* 222–23, pl. 46. It is dated not before the reign of Pepy I and most probably later because of mentioning the names of Pepy I on the doorway; Neferseshemptah/Seankhptahmeryre: A false door was found in Kom el-Sultan at Abydos, preserved now in Cairo Museum as CG 1404. It is dated by Baer to the reign of Pepy I or later (Baer, *Rank*, 93). We think it is dated to the reign of Pepy II or late Sixth Dynasty because the false door has a ewer and a basin resting on the ground line of the scene. A single ewer and basin on the ground line on the panel is dated to the reign of Merenre or Pepy II (Brovarski, "False Doors," 89). The false door has an abbreviated panel scene including the deceased sitting before the offering table and the ewer and basin. This feature is dated to the early reign of Pepy II. The writing of the *t3*-sign with two pellets underneath, as it is written on the upper lintel, is more common from the end of the Sixth Dynasty onwards. There are two figures of the deceased on the false door holding the staff alone. This posture was connected to tombs of late Sixth Dynasty as mentioned previously; Seankhenptah: A false door is preserved now in the Cairo Museum as CG 1445 (Borchardt, *CG 1295–1541,* 128–29). It is dated to the Sixth Dynasty (PM 3^2, 698), from Pepy I onwards (most probably Pepy II's reign) as we think because Seankhenptah had the epithet *im3ḫw ḫr Ptḥ-Zkr*. This epithet was attested in the Old Kingdom from the reign of Pepy I to the end of the Old Kingdom. This epithet was rarely known in the reigns of Pepy I and Merenre and was more connected to Pepy II's reign. In the offering formula, Anubis is written in the form of an animal on a stand, which appeared from the Sixth Dynasty, possibly Pepy I onwards (H. Fischer, *Dendera in the Third Millennium B.C* [New York, 1968], 84). In the Sixth Dynasty, the false door with cavetto cornice, torus molding and two or three jambs became the standard type for all officials. In the second half of the reign of Pepy II, two jambs only on each side were common (Strudwick, *Administration*, 36; Brovarski, "False Doors," 99). The use of the city determinative in the epithet of Anubis *imy wt* in the offering formula may suggest a date before the very end of the Sixth Dynasty (Kanawati, *Deir el-Gebrawi*, vol. 2, 86). Also the city determinative with the diagonal cross ⊗ is the usual design in the Old Kingdom, compared to the horizontal and vertical cross ⊕, which is a later development (Fischer, *Dendera*, 78–79). The feature of writing *prt-ḫrw* with the determinative consisting of three items only: bread, beer and cake, is a common characteristic and more connected to the Old Kingdom writing, predating Herakleopolitan Period (G. Lapp, *Die Opferformel des Alten Reiches* (Mainz, 1986), 91; Dawood, *Inscribed Stelae*, 162). The epithet *im3ḫw* is written in its complete form with the reed leaf, sickle, back bone, placenta and the quail chick. This unabbreviated form is Old Kingdom writing, predating the First Intermediate Period examples (Leprohon, "Priestess of Hathor," 45); Iri: S. Soleiman and A. El-Batal, *False Doors* (Cairo, 2015), 50–60, fig. 16, pls. 16, 30–34; Irenes: The false door of Irenes, preserved now in Cairo Museum CG 1400 (Borchardt, *CG 1295–1541,* 61, pl. 16). It is dated to the Sixth Dynasty or First Intermediate Period (PM 3^2, 736). We think it is not dated before the second half of Pepy II's reign because the false door has an abbreviated panel scene, including the deceased sitting before the offering table. This feature is dated to the second half of the reign of Pepy II onwards (Brovarski, "False Doors," 114–15);

[79] Weha: S. Hassan, *Excavations at Gîza 1933–1934*, vol. 5 (Cairo, 1944), 255–56; PM 3^2, 255; Idu II: Junker, *Gîza*, vol. 8, fig. 43.

[80] S. Soleiman and A. El-Batal, *Coffins and Architectural Elements* (Cairo, 2015), 16.

[81] J. Pirenne, *Histoire des Institutions et du Droit privé de l'ancienne Egypte*, vol. 2 (Brussels, 1934), 500; Mariette, *Mastabas*, 368–89; Borchardt, *CG 1295–1541,* 138–40, pl. 34; PM 3^2, 689.

[82] Baer, *Rank*, 239.

[83] A. Bolshakov, "Princess *ḥmt rʿ(w)*: The First Mention of Osiris?," *CdE* 67 (1992), 203–10.

[84] Brovarski, "False Doors," 108.

[85] Lapp, *Opferformel*, 91; Dawood, *Inscribed Stelae*, 162.

The offering formula of Heneni is written *prt-ḫrw nt.* This is a common offering formula, used to ensure that invocation offering comes forth for the dead. These offerings contain bread, beer and cake.[86] *Prt-ḫrw nt* is usually translated as "an invocation offering may come forth for" or "going forth of the voice with the offerings for."[87] Another possible translation could be that "the voice, bread, beer and cake of (the deceased) may go forth." It was wished that the dead person would first talk, then eat and drink. The opening of the mouth ceremony was known in the Old Kingdom[88] and its symbolic tools were discovered in some burial chambers. The mouth helps to speak, eat and drink. According to that, the text of Heneni could be read and translated as follows:

> *prt ḫrw t ḥnḳt pꜣt nt smr wʿty imy-r ʿrrwt Ḥnni*
>
> "May the voice, bread, beer, and cake of the sole companion and overseer of the gates, Heneni, come forth."

The presence of *nt* following *ḫrw t ḥnḳt pꜣt* gives weight to this suggested translation. It cannot be the proposition *n,* rather it is *nt*, the genitival adjective.[89] This genitival adjective *nt* is feminine to be agree in gender with *pꜣt*, the word immediately preceding it. Hence, it is better to translate *nt* as "of", not "for."

The use of *prt-ḫrw nt* in the offering formula of a male appeared from the Sixth Dynasty and continued into the Middle Kingdom.[90] The writing 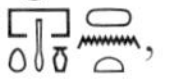, as on Heneni's monument, was common towards the end of the Sixth Dynasty or later.[91]

5. The Architecture of the False Door

The architecture of Heneni's false door also provides dating criteria. It has an inscribed supplementary frame consisting of a lintel and two jambs outside the cavetto cornice and the false door proper. This feature is not attested before the early part of the reign of Pepy II.[92]

In the Sixth Dynasty, the false door with cavetto cornice, torus molding, and two or three jambs of equal width became the standard type for all officials. In the second half of the reign of Pepy II, two jambs only on each side were common; the jambs became very narrow, usually with only one column of text.[93] The false door of Heneni has two narrow jambs of equal size with one column of text, which is a feature of the second half of the reign of Pepy II.

The panel of the false door of Heneni is a flaring T-shaped type. This type appeared as early as the end of the first half of Pepy II's reign.[94] The panel apertures of the false door are narrow and undecorated. This was the rule in the Sixth Dynasty.[95]

6. The Arrangement of the Scenes

The arrangement of the scenes on the false door of Heneni also provides dating criteria. On the panel of the false door, he is shown seated to the left of the offering table, facing right, his far (left) hand to his breast. This position is known in the Old Kingdom from Neuserre's reign into the late part of Pepy II's reign.[96] This abbrevi-

---

[86] Lapp, *Opferformel*, 91–93.

[87] A. Gardiner, *Egyptian Grammar* (Oxford, 1994), 170–73.

[88] A. Bolshakov, "The Old Kingdom Representation of Funeral Procession," *GM* 121 (1991), 41; A. Roth, "The *psš-kf* and the 'Opening of the Mouth' Ceremony: A Ritual of Birth and Rebirth, " *JEA* 78 (1992), 113.

[89] For the genitival adjectives, see E. Edel, *Altägyptische Grammatik*, vol. 1 (Rome, 1955), 137–38.

[90] Postel, "Formule d'offrande, " 255.

[91] Brovarski, "False Doors," 111.

[92] Dawood, *Inscribed Stelae*, 17.

[93] Strudwick, *Administration*, 36; Brovarski, "False Doors," 99.

[94] Brovarski, "False Doors," 111.

[95] Strudwick, *Administration*, 22.

[96] J. Swinton, *Dating the Tombs of the Egyptian Old Kingdom* (Sydney, 2014), 217.

ated panel scene, including the deceased sitting before the offering table with bread loaves, but without any other items, is dated to the second half of the reign of Pepy II.[97]

Heneni is shown sitting before the offering table wearing a long wig that exposes his ears. He appears three more times on the false door wearing the same style wig. This wig appears during the reign of Teti and became popular during the reigns of Pepy I and II.[98]

The chair upon which Heneni sits is without a cushion. Swinton suggested that this style is known from the early Kingdom to Teti's reign. However, we do not agree with this opinion because the chair without a cushion appears on the false door of Heneni that is of a later date. Heneni's chair also is without a back. Swinton suggested that this style of chair is attested from the early Kingdom to Unas' reign.[99] But again, we cannot agree because the false door of Heneni is later than the reign of Unas. The artist made a distinction between the front and rear legs of the lion on Heneni's chair. This custom is dated from the reign of Teti to the reign of Pepy II.[100] There are two representations of a single trapezium on its broad base in the chair leg supports. This style was depicted in the Old Kingdom and was commonly shown towards the end of that period.[101]

The offering table of Heneni has upturned edges. This style appeared once in the Fifth Dynasty, but it is a style of the Sixth Dynasty.[102] The way of placing the loaves or reeds on the offering table of Heneni can be dated from the reigns of Niuserre to Pepy II. The *ḫꜣ*-list of Heneni is inscribed above the offering table. This tradition of writing the *ḫꜣ*-list beside or above the table is attested in the Old Kingdom from late Fourth Dynasty to the end of Pepy II's reign.[103]

As for the standing figures of Heneni, on the innermost jambs he is shown with both arms at his side. This position is known from the late Fifth Dynasty onwards.[104] The deceased holding only a staff, as on the outer jambs, is known from tombs of the later Sixth Dynasty.[105] The two figures on the inner jambs of the false door are shorter than the two figures on the outer jambs. Showing taller and shorter figures on the jambs of the same false door probably started in the middle of the Sixth Dynasty.[106]

Discussion and Conclusion

It is here suggested that Heneni's false door dates from late in Pepy II's reign to the Eighth Dynasty. Yet the GIS cemetery from which it came is dated from the Fourth Dynasty to the early Sixth Dynasty, indicating that the tomb of Heneni was not part of the original design of that cemetery. The tomb was added later in the free space left between the late Fifth and early Sixth Dynasties tombs. The limited space between the tombs of Seshemnefer IV LG 53 and that probably of his son Sehotepu forced Heneni to build a small rectangular mastaba between these tombs.

The GIS cemetery started from the southern part of the Great Pyramid enclosure in the time of Menkaure, and it includes nine tombs in the main row. In late Fifth Dynasty and early Sixth Dynasty, the cemetery extended to the southeast. For the remainder of the Sixth Dynasty, individuals built their tombs between and to the south of the previous tombs. The tomb of Heneni represents the last Old Kingdom construction in the cemetery.

We need to find an answer for the question: Why did Heneni construct his tomb in Giza, and especially in this location, even though none of his titles is connected to any of the Giza pyramids? It seems that Heneni chose the location of his tomb to be with his former colleagues. We suggest that Heneni wanted to be buried

97 Brovarski, "False Doors," 114–15.

98 Swinton, *Dating*, 213; Cherpion, *Mastabas*, 57–58, 180–81.

99 Swinton, *Dating*, 272, 276.

100 Cherpion, *Mastabas*, 160.

101 Swinton, *Dating*, 278.

102 Cherpion (*Mastabas*, 172) mentioned two tombs: Washptah D 38 at Saqqara and Seshemnefer IV, LG 53 at Giza. The last tomb has been dated to the reigns of Izezi or to Unas, to the interval of the reigns of Unas and Teti, or more generally to the Sixth Dynasty.

103 Swinton, *Dating*, 235.

104 Strudwick, *Administration*, 68.

105 Harpur, *Decoration*, 127.

106 Altenmüller, *Mehu*, pl. 96; Harpur, *Decoration*, 274.

next to Sehotepu who had the same title (*zꜣb imy-r zšw*) and next to Sekhemka, the owner of Mastaba G VIII S, who had the same two titles *ḫry-tp nzwt* and *ꜥḏ mr*. So there was a family or a professional relationship between Heneni and these other two men.

Heneni held the position of lector priest, however without mention of any pyramid. He might have been employed part-time in the funerary complexes at Giza, and so he was buried there.

Heneni had honorific, administrative, and religious titles. His honorific titles are more a reflection of his status and relationship with the king than an indicator of a specific office. His religious and administrative titles prove that he served as a priest on a part-time basis, and that he worked in other administrative jobs in the state at other times.

Heneni's titles make it is evident that he was of modest rank, although some of his titles indicate that he served the king. His rank is emphasized by the location of his tomb, south of Khufu's pyramid, and not in the royal cemetery of Pepy II, which included, as was common, the tombs of the royal family of the king and his high officials. In the Sixth Dynasty, most of the high officials held titles associated with royal pyramids, but Heneni did not.

The limited space of the upper lintel of the supplementary frame and that of the false door of Heneni forced the sculptors to shorten the two offering formulae. The name of Anubis is usually followed by four epithets *tpy ḏw.f, imy-wt, nb tꜣ ḏsr,* and *ḫnty zḥ-nṯr* in the offering formula of the Old Kingdom if there is enough space. But Heneni's false door includes only *tpy ḏw.f* "he who is upon his mountain," because of the limited space.

Heneni's offering formula includes one wish attested twice. It is that the invocation offering may come forth. The limited space forced the sculptors of Heneni to inscribe only one wish, but most inscriptions for other persons had from two to four wishes.

The false door of Heneni dates from Pepy II to the Eighth Dynasty based on the location of the tomb, his personal name, his titles and epithets, the funerary formula, and the iconography of the false door.

The absence of the name of the contemporary king on the false door could be because Heneni lived in a period of transition, turmoil, and political instability. From the end of Pepy II's reign to the Eighth Dynasty there was often more than one king at the same time, or each ruled for only a short period. Perhaps he was born and began his career in the time of king Pepy II and lived until the Eighth Dynasty.

In addition to establishing a date for Heneni's tomb, the dating criteria suggest a new dating for thirteen other tombs: Sebeky at Heliopolis; Ankhuza/Ithi, Senedjemib/Inti, Idu II, and Nisuptah in the West Field at Giza; Irenakheti/Irenptah and Seshemnefer/Ifi in the Central Field at Giza; Nenkheftek at Deshasha; Neferseshemptah/Seankhptahmeryre at Abydos; Neferseshempepy at Dendera; and Irenes CG 1400, Pepysonb CG 1412, and Seankhenptah CG 1445 in the Cairo Museum.

Second Report on the Publication and Conservation of the Tomb of Ramesses III in the Valley of the Kings (KV 11)

Anke Weber
Humboldt-Universität zu Berlin

Judith Bunbury
Department of Earth Sciences, University of Cambridge

Klara Dietze
Universität Leipzig

Willem Hovestreydt
Netherlands Institute for the Near East, retired

Dora Petrova
Ruprecht-Karls-Universität, Heidelberg

Lutz Popko
Sächsische Akademie der Wissenschaften zu Leipzig

Gareth Rees
Oxford Archaeology East, Cambridge

Lea Rees
Freie Universität Berlin

Karin Schinken
Landesamt für Denkmalpflege, Stuttgart

Abstract

The Ramesses III (KV 11) Publication and Conservation Project is currently developing a site management, conservation and publication strategy for the severely damaged tomb of pharaoh Ramesses III in order to prevent further deterioration and to preserve this cultural heritage site for future generations. Along with first urgent measures of conservation, a geo-archaeological survey of KV 11 and its surroundings, as well as a geomatic and photogrammetric survey of the tomb itself, were carried out. The detailed recording of the current state of the architecture and wall decoration allowed for further reconstruction of scenes and texts. Moreover, an archaeological sondage in the burial chamber revealed additional information about the flooding and sedimentation processes. A field school with students of Luxor University offered training in digital recording methods and epigraphy, geo-archaeological survey and mapping methodologies, and conservation treatment and assessment. The following article outlines preliminary results in the fields of geology, conservation, recording, reconstruction, and excavation.

Journal of the American Research Center in Egypt 56 (2020), 213–244
doi: http://dx.doi.org/10.5913/jarce.56.2020.a014

ملخص

يعمل مشروع نشر وحفظ مقبرة رمسيس الثالث (KV 11) حاليًا على تطوير استراتيجية إدارة وحفظ ونشر لمقبرة الفرعون رمسيس الثالث المتضررة بشدة من أجل منع المزيد من التدهور والحفاظ على موقع التراث الثقافي هذا للأجيال القادمة، ومع تدابير الحفظ العاجلة الأولى تم تنفيذ المسح الجيولوجي الأثري للمقبرة KV 11 والمناطق المحيطة بها، فضلا عن المسح الجيوماتيكي و الفوتوغرامتري للمقبرة نفسها. سمح التسجيل المفصل للحالة الراهنة للعمارة والزخارف الجدارية بإعادة بناء المشاهد والنصوص. علاوة على ذلك، كشف المسح الأثري في غرفة الدفن عن معلومات إضافية حول عمليات الغمر والترسيب. قدمت مدرسة حفائر لطلاب بجامعة الأقصر التدريب على طرق التسجيل الرقمي والرسم والمسح الجيولوجي الأثري ومنهجيات رسم الخرائط ، ومنهجيات الترميم والتقييم. توضح المقالة التالية النتائج الأولية في مجالات الجيولوجيا والحفظ والتسجيل وإعادة البناء والحفائر الأثرية.

Introduction

The tomb of pharaoh Ramesses III (KV 11, fig. 1) is located in the Valley of the Kings, near the rest house. At the turn of the nineteenth–twentieth century, the rear part of the site was severely damaged by flash floods caused by heavy rainfall. Worst affected were the areas from corridor G to room L and especially the burial chamber (hall J), which is now threatened by rapid deterioration. To safeguard the tomb from further damage, urgent measures were required. For the sustainable preservation of the entire burial chamber and its small annexes, a geo-archaeological survey was carried out, alongside a first conservation assessment, in order to prepare for stabilization and conservation of the burial chamber. Therefore, a methodology combining archaeological and geo-archaeological techniques was employed. Based on the results from geo-archaeology and conservation assessment, the methodology presented in the first report[1] has been revised, and a new, detailed strategy for proceeding with the conservation and publication of this important cultural heritage site has been developed, combining archaeology and geo-archeology.

The geo-archaeological survey was conducted by Judith Bunbury in order to analyze the tomb's surrounding bedrock structures and to answer two questions:

(1) Was the water-soaking characteristic of the Esna shale responsible for the devastation of the tomb in the wake of the flood, as suggested in the first report?
(2) Is flood protection an urgent step in order to safeguard the tomb from future water ingress from above?

Initial conservation work was undertaken by Karin Schinken who recorded the tomb's condition and produced a detailed record of all damaged areas, including suggestions for preservation. By mapping the most affected parts of the tomb, she was able to provide an overview of causes of ongoing deterioration. Based on this information, an initial conservation plan was created.

An additional photogrammetric survey by Gareth Rees (Oxford Archaeology East) has provided a basis for mapping cracks and fissures. A 3D model of the tomb will support the future conservation and reconstruction work by generating orthophotos that will be used for digital drawings.

The reconstruction of the scenes and texts is a major part of the Site Management Plan and runs parallel to the conservation program. Willem Hovestreydt focused on the scenes in rooms H, I, K1, K2 and L, as well as on the decoration of pillars, while Anke Weber was working on the reconstruction of architectural elements in the burial chamber and the decoration of the ceiling. Lutz Popko has undertaken the task of reconstructing the texts and decoration of side-room Jc, which originally bore scenes from the Book of the Heavenly Cow. The Opening

Funding for the project for winter season 2019/2020 was received from the Antiquities Endowment Fund (AEF) of the American Research Center in Egypt (ARCE). Additional funding was provided by the Egypt Exploration Society (EES, Centenary Award 2019), which allowed the team to undertake complementary research in the British archives in order to combine the work of former researchers and travelers with work on site. The project is based at Humboldt-University Berlin and has been developed by the field director Anke Weber since 2011.

[1] Anke Weber, "First Report on the Publication and Conservation of the Tomb of Ramesses III in the Valley of the Kings (KV 11)," *JEA* 104.1 (2018), 65–69.

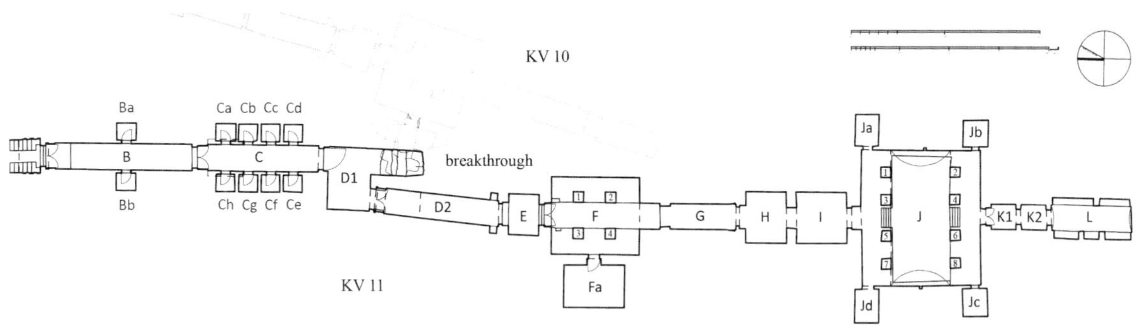

Fig. 1. Ground plan of KV 11 with the breakthrough in room D1 to the tomb of Amenemesse (KV 10). After The Theban Mapping Project.

of the Mouth Ritual will be reconstructed by Dora Petrova, who uses modern software like DStretch® in order to achieve this goal (see related article in this volume).

Initial archaeological field work was conducted by Klara Dietze and Anke Weber who cut a sondage in the burial chamber in order to expose the sediment layers and to reveal the original floor level. Research on the sarcophagus of Ramesses III and newly-located sarcophagus fragments is being carried out by Lea Rees, with the aim of recontextualizing these parts of the burial equipment.

Below, the first results of the 2019/2020 field season of The Ramesses III (KV 11) Publication and Conservation Project are presented in detail.

Geology

This season's fieldwork at KV 11 led to further insight into the forces at work in the Theban Mountain, allowing us to postulate the origins of the fault lines and other geological features.

KV 11 is excavated into the lowest parts of the limestone sequence of the Theban Mountain. These geological units were previously divided for field observation by the *Western Wadi Project* of the *New Kingdom Research Foundation*[2] as illustrated below (figs. 2 and 3). The approximate elevation and thickness in metres is given by the scale.

For the geological survey of KV 11 and its surroundings, the outcrop pattern of the units was noted according to the scheme in figure 2. In general, the tomb builders favoured the Wall Limestone, which tends to form a cliff suitable for a horizontal entrance and is white in color and relatively homogeneous in texture. It is a comparatively soft stone that is easily worked and decorated in raised or incised relief and its accessibility via horizontal tunnelling established Wall Limestone as a favourite among the tomb-builders. The same preference for the Wall Limestone was also seen in Wadi 300 and the Valley of the Queens, even though the outcrop pattern of the latter is complex, owing to a series of faulted blocks. There is occasional use of the Falcon Limestone (Wadi A) and, rarely, other units of agglomerate (Wadi Bairiya).[3]

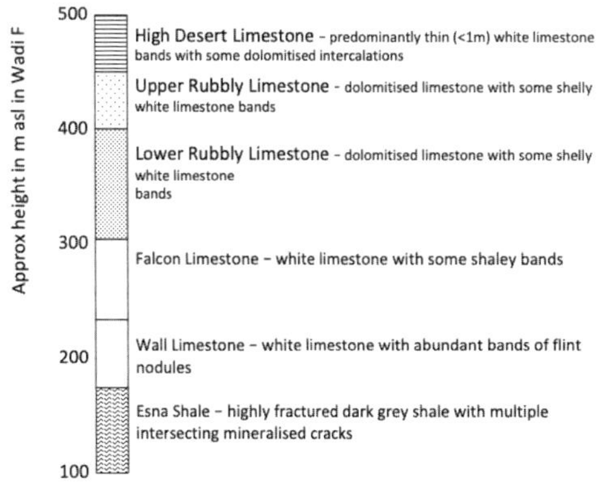

Fig. 2. Field units of the Theban Mountain delineated in Litherland (2015) and Bunbury (2016).

[2] Field seasons 2015–2020.

[3] Piers Litherland, *The Shaft Tombs of Wadi Bairiya: Volume 1, Preliminary report on the Clearance Work on the WB1 Site* (London, 2019), 70–72.

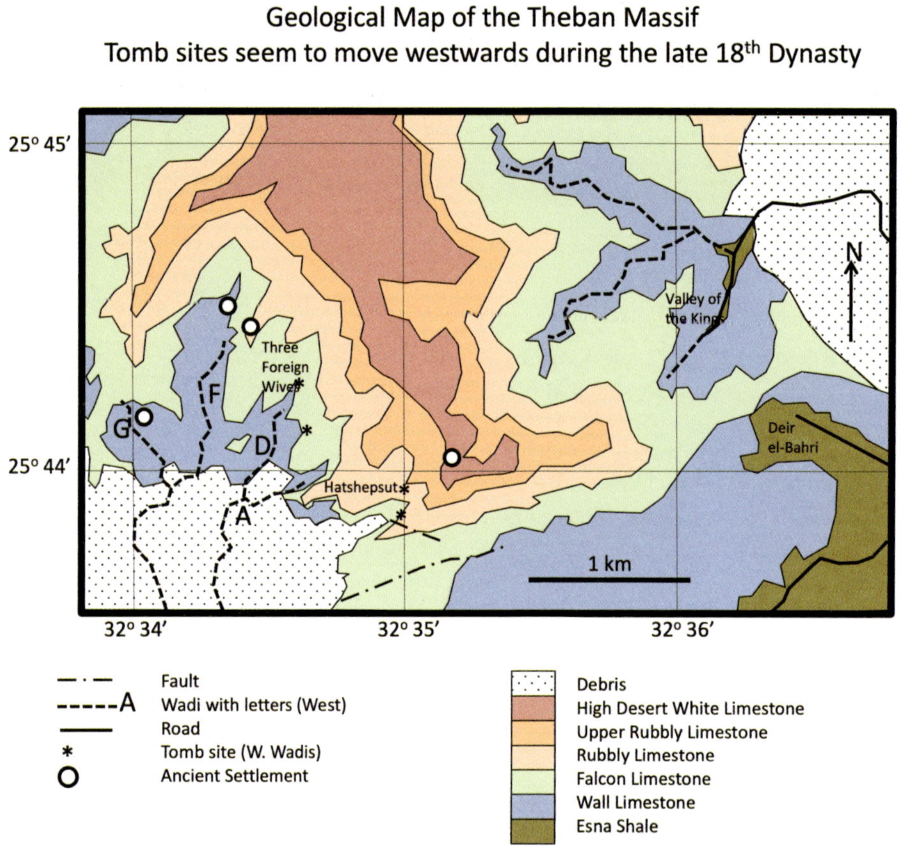

Fig. 3. Overview geological map of the area around the Valley of the Kings (field seasons 2015–2020).

The main units exposed in the Valley of the Kings are the sub-units of the Wall Limestone, with some of the Falcon and Lower Rubbly Limestone above and a limited outcrop of the Esna Shale in the Bus Park of the Valley below.

Mapping of the upper surface of the Wall Limestone suggests that the area of the Valley of the Kings should be considered as two fault blocks, as shown in the diagram below. To the east is a block of limestone into which Deir el-Bahari was placed and which is penetrated by KV 20. This block, identified here as the "Hatshepsut Block" is some 20 metres above the western fault block, here designated the "Rest House Block," into which most of the other tombs were excavated. The Rest House Block shows a variable dip, declining a few degrees to the north in the Thutmose III gully and more gently further north, where it is sub-horizontal. The structural units of the Valley of the Kings, showing the two main fault blocks, are designated here the "Rest House Block" and the "Hatshepsut Block." A slight fold marking a dip in an area of increased faulting and jointing is also shown in figure 4. The figure shows the two main fault blocks juxtaposed on a *Google Earth* image of the valley and combined with data from the *Theban Mapping Project*.[4] Down throw sides are marked with rectangles and folding with triangles.

The geology of the Valley of the Kings can be juxtaposed on a photograph of the area taken from the scarp to the south of the valley (fig. 5). The figure shows the geological units encountered, overlaying a photograph of the valley looking north. The correspondence of field designations with the units of the Thebes Formation

[4] Kent R. Weeks and Nigel J. Heatherington, *The Valley of the Kings: A Site Management Handbook* (Cairo, 2014), 4–56.

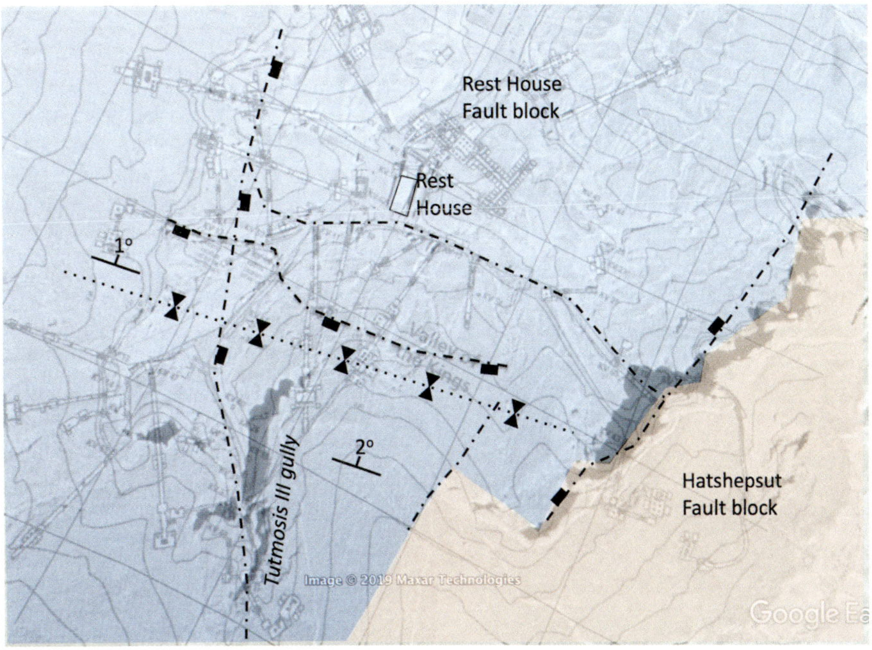

Fig. 4. Fault blocks of the Valley of the Kings area (November 2019 field season of The Ramesses III (KV 11) Publication and Conservation Project).

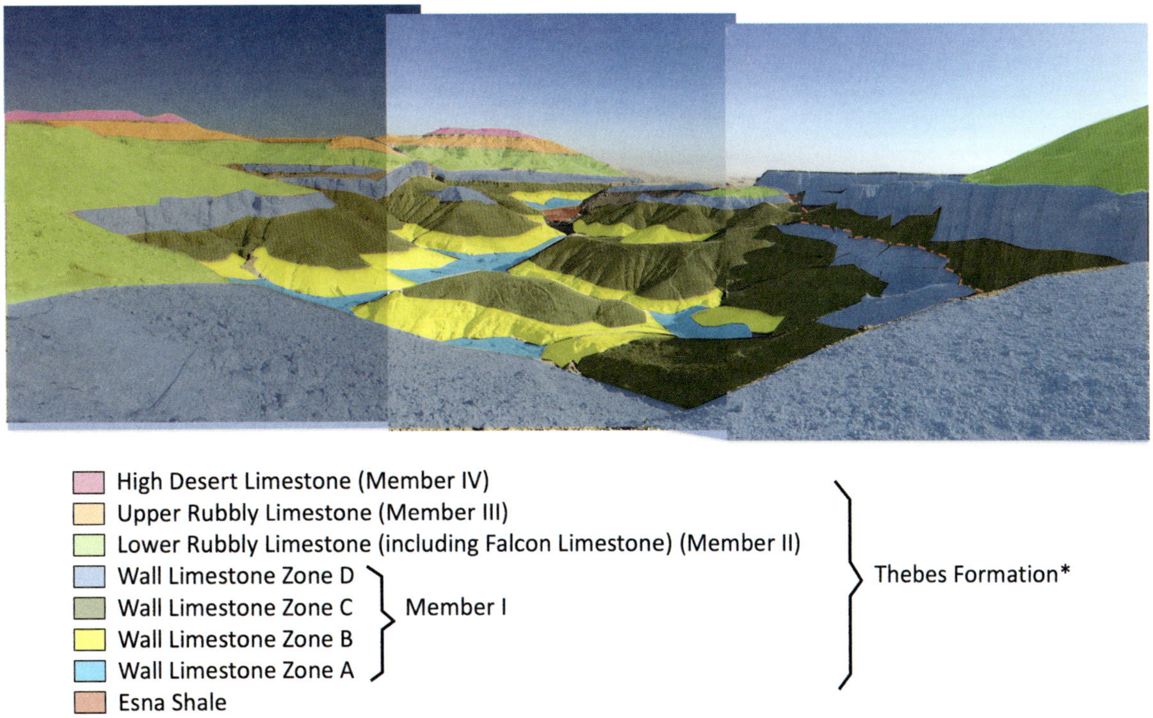

Fig. 5. Geological interpretation of the Valley of the Kings.

as given by Weeks and Heatherington[5] are shown in the key. Note to the right of the image the repetition of Member I, Zone D as a result of motion on the Hatshepsut Fault.

Internal Geology of the Tomb

In the Theban Mountain, faults occur on a range of scales from the large listric faults, with a significant throw (c 120 m) that displace the blocks in the Valley of the Queens and Wadi 300, to very small faults with negligible throw that are visible everywhere. For the purposes of this project, faults were mapped where there is significant throw and fault zones where a large number of small, sub-parallel faults or cracks occur in an area. The internal geology of the tomb is summarised in the composite cross-section shown in figure 6. Within Member I of the Thebes Formation (here: Wall Limestone) there are four subdivisions given in Weeks and Heatherington.[6] The lowest is Zone A, which sits upon the Esna Shale and is generally buff in colour, with few flints and very prone to weathering.

Above this, Zone B is white, rich in flints, and relatively resistant to weathering, while Zone C is softer and strongly jointed. At the top of Member I, the limestone is white with abundant flint nodules and also calcareous nodules. Zone D generally weathers out and forms many of the cliffs of the Valley of the Kings. The tomb builders in the Valley of the Queens and Wadi 300 seem to have favoured the Wall Limestone (Member I, Zone D) for tomb construction, but in the Valley of the Kings, most tombs commence in Zone B. Note, however, that in KV 11 the tomb construction soon moves into Zone A, where a combination of the friable nature of Zone A, the abundant faulting in the areas chosen for the larger rooms, and the later flooding have combined to produce dramatic damage to the tomb. The upper part of the burial chamber (hall J) is cut into the Zone B limestone and survives relatively well, in contrast to the top of the columns and the roof which have experienced extensive damage. This damage is consistent with the prevalence of the comparatively shaley Zone A limestone (visible as a buff layer that continues to 226 cm above the sill), into which floodwater can soak, thus causing expansion, cracking, and rock instability.

It is worth highlighting the transition from Zone B to Zone A of the Wall Limestone in the tomb and the areas where intense faulting crosses the tomb (see also fig. 8 [below] for relationship with KV 10). In hindsight, these areas of softer rock and faulting seem to have been prioritised by the original builders when finding a suitable location for the larger halls of the burial chambers.

This selection of location has also meant that these areas are also the most vulnerable to damage. Consideration was given to the view that the damage in the burial chamber was due to contact with the Esna Shale at the base of the room.[7] Although subsequent excavation may shed further light on this, the current interpretation suggests that this is unlikely and that the damage was a result of the interaction of flood water with the high shale content of the relatively soft Wall Limestone Zone A and the already faulted rocks of hall J (see above). We have calculated the thickness of the rocks in Zone A that are visible in the tomb and those of the total thickness of the unit that is visible in the parking lot of the valley. The difference between these two values suggests that there should still be some meters of Zone A below the floor of the tomb.

Consideration was also given to the idea that open cracks had allowed water to invade the tombs in the same way as was observed in KV 5.[8] However, the photograph in figure 7 shows the much greater extent of rock above the tomb in KV 11 when compared with KV 5, which reduces the likelihood of open cracks penetrating as far as hall J. The mineralisation of the joints discussed below make it more likely that there was limited water seepage through the mountain into the tomb.

The walls of corridor B to hall F in KV 11 are largely covered in original plaster or repairs, but a fault and joint survey of the neighbouring tomb (KV 10) provides some insight into the likely structures of these areas

---

5 Weeks and Heatherington, *Site Management Handbook*, 37.

6 Weeks and Heatherington, *Site Management Handbook*, 37.

7 Weber, "First Report," 63.

8 Weber, "First Report," 63. See also Weeks and Heatherington, *Site Management Handbook*, 36; Kent R. Weeks (ed.), *KV 5. A Preliminary Report on the Excavation of the Tomb of the Sons of Rameses II in the Valley of the Kings* (second edition) (Cairo, 2006), 147–89.

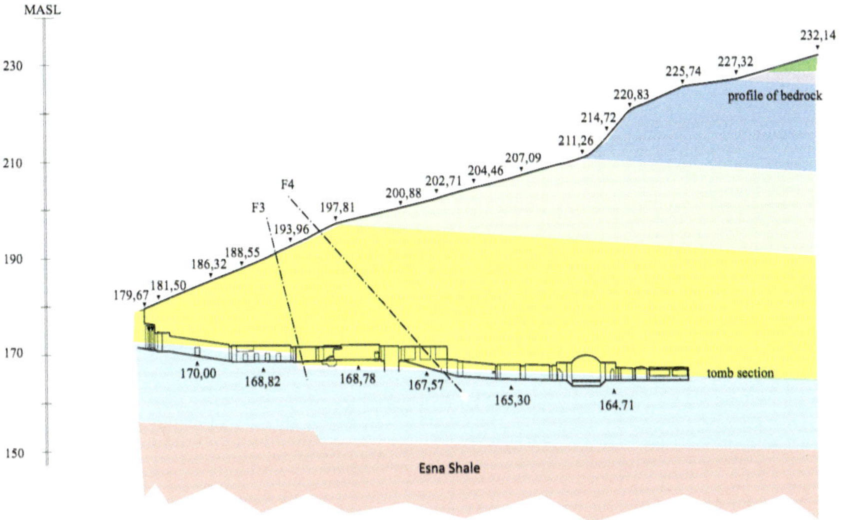

Fig. 6. Section of KV 11 showing the geology and the faulting (November 2019 field season of The Ramesses III (KV 11) Publication and Conservation Project).

Fig. 7. The profiles of KV 5 and KV 11 showing the depth of rock above the tomb in the two cases. Photo: Judith Bunbury.

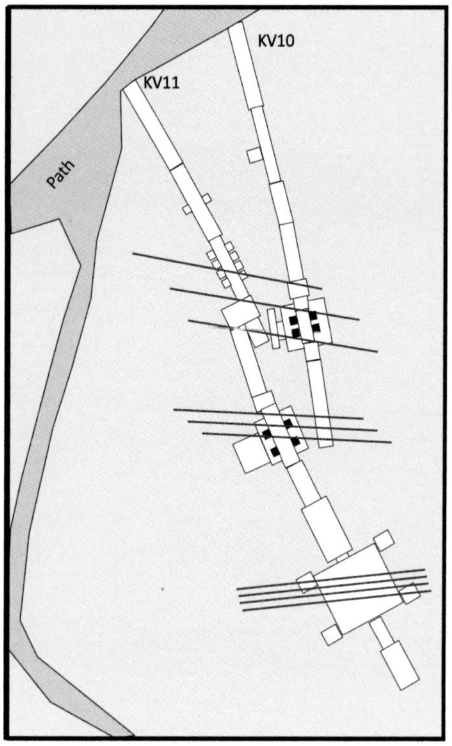

Fig. 8. Fault patterns across KV 10 and KV 11. Map after The Theban Mapping Project.

of KV 11 (fig. 8).[9] In KV 11, from room G to L there is better exposure of the faults and joints. Notably, the burial chamber has numerous small faults crossing it; some with a small throw, fault gouge, and some mineralisation. These cross the room in the direction WNW-ESE and are shown on the sketch plan below (fig. 9).

The main discontinuities in hall J are as follows:

JC1 (Joint in the ceiling 1). Major crack intersecting column 7. Some reddening of joint surface but offset minor. No movement after the addition of the decoration.

JC2. Very faint crack that does not disrupt the plaster in most places. Peters out in east wall and apparently discontinuous.

JC3. Persistent crack, quite broad and widened to around 1 cm. Red mineralisation but joint does not offset plaster. Expanded to 3 cm in east wall.

JC4. Persistent crack intersecting column 2. Snug joint with some red mineralisation, stronger at outside edge of crack although close inspection may reveal that this is a red plaster fill remaining from the initial construction.

JC5. Sub-horizontal crack that crosses JC4 with an apparent slight offset of this that displaces intact plaster and intersects and area of extreme roof damage outside side-room Jc.

The mineralisation of the faults suggests that much of the water leaving the crack does so by evaporation rather than by flow. Beyond hall J, the condition of the tomb deteriorates significantly and an intense zone of faulting and jointing intersects the rooms K1, K2 and L. These areas are much damaged. Joints in KV 10 and KV 11 were surveyed and the orientation of the majority of the joints is shown in the stereo-plot (fig. 10).

In general, there is a strong NNW-SSE trend in KV 11 with a secondary joint plane trending WNW-ESE. The change in trend may reflect the fact that much of the exposed rock in KV 11 is beyond the main fault in KV 10 hall F.

Fault zones often contain a fault gouge and, in some cases, either calcite or silica mineralisation. A foamy appearance to the rock in some faulted areas can be noted. This seems to result from the addition of water (possibly at depth and therefore higher temperature) to the rock. One can only speculate on the origin of the gas, but it may arise from small amounts of iron pyrites in the shale component that, dissolving, forms sulphuric acid that reacts with the calcium carbonate to release carbon dioxide.

Joints and Joint Fillings

Many joints are simple fractures in the rock and show no mineralisation or evidence of water flowing through them. However, some larger joints show MnO2 mineralisation with dendrites around 5 mm across forming (fig. 11). In some cases, movement of these surfaces has created a calcite polish known as a slickenside that demonstrates relative motion between the two faces. In the cases of greater movement, a rock flour fills in the cracks and a fault zone of a few millimetres to some tens of centimetres may form. These fault zones may also be mineralised with calcite and, in some cases, this is pink/red (fig. 12) due to the presence of iron oxide. In other cases (fault JC4 and fig. 14), salty efflorescence (fig. 13) may also occur in the fault zone. Some thought has been given to the source of water ingress into the tomb through these cracks.[10] It is clear that in some instances there

[9] We are grateful to Salima Ikram for her information on the geology of KV 10 from her field season.

[10] Weber, "First Report," 63.

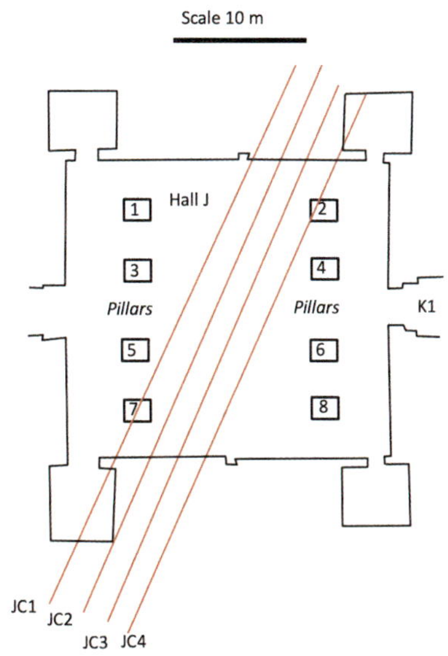

Fig. 9. Sketch plan of hall J showing main faults with the exception of JC5 which is sub-horizontal. Map after The Theban Mapping Project.

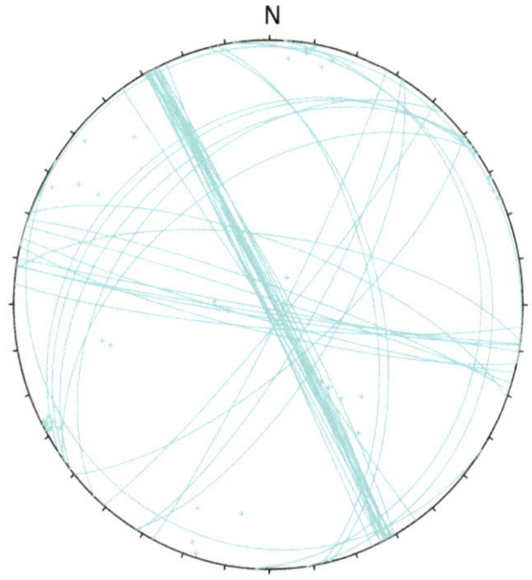

Fig. 10. Stereo-plot of joints in KV 11 indicating the direction of joint planes.

Fig. 11. Manganese dendrites (pencil, 15 cm, for scale) in joint surfaces. Photo by Judith Bunbury.

Fig. 12. Iron-stained calcite in joints overlying manganese dendrites. Pencil, 15 cm, for scale. Photo Judith by Bunbury.

has been a small amount of water percolation and evaporation around these cracks to produce mineralisation. However, there is little evidence for large open cracks, since these appear to be filled rapidly with clay minerals that swell into the cracks as clay minerals in the disrupted shale layers expand.

The unfinished area D1a also shows mineralised joint planes (fig. 14). The continuation of this zone in corridor D2, in particular the lintel, shows fault influence of the structure as well as fault damage to the plaster.

Fig. 13. Salty-efflorescence in joints. Pencil top, 5 cm, for scale. Photo by Judith Bunbury.

Fig. 14. Room D1a showing fault breaks (grey and red surfaces) in the ceiling. The nodules of Zone B limestone are also visible. Geologist for scale. Photo by Nelleke Hovestreydt.

Plaster

It was noted that a pinkish plaster was widely used in conjunction with rock chips to fill gaps where holes had opened up or where the surface was rough. The fine lime-paint/plaster was applied over the top of this pink plaster. The thicker plaster was therefore particularly used in areas of faulting and where the walls were cut into the Zone A limestone. There, plaster, where visible, can be considered a proxy for wall rock condition. A suitable base for the plaster is found in small *tafla* quarries all around the top of the Wall Limestone in the Valley of the Kings. A large number of small quarries into the *tafla* unit observed in this study is evidence for extensive use of these. Whilst the date at which holes were dug is difficult to date, the close comparison between the plaster extracted from the quarries and that used in the tombs suggest that they were probably used in antiquity as well as in more recent times.

Flood Deposits

Flood deposits in KV 11 have not yet been excavated, but examination of the sedimentary section in the recent disturbance of hall J suggests that there are 60 cm of sediments (fig. 15).

The upper part of the sediments is a lime-mud that shows polygonal drying cracks, while the lower part is fine sand. The sand is well-rounded, well sorted fine sand (grainsize phi=2.5). No lag at the base is yet visible. The lime-mud component is consistent with an origin in the Valley of the Kings, while the sandy component is more resonant of Nile river sand.

The geo-archaeological observations made in this field season, followed by constant monitoring in the upcoming seasons, serve as an important basis for the strategy developed for the conservation of the tomb.

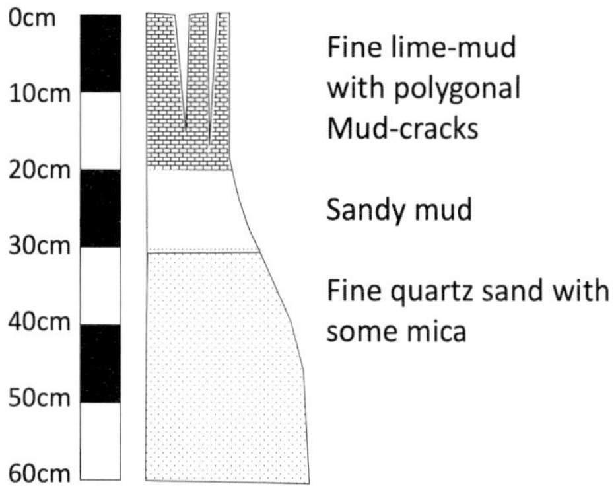

Fig. 15. Section of flood sediments currently visible in KV 11 hall J. Drawing by Judith Bunbury.

Conservation

Along with the geo-archaeological survey, stone deterioration was recorded inside the tomb in combination with an examination of the present condition and climate measurements. The collected data and information form the basis of our conservation strategy with suggested treatments for the coming years.

Originally, the tomb was richly decorated with paintings on pillars, walls and ceilings. Due to structural disintegration[11] of the bedrock and several episodes of flooding in the past, the rear parts of the tomb (rooms H to L) suffered heavy structural damage. Stone fragments have fallen down, as well as plaster and wall painting decoration. Apart from fragments of paintings in the upper areas of the walls and on ceilings, painted fragments on the lower portions of the walls were also found *in situ*. On the basis of visual analysis, it was possible to match broken stone fragments in the burial chamber (hall J) with the ceiling and the pillars. This helps to identify and understand the sequence of destruction, as well as to clarify the processes causing the damage. Due to structural problems of the bedrock (cracks, joints, soft parts etc.), the provisional focus of the ongoing work will be the stabilization of the tomb structure, followed by the plaster and paint layer conservation on the surface.

The principal aim of the project, apart from publication, is the stabilization and consolidation of the tomb to prevent further deterioration of the wall painting. Due to flooding in the past, a major part of the original decoration is already irrecoverably lost. The remaining fragments that still exist in their original position are therefore most important. They offer the last opportunity to pass on information about the materials used, working techniques, and contents of the decoration (*in situ*) to further generations. To date, the floor of the rear part of the tomb is completely covered with sediments, sand, limestone chips, and fragments, and it is most likely that small pieces of painted plaster are preserved underneath.[12] It is likely that an accumulation of collapsed plaster and wall paintings lie buried under limestone fragments adjacent to the walls (fig.16).

[11] See Birte Graue, Jannes Kordilla, Siegfried Siegesmund, "Stone Deterioration and Conservation of the Ancient Egyptian Tomb of Neferhotep (TT 49) in Thebes (Egypt)," *Zeitschrift der Deutschen Gesellschaft für Geowissenschaften* 15 (2007), 593–615.

[12] See the finds from our sondage which will be published in our next report (forthcoming).

Fig. 16. Room L, view into niche west with colourful wall painting fragments. Photo by Johannes Kramer.

Sources of Degradation

The principal causes of the damage in the rear part of the tomb are the unstable rock structure and the flooding.[13] The limestone, with its vertical and horizontal cracks, faults, and layering, is partially unstable: Open gaps and breakouts are visible in pillars, walls, and ceilings. The plaster, with its capability to soak up water and to absorb humidity from the air, reacted like a sponge during flooding, and with increasing water content the plaster became heavier and detached from the walls. In the burial chamber (hall J), plaster fragments are preserved close to the current floor level. They are present in the cavetto cornice of the isles surrounding the sunken central area,[14] which is still filled with sediments and sand originating from the flooding. Water not only works as a destructive agent by itself, it also transports water-soluble salts inside porous systems like natural stone and plaster. Salt crystallization is an additional factor for the detachment and deterioration of stone and plaster. Some walls in hall J show salt crystals growing out of cracks and faults.[15] The harmful effect of water-soluble salts is mainly based on the crystallization and volume increase in the pores. After cycles of crystallization and dissolution, crystallization pressure can lead to loosening of stone layers,[16] widening of fissures and cracks, and the blast down of surface layers of plaster or wall paintings. In comparison to the structural problems of the bedrock and the

---

[13] See Weber, "First Report," 62–65.

[14] For a photograph see Judith Bunbury and Karin Schinken, "Preliminary Report on the Geology, Stonemasonry and Plaster Remains in the Tomb of Ramesses III (KV 11)," in Anke Weber, Martina Grünhagen, Lea Rees, Jan Moje (eds.), *Akhet Neheh. Studies in Honour of Willem Hovestreydt on Occasion of His 75th Birthday* (London, 2020), 41, fig. 6.

[15] For an image in KV 11 see Anke Weber, "ARCE@KV 11," *Scribe Magazine*, 2021 (forthcoming).

[16] Wieslaw Domaslowski, *Preventive Conservation of Stone Objects* (Turin, 2003), 25–28.

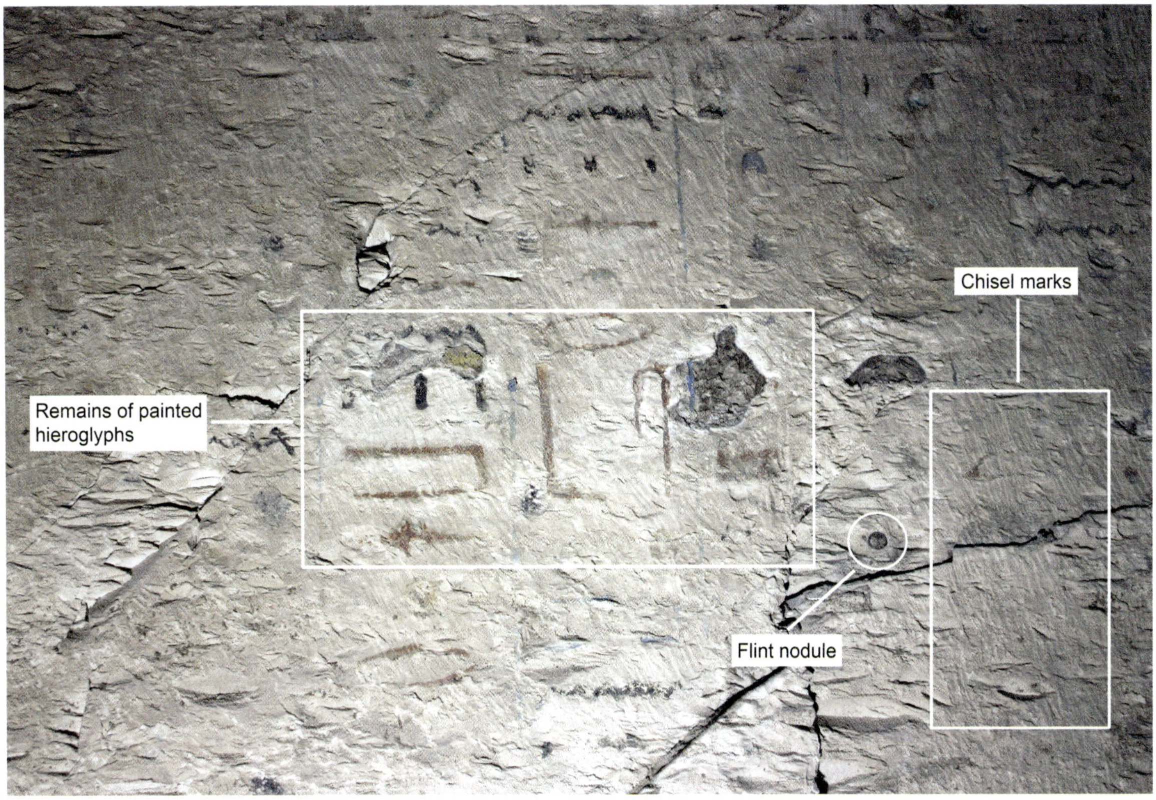

Fig. 17. Hall J, chisel marks, remains of painted hieroglyphs and underlying flint nodules. Photo by Karin Schinken.

flooding, crystallization seems to play a minor role, as a cause of destruction since there is only limited accumulation of salt on the stone or plaster surfaces. Nevertheless, the potential damage of crystallization processes must be considered for selecting compatible conservation materials and techniques.

Observable Working Techniques

During the field campaign, the focus was on collecting information about the condition of the limestone and wall paintings, remaining fragments, and ancient Egyptian working techniques, without any destructive intervention. A visual survey was carried out to identify, record and interpret tool marks, preparatory or construction markings,[17] and early repairs as a means to understand the work processes of the tomb builders.

As can be observed in the Valley of the Kings, above ground as well as underground, the limestone occurs typically in different qualities, from very solid and compact to brittle and fissured. Layers of flint nodules are visible as well. In the front part of KV 11, which is open to the public, the limestone is more stable than in the rear parts and, accordingly, the overall condition of the front part is better than that of the rooms in the rear part.[18] The general tendency of the limestone to form horizontal cracks and scales, combined with naturally occurring faults, enabled the ancient Egyptian stonemasons to cut the bedrock with less labour and force. The limestone's

[17] Comparable to red or black construction lines known from the tomb of Nefertari (QV 66). See S. Rickerby, "Original Painting Techniques and Materials Used in the Tomb of Nefertari," in M. Corzo and M. Afshar (eds.), *Art and Eternity: The Nefertari Wall Paintings Conservation Project, 1986–1992* (Singapore, 1993), 45.

[18] See the contribution concerning the geology of the tomb above.

Fig. 18. Room L, preparatory horizontal line. Photo by Karin Schinken.

Fig. 19. Room L, south-west corner, wall painting fragment overlaying black point grid. Photo by Johannes Kramer.

characteristics worked like rated break points,[19] which were perfectly known and used by the ancient workers who hammered out the rectangular rooms, niches, and floors. The faults, cracks, and fissures were already visible during the construction of the tomb. A rough plaster was therefore used to level breakouts, cracks, or holes.[20]

This levelling coat was then covered with a finer and lighter plaster, after which a kind of wash and/or the paint layer was applied. In areas with better limestone quality and rather less cracks and faults, only one or no layer of plaster was applied. Different types of chisel marks are well preserved on many walls in the tomb (see, for example, the diagonal lines from left to right visible in figure 17). For the moment, they can only be noticed but not identified. Future observation will clarify which kinds of tools were used, in which type of application, and for which task. In a later stage, better understanding of the application of multi-layered plaster will make it possible to reconstruct the building process of the tomb. Instances of compensation for irregularities in masonry and different types of repair or adjustment are well preserved in KV 11. Examples include the outline of a dovetail connection to cover a crack and the bricking-up of damaged parts of the walls,[21] located in hall J. Flint nodules were not removed from the walls in preparation for the painting process; instead, they were flattened and painted over (fig. 17, lower right). Walls and pillars which have lost their decoration (e.g., fig. 17) show, apart from tool marks, preparatory markings such as a horizontal black line (room L, fig. 18) and a grid of painted black points[22] (fig. 19). This kind of information thus allows us to gain insights into the process of constructing and decorating the tomb. First conclusions are that the workmen responded to difficulties posed by the characteristics of the stone with a pragmatic approach, by following the weaker limestone, repairing cracks, masking irregularities and applying multiple layers of plaster. By creating a sunken relief in the plaster, the effect of the paintings is comparable to fine stone masonry in tombs of better quality stone.[23]

Preventive Conservation Measures: Climate Control

Apart from conservation and restoration, preventive conservation is an important task in preserving an object and making conservation treatment long-lasting. During work inside the tomb, a start was made on climate control by measuring the temperature and the relative humidity. Owing to the large amount of wall painting fragments

---

[19] A soft structure or weakness constituting a predetermined breaking point.

[20] For a photograph see Bunbury and Schinken, "Preliminary Report," fig. 1.

[21] See Weber, "First Report," 64, fig. 2.

[22] Average diameter of nearly 1 cm; the distance varies between 12 and 20 cm. Also visible in fig. 21.

[23] First results are presented in Bunbury and Schinken, "Preliminary Report." Further studies will allow to distinguish more precisely between different stages of construction and decoration, and will hopefully help to identify different groups of workmen involved in building the tomb.

in hall J, a data logger was installed in this particular part of the tomb. To minimize the influence of dust, dirt, and lights, the data logger[24] was installed at a height of approximately four meters. It constantly records the temperature and the relative humidity and estimates the dew point.

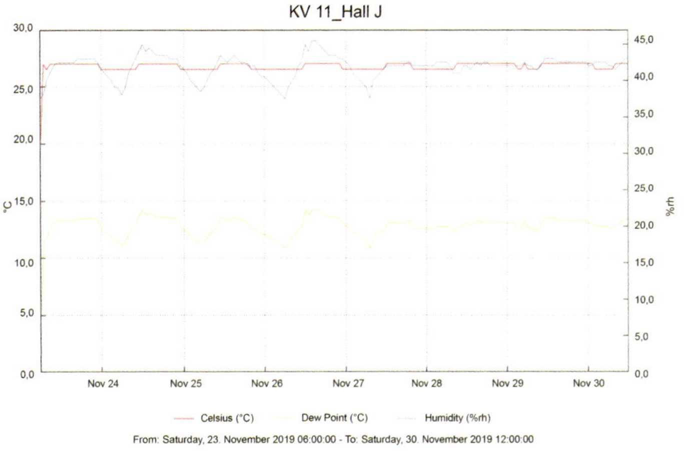

Fig. 20. Climate graph, hall J, pillar 5. Four metres above floor level. Temperatures are given in degrees Celsius.

The results of the first read-out of the memory on 30 November 2019 are illustrated in figure 20. While the temperature varies slightly around 26 to 27 c., the graph of the relative humidity (blue) in the first half oscillates between 39% and 45%. The measurement was carried out over a period of one week and provides first indications that frequent changes of humidity occur that can provoke the crystallization and solution cycles of salts. Another evaluation will take place after a long-term measurement cycle of one year. The graph demonstrates that the work of our team in hall J did not affect the climate (on the 29th the team was not working and the climate is almost comparable to the days of the 28th and the 30th). Each type of salt is soluble at a specific point: the Deliquescence Relative Humidity (DRH). Analysis of the various types will help in the precise risk estimation of the visible salts. The goal is to reduce the crystallization and solution cycles to a minimum. This will be achieved by creating a stable climate, for example with low relative humidity. Climate trends from November 2019 to January 2020 suggest that low relative humidity remains relatively stable, whereas the natural climate in this part of the tomb in the winter months varies to a certain degree (fig. 21). The connection between outside climate and daily changes will be investigated in the future.

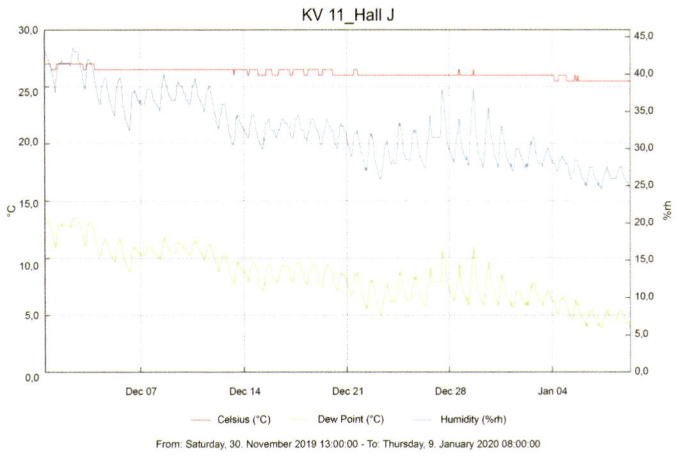

Fig. 21. Climate graph, hall J, overview November 2019-January 2020.

Materials Used: Plaster, Pigments, and Binder

The dark shaded levelling plaster contains some millimetre-sized limestone fragments as fill material. They are visible as whitish debris in a homogeneous, lightly reddish-yellow plaster matrix. The colour corresponds to the natural *tafla* source above KV 11. It seems likely that local material was used for the plaster preparation. Therefore, gypsum or lime can be considered as binding material.[25] The results of former conservation projects suggest

[24] Easy Log EL-USB-1, Lascar Electronics Ltd. United Kingdom.

[25] Rickerby, "Original Painting Techniques."

that a combination of gypsum and lime is conceivable. In contrast to the plaster in the tomb of Neferhotep (TT 49) or the tomb of Nefertari (QV 66), straw is microscopic and not visible. Until laboratory analyses are carried out, we assume that natural pigments in combination with gum arabic were used as painting material.

Condition of Wall Painting Fragments and Conservation Planning

The plaster and the paint layer are in a fragile condition. The plaster is partially detached from the limestone; the edges are removed and cracks run through from the stone to the paint layer. Additionally, flaking of the paint layer can be observed. Scaling and ongoing cracking of the limestone leads to loss of wall painting fragments. On the west wall in the burial chamber (hall J) where the biggest part of wall painting still exists, the decay is ongoing as well. A comparison of earlier photos[26] with the current condition (fig. 22) shows that the height of their position does not protect or preserve the wall paintings. As mechanical stress due to touching by hand cannot occur at this height, there must be other causes such as humidity changes, vibration, action caused by salts and the ongoing deterioration of the stone and the binder of the plaster.

The investigation of the preservation of wall paintings in this field season was documented with photography and notes, forming the basis of a damage mapping catalogue that will be constantly updated in the coming seasons. Additionally, analysis of the plaster, pigments, and binding material will be carried out to generate a body of information to adjust the modified conservation plan, including compatible consolidants.

Once the results of the material analysis are available, the detailed planning and selection of conservation materials will begin. In general, all conservation materials should be as similar as possible to the original material used. This will offer the best possible compatibility between old and new. Mineral consolidants, for example, should be preferred to synthetics. We are going to run small test areas prior to applying it to larger. In this way, unexpected interaction due to local characteristics can be avoided and materials and recipes can be improved for best results in color, structure, and applicability. In the course of work on the test areas, time and material records will provide important information for operating expenses in the future. Based on this experience, time schedules, requisition of material, manpower needed, and costs will be estimated.

The main stages of work in the future are planned as follows:

(1) minimally invasive sampling and material analysis (by agreement with the Ministry of Tourism and Antiquities);
(2) climate records, one year cycle;
(3) ongoing documentation of the current condition of the wall paintings, including damage mapping;
(4) stabilization of the tomb structure:
  (a) checking all surfaces in rooms H-L and side-rooms (ceilings, walls, pillars, niches, door jambs) by percussion test;
  (b) gluing loose stone fragments in place with a point cast epoxy resin bonding;
  (c) closing relevant cracks with cement-free mortar, exceptional force back connections due to advice and request of a structural engineer;
  (d) if checked and required by the structural engineer, installation of additional support for pillars and door jambs;
(5) installation of test areas for dry and wet cleaning, salt reduction, crust reduction, consolidation of plaster and paint layer, laying back of paint layer, backfilling of plaster, reattaching plaster, jointing, gluing stone fragments;
(6) pre-stabilization of the wall paintings in their position;
(7) controlling and evaluation of the test areas;
(8) modification of test materials, recipes and techniques;
(9) cleaning of all surfaces of stone, plaster and wall painting;

[26] Marek Marciniak, "Deux campagnes épigraphiques au tombeau de Ramsès III dans la Vallée de Rois (no. 11)," *ET* 12 (1983), 299, fig. 2.

Fig. 22. West wall of hall J (November 2019), showing places where wall painting has been lost since the early 1980s. Photo by Johannes Kramer.

(10) full conservation treatment of stone, plaster and wall painting fragments, documentation and publication of the work carried out.

Photogrammetry and Total Station Survey

The aim of the photogrammetric survey of the tomb was to provide a baseline digital 3D model for future conservation work, along with orthophotos of the walls to be used for mapping geological faults and other threats to the stability of the tomb, as well as digital epigraphy of the wall decoration. The latter can be achieved by producing orthophotos for digital line drawings and as such is an important part of the conservation as well as the publication process.

The survey took place over thirteen days and was undertaken using a Nikon D5300 DSLR camera using a Nikon AF-S micro Nikkor 40m and an 18–55 mm lens, fixed in the 18mm position. For the purposes of the survey, the tomb was divided into twenty-four overlapping zones, each of which was photographed as a single entity, with the survey beginning in the rear part of the tomb in room L and progressing towards the front entrance, corridors B-C. The lighting in the tomb varies considerably, particularly between the accessible areas (B-F/Fa) which are up-lit from the floor level with strip lights, and the unlit rear part of the tomb (H-L). Each zone in the rear part was lit using three high powered LED flood lights to provide the highest quality detail on the decoration and the current state of deterioration. The burial chamber, hall J, proved particularly challenging due to the shadows cast by the columns demarcating the northern and southern aisles; survey of these areas was conducted under various lighting set-ups to ensure that all sides of the columns were sufficiently recorded. Over 50,000 photographs were taken during the survey, of which 40,660 were used for the final processing. Between 670 and 4813 photographs were taken per zone.

The survey areas were georeferenced and scaled using ground control points placed into each zone. Barcoded targets provided by Agisoft Metashape Pro software were placed throughout each zone and were supplemented by reflective retro targets placed along the wooden edging of the walkway in the accessible part of the tomb.[27] These will provide more permanent reference points for future surveys.

The ground control survey was conducted using a Leica TS06 total station. The local coordinate system, established by the Theban Mapping Project (TMP), was used for the survey in order to allow future comparison with other data sets. Two permanent stations were established outside of the entrance of KV 11 (R3-1 and R3-2) to form a control network along with the TMP stations VK11 and VK2.[28] The total station survey also allowed the creation of a measurable 3D model.[29] The initial processing of the photogrammetry was carried out using the TMP reference system, but final results will be georeferenced to UTM WGS 84 36N using the coordinates published by the University of Turin mapping team.[30] Nine fixed points were established in the tomb using a linear traverse in order to record accurately the positions of the ground control.

The photogrammetric data were processed using AgiSoft Metashape Pro software. The photographs from each survey zone were processed independently. Nikon propriety format RAW photographs were converted into tiff format in order to conduct the first stages of processing and geo-referencing. Processing of the photogrammetric data will take many months, and so only preliminary results are available. More details will be published in our upcoming report.

For each of the twenty-four zones, an aligned, geo-referenced point cloud and 3D mesh has been created. Particular note is made here of corridors B and C, side-rooms Ba, Bb, and side-rooms Ca to Ch, which were aligned as a single entity (figs. 23a and 23b), and well chamber E, which was aligned in its entirety down to the rubble below, under the modern walkway bridge.

The final results will consist of a series of scaled and georeferenced images of the walls, floors, and ceilings of each survey zone, along with a digital 3D model of the entire tomb. Our aim is to combine this model in the future with models that have been made of the sarcophagus of Ramesses III (Musée du Louvre, Paris, Inv. No. D1) and its lid (The Fitzwilliam Museum, Cambridge, Inv. No. E.1.1823) to reunite these pieces virtually in their original setting.[31] This will enable the recontextualising of the burial equipment within the tomb in a digital environment. The virtually reunited sarcophagus will be made available online and in museums, enabling people who could not otherwise visit the tomb or the sarcophagus to view and study them.

[27] The total station survey was conducted by Garthe Rees with the assistance of Nelleke Hovestreydt and Judith Bunbury.

[28] It was not possible to locate TMP station KV 11, and it is assumed that it has been removed.

[29] The length of the tomb based on the new measurements is 113.93 m from the entrance gate direct to the rear of room L.

[30] Francesco Porcelli, Luigi Sambuelli, Cesare Comina, Antonia Spanò, Andrea Lingua, Alessio Calantropio, Gianluca Catanzariti, Filiberto Chiabrando, Federico Fischanger, Paolo Maschio, Ahmed Ellaithy, Giulia Airoldi and Valeria De Ruvo, "Integrated Geophysics and Geomatics Surveys in the Valley of the Kings," *Sensors* 20.6 (2020), 5.

[31] The model of the lid is available at https://sketchfab.com/3d-models/ramesses-iii-sarcophagus-lid-886d5fceec5847618a054b2389d84751 (accessed 14.02.20). FThe model of the coffer is available at https://sketchfab.com/3d-models/ramesses-iii-sarcophagus-louvre-paris-9b2ad0810bc24e14aa10202d6e9cd56f (accessed 14.02.20). For more information, see Gareth Rees, "Reuniting and Recontextualising the Sarcophagus of Ramesses III Using Photogrammetric Modelling," in Anke Weber, Martina Grünhagen, Lea Rees, and Jan Moje (eds.), *Akhet Neheh. Studies in Honour of Willem Hovestreydt*, 57–63.

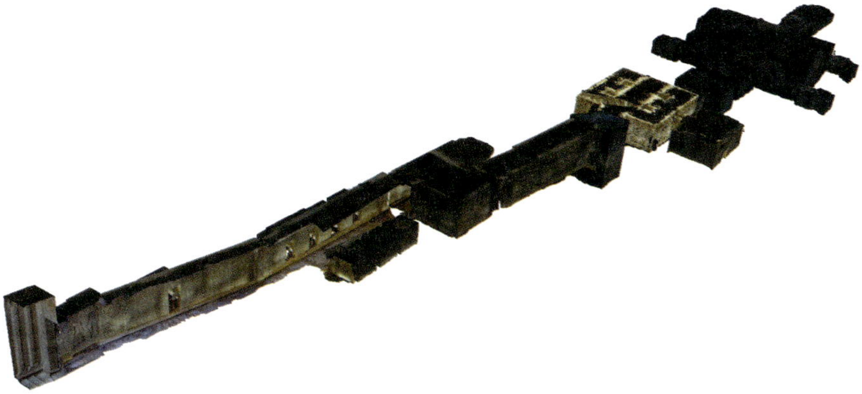

Fig. 23a. Shaded mesh of KV11 viewed from the northwest by Gareth Rees.

Fig. 23b. Detail of the shaded mesh of Corridor B\C with cut-away view into chamber Ch, viewed from northwest by Gareth Rees.

Reconstruction

One of the aims during this season was to prepare a photogrammetric record of the tomb and to create a model showing its physical condition.[32] At the same time, this provided an opportunity to assess the condition of the tomb's decoration and the prospects for reconstruction and future restoration.

Reconstruction of Rooms H to L

From the foregoing sections, it will be clear that there is a striking difference between the state of preservation of the tomb's outer parts and those at the rear (corridor G to room L). After the sloped descent in pillared hall F, the succeeding corridors and rooms, which were all constructed at a lower level, have suffered extensive and severe damage from the invading floods. Naturally, the decoration has suffered as well. As in all parts of the tomb, the decoration of the rear compartments was executed in slightly raised relief, modeled in a plaster layer applied to

[32] See the contribution of Gareth Rees concerning photogrammetry, above.

the walls and pillars. With few exceptions, very little of the plaster has remained, mostly in the topmost sections where the walls touch the ceiling.[33] Nevertheless, traces of texts and figures are still visible where the artisans happened to cut through the plaster into the stone surface, and in places patches of plaster are still extant with the colors preserved intact.

At first sight, the damage to the rear part seems so severe that reconstruction of the decoration may present an almost impossible task. Most often, we can only recognize unevenly distributed fragments of divine or human figures, and it would be impossible to reconstruct whole scenes or a complete wall on this basis alone. It is fortunate, therefore, that much of the lost decoration was either described or copied by early travelers and scholars who visited the Valley of the Kings before the floods that destroyed so much of KV 11.

Several studies have demonstrated how much can be achieved from a close study of this documentation.[34] For KV 11, the principal sources are Jean-Francois Champollion's *Notices descriptives* and the supplementary notes by Eugène Lefébure. Other important sources are the notes and drawings produced by Robert Hay and his collaborators. Significant contributions were made as well by John Gardner Wilkinson and James Burton. The extent and scope of this documentation is somewhat surprising, as most visitors at that time were interested primarily in the front parts of the tomb, notably the ten small side-rooms flanking corridors B and C. In the course of our work, this body of documentation proved to be an invaluable aid in finding and identifying traces of decoration that we might otherwise have overlooked.

Though still preliminary, the results of this first season are encouraging. We are confident that most of the decoration, while heavily damaged, has been preserved to such an extent that most of the scenes can be reconstructed with a high degree of reliability. For every wall in the rear part of the tomb, we can say with certainty what scenes were depicted and what deities were represented. The same holds for the decoration of the eight pillars of the burial chamber.

A full recording of the remaining traces will take time, but a start has been made on a provisional basis. The traditional practice of tracing on transparent sheets fixed over the original base image is no longer an option, but photogrammetry has proved to be an excellent alternative. In the case of the heavily damaged walls of KV 11, it has even distinct advantages over older methods.

Figure 24a presents an orthophoto of the west wall of room I, which immediately precedes the burial chamber. The damage to the wall is clearly visible: large chunks of rock have broken away. The contents of the scene are known from descriptions by Champollion,[35] Hay,[36] Wilkinson,[37] and Lefébure.[38] The king was shown holding hands with four different gods: Atum, Anubis, Thoth, and Horus. In a few cases, traces of the god's legs are still visible, showing that god and king are not standing opposite each other. Instead, they are walking in the same direction, the god's upper body being turned around to face the king. In two cases the king wears a billowing skirt which, at least in the left-hand scene, reaches down to the ankles.

The hieroglyphic captions to the scenes have only been partially preserved. An interesting detail is that in the rightmost scene, where Horus is facing the king, traces of the king's nomen show that the name is given in a more compact form than in the outer sections of the tomb. Other preserved traces suggest this is typical of the tomb's rear part in its entirety.

Figure 24c shows a provisional reconstruction of the wall, based on an equally provisional epigraphic recording (fig. 24b) which will have to be collated later on. It might be objected that such a reconstruction seems premature, and it is true that some elements are somewhat hypothetical – notably the king's dress in Groups 2 and 4. As in many other cases, however, the actual remaining traces on this wall are so sparse that even with a full and detailed epigraphic recording it will remain difficult to visualize the original aspect of the decoration. In spite of possible imperfections, the reconstruction derives its principal value from the fact that, in combination with

[33] See the contribution of Karin Schinken above.

[34] A meticulous study presenting much of the evidence for KV 11's rear parts is Florence Mauric-Barberio, "Reconstitution du décor de la tombe de Ramsès III (partie inférieure) d'après les manuscrits de Robert Hay," *BIFAO* 104 (2004), 389–456.

[35] Jean-François Champollion, *Monuments de l'Égypte et de la Nubie: Notices descriptives* (Paris, 1844), 419.

[36] London, British Library, Add. MSS. 29820, fol. 112 ro.

[37] Oxford, Bodleian Libraries, MS. Wilkinson. dep. c. 5, fol. 100 ro.

[38] Eugène Lefébure, Les Hypogées royaux de Thèbes: Notice des Hypogées, *MMAF* 3/2 (Paris, 1886), 108.

Fig. 24a. Room I, West Wall. Orthophoto by Willem Hovestreydt.

Fig. 24b. Room I, West Wall: tracing of the decoration. Drawing by Willem Hovestreydt

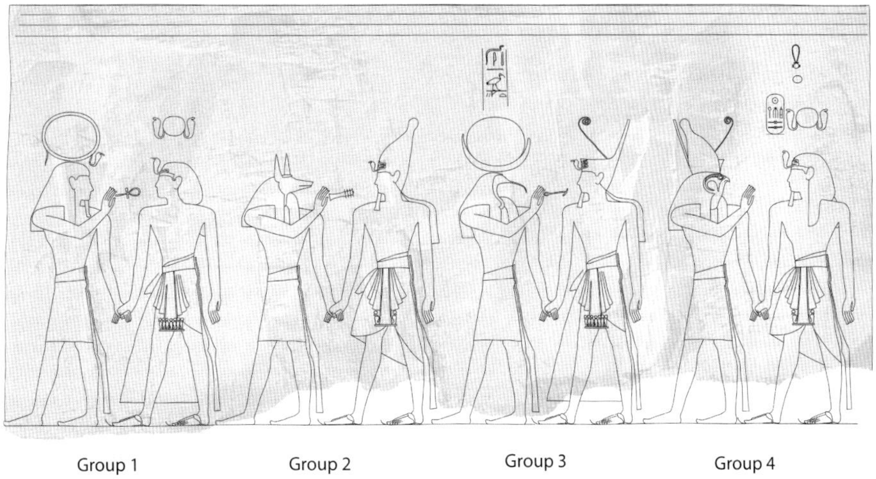

Fig. 24c. Room I, West Wall: reconstruction of the decoration. The king's dress in Groups 2 and 4 is hypothetical. Drawing by Willem Hovestreydt.

similar reconstructions from other walls, it can serve as a heuristic tool.[39] As such, it can help to identify remaining elements of the decoration, either *in situ* or still to be discovered under the thick layer of rubble covering the floor. It can also help to clarify the interrelationships between different scenes in the rear parts of the tomb. In KV 11, such relationships have proved to be particularly strong.[40]

The Ceiling of the Burial Chamber

The workmen of the tomb of Ramesses III were aware of the bad quality of limestone in the Valley of the Kings, but they accepted it because it allowed an easier preparation of the large rooms.[41] Subsequently, they had to deal with some difficulties caused by the geological properties of the limestone. A number of breakouts in walls and ceilings have been detected and recorded during our winter season. On some parts, reddish mortar was spread on the ceiling of the burial chamber. In some cases, marks from applying the mortar with the fingers are still visible (fig. 25). The mortar seems to be a composition of local materials and certainly mainly consists of *tafla*[42] which is a reddish, very friable shale.[43]

The ceiling of the burial chamber can be examined for its faults and breakouts in order to replace limestone fragments virtually, but most importantly for reconstructing the scenes, which are almost completely destroyed. By using software such as photogrammetry coupled with DStretch® and by preparing a digital drawing right in front of the paintings and directly below the ceiling, it was possible to record the last traces of decoration which might lead to a reconstruction of the scene (fig. 26).

So far, we can say that the scene must have been comparable to the ceilings of the burial chambers in KV 2 and KV 14. Two pathways can be reconstructed. Inside them, there are yellow half-disks that appear to be rising or setting suns. According to numerous single hieroglyphs and parts of the former decoration, the ceiling must have shown almost the same scene as in the tomb of Tawosret and Sethnakht (J1) and the tomb of Seti I. However, the investigation is still in progress and further results will be published in our future reports. More results will be available and closer analysis possible when the full set of orthophotos for the tomb are processed.[44]

The Book Of The Heavenly Cow

The burial chamber of KV 11 (hall J) has four side-rooms, as did most of the royal tombs in the Valley of the Kings. Side-room Jc[45] is located in the southwestern corner and it contains a copy of the so-called Book of the Heavenly Cow or The Destruction of Mankind—a text that has received much attention since Édouard Naville published the copies from Seti I and Ramesses III.[46] The copy in KV 11 was already in bad condition when Naville visited the tomb in 1882, and Charles Maystre reported in 1941 that it is "anéanti."[47] Fortunately, his statement was slightly exaggerated, and Elisabeth Staehelin and Hermann Schlögl were able to cross-check the original and even to correct the old transcription of the text. Their transcript was used by Erik Hornung in his synoptic edition.[48] Over the years, however, the condition of the side-rooms deteriorated, and the decoration is almost destroyed today. The cleaning and restoration of this area, therefore, is considered amongst the most urgent tasks of our further work in this tomb.

Side-room Jc was cut into the contact zone between the Wall Limestone Zone A and B, which is also visible in hall J.[49] The vertical open joints that are typical for the limestone are visible in side-room Jc as well; they forced the ancient Egyptian workmen to cover the walls partially with plaster before they decorated them.[50]

The side-room measures ca. 2.85 m (east–west) × 2.66 m (north-south) and is accessible from the burial chamber by a low doorway, which is today severely destroyed. The flood events mentioned by Anke Weber submerged

---

[44] See the contribution of Gareth Rees, above.

[48] Erik Hornung, *Der ägyptische Mythos von der Himmelskuh: Eine Ätiologie des Unvollkommenen*, OBO 46 (Freiburg-Schweiz-Göttingen, 1982), especially ix and 35.

[49] See Bonnie M. Sampsell, *The Geology of Egypt: A Traveler's Handbook* (Cairo-New York, 2014), 78–82 for the situation in the Kings' Valley in general, and the contribution of Judith Bunbury in this report.

[50] See the contributions of Judith Bunbury and Karin Schinken concerning the geology and conservation, above.

side-room Jc in the past,[51] and limestone blocks detached from the ceiling as a consequence, making it currently impossible to draw conclusions about its original appearance. The debris now covers the floor of side-room Jc and the lower part of the wall decoration. The height of the room cannot, therefore, be given with certainty—the walls are visible up to a height of ca. 0.85 m, measured from top corner to debris level in the northeastern corner of the room.

Fig. 25. Mortar filling on the ceiling of hall J with visible fingerprints of the workmen. Photo by Anke Weber.

Additional damage was caused by bats that used side-room Jc for roosting in the past. Wilbour reported in April 1881 that "the remains of bats which choked the hieroglyphics on the wall [of side-room Jc, L.P.], were not pleasant to breathe."[52] Today, remains of guano are not clearly visible but might have been washed off by the floodwater. However, one bat died in the side-room and is naturally mummified, still sticking at the middle of the south wall, between columns 63 and 64 of the Book of the Heavenly Cow, right at the passage where the ibis and the moon of Thot are created and Thoth shall embrace the sky—a fitting place of death for a flying nocturnal animal.

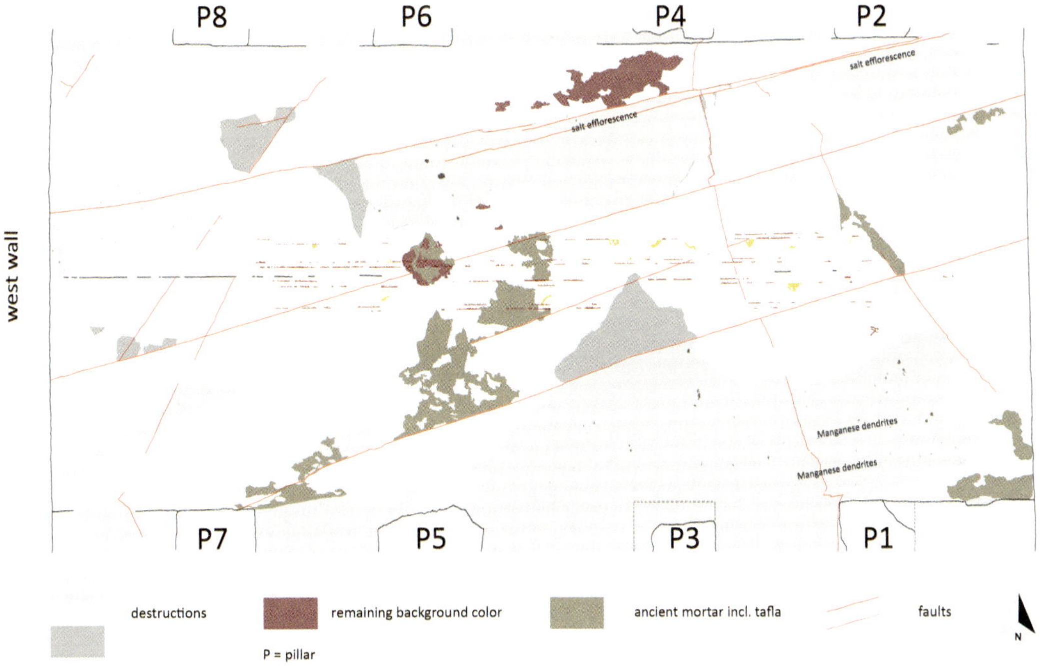

Fig. 26. Preliminary line drawing of the ceiling in hall J including faults, remains of plaster, antique repairs, breakouts and the remaining decoration. Drawing by Anke Weber.

---

[51] See Weber, "First Report," 65–66, figs. 3 and 4.

[52] Charles Edwin Wilbour, *Travels in Egypt [December 1880 to May 1891]: Letters of Charles Edwin Wilbour*, with the assistance of Jean Capart (Brooklyn, 1936), 64. See also Naville, "L'inscription de la destruction des hommes dans le tombeau de Ramsès III," 413.

Due to these destructions, Maystre's judgement is more correct today than it was in his time, and side-room Jc is in a precarious condition. A first examination in January 2020 revealed that most of the decoration has vanished: Columns 1 and 2 of the text were destroyed when the upper half of the northern doorframe broke off. Apart from this destruction, the northern half of the east wall is the best preserved one, together with the south wall, and many text columns could be identified on these two walls. The northern and western wall, by contrast, show only single signs or sign traces, dispersed over several columns.

The vignette of the Heavenly Cow, which occupies most of the western wall, has almost disappeared. The outlines of the head and the frontal horn are still visible, but only tiny traces of the dorsal and the ventral lines and of the rear legs could be identified. Some additional blurs might belong to the accompanying figures, but could also be just natural color changes of the limestone. The bad state of preservation is most unfortunate, because the remaining parts still preserve color fragments; the most striking one is the blue color of the cow's horns.

Nothing is left from the second vignette, the depiction of the threefold king and the support of heaven, which once occupied the southern half of the east wall.[53]

Priority tasks for future seasons will include securing the ceiling and removing the limestone debris mentioned above. Special attention will be given to the debris next to the entrance, where the remains of the broken doorframe might still be situated, and to the lowest level of the limestone debris, were fragments from the surface of the ceiling might be expected.

In a next step, another collation of the texts is necessary in order to identify all remaining traces of hieroglyphic signs and depictions and to examine the lower parts of the columns which are still covered by debris. Two possible, though marginal, corrections of Hornung's edition were detected during the first collation in January 2020, and this proves a further collation of the text useful. DStretch® yielded good results in restoring the parts of the Opening of the Mouth Ritual in corridor G which are no longer visible by eye.[54] First, preliminary tests with this software in side-room Jc were less successful, because the plaster itself is destroyed on many parts of the walls, along with the text written on it. It is possible that a better illumination of the walls might lead to a more positive outcome in the next season.

The examination of the decoration pattern in side-room Jc will add further details to the interpretation of the text. As is already known, the KV 11 copy of the Book of the Heavenly Cow is shorter than the copy in the tomb of Seti I: the description of the vignette is reduced to the final sentences, and the concluding *ba*-theology, magical incantation and postscript are omitted. The reason for these differences is an open question. Are they due simply to the available space? Or are they based upon different sources?[55] Fortunately, the grid is partially still visible in side-room Jc, and it is significant that the column lines do not follow it. Further examination of these deviations might contribute to this issue.

The vignette of the Heavenly Cow also deserves closer attention, because its dimensions were important enough to be noted in the original description of the vignette.[56] The exact reading of the passage in question is a matter of debate, and the dimension given in the final text does not suit the actual dimension of the vignette.[57] It would be a worthwhile task, therefore, to reconstruct the dimension of the vignette in KV 11 and to compare it with the other known vignettes.[58]

---

53 See Hornung, *Der ägyptische Mythos von der Himmelskuh*, 86–87 for this vignette.

54 See Dora Petrova, "A Lost Dipinto from the Tomb of Ramesses III …" in this volume.

55 See already Nadine Guilhou, *La vieillesse des dieux* (Montpellier, 1989), 132 for these questions.

56 Col. 44–45 in the version of Seti I, Hornung, *Der ägyptische Mythos von der Himmelskuh*, 14–15.

57 Lutz Popko, "Grammatische und lexikalische Notizen zum Buch von der Himmelskuh," *GM* 225 (2010), 90–91.

58 Monumental versions are known from the shrine of Tutankhamun and the tomb of Ramesses II. The copy of the text in the tomb of Ramesses VI is not accompanied by a vignette (in fact, this version only starts after the description of the vignette). A non-monumental, fragmentary vignette can be found on pTurin Cat. 2060/074+ / CGT 54078, Sara Maria Demichelis, "I papyri del Museo Egizio," in *Museo Egizio* (Modena, 2015), 261, fig. 338. The fragments of the text, however, do not contain the passage in question. (I thank Susanne Töpfer, Museo Egizio, for sending me photos of this papyrus.) Papyrus Turin Pleyte-Rossi lxxxiv / Cat. 1982 / CGT 54077 does not contain the vignette, pace Madeleine Bellion, *Égypte ancienne: Catalogue des manuscrits hiéroglyphiques et hiératiques et des dessins, sur papyrus, cuir ou tissu, publies ou signalés* (Paris, 1987), 363. Bellion furthermore mentions pTurin Cat. 1826 with yet another vignette, following Alessandro Roccati, "Les papyrus de Turin," *BSFE* 99 (1984), 27, n. 35. The iconography of the cow, however, speaks against Roccati's suggestion: Firstly, the cow wears the combination of sun disc and double feathers between her horns on pTurin Cat. 1826, which is missing in the versions of Tutankhamun,

The results of analyzing both, text and vignette, will also help to determine their setting within the "semantics" and the "syntax"[59] of this tomb in particular and of royal tombs in general: The text is placed in the first annex room to the right of the burial chamber in the tombs of Seti I and Ramesses II, but in the second side-room to the right in the tomb of Ramesses III.[60] This relocation is presumably not coincidental, and the analysis of the setting of this text within the general decoration program of KV 11 might add some pieces to this puzzle.

The Opening of the Mouth Ritual

In corridor G of the tomb of Ramesses III (KV 11) the ritual of the Opening of the Mouth is situated. The height of the corridor is 3.07 m, the width is 2.64 m, and the length is 6.88 m. On each side of the entrance, there is a thickness containing traces of what appear to be the introductory scenes of the Opening of the Mouth ritual. The height of the thickness is 3.17 m, the width is 2.14 m, and the length is 1.07 m.[61] On the left (east) side there are traces of a falcon god wearing the sun disk on his head, while on the opposite right (west) wall, a goddess holding two vases is depicted.

The condition of the rear part of the tomb, which starts with the beginning of the corridor and ends with the burial chamber, is critical due to the effects of the heavy flooding events.[62] As a result, access to the rear part of the tomb is restricted and the reconstruction of the scenes is based entirely on the photos taken during the winter campaign of The Ramesses III (KV 11) Publication and Conservation Project in 2019/2020 and the notes of Champollion and Lefébure.[63] The photogrammetry performed by Gareth Rees and the very skillful merging of the photos by Johannes Kramer resulted in two very high quality pictures of the entire left (east) and right (west) walls of the corridor. Based on these, it could easily be determined that the inscriptions in corridor G have suffered severe damage and that only a small part is still visible, with traces of red and blue ink.

At this early stage of the investigation, the left wall, which is the better preserved of the two, was the main objective. A small number of reliefs still remain, including traces of the cartouches of Ramesses III. Only a few groups of signs preserved on the white plaster are visible to the naked eye. The traces of ink left under this plaster on the limestone wall, which is covered in chisel marks, are of particular interest. With the help of the image enhancement technique DStretch® (especially in colorspaces LDS and LAB), additional parts of the text became visible, as well as many marking dots placed to fit the scenes within the layout of the wall.

The enhanced picture showed that the first nine scenes of the Opening of the Mouth ritual were placed on the left (east) wall in corridor G and that their reconstruction is now possible.[64] Double vertical lines divide the title and the individual scenes, while the rest of the text follows the division of the scene as in KV 17 (Seti I) and KV 14 (Tausret/Sethnakht). The texts are inscribed below a corresponding image section that includes the

---

Seti I, Ramesses III and pTurin CGT 54078 (the version of Ramesses II was never published; the rough sketch of the version of Ramesses II in Maystre, "Le Livre de la Vache du Ciel dans les tombeaux de la Vallée des Rois", 55, at least, does not indicate it). Secondly, the cow is labelled as *jh.t-wr.t*: "the big cow" on pTurin Cat. 1826, whereas this name is missing in the other depictions. And finally, the cow is oriented to the right on pTurin Cat. 1826 but always oriented to the left in the vignette of the Book of the Heavenly Cow (explicitly remarked by Hornung, *Der ägyptische Mythos von der Himmelskuh*, 83). For a simplified vignette in the Book of the Fayum, see Hornung, *Der ägyptische Mythos von der Himmelskuh*, 84–85.

59 For these concepts, see Jan Assmann, "Geheimnis, Gedächtnis und Gottesnähe: Zum Strukturwandel der Grabsemantik und der Diesseits-Jenseitsbeziehungen im Neuen Reich," in Jan Assmann et al. (eds.), *Thebanische Beamtennekropolen: Neue Perspektiven archäologischer Forschung. Internationales Symposion*, Heidelberg, 9. – 13.6.1993, SAGA 12 (Heidelberg, 1995), 281–93, and Derchain's "grammaire du temple" and his "syntaxe naologique" (Philippe Derchain, "Un manuel de géographie liturgique à Edfou," CdÉ 37, no. 73 (1962), especially 33–36, and Derchain, "Réflexions sur la décoration des pylônes," *BSFÉ* 46 (1966), 17).

60 See Guilhou, *La vieillesse des dieux*, 131 for this question.

61 The dimensions are available on the web page of The Theban Mapping Project. http://www.thebanmappingproject.com (accessed 02.01.2019).

62 Especially the flood events between 1890 and 1914. See Weber, "First Report," 62–65.

63 See notes 65 and 66.

64 The reconstruction is available here: D. Petrova, "From Invisible Traces to Invincible Ritual. Reconstructing the Opening of the Mouth Ritual in the Tomb of Ramesses III," in Weber, Grünhagen, Rees, Moje (eds.), *Akhet Neheh: Studies in Honour of Willem Hovestreydt*, 115–22.

depiction of a royal statue put on a mound of sand on a rectangular base, except in scene 8. All images show the king as the recipient of the ritual facing left, wearing a triangular apron and the double crown in scene one or the *nms*-headcloth in all other scenes. For the reconstruction of the nine scenes the notes of Champollion [65] and Lefébure [66] were used in combination with the much better preserved variants of the Opening of the Mouth ritual preserved in the tombs KV 17 and KV 14.

During the reconstruction of the scenes on the left wall in corridor G, a hieratic *dipinto* was discovered written across the depiction of scene three of the ritual (see article by Petrova in this volume). By using DStretch®, more of the text became visible, revealing "regnal year 3, month 2 of Akhet, (day) 13." Unfortunately, the name of the king is not preserved. The text is of importance not only because it might shed more light on the question of how far the construction of the tomb went under the reign of Sethnakht but also whether the *dipinto* was written during his successor, Ramesses III. The inscription also provides us with insights into the nature of an architectural feature called *nfr.w*, which is translated as "the innermost," and on how it was envisioned within the plan of the tomb. Due to its importance, this discovery will be singled out in the contribution following the report.

Reconstruction of Architectural Elements and the Chronology of Flooding Events

One of the main aims of this project is the reconstruction of architectural elements in the tomb's rear part. To achieve this goal, it was necessary to implement a complex numbering system for the huge amount of stones that have accumulated in the burial chamber and the annex rooms and side-rooms. A low resolution orthophoto served as a basis for a line drawing including all diagnostic stones that cover the current floor level. By developing lists with stone identification patterns and areas where the stones should be replaced, we were able to install a number of block yards (*Steingärten*) for intermediate storage and future assignment of the architectural elements. Several fragments of pillars and the ceiling were identified on the basis of chisel marks and remaining decoration. Furthermore, we were able to retrace the collapse events by investigating the positions of the stones and whether they fell on top of the dry sediments or into the wet mud. Many of those fragments must have collapsed onto the flood sedimentation while it was still moist, as its top skin was firmly bonded with the stones. By observing the limestone fragments and the surrounding debris, it was possible to identify certain flood streams and the places into which they flowed. In this way, it was possible to draw a clear picture of the chronology of the flooding events and the subsequent years of deterioration.

Excavation

The results of the archaeological sondage conducted in KV 11 during the 2019/2020 field season will be discussed in more detail in our forthcoming "Report on the Publication and Conservation of the Tomb of Ramesses III in the Valley of the Kings (KV 11)." Therefore, the following remarks are only preliminary and serve as an overview in advance of the more detailed publication.

The archaeological work conducted in the burial chamber (hall J) served as a preliminary step for future excavation. Since the tomb's rear part is heavily destroyed, presumably by a number of flash floods occurring between 1890 and 1914,[67] it was necessary to begin with the clearance of the affected rooms (H-L).

Several small sondages helped to understand the flooding events and will aid the development of a full excavation strategy. Neither the height of the original ground level nor the overlaying sedimentation layers in the burial chamber (hall J) had ever been measured. The main objective was thus to provide exact measurements of these levels and a detailed documentation of the sedimentation process. In order to achieve these aims, a first sondage was excavated in order to determine and measure the deposition of limestone debris, dried out flood

[65] Champollion, *Monuments de l'Egypte*, vol 1, 416–17.

[66] M. E. Lefébure, *Les Hypogées Royaux de Thébes*, vol. 3, MMAF (Paris 1889), 87–120.

[67] Anke Weber, "First Report," 63.

sedimentation, and a sand layer. The area of a recent disturbance[68]—a pit cut into the ground probably after the year 2000[69]—was chosen (fig. 27).

The excavation layers are visible in figure 15. Eventually, after removing the disturbed sediment, for the first time since more than 100 years, the original floor level of the burial chamber has been revealed below an undisturbed sand layer, which also consisted of debris and dropped limestones.

The sand itself consists of fine quartz with some mica and, according to Judith Bunbury, it must have been secondarily brought into the burial chamber.[70] By extending the dimensions of the sondage in which the hole is located, it came to light that the whole ground must be covered on a similar level with this sand layer.[71] The survey even revealed that the aisles behind the pillars are covered with sand. Furthermore, finds of plant remains coated in sediment mud in cracks of two pillars (P4 and P5) of hall J provide the lowest level of one of the main floodings. Thus, the flood waters must have risen at least up to 2.6m above the floor surface of the burial chamber.

The excavation of the sand layer brought a number of interesting finds to light, including two rose granite sarcophagus fragments that were found on top of the original ground level (fig. 28). Another fragment that was found on the surface of the pit in 2016 belongs to the same corpus. The fragments appear to have been intentionally smashed.

Fragments of Sarcophagus Lids Found In Hall J

As mentioned above, the fragment (J-V-1-1) was first spotted in 2016, lying on top of the sediment layer next to the recently dug intrusive pit.[72] The object was probably removed from its archaeological context and then placed on the edge of the pit. It measures 16.7 × 17.1 × 17.6 cm (height, width, depth) and consists of light pink rose granite with feldspar, quartz and mica components.[73] On its upper side, a long, slightly curved, raised part is sculpted out of the stone; a winding, incised line and a band of inscription, quoting the sentence *n*(*n*) *ḫft.j n=k* ("You do (or: will) not have any enemies"), are running along the vertical side; the curvature on the inside of the lid is carefully polished (fig. 29, top). The two other fragments (J-V-4-1 and J-V-4-2) were found in the 2019/2020 season, in the sand layer underneath the layer of baked sediments (see fig. 28, above). Fragment J-V-4-2 measures 21.0 x 17.8 x 14.0 cm and consists of a rose granite with inclusions of feldspar, quartz, and mica in parallel formation.[74] It shows a similar sculpted part to J-V-1-1 on top and a polished, slightly curved surface on its underside, which used to be the inside of the sarcophagus (fig. 29, middle). Fragment J-V-4-1 has maximal measurements of 20.8 x 23.5 x 10.5 cm and closely resembles the stone material of J-V-1-1. It once formed a rectangular corner piece of a sarcophagus lid with an equally rectangular rim that was lowered into the coffer (fig. 29, below). It bears bands of inscriptions on the two perpendicular vertical sides, reading *jpw* […] (dem. pron. m. pl. "these," followed by two unidentified signs) and [*j*]*w=k m ꜣḫ* ("You are the transfigured *ꜣḫ*-spirit").

A comparison between the sarcophagus lid of Ramesses III in the Fitzwilliam Museum and the newly found fragments highlights important parallels: the sculpted parts on the upper side of fragments J-V-1-1 and J-V-4-2 closely resemble the bodies of the human-headed serpents and the snake next to Nephthys on the lid in the Fitzwilliam Museum. The winding incised line underneath the band of inscription on the vertical side of fragment J-V-1-1 can be identified as an ouroboros, just like on the Cambridge lid. Most strikingly, the same inscription

---

68 See Weber, "First Report," 65.

69 Hitherto, the photographs taken by Araldo de Luca in hall J in 2000 serve as a terminus post quem (photograph nos. 30367–30368, cf. https://www.araldodeluca.com/de/bild/30367 and https://www. Araldodeluca.com/ de/bild/30368). The first visit of the field director, Anke Weber, to the tomb's rear part in 2014 provides a terminus ante quem as the disturbance was already present at this time. More detailed information will be given in the upcoming report.

70 The conclusion derives from the type of sand and its grain size. Neither is found in the wadi, so both must come from another place.

71 See the digging grid of hall J in Weber, "First Report," 68, fig. 9.

72 The fragment was first spotted by the field director during her preliminary work of her Ph.D. project. In the 2019/2020 season, we had the chance to study and document it properly with drawings, photographs and a photogrammetric 3D model.

73 On a macroscopic level, the material seems to resemble Klemm & Klemm No. 961. See Rosemarie Klemm and Dietrich D. Klemm, *Steine und Steinbrüche im Alten Ägypten* (Berlin, 1993), 326, 448, pl. 10.1.

74 Maybe close to Klemm & Klemm no. 710 or 748. See Klemm and Klemm, *Steine und Steinbrüche*, 327, 448, pl. 10.3–4.

Fig. 27. Photogrammetry model of the recent disturbance in hall J by Willem Hovestreydt.

nn ḫft.i n=k is to be found on this fragment, as well as on the viewer's left side of the lid in the Fitzwilliam Museum.[75] So far, we know of no other exact parallels to this passage; certainly is not to be found on any other royal sarcophagus of this date and type.[76] The closest analogy comes from the Book of the Dead spell 178, where it says *nn ḫft.jw=k* ("You are without enemies.").[77]

However, the fragment J-V-1-1 and its inscription have much smaller dimensions than the lid, which is more than double in size. The vertical side of the lid in the Fitzwilliam Museum measures 39 cm and the inscription line 18 cm, whereas the vertical side of fragment J-V-1-1 can be reconstructed not measuring more than 25 cm (15 cm are preserved and it is only the ouroboros missing), with an inscription line of 7.3 cm. Moreover, the execution of the hieroglyphs, especially their style and depth, but also their organization, differ strongly: Whereas the hieroglyphs on the lid are arranged vertically into one text block, they are more widely spread into two fields on the fragment found in the tomb.

Fragment J-V-4-1, on the other hand, has a completely different design than J-V-1-1 and the Cambridge lid. There is no ouroboros on its vertical side, nor do the dimensions of the band of inscription, measuring 9.5 cm, fit either of the two. Because of the rectangular angle of the rim and the corner, this piece cannot be

75 Suggested translations of the lid's inscription can be found in Wallis Budge, *A Catalogue of the Egyptian Collection in the Fitzwilliam Museum, Cambridge* (Cambridge, 1893), 2; Samuel Birch, "On the Cover of the Sarcophagus of Ramesses III. Now in the Fitzwilliam Museum," *Cambridge Antiquarian Communications* III (1879), 373–74; Penelope Wilson, "Ramesses III, Giovanni Belzoni and the Mysterious Reverend Browne," in Paul Starkey and Nadia el-Kholy (eds.), *Egypt through the Eyes of Travellers* (Durham, 2002), 49–56.

76 Of the cartouche-shaped Ramesside royal sarcophagi only those of Seti II and Ramesses IV bear an inscription on the vertical side.

77 See the transcription and German translation from Burkhard Backes in Thesaurus Linguae Aegyptiae (TLA) (Version 31.10.14) http://aaew.bbaw.de/tla/index.html (accessed 21.02.2020). A similar passage is known from Book of the Dead spell 181, where the deceased is equated with Osiris: *nn ḫftj.w=f r=f nn ḫft.jw=f r=k* ("As he has no enemies against him, you have no enemies against you."). An early variant of this idea might be found in the pyramid texts of the Old Kingdom, where PT 368 in the pyramid of Teti and PT 588 in the pyramids of Merenre and Neith state *rdj.n=s wn=k m nṯr n ḫft.j=k m rn=k n(.j) nṯr* ("She [the goddess Nut] made you into a god, you do not have an enemy in your name 'God'.").

Fig. 28. Profile of the recent disturbance (view south) including the finds of two sarcophagus fragments. Photo by Anke Weber.

part of a cartouche-shaped sarcophagus, but rather of one with at least one rectangular end (probably the foot end, whereas the head end may have been arched or rectangular). So far, no exact parallel for the inscription [*j*]*w*=*k m ꜣḫ* could be found.[78] For fragment J-V-4-2, its thickness of only 14 cm also makes it unlikely that it once belonged to the Fitzwilliam lid. Moreover, the beginning of the curvature suggests that the sculpted serpent on top was placed rather close to the edge of the upper side of the sarcophagus lid, similar to fragment J-V-1-1, whereas on the Cambridge lid, the two goddesses are taking up this space. Overall, it can be concluded that the newly found objects cannot be joined with the lid displayed in the Fitzwilliam Museum, and they probably do not fit together either.

Along with our recent findings, a number of rose granite fragments have already been discovered in the 1980s during Edwin C. Brock's excavations in the well chamber (room E) of KV 11.[79] When Lyla Pinch-Brock lately revisited his finds, it became clear that several pieces closely resemble the fragments found in the burial chamber. Some of them seem to be worked in a similar size and style, bear inscriptions, and display sculpted bodies of

[78] Thematically similar may be the phrases of Book of the Dead spells 135, 136 and 91, mentioning that the deceased will become a transfigured *ꜣḫ*-spirit by knowing that particular spell. They, however, use the 3rd p. sg. and the verbs *wnn* or *ḫpr* to describe the process of the transformation, not its result. See the transcription and German translation from Burkhard Backes in Thesaurus Linguae Aegyptiae (TLA) (15th update, Version 31. October 2014) http://aaew.bbaw.de/tla/index.html (accessed 27.02.2020).

[79] His excavations remained unpublished, but references to Brock's work can be found in Jean Leclant and Gisele Clèrk, "Fouilles et travaux en Ègypte et au Soudan, 1986–1987," *Orientalia* 57 (1988), 353, n. 266, who refer to the circular of the German Archaeological Institute from 1987 (DAI Rundbrief), 22. Also see Eleni Vassilika, *Egyptian Art* (Cambridge, 1995), 86 and A. Dodson, "Sarcophagi," in R. Wilkinson and K. Weeks (eds.), *The Oxford Handbook to the Valley of the Kings* (Oxford, 2016), 253.

serpents.[80] So far, however, it remains unclear, whether any of the newly found fragments can be joined with Brock's finds.

For now, it also remains unclear whether the fragments of different sarcophagi found in KV 11 were once (re) used for Ramesses III himself, forming a sarcophagus ensemble similar to that of Merenptah,[81] or whether they belonged to burials of different people. After all, many royal sarcophagi were severely damaged—maybe even deliberately smashed—in antiquity, and fragments thereof scattered in various places in the Valley of the Kings. Famous examples include the sarcophagus of Ramesses VI, found dispersed throughout the whole *wadi*, and the sarcophagus of queen Takhat, found shattered in the tomb of Amenmesse (KV 10).[82] Hopefully, excavations in the burial chamber will help to gain new insights into the original owners of these sarcophagi, of which fragments found their way into KV 11.[83]

Conclusions

This field season in KV 11 achieved promising results, forming the basis of a Site Management Plan and a strategy to conserve and publish the tomb. The assumption that the immense pressure of the soaked Esna Shale beneath the tomb caused the destruction of the rear part of the tomb has to be revised.[84] Instead, the geoarchaeological survey revealed that the water-soaking characteristics of the Wall Limestone in the lower part of the tomb (Zone A) have been responsible for it. Furthermore, it was determined that a flood protection intervention is not necessary at the moment because the cracks leading from the rock surface to the burial chamber are narrow and filled with debris, so that water evaporates before it reaches the inner part of the tomb. Therefore, our future work will concentrate on the conservation and reconstruction of wall paintings and reliefs. When the photogrammetric model is finished, orthophotos will serve as a basis for digital line drawings that will be of fundamental help for the conservation and reconstruction work. The reconstruction work runs parallel to the conservation and is based on photogrammetry, notes, and records, as well as drawings of early researchers and travelers. According to present estimates, we will be able to reconstruct c. 95% of the original scene material of KV 11. A damage catalogue accompanied by a detailed plan for conservation treatment form the basis for the sustainable conservation of the tomb in the upcoming seasons. The detailed analysis of finds like the sarcophagus fragments will possibly help to reconstruct the burial equipment of Ramesses III or even other royal burials. With the risk management maps, conservation methods, and our Site Management Plan, we will be able to reconstruct the tomb systematically, make it structurally safe and accessible again for visitors, and provide additional information material for tourists in the future. After the final processing of the data collected in this season, subsequent reports will present the final 3D model of the tomb, a detailed description of the sondage, and further results of our field work.

[80] We would like to thank Lyla for sharing this information with us during the 3rd Workshop of The Ramesses III (KV 11) Publication and Conservation Project in Berlin in February 2018.

[81] See Edwin C. Brock, "The Tomb of Merenptah and its Sarcophagi," in Nicholas Reeves (ed.), *After Tut'ankhamun: Research and Excavation in the Royal Necropolis at Thebes* (London, 1992), 122–40.

[82] See Edwin C. Brock, "Conservation of the Sarcophagus of Ramesses VI. Piecing together a Three-Dimensional Puzzle," in Randi Danforth (ed.), *Preserving Egypt's Cultural Heritage: The Conservation Work of the American Research Center in Egypt* (San Antonio, 2010), 63–67; Edwin C. Brock, "The sarcophagus lid of queen Takhat," in Zahi Hawass (ed.), *Egyptology at the Dawn of the Twenty-First Century. Proceedings of the Eight International Congress of Egyptologists, Cairo, 2000*, vol. I (Cairo, 2003), 97–102.

[83] Various authors have already suggested that missing fragments of the Cambridge lid are still expected to be found in KV 11. See Bojana Mojsov, "The Monuments of Ramesses III," in Eric H. Cline and David O'Connor (eds.), *Ramesses III. The Life and Times of Egypt's Last Hero* (Ann Arbor, 2012), 277, 303, n. 37; Elisabeth Thomas, *The Royal Necropolis of Thebes* (Princeton, 1996), 127.

[84] Weber, "First Report, " 62–69.

Fig. 29. Drawings of the sarcophagus fragments J-V-1-1 (top), J-V-4-2 (middle), and J-V-4-1 (below), found in KV 11. Drawings by Lutz Popko and Anke Weber; digital drawings by Anke Weber.

Acknowledgements

We are grateful to the Ministry of Tourism and Antiquities; the Minister of Antiquities, His Excellency Prof. Dr. Khaled el-Enany; the Director of Foreign Missions Affairs, Dr. Nashwa Gaber; the Secretary General, Dr. Mostafa el-Waziri, and the Permanent Committee for receiving the concession for KV 11. Furthermore, we would like to thank the local administration at Luxor for their constant support: Mr. Fathy, Ramadan Ahmed Ali,

Ali Redda, Hussein Fawzy, Negm Eldin Saedey, and Mohamed Abu. We are also very grateful to Kent Weeks for providing necessary data for our surveys, as well as Antonio Morales from the MKTP for lending us the Total Station of his project. Special thanks as well to J. Brett McClain and Nigel Strudwick for supporting our work in the scientific advisory board, and especially to Brett who proofread this article. The staff of Chicago House at Luxor, especially Ray Johnson, was always very supportive and we owe them our gratitude. We are also grateful to the administration of Humboldt-Universität zu Berlin as well as Silvia Kutscher and Frank Kammerzell for their administrative support. Most importantly, we would like to thank the American Research Center in Egypt for providing funding with their Antiquities Endowment Fund for this field season and the Egypt Exploration Society for their Centenary Award which allowed us to collect relevant archive material. Finally, we are very thankful to our Egyptian workmen and especially to our *rais* Ahmed Hussein without whom all our results would not have been achieved.

Book Reviews

Giovanni R. Ruffini. *Life in an Egyptian Village in Late Antiquity: Aphrodito Before and After the Islamic Conquest* (Cambridge-New York: Cambridge University Press, 2018). ISBN 9781107105607. Pp. ix + 233, black and white illustrations.

This volume is a study on life at Aphrodito, a village of the Antaiopolite nome of Upper Egypt, during the sixth century CE. Ruffini makes extensive use of documentary evidence that was found at the village of Kom Ishqaw (ancient Aphrodito) in the early twentieth century, particularly the well-known archive of a local headman, as well as aspiring poet, named Dioskoros. The aim of the author is to provide a social history, at the micro level, of Aphrodito, which was chosen as an ideal case-study for this type of historical analysis thanks to the rich body of documentary evidence that has survived to this day. What emerges from this book is a meaningful and vivid picture of daily life in an Egyptian village in late antiquity. As is made amply clear by Ruffini, the focus is not so much on the urban elite and their viewpoints, but rather on the lives of the "typical" men and women of the time (p. i), which is to be expected considering that papyrological sources play a preeminent role in this study.

The content of the book is structured into twelve chapters organized thematically. These are preceded by a brief preface, lists of contents, figures, and map, as well as a "Cast of Characters." Following the last chapter are an extensive bibliography, a general index and an *index locorum*, all useful tools to navigate the book. A map of late Roman Egypt is provided before Chapter 1; black and white illustrations are placed within the individual chapters.

Chapter 1, *Aphrodito in Egypt*, sets the tone by introducing a story of violent murder and the related charges levied, in particular against a soldier named Menas. The truculent account makes it clear, from the very beginning of the book, that the voices revealed here, as in the ancient documents on which the volume is built, are those of "ordinary" people, their daily concerns, struggles, small and big victories and losses. This is the picture that emerges in Ruffini's work, despite the fact that the archive belonged to a relatively privileged elite family. The chapter then introduces the town of Aphrodito, once an administratively recognized city but reverted to the status of village by the sixth century. A brief history of the excavations carried out at the site is offered, together with a brief analysis of the types of ancient written sources that were found at Aphrodito/Kom Ishqaw. The author highlights the limits of the evidence in portraying a complete picture of public and private life of a village in late antique Egypt. The documents from this town cover a relatively short period of time compared to that of other archives; also, some groups of people, particularly women and children, are either underrepresented or almost completely absent in these sources. Yet, the evidence from Aphrodito offers a unique way to look at a world characterized by the contrasting forces of chaos and order (p. 4). According to Ruffini, this is a world of personal relationships and connections based on trust, rather than an environment driven by class struggle (pp. 25–26). This is the picture of "social late antiquity" based on the daily life of largely non-elite individuals (p. 27). There does not seem to be particular reasons, according to the author, to believe that Aphrodito was a unique settlement; therefore, it can be a useful case study to investigate the social and economic history of rural Egypt in late antiquity on a larger scale (p. 22).

Chapter 2, *A World of Violence*, deals with acts of violence and law-breaking as attested in the documentary evidence from Aphrodito. What matters even more seems to be what strategies men and women of the village employed to react and resolve such episodes of violence. One approach was to appeal to higher local, regional, and even imperial authorities to act as mediators in legal disputes of all sorts. Thus, the focus is on the importance and role of patronage in responding to social conflict, in the context of a world that, however, may not have been characterized by so much anarchy and violence as a cursory look at the written evidence would suggest (p. 41).

Chapter 3, *A World of Law*, is closely related to the previous chapter, inasmuch as it emphasizes the weight of law and of the forces of local and imperial government in addressing disputes among the villagers of Aphrodito, often including the inhabitants of nearby settlements. Ruffini presents in this chapter the main features of the administrative and fiscal system of sixth-century Egypt and, more specifically, highlights the conflict, omnipresent in the documentary material from Aphrodito, that existed among regional and village authorities regarding tax collection. It is

Journal of the American Research Center in Egypt 56 (2020), 245–258
doi: http://dx.doi.org/10.5913/jarce.56.2020.r015

apparent how this was a particularly heartfelt matter for a village that was, at least on paper, fiscally independent from the capital of its nome.

In Chapter 4, *Dioskoros, Caught in Between*, the focus is again on the headman Dioskoros, in particular his official complaints concerning thefts and trespassing over his properties. This part of the volume provides a vivid picture of the difficulties characterizing the relations among different groups of people, chiefly shepherds and landowners, both within Aphrodito and from nearby villages. The documents highlight, in Ruffini's opinion, how "local social pressures" conflicted with and undermined the weight of the law at the level of the village, leading to alternative means in order to achieve resolutions to such conflicts (p. 73).

Chapter 5, *Working in the Fields*, deals with agricultural estates and the relations between landowners and tenants. It also touches upon the subject of tax collection and the issues that stem from it (at a local level). Ruffini believes that the evidence from Aphrodito does not support the view of rural Egypt as a world dominated by a few very large estates (such as, for example, that of Flavius Apion in Oxyrhynchos) with their owners oppressing those with less or no economic means.

In Chapter 6, *Town Crafts and Trades*, the focus shifts from farmers and landowners to those occupations not directly related to farm work. The chapter highlights the existence of professional groups that are less represented, yet still visible, in the documentary evidence. An important point made by the author is the difference in the degree of specialization of labor, which was considerably higher in the bigger cities of southern Egypt than in villages like Aphrodito (p. 106). Another essential takeaway of this chapter is that Aphrodito reveals a society in which people were, at a local level, very familiar with each other and where trust was the defining feature of social and economic interactions.

The religious landscape of Aphrodito is at the center of Chapter 7, *Looking to Heaven*. Evidence for the degree of Christianization of the village by the sixth century CE comes in large part from onomastics, as well as from information about local churches and patrons' donations to religious institutions such as monasteries. The latter became major players in the economy of the village and of the surrounding region, following a pattern attested throughout Egypt. The geography of Christianity at Aphrodito is far from being well-known, Ruffini reminds us, yet there is clear evidence of close connections between villagers and institutions like churches and monasteries. Christianity was undoubtedly a pervasive presence in the life of sixth century Aphrodito, but revealed itself more in matters of day-to-day life, at least on the basis of the available evidence (p. 127).

Chapter 8, *From Cradle to Grave*, tackles what can be reconstructed about several aspects of life at Aphrodito, in particular birth, death, health and disease, marriage, and divorce. What characterizes all of these facets of the human experience in the written record is that they are generally conceived and treated as legal transactions, with little to no space left for the expression of emotions and feelings such as love. As mentioned earlier on, women are underrepresented, although not absent, in Dioskoros's archive.

Chapter 9, *Aphrodito's Women*, emphasizes how businesswomen rarely appear in the documentary sources, which nonetheless testify to the existence of "well-born" women. These were individuals of high socio-economic status and were often actively involved in matters related to their family business. Although more evidence is available for a female elite in Antinoopolis and the areas surrounding Aphrodito, the existence of wealthy, high-status women in that village is attested in the documentary record; they were, however, a minority compared to a large percentage of economically impoverished women. More broadly, Ruffini investigates, in this chapter, the gender roles of women, including widows, in Aphrodito and their depiction in the available documentary and literary sources.

In Chapter 10, *Big Men and Strangers*, Ruffini engages once more with the image of Aphrodito as a world characterized by uncertainty, abuse, and violence. These conflicts, often concerning available resources, arose among villagers and between villagers and outsiders. It is to find protection and achieve conflict resolution that the inhabitants of Aphrodito, including Dioskoros, sought after powerful and influential men, from a local and regional level all the way to the imperial capital, Constantinople.

Chapter 11, *Life in the Big City*, shows the deeply interconnected world of Dioskoros and his village, Aphrodito. The focus is on the city of Antinoopolis, the capital of southern Egypt, where Dioskoros moved at a later stage in his career, before returning to Aphrodito once again. As Ruffini tells us, Antinoopolis was a significantly more cosmopolite world than Aphrodito, offering more opportunities not only in terms of business, but also in entertainment and education. A significant portion of the chapter is reserved to a discussion of what is known—or can be inferred—about the legal, as well as literary, education of Dioskoros, whose writings showcase an interesting mix (albeit of debatable quality) between law and poetry (p. 157).

The book ends with Chapter 12, *Conclusion*, in which the author deals with evidence about Aphrodito in the early Islamic period (although less extensively—perhaps—than one might have expected based on the subtitle of the book). What emerges from documentary evidence of the late seventh and early eighth century is, according to Ruffini, a world that did not dramatically change following the Islamic conquest. Nevertheless, the same sources point to some differences, including a stronger presence of the army and, more broadly, of direct orders from the new central government (p. 207). Another important conclusion drawn by the author is that Aphrodito was likely not so dissimilar from the many other villages that formed a large part of rural Egypt, as well as of the Roman world, in late antiquity. It is this world, in which people lived and were affected by very pragmatic concerns (although not impermeable to the influence of the bigger towns and cities) that this book has so beautifully described at the level of micro-history.

Ruffini's work is a welcome addition—as well as a valuable contribution—to the study of Egypt in late antiquity. It builds on the work done in recent decades by leading papyrologists such as R. Bagnall, J.-L. Fournet, J. Keenan, and L. S. B. MacCoull just to name a few, and offers an inspiring discussion of a deeply fascinating period, which intersects Classical Greco-Roman traditions at one end and the Islamic world at the other.

The book will be of definite interest to an academic audience, including both scholars and undergraduate and graduate students, with an interest in late Roman Egypt and, more broadly, the Mediterranean world of late antiquity. A wider, interested audience will also find the volume an accessible and fruitful read. Indeed, this book could not offer better proof of how documentary evidence is instrumental in bringing ancient society back to life, in a way that can be together meaningful and utterly enjoyable.

Nicola Aravecchia
Washington University in St. Louis

Glennise West, *The* Tekenu *and Ancient Egyptian Funerary Ritual*. Archaeopress Egyptology 23 (Oxford: Archaeopress, 2019). ISBN 9781789691825. Pp. 300, 362 figures (color and black & white), 1 table.

This publication is a reworked PhD thesis that investigates the *tekenu*, an enigmatic object that is sometimes shown as part of the funeral procession in Egyptian tomb scenes. Represented as an amorphous sack-like object that can also evince anthropomorphic features, it was dragged by priests to the cemetery along with the coffin and box containing the canopic jars. Unlike the latter items that are archaeologically well attested, a *tekenu*-shaped object has never been confidently identified amongst a tomb or mortuary-related assemblage. Nor is the *tekenu* mentioned in any funerary text apart from the abbreviated texts accompanying the scenes. These factors have naturally encouraged speculation concerning the *tekenu*' s nature as well as its role in funerary rituals and beliefs, but this volume from Archaeopress is the first full-length monograph devoted solely to this curious icon.

The beginning of the first chapter offers a very general overview of Egyptian funerary practice and belief. Strangely, the *tekenu* itself is not mentioned until page 4. The aim of this long introduction, which includes a summary of the elements that constituted an individual, eventually becomes apparent: The revivification of the deceased required the reunification of the body with the *ka*. It is "therefore conceivable that the non-royal might desire some reference to the Ka within the repertoire of his tomb decoration" (p. 3) implying that there was no reference to the *ka* in the tomb. This problematic claim signals the final conclusions regarding the function of the *tekenu* (see below). After discussion of some of the challenges of the study (pp. 4–5), the author moves onto a literature review (pp. 6–21). This is certainly useful as on overview of different interpretations of the *tekenu* and one is struck here by the variety of explanations that the ambiguity of the evidence allows for. For example: the *tekenu* as a sacrifice; as a component of a skin ritual; as a relic of prehistoric ritual practices; as a disguised priest; as a divine icon; or as a so-called corn Osiris. These explanations are ultimately rejected (pp. 19–21) with surprisingly little critical analysis of the underlying arguments or examination of the relevant evidence. As a result, the reader is left wanting more and is less inclined to be convinced by the author's own alternative interpretation.

A case in point is the idea proposed by experts in Egyptian funerary practice such as Assmann, Hornung, and Ikram (among others) (pp. 20, 266) that the *tekenu* represents embalming waste taken to the cemetery to be buried apart from the body. This theory is summarily rejected, as according to the author "One would expect some physical evidence of the *tekenu* if it contained 'leftovers' from the mummification process" (p. 20). There is no further qualification so it is unclear whether the author is unaware of the vast evidence for burials of embalming waste from Egyptian cemeteries, or having reviewed all this evidence, has decided there can be no connection with the *tekenu*. In any case, given the author's own conclusion that the *tekenu* appears to be covered in a cloth or skin (p. 189) that effectively disguises its true material nature, it is difficult to understand how the author can be so certain of this point. Strangely, much more space is devoted to discussing and rejecting a theory for which there is no valid evidence and that has not been accepted by mainstream Egyptologists, namely that the *tekenu* was a shamanic priest who would be ritually reborn as an entheogenic mushroom (pp. 14, 20).

Two very brief chapters follow the introductory chapter. Chapter 2 (two and a half pages) is devoted to aims and methods, whereas Chapter 3 (ten pages) is devoted to a *tekenu* typology. "Aims and methods" is effectively a description in extended point form of how the book was researched and how the catalogue is organised. Importantly, the author stresses that chronology plays no part in the organisation of the catalogue, as there is no diachronic analysis (p. 23). Given that representations of the *tekenu* span approximately 2,000 years, a period when we know that ideas and practices relating to the afterlife changed dramatically, this might have been an interesting type of analysis to apply. The chapter on Typology (pp. 25–35) is more substantial. Importantly, the author bases her four main types on scenes where an object is labelled as a *tekenu* (twelve cases). Thus, securely identified, the author can work outwards to discuss the occurrence of these types from forty-four different tombs. These representations are conveniently organised and illustrated in some very good figures (pp. 30–34) that give the reader an overview of all known *tekenu* depictions at a glance. The use of colour images, wherever these were available, greatly enhances the value of this section. The stringent criteria for identifying the *tekenu*, however, were not strictly applied. The identification of Type 4 "standing human figure" is controversial at best given it only occurs once and in a context where the relationship of the labels to the image is unclear (pp. 86–87, see below).

Chapter 4 is a complete, fully illustrated catalogue of all known occurrences of the *tekenu*, whereas Chapter 5 is an analysis and interpretation of these. The catalogue is well designed, and the author draws on extensive research amongst both published and unpublished sources. The level of descriptive detail is thorough, and the rich illustrative material ensures that this chapter will be a reference work for future research. Unfortunately, the practice of using red boxes with thick contours and hanging shadows to draw attention to elements of the figures detracts from the usefulness of some of the illustrations. In contrast to the description, the analytical components of chapters 4 and 5 fall short of an authoritative treatment, especially concerning the reading of the texts that accompany the scenes. In lieu of proper source criticism, the author resorts to comparing translations. Why one translation is accepted over another is unclear: For example, the author's own translation of a badly damaged text in TT20 (p. 88) "producing water over/on him for his city, when he [? passes away]" is preferred to Helck's "The fur is on [when] he [goes] out of his town" without further discussion (Wolfgang Helck, *Untersuchungen zur Thinitenzeit*, Ägyptologische Abhandlungen 45 [Wiesbaden: Harrassowitz, 1987], 34). This is a problem as the connection of the *tekenu* with ritual purifications is later taken as fact (p. 214). Elsewhere (pp. 177–78), two possible translations of *ḏt* ("body" and "eternity") are given but the issue is not satisfactorily resolved. Later (pp. 214–15), the author relies on the translation "body" to argue that the *tekenu* re-joins the corpse. This analytical weakness also pervades some of the iconographic analysis. For example, the identification of a standing human figure in TT20 as a *tekenu* (Type 4; pp. 4, 213) uncritically follows the suggestion of Serrano Delgado (José M. Serrano Delgado, "A contribution to the study of the tekenu and its role in Egyptian funerary ritual," *ZÄS* 138 [2011], 150–62). While it is an interesting theory, other interpretations remain unexplored and the unique type then plays an outsized role in the reconstruction of the "journey of the *tekenu*" (pp. 222–23).

Chapter 6 discusses the special scenes in TT20 and TT100. Given the interesting discussion of evidence that points to the burial of the *tekenu* separate from the body with other items including a sledge and hair (p. 220) a review of archaeological evidence for extra-sepulchral deposits would have been worth including.

Chapter 7 investigates the origins of the *tekenu*, including the possible associations that the *tekenu* had with prehistoric bovine burials in the Sudan, Early Dynastic anthropoid figures, as well as the so-called biloped emblem with which it shares some similar iconographic traits. The conclusions are for the most part highly speculative. This is unsurprising given that most of these topics are as enigmatic, if not more so, than the *tekenu* itself. The argumentation is not always convincing: the linking of the alleged disappearance of co-burials of humans and bovids in the Late Old Kingdom to the first appearance of the *tekenu* (p. 239) is purely circumstantial, and the circumstances are unclear. Another argument for a potential relationship of the *tekenu* to shrouded figures depicted in royal festival scenes is circular as it relies on a functional parity proposed by the author. More convincing is the rejection of any relationship to the Opening of the Mouth Ceremony in Chapter 8. The final chapter presents a short selection of Pyramid Texts and argues that the *tekenu* was an effigy used to transport the *ka* to the tomb. Circumstantial evidence is cited to link the journey of the *tekenu* and the body to the tomb with the ascent of the King and his *ka* to the sky. As the *tekenu* is not mentioned in the Pyramid Texts, and the *ka* is not mentioned in any of the texts that refer directly to the *tekenu*, this is a difficult argument to make and seems less plausible that some of the current ideas concerning the *tekenu* that are rejected out of hand in Chapter 1. As most of the sources for the *tekenu* are of the New Kingdom, the absence of a discussion of any New Kingdom funerary texts is puzzling, but is presumably due to the synchronic outlook of the entire volume.

The great worth of this volume is that it gathers all the sources for the *tekenu* in one place and presents them with copious illustrations, many of them in colour. The catalogue is certainly the longest and most-detailed part of the book and will be of considerable use to anyone who is interested in Egyptian funerals and their representation on tomb walls. Unfortunately, the other parts of the book are much more uneven and suffer from methodological weaknesses that adversely affect both analysis and interpretation. Those hoping that this book will provide a compelling answer to the question "what is a *tekenu*?" will be disappointed. The *tekenu* remains firmly shrouded and impenetrable, just as the artists who painted the funeral scenes discussed in this book probably intended.

Christian Knoblauch
Swansea University, Wales, UK

Julia Budka (ed.), *AcrossBorders 2: Living in New Kingdom SAI*. AESL 1 (Vienna: Austrian Academy of Sciences Press, 2020). ISBN 9783700184027. Pp. 599, 2 folding plans, illustrations, maps.

AcrossBorders 2 is the second installment of extensive archaeological publication of the New Kingdom settlement and environ of Sai Island, thanks to a European Research Council grant from 2013–2017. With its location halfway between the Second and Third Cataracts in Nubia, on the border of Egypt and Nubia, Sai Island is an ideal location to study questions of multiculturalism, cultural-entanglement, and Egyptian imperialism, in addition to life in a border region. Budka and her team strive to address these themes and many others through archaeology and science on both a micro and macro level.

The second volume, *Living in New Kingdom Sai*, complements the first. It adds archaeological analysis of areas SAV1 East and SAV1 West. It supplements the archaeological analysis of area SAV1 North, primarily discussed in the first volume. The small finds and stratigraphy are discussed in detail. Most importantly, it publishes the primary data for multiple scientific analyses for all regions in order to address what life was like at Sai. This volume includes analysis of the region's geoarchaeology and micromorphological sediment, architectural studies, ceramic analysis and petrographic analysis, ethno-archaeological approaches to Strontium Isotope Analysis and Instrumental Neutron Activation Analysis (INNA). This is an exceedingly important archaeological reference book that every library supporting these studies should have. The archaeological work and publication are of the highest quality and stand as examples for other excavations to match.

The book is divided into eight chapters; most were written by Julia Budka. I note where other specialists authored chapters below. Each is the final publication of this material and provides extensive amounts of primary data for other researchers to access.

"Chapter 1: Introduction" lays out the background to the volume. It talks about the team's investigations of Sai as a key settlement for understanding how the colonial policies of Egypt impacted Nubia during the New Kingdom. The site was in use from Prehistory to the Ottoman era due to its strategic location. As the New Kingdom is the focus of their research, copious evidence from the Dynasty 18 reigns of Ahmose to Amenhotep III is discussed. Yet most of Chapter 1 outlines what the reader needs to know to understand the quality and depth of the team's work. It summarizes excavations prior to 2013, especially those of the French SIAM project. It details the archaeological methods used for excavation, surface collection, photography, mapping, 3D scanning, geoarchaeological survey, and geological sampling. And it explicitly discusses the project's well-thought-out archaeological goals, based on research questions and hypotheses, and how they planned to achieve them. The project, as a whole, is looking to give a "bottom-up" understanding of this multicultural society by taking both a micro and macro approach.

"Chapter 2: Geologic Realities for the New Kingdom Town of Sai Island" (by Budka and Martina Ullmann) includes detailed geoarchaeological research in Sai's natural features and environment focused on how humans adopted and adapted their surroundings. Budka's team has conducted many micromorphological and petrographic studies all over the island. Their first major goal was to locate where the famous Sai Sandstone, used in building projects from Esna to Gebel Barkal, came from by compiling and analyzing the textual evidence for the use of Sai's sandstone and taking samples from all over the island. Two or three locations were likely, but one large quarry was found on the east side of the island. Their second major geoarchaeological goal was to find where ships landed at the island. No formally constructed harbor existed, but instead they identified three naturally occurring locations to dock boats. The main one was on the east side of the island, in a location that helped the people of Sai control river traffic, load and unload boats, and it was located close to the large sandstone quarry, making the exporting of sandstone easier.

"Chapter 3: The New Kingdom Town – The Excavation and the Architecture" details excavations that Budka's team carried out from 2013–2017 in three different areas: SAV1 East, SAV1 West, SAV1 Northeast.[1] The interior of Sai's temple-town is orthogonal and displays several similarities to Buhen, Amara West, and Sesebi. All excavated areas break into three different archaeological phases, dating from the beginning to the end of the Eighteenth Dynasty. It was an active, evolving city. SAV 1 Northeast is a small section of the town wall dating to the middle of Dynasty 18. SAV1 West contains the exterior wall with an interior "wall-street" separating the enclosure wall from the buildings. The micromorphology showed that this "wall-street" was a heavily used traffic route during Dynasty 18. The team excavated six domestic structures in SAV1 West, all of modest, mud-brick construction. Like SAV1 North's domestic units, those in SAV1 West show evidence for household activities such as milling and bread baking. The contemporary area in SAV1 East, however, is of a different character, even though it was still made of mud-brick. It is located on the east side, only 30–50 meters north of Temple A and near the ports. Its architectural remains also aligned with the temple and were likely built at the same time. Although this area underwent continuous renovation in each phase, it contained workshops and storage magazines; its cellars were dug into the foundation and held many seal impressions, some mentioning the names of kings. The area contains evidence for

[1] Excavations conducted in SAV1 North were discussed in the first *AcrossBorders* volume and in other publications.

the cooking of food, including animals, as is seen both in the small finds and the micromorphology. Budka believes that this area was connected to the official administrative function of Sai Island and was associated with Temple A's storage facilities.

"Chapter 4: The Material Remains from the New Kingdom town" offers a full discussion of all small finds (ceramic and non-ceramic) dating to the New Kingdom found by the AcrossBorders project. Approximately half of the finds date from post-New Kingdom to Ottoman contexts. The chapter includes many line drawings, photographs, and select lists of finds in addition to a full list of their nearly 5,000 recorded objects which is available online (https://voi.org/10.1553/AcrossBorders2_Appendix_List-of-Finds). In general, the material assemblage is very similar to what is found in other New Kingdom settlements such as Elephantine, Amarna, Askut, Buhen, and Amara West. The majority of finds also relate to activities of weaving, fishing, and grinding grain. Unsurprisingly, the objects found most frequently include pottery, bone, charcoal, and stone tools. But more unusual finds were made as well, such as jewelry, seals and seal impressions, stone and faience vessels, scarabs, stelae fragments, figurines (especially zoological ones), and tokens or gaming pieces. Stone tools and macro-lithics are discussed in detail, as well as plaster and mortar. Moreover, the majority of finds at Sai are of the Egyptian type, despite the fact that this town is located in Nubia, an "inconsistency" which is normal for this period. Budka divides the pottery fabric into six main groups according to where the clays originated and thus could differentiate imported wares from local wares. Both Egyptian (wheel-made) and Nubian (hand-made) pottery exists throughout all contexts at Sai, and hand-made cooking pots and storage vessels are quite common. Additionally, hybrid vessels or imitation wares are common. Thus, we see that Egyptians and Nubians were creating a multicultural society at Sai.

"Chapter 5: The Environmental Remains" (by Frits Heinrich, Annette Hansen, Julia Budka, Helmut Sattmann, and Sara Schnedl) shares the scientific tests of archaeological materials to learn about life and death at Sai. The team completed a vast amount of archaeobotanical studies to look at various relationships between plants and people; all data are presented in extensive tables. Samples came from many different locations, but some of the best were from mud bricks because they produce a closed context for botanicals. Mud bricks were made at a fairly standard size in at Sai, and wild grasses and weeds were used as temper. Wood was often used as timber. The Sai people cultivated both barley and emmer wheat; however, more barley was used than emmer, which is unusual because in most contemporary parts of Egypt, more emmer was grown than barley. They also ate lentils, doum palm, date palm, cucumbers, grapes, and watermelon. People at Sai also ate cattle, sheep/goats, and pigs. The proportions among these three domestic animals eaten changed at different points of time and in different contexts, which might be significant to their lived history. Fish, birds, and reptile bones also were found and were likely remains from their diets, and examples of mollusks were often found in cellars and storage places. Also recovered were bones of some wild animals, including occasional hare, hippo, baboon, and gazelle bones. Considering that gazelle were among Nubia's standard tributes to Egypt, it is not surprising that some gazelles were found at Sai. Human remains were rare at Sai because the team was excavating within a town; adults were buried in cemeteries outside of towns. However, the bones of infants and children were found buried in ceramic vessels in houses, which was a normal practice for Egyptians. Many of the human remains point to an unhealthy, hard life. They display evidence of stress, infectious disease and poor nutrition, and two show that they died from head trauma.

"Chapter 6: People on Sai: Prosopographical Contributions to the 'social fabric' of Sai in the New Kingdom" (by Johannes Auenmüller) examines the names and titles of people who came from New Kingdom Sai in an effort to understand their administrative structure and social connections. The seventy-four textual sources cataloged and discussed from this chapter incorporate objects found over the last 150 years in addition to a few from the current excavations. Interestingly, the majority of inscriptions date to the reigns of Hatshepsut/Thutmose III or Ramesses II, which seems to be the "heyday" for Sai's importance as a "bridge-head" to Kerma and a reflection of Egypt's political interest in controlling Nubia. The person in charge of Lower Nubia, including Sai, was the King's Son of Kush, and five of the King's Sons are attested in the evidence from Sai. Second in command was the Deputy of Kush and two deputies are mentioned in connection with Sai. But both of those officials were regional; Sai was actually controlled by a mayor. Because Sai, and other Lower Nubian temple-towns at this time were administered as *mnn.w*-fortresses, a mayor held the highest level of local authority. Four mayors are known by name. A handful of lower level people are also known from objects that are mostly related to burials; these include priests, scribes, and a few women. Because of Sai's location near Nubian gold mines, it also supplied those expeditions. Thus, one gold worker's tomb with many objects was found in Sai. To elucidate his role more, this chapter includes a full discussion of all gold workers from New Kingdom Nubia.

"Chapter 7: The New Kingdom town in its Macrocosm—Sai within Upper Nubia" is a short and helpful overview that everyone should read. It places Sai into the larger contexts of political, regional, economic, cultural, and religious history while highlighting places of evolving, complex, intercultural entanglements. Essentially, Sai Island was a temple-town community built by Egyptians, run by a mayor and overseen by the King's Son of Kush. It functioned very similarly to and in connection with the nearby towns of Sesebi, Tombos, Soleb, and Amara West. With the colonization of Nubia in the New Kingdom, Egyptian kingship changed to incorporate the control of this area into the royal ideology. And so, we find the deification of the pharaoh in Nubian temples. Sai was the main city of Egyptian administration especially during the reigns of Thutmose III to Amenhotep III. The Egyptians were interested in this place because it was in a strategic location both for the control of the Nubians to the south and the control of goldmining to the east. The invention of gold grinding mills in the New Kingdom opened up new regions for gold extraction. Additionally, sandstone from Sai was exported to sites in Nubia and Upper Egypt. The elite cemetery at Sai gives evidence for Egyptian officials and religion. The non-elite cemetery shows cultural entanglement and a mix of both Egyptian and Nubian traditions, but with the Egyptian religion being adopted by local Nubians. The cemeteries and skeletons also show sexual entanglement and multicultural families.

"Chapter 8: Sai as an Egyptian Microcosm in Nubia" is the cumulative analysis of all of the archaeology, science, comparison, and theory from the previous chapters, to reveal how people lived at Sai. Most scholars will benefit from this chapter. It also ends with a concise summary of the entire book, as well as Sai's history and chronology. It might be a good strategy to read this summary first, and then dive into the rest of the book. In this chapter, Budka explores if we can tell who lived at Sai, how they lived, and how multiple cultures interacted in a town. Discussions of women and children, state and domestic religion, and domestic activities shed light on those questions, as do comparisons of life and material culture at Sai with other New Kingdom towns, especially Elephantine and Abydos in Egypt as well as Sesebi, Amara West, and other towns in Lower Nubia. All evidence points to a multicultural society in which the Egyptians were the dominant culture.

My only minor critique of *AcrossBorders 2* is that, even though in Chapter 8 Budka discusses the importance of moving away from earlier biases and the simple categories of "Nubian" and "Egyptian," advocating for a deeper discussion of complex, cultural entanglement, these categories are so ingrained that they still deeply frame the discussion. We see them, for example, in the comparisons between towns where Sai is compared to contemporary towns in Egypt and others founded by Egyptians in Lower Nubia, but not to a Nubian town. Even an asynchronous comparison to a Nubian town from the Middle Kerma or Classic Kerma periods would have provided the other needed point of view. However, on the whole, this is a seminal book, expanding our understanding of life in a New Kingdom border town through archaeology.

Kate Liszka
California State University San Bernardino

Reg Clark. *Securing Eternity: Ancient Egyptian Tomb Protection from Prehistory to the Pyramids* (Cairo: AUC Press, 2019). ISBN 978-9774169021. Pp. 346, 150 color photographs and tomb plans.

When mentioning "tomb protection" within an ancient Egyptian context, one automatically thinks of the sphere of religion and ritual, namely the magical performance, objects, decorations, and texts that were meant to protect the tomb in order to let the body as well as the spiritual components of the deceased survive in eternity. The reason for such a quick assumption is the great popularity of ancient Egyptian funerary religion today, and the abundance of textual and material artifacts with magical purpose found in burial contexts of all ages, from prehistory to the later periods of ancient Egyptian history. However, the ancient Egyptians were also clearly concerned with a more practical kind of protection. One which did not focus on obtaining the blessing of the gods through magic, but which was based on the development of complex and smart techniques of construction for the substructure and superstructure of the tomb itself, in order for the latter to remain inaccessible and secure through time.

The book under review is a new, exhaustive study on the fascinating historical development of techniques aimed at tomb security, both on a royal as well as on a private level. In the Preface, the author writes that this is a book written for the "Egyptophile student" and the "general reader." However, his detailed analysis and an in-depth account on the evolution of tomb architecture from the Predynastic period to the reign of Sneferu in the Fourth Dynasty makes this book a welcome contribution within the scholarly community as well. Although many previous studies on tomb architecture have discussed the same topic, none has attempted to compare theories of construction and security measures among many different typologies of burial contexts, both royal and private.

The author's choice to limit his study only to the earliest historical evidence (Prehistory to the early Fourth Dynasty) is understandable, given the vast and complex archaeological burial contexts he has to compare from southern to northern Egypt. The complexity of interpreting these early burial contexts is due especially to the fact that one has to deal most often with incomplete archaeological evidence and partially or almost totally destroyed tomb architecture under- and above-ground. Moreover, as the author states in the Introduction (pp. 1–2), the period under consideration in this book is when the main architectural characteristics and techniques of ancient Egyptian tombs were developed, from pit to mound to a complex superstructure, such as the pyramid. It would however be desirable, in the future, if a comprehensive and descriptive study that would continue this kind of analysis would appear, by taking into consideration also the very peculiar tomb structures of the other periods of pharaonic history, in order to understand in more detail how the technical achievements of tomb security produced in the earlier periods were employed and changed by the architects of later periods in different regions in Egypt.

This book is a very well-organized study, whose chapters follow a linear, chronological, and thematic analysis, starting with discussing the need for tomb security in ancient Egyptian society (Chapter 1) and continuing with the description of the various types of tomb architecture attested in Egypt for each period taken into consideration (Chapters 2 to 7). Finally, in the last chapter (Chapter 8), the author resumes the main issues discussed in the book: the series of architectural responses to tomb robbery and the techniques for securing the substructure, the access route, as well as the superstructure, when these two latter were present. He concludes by pointing out how the need for tomb security and the fear of tomb robbery have been the main reasons for innovation and development of tomb architecture.

The book is accompanied by extensive endnotes where the author includes and discusses a very detailed and exhaustive bibliography. The numerous tomb plans and sections added to the tomb descriptions help the reader to understand the series of different architectural solutions for enhancing tomb security while two excursuses on more specific techniques such as the use of backfills, blockings, and portcullises in tomb architecture, complement the tomb descriptions with more technical information.

In Chapter 2, the author shows that it is because of the emergence of an elite with larger and more equipped tombs during the Naqada period that the need for tomb security starts to be taken into consideration. While reading through this book on all the efforts that ancient Egyptian architects made for developing architectural techniques aimed at ensuring protection against tomb robbery throughout the centuries, one cannot avoid thinking how, in the end, royal and non-royal tomb owners were concerned about one and the same danger: that their "house of eternity" could be violated and their funerary cult would cease to be carried on, no matter how influential they were in society or how loved and pious they were in front of the gods. It would be interesting to continue this kind of study by looking at tomb structures and their securing techniques in the later Old Kingdom and throughout the New Kingdom, when tomb decoration includes more consistently magical spells and iconographical motives whose distribution on tomb walls and spaces is not casual but always related to specific architectural spaces.

In conclusion, this book adds interesting new information and points of analysis to a field, the archaeology of death, which remains one of the most fascinating within the study of the past and of ancient Egypt in particular.

Rita Lucarelli
University of California at Berkeley

Roger S. Bagnall and Gaëlle Tallet (eds.). *The Great Oasis of Egypt: the Kharga and Dakhla Oases in Antiquity* (Cambridge: Cambridge University Press, 2019). ISBN 978-1-108-48216-5. Pp. xviii + 344, 131 figures, 5 tables.

The Kharga and Dakhla oases of Egypt's Western Desert are, on first appearance, something of a contradiction. The harsh environment surrounding them does not seem conducive to the same way of life as we see on the Nile, yet the communities which grew around the oases were nevertheless prosperous throughout antiquity. Moreover, thanks in part to their very place on the "fringe" of the Egyptian world, the oases remained a focal point for trade. The result, according to Roger Bagnall and Gaëlle Tallet, is a region "characterized by both extreme isolation and wide-ranging connectivity" (p. 5). A similar contrast can be applied to scholarship on the oases as well: though far from the mainstream, these sites furnish ample connections both to each other and to Egyptian society at large. The goal of this collection, then, is to dissect what makes the oases distinctive, as well as to show their applicability to broader scholarship.

This is accomplished through a set of sixteen chapters, written primarily by specialists currently working at one or more oasis sites; these are further divided into four thematic and methodological sections. Naturally the oases' isolation and connectivity also serve as guide here: environmental factors are at the center of Part 1 (Chapters 2–4), while both Parts 2 (Chapters 5–7) and 3 (Chapters 8–12) discuss systems of exchange. Finally, Part 4 (Chapters 13–16) tackles the far more nebulous problem of cultural influences upon the oases, and how to place "oasis culture" into a broader Egyptian and Libyan context.

Thematically, oasis ecology and environment are excellent starting places for the volume, given the clear impact of both on the oases' economy and settlement patterns. Jean-Paul Bravard's contribution (Chapter 2) demonstrates this very well through its overview of geology and hydrology. Isolation is immediately apparent: the oases are surrounded by desert, and are not even themselves a unitary feature, but rather a constellation of growing and shrinking springs. Their harshness is further underlined by the numerous pathologies found in Françoise Dunand and Roger Lichtenberg's osteological study (Chapter 3). The oases perhaps *were* too harsh for settled life to be sustainable, at least as known in the Nile valley: Bravard finds a precipitous decline in arable soils over the course of the third century CE. Erosion, coupled with lowering water tables, may have rendered large-scale agriculture impractical, leading to the abandonment of cities like Trimithis (modern Amheida) at the end of the Roman period and a shift towards a more caravan-focused economy.

The city of Trimithis is the focus of Paola Davoli's contribution (Chapter 4), the last in this section. Thematically, this chapter feels somewhat out of place, as its focus is firmly on urbanism rather than the environment. Nevertheless, this chapter provides a thorough overview of the fourth century CE remains, including a preliminary city plan and tentative spatial analysis. This chapter will be of greatest interest to Roman historians and archaeologists, especially those interested in ancient urbanism. As the author notes, the site provides an exceptional view of a late antique city. Since Trimithis is one of the most important sites in the region and reappears frequently in the following chapters, it also serves as useful background for any reader.

If Part 1 dealt largely with the oases' isolation, Parts 2 and 3, thanks to their economic focus, are all about connectivity. Part 2 approaches this through the lens of redistributive processes: tribute (Chapter 5), provisioning (Chapter 6), and taxation (Chapter 7). The first of these, by Roger Bagnall and Gaëlle Tallet, charts the administrative history of the oases, with an emphasis on the site of Hibis. There is little definitive evidence for a Pharaonic administrative center in Kharga, though they suggest that Hibis became one following the foundation of its temple of Amun in the Saite period. Hibis itself is largely unexcavated outside of the Amun temple; as such the authors have had to infer connectivity and centralization largely from temple records and iconography (alongside a few major inscriptions like the Greater Dakhla Stele). What evidence there is suggests that the temple of Amun served as economic center for the oases, and in turn sent the oases' tribute to the temples of Upper Egypt. While the Greco-Roman period does bring slightly more clarity, including a unified "Great Oasis" district, the region remains notable for its irregularities and historical obscurity. The authors conclude that they cannot say when, over even if, Hibis became the sole nome capital.

Chapters 6 and 7 present the oasis economy through its papyrological evidence. Rodney Ast (Chapter 6) provides an excellent analysis of the structure of Late Roman agriculture, drawing upon the Hibis Codex (SB 14.11938), the Kellis Agricultural Account Book (KAB), and numerous ostracon "well tags" found pressed into amphora seals. Much of his analysis focuses on terminology: first Greco-Egyptian words for wells, then Roman military titulature. As much as the Roman army appropriated the oases' agricultural surplus through coercion, Ast makes it clear that their provisioning system only functioned through the mediation and active participation of local elites. Coercive systems also loom large in Damien Agut-Labordère's contribution (Chapter 7) on temple taxation; the chapter is also notable both for its use of Demotic ostraca and the fact that it sheds light on taxation in the otherwise poorly documented Persian period—including a unique tax on lighting oil.

Wine—"Seth's gift"—was clearly a vital part of the oasis economy and was seemingly one of its major exports; fittingly, the five chapters of Part 3 discuss oasis ceramics in detail. Of particular importance is Chapter 8, a report by Salima Ikram on the North Kharga Oasis Darb Ain Amur Survey (NKODAAS). Like Bravard in his discussion of geology, Ikram does a good job of showing that the oases were not always a unitary feature, but rather a set of disparate locations connected through the movement of people and goods. The three following chapters provide more information on the pottery itself: production and typological patterns (Pascale Ballet, Chapter 9), imported amphorae (Clementina Caputo, Chapter 10), and locally produced kegs (Irene Soto Marín, Chapter 11). Both Ballet and Soto Marín emphasize the importance of these keg or *siga*-type containers, which seem to have been used in both the production and transport of local wine. Amphorae were not common in the oases, Caputo finds; nevertheless, they do reveal distribution patterns. Egyptian vessels make up most of the extant examples from Trimithis, in particular Middle Egyptian LRA 7s, though there were a few examples from the Aegean, Levant, and even Italy and Tunisia. The section concludes with Yaël Chevalier's contribution (Chapter 12), a return to the desert routes of North Kharga. She finds that the site of el-Deir was both a local production center (once again, the ever-present *siga*) as well as an important point of exchange on the tracks connecting Kharga with Dakhla, Middle Egypt, and Nubia. As at Trimithis, ceramics from the Eastern Mediterranean attest to deep connectivity in the Late Roman period. Overall, these five chapters provide concrete quantitative and qualitative evidence for the oases' integration into inter-regional economic systems as both large-scale exporters and importers of wine.

Continuity and change are the central issues of the final section. Examples of peculiar Oasite practices are evident in earlier sections (as in the persistent veneration of Seth), but despite the section's title ("An Oasis Culture?") the chapters of Part 4 focus less on how the oases differed from the rest of Egypt, and more on how Oasite cultural practices evolved over time. In this Olaf Kaper's contribution (Chapter 13) is something of an outlier, as it is the only one to examine pharaonic examples, in this case temple building under Dynasties 18, 19, and 20 (with brief excursuses to the Late period). He finds that while the oases almost certainly fell out of Egyptian control periodically, this left few material remains; our only evidence for Libyan occupation is a decrease in the quality and quantity of temple construction, alongside a decrease in exports and imports. Also of interest is the evidence Kaper provides for a scribal school at the Temple of Thoth at Trimithis—another point of cultural connectivity with Egypt.

The remaining three chapters are firmly within the Roman period, and each tackles in its own way the evolution of elite Egyptian identity in Late Antiquity. Spectacular cultural artifacts are not lacking: Françoise Dunand and Fleur Letellier-Willemin (Chapter 14) present new cartonnage mummies as well as what they identify as a Christian cemetery at el-Deir, Rafaella Cribiore (Chapter 15) describes a well-preserved "schoolhouse" at Amheida, and Susanna

McFadden (Chapter 16) gives an overview of the extensive wall-paintings at the House of Serenos. McFadden gives an apt conclusion not just for her own chapter, but for this section and the volume as a whole. She comments that Alexandria's assumed monopoly on Greco-Egyptian art should be reconsidered. That is, not all high-quality art came directly from Alexandria, and not every skilled artist was looking to Alexandria for inspiration. While we should not discount the influence of the center on the periphery—political, economic, or cultural—we should always be aware of how this is reproduced, reworked, and rendered local by communities on the margin. Thus, in funerary practices as well as literary consumption and production, we also see trends which reflect a traditional mainstream (whether mummification techniques or allusions to Homer), but which have been made intimately local and learned (and used) within the community.

Taken as a whole, this volume is of greatest value to Roman historians and archaeologists, especially those studying Late Antiquity. While the oases do have a long pharaonic history, the sites central to the volume (Trimithis, el-Deir, the North Kharga routes) all provide particularly abundant Roman materials. Naturally it is also relevant to those studying desert communities elsewhere in antiquity, and Egypt's Eastern Desert immediately springs to mind as a parallel. Above all, its appeal perhaps lies in how it shows the deep connection between environment and exchange, resulting in a view of the oases as a sort of Egyptian micro-region along Egypt's western fringe. Or, to borrow another concept from Horden and Purcell, it illustrates the "insular nature" of the oases: their physical isolation only encouraged deeper economic connectivity.

Ryan Evan Reynolds
PhD Candidate, University of California at Berkeley

Marianne Eaton-Krauss. *Bernard V. Bothmer, Egyptologist in the Making, 1912 through July 1946. With Bothmer's own account of his* Escape from Central Europe *in October 1941*. Investigatio Orientis 3 (Münster: Zaphon, 2019). ISBN 9783963270482. 174 pages, 18 figures, 4 color plates.

This volume is a very welcome addition to the increasing number of studies on the intellectual, institutional, and personal history of Egyptology in the twentieth century. It focuses on the early life of Bernhard von Bothmer (from 1946 on, Bernard V. Bothmer), "[f]rom the mid-1950s through the 1980s. (…) the North American among the four most influential historians of ancient Egyptian art" (alongside Cyril Aldred, Hans Wolfgang Müller, and Jacques Vandier). Bothmer (1912–1993), who became Curator and Chairman of the Department of Ancient Art of The Brooklyn Museum and after his retirement from the museum, *Lila Acheson Wallace Professor of Ancient Egyptian Art* at the Institute of Fine Arts, and his younger brother Dietrich von Bothmer (1918–2006), Curator of Greek and Roman Art at the Metropolitan Museum of Art and Chairman of the Department, were both leading figures in the study of ancient art in the United States. Dietrich von Bothmer studied in Oxford and, when caught by the outbreak of the war during a museum tour in the United States, completed his doctorate at Berkeley, received US citizenship and joined the US army before assuming employment at the Metropolitan Museum of Art in 1946. In turn, Bernhard von Bothmer pursued his studies between 1931 and 1938 in Bonn and Berlin. Unable to complete his doctorate before leaving Germany in August 1939, he ultimately arrived in the United States in October 1941, where, after serving in the army, he started his museum career at The Brooklyn Museum in August 1946.

Based on B.V. Bothmer's pocket diaries, personal documents and correspondence, Eaton-Krauss provides a minutely detailed chronological reconstruction of Bothmer's life until 1946, in six chapters: 1) From childhood through secondary schooling; 2) Bernhard and the Stefan George Circle; 3) At university and in the museum; 4) Leaving Germany; 5) From Ascona to America; and 6) New York City and beyond. As an appendix, Bothmer's colorful own account of his "Escape from Central Europe" is published for the first time (pp. 125–51).

While the book under review is admirably detailed in chronicling the events, visits, and acquaintances made by Bothmer within these thirty-four initial years of his life, it remains almost exclusively descriptive and without much analysis and contextualization. It is left to the reader to understand what the "making" of the "Egyptologist in the making" actually means. To be more specific, I will provide here three examples of contextualization for the period of 1928–1939, when Bothmer was aged sixteen to twenty-seven: his affiliation with (the circle around) the poet Stefan George; the political situation in the first years of Nazi Germany; and his university education in Berlin.

An entire chapter is devoted to "Bernhard and the Stefan George Circle," but the impact of George and members of the circle on Bothmer continued beyond the period covered by the book. Testament to this importance is the fact that as early as 1933, Bothmer started to compile a bibliography of all references to the poet and his reception, and continued to work on it after 1946 (pp. 84–85). The time when Bothmer was involved in the circle during George's last six years (1928–1933), when he was aged sixteen to twenty-one, must have been formative for him. George has recently seen a much intensified scholarly reception. To use Kraemer's 2015 summary, he was one of the most prominent literary-social individuals of early twentieth century Germany, at one point compared to Goethe and Hölderlin, charismatic with his holistic pedagogy and elitist intellectualism, "with a poetry inspired by a radical antimodernism as well as the experience of a profoundly outlawed and illegal sexuality," later ostracized for his protofaschist ideology (Max Kraemer, "Review of M. S. Lane, Martin Ruehl (eds.), *A Poet's Reich: Politics and Culture in the George Circle*. Rochester: Camden House, 2011" [H-German, H-Net Reviews. August, 2015] URL: http://www.h-net.org/reviews/showrev.php?id=40347). Hardly anything of this intense research is given here as a context. The chapter starts with the statement that "[a]mong the last youths acquainted with the German poet Stefan George (1868–1933), Bernhard was reportedly the one who most deeply affected him," and conversely, "The Master, as members of the Circle referred to him, occupied a unique place in Bernhard's life beginning in January 1927 when they first met in the atelier of the sculptor Alexander Zschokke" (p. 29). While Eaton-Krauss informs the reader that George and his Circle have increasingly attracted the attention of historians of the Weimar Republic and the Third Reich (for which, see below), she does not disclose anything about a fact certainly essential for Bothmer's development as an adolescent—the obvious pederasty underlying the George Circle. Bothmer was acquainted with the poet by George's friend, Ernst von Morwitz who remained a mentor of the Bothmer brothers for decades—Morwitz eventually entrusted his *Nachlass* to Dietrich von Bothmer. Morwitz would identify handsome adolescents from families of the German nobility who could be introduced to "The Master." One volume of poetry by George, "Der Stern des Bundes," was used as an education guide for the circle. According to the now magisterial biography of George by Thomas Karlauf, this volume of poetry was "the monstrous attempt, to declare, with pedagogical zeal, pederasty the highest spiritual form of existence" (*Stefan George. Die Entdeckung des Charisma* [Munich: Blessing, 2007], 394).[1] Thomas Mann found George's "mystification of pederasty" distasteful. Since the members of the circle used coded language—Eaton-Krauss mentions in a footnote Morwitz's nick-name "Schwarze Wonne" (Black Bliss) and George's use of the term "Süsser" (sweetie) for the adolescent circle members, without pointing to the sexual connotations (p. 30 n. 66)—it is not clear today if homosexuality was practiced within the group (with members who in some cases were as young as thirteen). As Ute Oelmann and Carola Groppe write in their new edition of the correspondence between George and Morwitz: "While the choice of children and adolescents was motivated by homoeroticism and pedophily, the letters do not contain concrete hints that this was practised sexually. It has to remain unclear if the affection for male adolescents who were docketed as handsome by the circle and by George himself actually led to sexualized violence against them or not (…) Many passages in the letters make it clear that this issue was recognized as a problem. It is impossible to say, though, if this concern was rooted in criminal law or ethical considerations by George and Morwitz" (Ute Oelmann and Carola Groppe (eds.), *Stefan George—Ernst Morwitz: Briefwechsel (1905–1933)* [Berlin: de Gruyter, 2020], 43).[2] George's special affection for Bothmer is clear from several of his letters from 1927 (e.g., letter of May 1, 1927: „An den lieben B. denk ich jeden Tag..." [About dear B[othmer] I think every day", p. 35]; also June 22, 1927). At least one of the last (three) poems written by George in 1928 as part of the cycle "Das Neue Reich" is assumed to relate to Bothmer: "Das Licht [The Light]."[3] We thus do not have evidence in support of the assumption that the relationship of Morwitz and George (or for that matter, other members of the circle) with several of their young "mentees" included "sexual impropriety" (ruled out by Eaton-Krauss in a mere footnote, p. 31 n. 70). However, stating (p. 31) that Morwitz's "true calling in life was pedagogical, to give carefully selected boys of promise the guidance necessary so that they might enjoy the 'beautiful life' as envisaged by The Master," including "emotional closeness" with mentees such as the Bothmer brothers whom Morwitz called his "spiritual sons [geistige Söhne]," needs to be qualified (given that pederasty was pedagogically veiled precisely as the highest "spiritual" [geistig] form of existence!).[4]

There has been a controversial debate, both among members and opponents of the George Circle and in recent scholarship, about George's attitude towards Nazism. This discussion focused on the question of whether his visions for "Das Neue Reich" (The New Reich, title of his last poetry cycle) and "Das Geheime Deutschland" (Secret Germany) can be seen as having paved the way for National Socialism. Eaton-Krauss cites a letter by Bothmer from 1933 in which he is critical about George's political views, particularly the poet's passive attitude and indifference towards the events in

[1] „der ungeheuerliche Versuch, die Päderastie mit pädagogischem Eifer zur höchsten geistigen Daseinsform zu erklären".

[2] „War die Auswahl von Kindern und Jugendlichen homoerotisch und pädophil motiviert, so enthalten die Briefe dennoch keine konkreten Hinweise auf eine entsprechende sexuelle Praxis. Es muss ungeklärt bleiben, ob die Zuneigung zu als schön klassifizierten männlichen Heranwachsenden im Kreis und durch George zur sexualisierten Gewalt gegenüber diesen wurde oder nicht... Dass hier ein Problem bestand, wird an vielen Briefstellen deutlich. Ob dieses Problem in Gründen des Strafrechts oder in ethischen Erwägungen von George und Morwitz gesehen wurde, lässt sich nicht sagen."

[3] See Wolfgang Frommel and Renata von Scheliha, *Wolfgang Frommel – Renata von Scheliha: Briefwechsel 1930–1967* (Amsterdam: Castrum Peregrini, 2002), 120, 128, where also „In stillste Ruh" is believed to be about Bothmer; equally Eaton-Krauss p. 33 with n. 82 (whereas George scholarship usually sees in it a reflection of George's mythicized idol Maximin). Cf. also Marita Keilson-Lauritz, *Von der Liebe die Freundschaft heisst: Zur Homoerotik im Werk Stefan Georges* (Berlin: Rosa Winkel, 1987), 58.

[4] In the case of Bothmer's friendship with Silvio Markees, four years his senior, concerns about a homosexual relationship arose among relatives (p. 25 with n. 53).

Germany that he thought needed to be accepted as fate (p. 70), only to state in n. 274: "This is not the place to discuss this controversy [George's attitude towards Hitler's assumption of power] nor am I qualified to do so ... Note, too, Morwitz's assertion that George realized the consequences of Hitler's policies which led him to seek personal freedom for himself in Switzerland." This latter assertion has long been debunked (see Karlauf, *Stefan George. Die Entdeckung des Charisma*, 615). In this reviewer's opinion, it would have been essential to provide a succinct review of this debate in order to contextualize Bothmer's political views and circumstances in the early 1930s when his studies at the university coincided with the first years of the Nazi regime. After all, his escape from Nazi Germany was motivated politically. Jewish members of the circle (such as Morwitz and the historian Ernst Kantorowicz who both emigrated to the United States in 1938; p. 77) had to flee the country. Other associates of Bothmer's in the George Circle were the three Stauffenberg brothers of which one, Claus, was to carry out the failed assault on Hitler on July 20, 1944 (see Manfred Riedel, *Geheimes Deutschland: Stefan George und die Brüder Stauffenberg* [Berlin: Kulturverlag Kadmos, 2006]; Thomas Karlauf's contribution to the volume *A Poet's Reich* quoted below).

Several contributions in the 2011 volume, *A Poet's Reich: Politics and Culture in the George Circle* (M. S. Lane and Martin Ruehl (eds.) [Rochester: Camden House, 2011]), demonstrate that George's political vision and the ideology of National Socialism showed significant overlap but also disparity on many issues. While George would likely not have approved of the holocaust or even the persecution of Jews, he still claimed the ancestorship of Nazism and certainly did not oppose the politics of persecution that started in 1933 (Ruehl, Norton, Hoffmann, Karlauf). For members of the George Circle—particularly its Jewish members—it was difficult to discriminate between George's "New Reich" and the "Third Reich." Carl von Stauffenberg realized this only after the defeats of 1942–1943 when he recognized Hitler as a false leader and planned his assassination (in which he may have pursued George's imperative to be a "man of action"). Jan Stottmeister has recently emphasized that while it is true that George did not give in to the overtures of the Nazi regime, he also never objected to his own and his ideology's appropriation by them. He characterizes him as an "amoral cynic who enjoyed ambiguities" when a clear political stance would have been necessary in 1933. This ambiguity also applied to the swastika which was used as a cover vignette on publications of the George circle. At the latest with the Nazis' assumption of power, George's visions of a "New Reich" and the swastika could no longer be perceived without their association with the Nazi regime (Jan Stottmeister, *Der George-Kreis und die Theosophie. Mit einem Exkurs zum Swastika-Zeichen bei Helena Blavatsky, Alfred Schuler und Stefan George* [Amsterdam: Castrum Peregrini, 2014], 387–88, 398). George's intentional ambiguity and indifference—as criticized by Bothmer in his letter—was a major concern to his circle and its Jewish members. When asked (in September 1939 in Switzerland) to protest the hardship of the Jews in Germany, George said that when contemplating the destiny of Germany in the next fifty years he did not think that the "Judensach" (the issue with the Jews) would appear particularly relevant to him (Ulrich Raulff, *Kreis ohne Meister: Stefan Georges Nachleben* [Munich: Beck, 2009], 72–79; the Bothmer letter cited and commented upon on p. 73).

Were these views not a topic of conversation between Bothmer and his close friends in the circle? Quite definitely so. On p. 53, Bothmer is cited as assessing Woldemar Uxkull's piece, "The Revolutionary Ethos in the Work of Stefan George," "which implicitly associated George's last poetry cycle *Das Neue Reich* with the Third Reich," as "appallingly dumb and completely out of the question" ["entsetzlich dumm and ganz indiskutabel"]. Sketching the controversies within the George circle about the Nazi regime in these years in more detail would have provided much context for Bothmer's own position. For example, the Stauffenberg brothers are not mentioned in the present book; however, Bothmer certainly met and talked to them (meetings with Alexander von Stauffenberg in the university library are referred to by Ulrich Raulff (*Kreis ohne Meister: Stefan Georges Nachleben*, 279 n. 21, according to a letter by Morwitz to Walter Kempner dated 26 November 1934). It would have been helpful here to rebut explicitly an assumption made in the earlier literature, including by this reviewer, namely that Bothmer was denied his doctorate for his political activism against the Nazi regime (Thomas Schneider, Ägyptologen im Dritten Reich: Biographische Notizen anhand der sogenannten "Steindorff-Liste" *JEgH* 5 [2012], 119–246, at 156–57 with references[5]). This was clearly not the case, and the documentation provided by Eaton-Krauss shows that it was not because of the dispute within the discipline, either (as claimed by Susanne Voss, "Wissenshintergründe…: Die Ägyptologie als 'völkische' Wissenschaft entlang des Nachlasses Georg Steindorffs von der Weimarer Republik über die NS- bis zur Nachkriegszeit," in Susanne Voss and Dietrich Raue, eds., *Georg Steindorff und die deutsche* Ägyptologie *im 20. Jahrhundert. Wissenshintergründe und Forschungstransfers* [Berlin: de Gruyter, 2016], 106–332, at 308). Rather, Bothmer was personally struggling to bring his doctoral thesis to a completion (p. 70) and suffered setbacks due to his health. He came down with an illness in early November 1938 after accompanying Morwitz (who emigrated) to England and meeting his brother Dietrich (recipient of a Rhodes scholarship at Oxford), spent two weeks at a sanatorium, was deemed too ill for a renewal of his museum

[5] Reprinted in Thomas Schneider and Peter Raulwing, *Egyptology from the First World War to the Third Reich: Ideology, Scholarship, and Individual Biographies* (Leiden-Boston: Brill, 2013).

contract in early 1939, and then had a motorcycle accident in May 1939. His intended doctoral exam could not be held before Bothmer left Germany for Switzerland on August 7, 1939. His personal condition was aggravated by, among others, the departure of Morwitz, Silvio Markees, his brother, and certainly also by the overall political context. Dramatic is the scene on November 10, 1938, when Bothmer is driven to the sanatorium along the destruction visible after the previous night of the November pogrom, the *Reichskristallnacht* (pp. 81–82). There was also the earlier suicide of his sister Marie on 5 July 1936, strangely relegated into a mere footnote by the author (Bothmer and a friend had been swimming on July 5, 1936, when "Bothmer returned to the family apartment to discover that his sister Marie had taken her own life," n. 290).

Chapters 3 *(At university and in the museum)* and 4 *(Leaving Germany)* are dedicated to the time of Bothmer's academic education and his work at the Berlin museum. After initially studying law, Bothmer's Egyptological "making" occurred at the University of Bonn, where he received his first instruction by Hans Bonnet, and subsequently in Berlin (1932–1939). From April 1933 on, he was also employed as a *wissenschaftlicher Hilfsarbeiter* at the Egyptian museum, which was instrumental in nurturing his interest in Egyptian art. These years see clearly academic, personal, and political issues compounded. While the two chapters present many facts regarding the timeline of events, Egyptological acquaintances in Berlin and abroad, and personal problems, it might have been conducive to an understanding of Bothmer's "making" to arrange the material from a thematic rather than chronological angle of view. For example, academically, Bothmer's interest in art history exposed him to the open conflict between the philological Berlin School (with his erstwhile supervisor Kurt Sethe, and after Sethe's death, Hermann Grapow) and proponents of Egyptian archaeology. This controversy has been examined recently (Voss, "Wissenshintergründe…: Die Ägyptologie als 'völkische' Wissenschaft," 253–63) but is omitted in the present volume. Chapter 3 mentions about thirty individuals from Egyptology or the Berlin art scene whom Bothmer met during his study years; of these, the friendships with Hans-Wolfgang Müller and Rudolf Anthes are presented in more detail (pp. 66–69). Still, it is mostly left to the reader to develop a more thorough idea of how Bothmer's interests—in particular, his interest in Egyptian statuary—developed. For example, no mention is made that from 1935–1936, Käthe Bosse was employed at the museum (and was thus a colleague of Bothmer's). She had just defended her doctorate on Late Egyptian sculpture, precisely Bothmer's subsequent specialty (published in 1936 as *Die menschliche Figur in der Rundplastik der* ägyptischen *Spätzeit von der XXII. bis zur XXX. Dynastie*); later Bothmer was counted among Bosse and her husband J. Gwyn Griffiths' best friends (Käthe Bosse-Griffiths, *Amarna Studies and Other Selected Papers* (ed. J. Gwyn Griffiths) [Fribourg: University Press; Göttingen: Vandenhoeck & Ruprecht, 2001], 9). I assume it is also likely that Bothmer met art historian and Egyptologist Hedwig Fechheimer, author of *Die Plastik der Ägypter* (Berlin: B. Cassirer, 1923), whose nephew Clemens Bruehl, member of the post-war circle around Wolfgang Frommel which continued George's legacy, became a friend of Ernst Morwitz and Silvio Markees (Sylvia Peuckert, *Hedwig Fechheimer und die ägyptische Kunst. Leben und Werk einer jüdischen Kunstwissenschaftlerin in Deutschland* [Berlin: de Gruyter, 2014], 257–66).[6] In a much more general and personal perspective, I wonder whether the momentous relevance of sculpture for the George circle and George's political aesthetics—the atelier was the meeting venue for the members of the circle; Bothmer also entertained a close friendship with the sculptor Alexander Zschokke (pp. 37–49; he also posed for him as a model for a bronze statue)—may actually have been the most consequential factor in Bothmer's academic interests (cf. Ulrich Raulff and Lutz Näfelt (eds.), *Das geheime Deutschland. Eine Ausgrabung. Köpfe aus dem George-Kreis. Ausstellung Literaturmuseum der Moderne, Marbach am Neckar, 13. März 2008 bis 31. August 2008* [Marbach am Neckar: Deutsche Schillergesellschaft, 2008]).

These points are not meant to diminish the value of Eaton-Krauss's monograph as a veritable quarry of information on Bothmer's early life and career. Rather, as Michael Hesse has emphasized in his review (https://bmcr.brynmawr.edu/2008/2008.11.27) of Karl Christ's biography of Alexander von Stauffenberg—like Bothmer a member of the George circle and scholar (*Der andere Stauffenberg: Der Historiker und Dichter Alexander von Stauffenberg* [Munich, Beck, 2008])—they emphasize that much study will still be needed to fully understand the interplay of life and scholarship of such a "highly complex personality."

Thomas Schneider
University of British Columbia

Omar D. Foda. *Egypt's Beer: Stella, Identity, and the Modern State* (Austin: University of Texas Press, 2019). ISBN 978-1-4773-1955-0. Pp. vii + 252, numerous black and white illustrations.

In *Egypt's Beer* Omar D. Foda's primary objective is to explore how Stella became Egypt's "national beer" and main-

[6] The acquaintance of Bothmer and Fechheimer is indirectly confirmed by Bothmer's later recollection that Hermann Junker frowned upon Fechheimer's visits to the Egyptian museum after 1933 (R. Krauss, "Ludwig Borchardts Fälschungen-Recherche von 1930 aus den Quellen neu erzählt," *EDAL* 3 [2012] 121–61, at 154–55 with n. 193).

tained that status despite a decline in public reputation from the late-1980s onwards. More than just a corporate narrative of Crown and Pyramid (the companies that produced the beer), the author utilizes Stella as a case study to engage Egypt's broader political and economy history and explain the outlook of the nation's developing middle class, as well as society's relationship to changing policies of socialism and capitalism. As one might expect from the subject matter, the book aims to be accessible to non-academic readers, but it also succeeds in providing the type of theoretical rigor that makes it a launching pad for further academic research.

Foda's introduction expresses the overarching narrative clearly, which is that having a "national beer" was important for a country trying to emphasize its modernity and to distance itself from its Islamic roots by identifying with Europe. As the values of the middle class shifted from secularism back to Islam, however, Stella came to be rejected as a foreign intrusion and, coupled with a decline in quality after 1985, the brand became marginalized in society. The author's story begins with the British occupation and the concomitant commercial, infrastructural, and technological developments that intersected with the growth of an indigenous, secularized middle class, urbanization, and an influx of foreigners to create a larger market for alcohol.

The theme of the second chapter is the "foreign-backed consolidation of the beer industry" (p. 32) that transformed the uneven efforts of local entrepreneurs into an organized business model that targeted the burgeoning middle class. This marketing campaign produced "a high-quality, low-cost, and evocatively branded product supported by a strong and effective sales system" (p. 49) that helped Stella compete with foreign beers, as well as alternatives such as coffee and whiskey. Chapter three discuses the growing acceptance of beer by highlighting its appearance in cinema, and also explores how Dutch brewer Heineken established a solid foundation for the business as government interest and involvement loomed on the horizon.

The author next engages the process of Egyptianization under Gamal Abdel Nasser, who perceived the development of a national beer as an important symbol of the country's modern and secularized economy. The subsequent chapter details the "normalization of beer in Egyptian culture" (p. 108) and how Nasser molded the industry to be subservient to the state, a model he used for Egyptian corporations in general. This culminated in the nationalization of the Crown and Pyramid breweries in 1961 (subsequently renamed Al-Ahram) and the installation of Foda's grandfather (also named Omar Foda) as head of the national beer industry.

Despite the state-mandated overemployment that was the hallmark of Nasser's socialist programs, the company remained profitable into the era of Anwar Sadat, which the author attributes to Heineken's operational legacy, the efforts of his grandfather, and the emergence of a consumption-focused class under Sadat's "opening" of the economy to more foreign and capitalist investment. Stella as a brand reached its peak in 1987, after which "a lack of leadership, a general financial downturn, and the Islamization of Egyptian public culture" (p. 164) led to the quality of the product decreasing and reduced market demand. The company became privatized in the late 1990s and began emphasizing Stella's Egyptian and scientific characteristics, while also producing a non-alcoholic beer to engage a newly religious segment of society. Nonetheless, al-Ahram remains a transnational company and has been unable to recapture the popularity it held prior to the 1990s.

Foda's final chapter summarizes his major arguments concisely and provides an overview of the narrative and its broader significance. It is a fitting conclusion to a work that maintains a balance between accessibility and academic rigor throughout, one that touches upon theory and the broader history at key junctures, but does not overwhelm. As with all approaches that attempt to find a middle ground between these two elements, readers who desire a strictly popular or academic perspective may be disappointed; most, however, should be pleased with the author's balancing act.

The text does sometimes lean towards including everything Foda could uncover about his subject, and thus it does include numerous technical details that can be difficult for the uninitiated to take in all at once. Nonetheless, it is sufficiently well-written to hold the reader's attention. I also would like to have known the author's relationship to the brewer Omar Foda (who is mentioned as an important figure in the introduction) much earlier in the book; it is not stated that they are grandson and grandfather until two-thirds of the way into the narrative. I do not think that the relationship is a problem—in fact, this book probably could not be so well written without material that is available only through personal family archives—but the nature of the relationship is an important consideration when analyzing the story. The fact that it comes so late makes it feel as if it were trying to be masked and leaves the reader in the dark when attempting to interpret the objectives. Overall, however, *Egypt's Beer* is an engaging read that provides an important contribution to the growing body of academic works that highlight popular culture's important relationship to, and impact on, society, politics, and the economy.

Paul Tchir
PhD Candidate, University of California, San Diego